THE NEW BOOK OF KNOWLEDGE ANNUAL

THE NEW BOOK OF KNOWLEDGE ANNUAL

The Young People's Book of the Year

Grolier Incorporated, Danbury, Connecticut

1999

Highlighting Events of 1998

ISBN 0-7172-0632-7
ISSN 0196-0148
The Library of Congress Catalog Card Number: 79-26807

PRINTED AND MANUFACTURED IN THE UNITED STATES OF AMERICA

STAFF

CONTENTS

CONTRIBUTORS

BORTZ, Alfred (Fred)
Author, science books for children
MAGNETS AND MAGNETISM

CAREY, George W.
Professor of Government, Georgetown University; Author, *The Federalist: Design for a Constitutional Republic; A Defense of the Constitution*
WATERGATE

COCKCROFT, James D.
Professor, State University of New York (Empire State College); Author, *Latinos in the Making of the United States; Latinos in Beisbol; Latin America: History, Politics, and U.S. Policy*
HISPANIC AMERICANS

COFFIN, Cheri L.
Family Films Coordinator and Family Programs Assistant, Department of Education, Museum of Modern Art
CUBISM

DIERKS, Carrie
Science writer; Editor, *Ask Isaac Asimov* series
HAWKS

HART, David L.
Senior Technical Editor, San Diego Supercomputer Center; Coauthor, *MacOS8 Web Server Cookbook*
COMPUTERS

HAVIGHURST, Walter
Research Professor Emeritus of English, Miami University (Oxford, Ohio); Author, *First Book of Pioneers; First Book of the Oregon Trail*
PIONEER LIFE

KETTELKAMP, Larry
Director, Bookarts Associates; Instructor, Rider College, Lawrenceville, New Jersey; Author and Illustrator, *Kites; The Magic of Sound; Electronic Musical Instruments: What They Do, How They Work; Lasers: The Miracle Light; Modern Sports Science*
(Reviewer) KITES

KURTZ, Henry I.
Author, *John and Sebastian Cabot; Defending Our Country: The U.S. Army; Captain John Smith; The Art of the Toy Soldier*
THE SPANISH-AMERICAN WAR
A SPY FOR THE UNION

MOGIL, H. Michael
Meteorologist, How the Weatherworks; Coauthor, *The Amateur Meteorologist: Explorations and Investigations*
CLIMATE

PARRY, B. Brooke A.
Research Assistant, School of Forestry and Environmental Studies, Yale University
RAIN FORESTS

PASCOE, Elaine
Author, *South Africa: Troubled Land; Neighbors at Odds: U.S. Policy in Latin America; Racial Prejudice; The Horse Owner's Preventive Maintenance Handbook; Freedom of Expression: The Right to Speak Out in America*
AROUND THE WORLD

PIORKOWSKI, Nona
Editor, *Crafts 'n Things* magazine
POPULAR CRAFTS

RAMPON, William J.
Associate Professor, Department of Geography, West Chester State College (Pennsylvania)
OVERLAND TRAILS

TESAR, Jenny
Author, *Endangered Habitats; Global Warming; Scientific Crime Investigation; The Waste Crisis; Shrinking Forests; The New Webster's Computer Handbook; What on Earth Is a Meerkat?; Spiders*
EARTH WATCH
SPACE BRIEFS

VAN RYZIN, Robert
Managing Editor, *Numismatic News*, Krause Publications; Author, *Striking Impressions: A Visual Guide to Collecting U.S. Coins*
COIN COLLECTING

VOGT, Kristiina
Professor of Ecosystem Ecology, Yale University; Coauthor, *Ecosystems: Balancing Science with Management*
RAIN FORESTS

WHITE, Mark J.
Assistant Professor of History, Eastern Illinois University; Author, *The Cuban Missile Crisis; Missiles in Cuba*
CUBAN MISSILE CRISIS

IN THE PAGES OF THIS BOOK . . .

How closely did you follow the events of 1998? Do you remember the people who made news during the year? What about the trends—what was in and what was out? Who won in sports? What were the top songs, films, and television shows? What important anniversaries were celebrated? All these helped make up your world in 1998—a year that was like no other.

Here's a quiz that will tell you how much you know about your world—about what took place during the past year and about other things, as well. If you're stumped by a question, don't worry. You'll find all the answers in the pages of this book. (The page numbers after the questions will tell you where to look.)

In January 1998, Pope John Paul II made a historic trip to (China/Cuba/Chile). (*17*)

On October 29, astronaut _______ became the oldest person to travel into space. (*36, 94, 114*)

Two of the biggest film hits of the year were based on historical events. One movie told the story of a group of Africans sold into slavery in 1839. The other was about the sinking of a luxury ocean liner in 1912. Name these movies. (*200*)

Scientists reported in July that they had created more than 50 cloned (hamsters/gerbils/mice). (*28*)

Two famous captured whales, named _______ and _______, began separate journeys to freedom in 1998. One was returned to the ocean, and the other was placed in a sea pen in Iceland and will hopefully be set free at a later date. (*92*)

January marked the 150th anniversary of the discovery of gold in California—a landmark event that sparked the California gold rush. What name was given to the people who went to California in search of gold? (*190*)

Shirley and Frank Capaci of Streamwood, Illinois, gave new meaning to the word "lucky." They won the largest single (lottery payment/tax refund/Jeopardy jackpot) in U.S. history. (*63*)

It was a year to remember for baseball fans. St. Louis Cardinal first baseman _______ and Chicago Cub rightfielder _______ both shattered the single-season home-run record. (*158, 169*)

Which TV shows won 1998 Emmy Awards as best comedy and drama series? (*264*)

In the next five to ten years, (strawberries/chocolate/cereal) may become a rare and expensive treat. (*127*)

February 15 marked the 100th anniversary of the sinking of the U.S.S. *Maine* in the Havana, Cuba, harbor. This event triggered the _______ War. (*210*)

Which film won the 1998 Academy Award for best motion picture? (*244*)

The Y2K bug is a computer glitch that some people fear will disrupt computer systems everywhere at the stroke of midnight on December 31, 1999. What does Y2K stand for? (*106*)

At the Winter Olympics, Tara Lipinski won a gold medal in women's (speed skating/ski jumping/figure skating)—and became the youngest person ever to win a gold medal in that event. (*161*)

On June 3, a monument to a great Native American leader was dedicated in the Black Hills of South Dakota.

When completed, the memorial will be the largest statue in the world. What great warrior does the statue depict? (*27*)

One of the year's most talked-about female musicians was (Madonna/Paula Cole/Sarah McLachlan). She was awarded two Grammys. (*268, 271*)

In May, about 108 million people watched the last episode of _______. This popular TV series—billed as a "show about nothing"—went off the air after a nine-year run. (*256*)

The United Nations declared 1998 the International Year of the Ocean. Can you name the world's five oceans? (*96*)

The longest suspension bridge in the world opened in (Japan/Malaysia/the United States) in April. (*23*)

The animated film _______ told the tale of a young girl in ancient China who disguises herself as a soldier and ends up saving her country. (*262*)

Americans were delighted when a new member of the First Family moved into the White House—a chocolate Labrador retriever. What's the name of the new presidential pooch? (*84*)

Vast forest fires in Indonesia threaten the survival of (elephants/orangutans/pandas). (*126*)

Five previously unknown pages from the famous diary of holocaust victim _______ were made public in 1998. (*64*)

On August 7, terrorists exploded two bombs within minutes of each other outside the U.S. embassies in two African nations. Name the countries. (*30, 52*)

On December 19, the U.S. House of Representatives voted to impeach President Bill Clinton. Clinton was only the second president in U.S. history to be impeached and thus face the threat of being removed from office by Congress. Who was the other president? (*43*)

(Scottie Pippen/Dennis Rodman/Michael Jordan) was named Most Valuable Player for both the regular season and the playoffs of the National Basketball Association. (*172*)

The year 1998 was a dreadful one for people with triskaidekaphobia. They were especially nervous on three particular Fridays in February, March, and November because triskaidakaphobia is a fear of the number _______. (*102*)

In the fall, a cease-fire brought a halt to fighting in an ethnic conflict in Kosovo. In which eastern European country is Kosovo located? (*58*)

On Election Day, political experts were stunned when Jesse Ventura, a former professional (wrestler/hockey player/lifeguard), was elected governor of Minnesota. (*62*)

People flocked to automobile showrooms in March to see the New _______ —an updated version of a classic car that sold more than any other car in history. (*21*)

Teenage pop stars Brandy and Monica sang a duet that skyrocketed to the top of the Billboard charts. Name that song. (*267*)

Tennis player (Martina Hingis/Lindsay Davenport/Jana Novatna) won the U.S. Open. (*185*)

In December, the space shuttle *Endeavour* carried American astronauts into orbit so that they could begin assembling the *International* _______. (*38; 108*)

THE WORLD IN 1998

As America's First Family—First Lady Hillary Clinton, daughter Chelsea Clinton, and President Bill Clinton—left for vacation in August 1998, controversy and scandal swirled around the White House. The president had just admitted that he had misled people in an effort to conceal an improper relationship with a former White House intern. Four months later, on December 19, the House of Representatives voted to impeach Clinton. Clinton thus became the second president in U.S. history to be impeached.

THE YEAR IN REVIEW

Nations are linked in many ways today—by trade, by alliances, by high-speed communications and transportation. Events in one country often affect people far away. That was the case in 1998, when economic troubles in Asia, the threat of nuclear weapons, and other developments raised worldwide concern. For people in the United States, however, the events of 1998 were overshadowed by a growing cloud of controversy surrounding the White House.

On December 19, 1998, Bill Clinton became the second president in U.S. history to be impeached. On that day the U.S. House of Representatives adopted two articles of impeachment, or formal charges of wrongdoing, against him. The vote was along party lines, with Democrats backing the president and Republicans, who held a majority in Congress, voting for impeachment. Clinton thus faced the prospect of a trial in the Senate, and possible removal from office, in 1999. The controversy grew out of charges that the president had lied about an improper relationship he had had with a former White House intern.

Many Americans voiced impatience with the controversy and with the extensive media coverage it received. November elections, in which the Democratic Party made a strong showing, also indicated that people were content with the state of the country. In fact, Americans had much to be happy about. The economy was healthy and growing. Unemployment was low. But those who looked overseas could see storm clouds on the horizon.

A financial crisis that erupted in East Asia in 1997 worsened in 1998, raising concern for the world economy. Many Asian nations had booming economies through the 1980s, but in the process they had borrowed too much money from abroad. In the late 1990s the effects of the borrowing and spending spree hit home. Banks and businesses couldn't repay foreign loans, and investors began to pull out. Currencies and stock markets tumbled in value.

There were also political effects in several countries. President Suharto, Indonesia's longtime ruler, was forced from office. Economists forecast a long recession for the region, and they predicted that other nations would suffer from the Asian financial "flu."

Nuclear weapons were another cause for worldwide concern in 1998. In May, India and Pakistan set off a series of underground nuclear weapons tests. Although these countries, which have been rivals for 50 years, were thought to be developing nuclear weapons, neither had previously admitted it. The tests highlighted the problem of the spread, or proliferation, of these deadly weapons. Many nations have agreed not to develop nuclear arms, but a handful of countries are thought to be secretly trying to build them. Among those nations are Iran, Iraq, and North Korea, all of which have threatened their neighbors and have been linked to international terrorism.

Since Iraq's defeat in the 1991 Persian Gulf War, U.N. inspectors have been searching that country for chemical, biological, and nuclear weapons. However, Iraq had brought the inspections to a halt several times during 1998, and the United States had threatened military action in retaliation. At the end of the year, U.N. inspectors reported that the Iraqis were still not cooperating, and on December 16 the United States and Britain launched air strikes against Iraq. The attack lasted four days and was aimed at setting back Iraq's weapons program and its ability to threaten its neighbors.

Elsewhere in the Middle East, Israel celebrated a special event in 1998—the 50th anniversary of its founding as a homeland for the Jewish people.

Israelis could take pride in the remarkable success of their country. But the anniversary also signaled the 50th year of conflict between Israelis and Palestinian Arabs, displaced when Israel was created.

Under past agreements, Palestinians had achieved a measure of self-rule in the West Bank and the Gaza Strip, territories Israel had occupied since 1967. The peace process that led to those agreements stalled late in 1996, however, and militant Islamic groups continued to stage terrorist attacks against Israelis. Finally, in October 1998, the Mideast peace process seemed to be getting back on track. Israeli Prime Minister Benjamin Netanyahu and Palestinian leader Yasir Arafat signed an important agreement at the White House in Washington, D.C. Under its terms, Israel began to turn additional West Bank land over to Palestinian control. But the agreement hit snag after snag, as deep distrust and a new rash of terrorist attacks threatened to undo it.

In August 1998 the United Nations stepped up its aid to Sudan, where as many as 2.6 million people faced starvation. Sudan was in the tenth year of a famine that stemmed mostly from a long-running civil war. The war has pitted the government, which is controlled by Muslim Arabs in northern Sudan, against rebels from the south. The southerners have long been denied equality, and they felt the worst effects of the famine. Even with almost 15,000 tons of food being sent each month by international agencies, people were dying because help failed to reach them in time.

Russians tightened their belts as they continued to struggle with economic and political woes. Russia's currency plummeted in value in 1998, and many workers went unpaid because their employers had no cash. Meanwhile, the government was in turmoil. By year's end it was clear that Russian president Boris Yeltsin was in poor health, and people began to wonder how much longer he would remain in power.

Bosnia and Herzegovina, a tiny European nation that was torn by ethnic fighting in the mid-1990s, struggled to hold onto a fragile peace in 1998. Meanwhile, new violence broke out in neighboring Serbia, where the government cracked down brutally on ethnic Albanian rebels in the province of Kosovo. An international outcry brought a cease-fire in the fall, but not before hundreds of people had been killed. The news was brighter in Northern Ireland, where an April peace agreement marked the end of the "Troubles"—almost 30 years of fighting between Roman Catholics and Protestants.

The weather grabbed more than its share of headlines during the year. El Niño, a weather disturbance brought on by a warming of Pacific Ocean waters, made for a hard winter in many areas in 1997–98. In North America, the West Coast was battered with devastating storms, and much of the South was drenched as well. Parts of the Northeast escaped unscathed, but eastern Canada and northern New England suffered crippling ice storms.

Despite the gloom cast by El Niño storms, people were cheered by the spectacle of the 1998 Winter Olympics, held in Nagano, Japan. Germany topped the list of medal winners, with a total of 29. U.S. athletes took home 13 medals, among them the gold in the first-ever women's Olympic ice-hockey tournament. Tara Lipinski, 15, became the youngest athlete to capture the gold in women's figure skating.

Spirits were lifted again in the fall, by the most celebrated U.S. space mission in years. John Glenn, who in 1962 had been the first American to orbit the Earth, returned to space aboard the shuttle *Discovery* on October 29, 1998. At age 77, he was the oldest person ever to travel into space. Americans and people everywhere hailed his achievement.

JANUARY

5-9 Severe ice storms swept through eastern Canada and the northeastern United States, causing at least 25 deaths and more than $1 billion worth of damage. It was the worst ice storm on record in Canada, and that nation's costliest natural disaster ever. The hardest hit areas were in Quebec, Ontario, and New Brunswick, where thick coats of ice toppled electric transmission towers, leaving millions of people without power.

22 In a federal court in Sacramento, California, Theodore J. Kaczynski pleaded guilty and admitted that he was the serial bomber known as the Unabomber (for the initial letters of his chief targets: people connected to universities and airlines). Between 1978 and 1995, he had placed or mailed sixteen bombs that killed three people and injured 23 others. He was sentenced to life in prison without the possibility of parole.

31 The U.S. space shuttle *Endeavour* completed a nine-day mission. The main objective of the mission was to link up with the Russian space station *Mir* and bring home astronaut David Wolf, who had been stationed aboard *Mir* for four months. The crew consisted of Michael Anderson, Bonnie Dunbar, Joe Edwards, Jr., James Reilly 2nd, Terrence Wilcutt, Salizhan Sharipov of Russia, and Andrew Thomas, who replaced Wolf aboard *Mir*.

A wave of ice storms crippled eastern Canada in early January. The storms shut down roads, railways, schools, and businesses and forced thousands of people to seek temporary shelters.

The Pope Visits Cuba

On January 21, tens of thousands of cheering people lined the streets of Havana, Cuba, to welcome Pope John Paul II, head of the Roman Catholic Church. The Pope arrived in Cuba's capital for the start of a five-day visit, at the invitation of President Fidel Castro. It was the Pope's first trip to the Caribbean island nation. Highlights of the visit included the historic meetings between the two powerful leaders: Pope John Paul, 77, who had been a strong critic of Communism in Eastern Europe, and Castro, 71, head of the only Communist state in the Western Hemisphere.

During the visit, the Pope led four outdoor masses. He spoke about spiritual and family issues and criticized Castro's suppression of religious and personal freedoms. The Pope also urged the United States to end its economic blockade of Cuba, which prevents U.S. products from being sold in Cuba, and Cuban products from being sold in the United States. (On March 20, in response to the Pope's pleas, U.S. President Bill Clinton announced that the United States would ease some restrictions on aid to Cuba, although it wouldn't lift the economic embargo. Clinton said that humanitarian flights to Cuba could resume and that Cuban-Americans could send up to $1,200 a year to relatives living in Cuba.)

Government changes in January: In national elections in **Lithuania,** Valdas Adamkus was elected president. An emigrant who returned from the United States, Adamkus succeeded Algirdas Brazauskas, who had been president since 1993. . . . In **Pakistan,** Mohammad Rafiq Tarar became president. He succeeded Farooq Leghari, who had been president since 1993. . . . In **Vietnam,** Le Kha Phieu became General Secretary of the Communist Party, the country's top position. He succeeded Do Muoi, who had been secretary since 1991.

FEBRUARY

4 A powerful earthquake measuring 6.1 on the Richter scale of ground motion struck northeastern Afghanistan. More than 4,500 people were killed, and 30,000 were left homeless. (On May 30, an even stronger earthquake, measuring 6.9 on the Richter scale, hit the same area. About 5,000 people were killed, and 45,000 were left homeless.)

22 Iraq signed an agreement with the United Nations that gave U.N. arms inspectors access to suspected weapons sites. The agreement eased a crisis that had begun in January when Iraqi President Saddam Hussein refused to allow the inspectors into areas where they believed weapons were being produced. The United States threatened to take military action, saying that Iraq was violating the treaty that ended the 1991 Persian Gulf War. Under the terms of that treaty, the inspections were required to ensure that Iraq destroyed its supplies of weapons of mass destruction, especially chemical and biological weapons.

Government changes in February: In national elections in **Costa Rica,** Miguel Angel Rodriguez was elected president. He succeeded José María Figueres Olsen, who had been president since 1994. . . . In **Laos,** Premier Khamtai Siphandon was

U.N Secretary General Kofi Annan meets with Iraqi leader Saddam Hussein. A crisis was averted when Saddam agreed to allow U.N. inspectors to check out suspected weapons sites.

This multiple-exposure photo shows three phases of the total eclipse of the sun—before, during, and after (*beginning at top, right*). People used protective glasses to view the eclipse.

Day Turned into Night

A rare total eclipse of the sun darkened the daytime sky in many parts of the world on February 26. The eclipse began in the Pacific Ocean southeast of Hawaii, then moved across South America, the Caribbean, and most of the Atlantic Ocean. People along the path of the eclipse watched through protective glasses, while scientists used telescopes to study the sun's corona, or outer atmosphere.

A solar eclipse occurs when the moon moves between Earth and the sun. The moon blocks the sun's light, casting a shadow that races from west to east across a narrow strip of Earth's surface. The moon doesn't always cover the sun completely. Because the moon's orbit is oval, its distance from Earth changes as it travels. Only if an eclipse takes place when the moon is close to Earth will the moon completely block out the sun, causing a total eclipse. Total darkness at any one point along the eclipse's path lasts for about two to seven minutes. During this time, the sun's corona is visible as a beautiful white halo around the moon.

named president. He succeeded Nouhak Phoumsavan, who had been president since 1992. Sisavat Keobounphan was appointed premier.... In **Sierra Leone,** the military government led by Johnny Paul Koromah was ousted by Nigerian-led West African troops. President Ahmed Tejan Kabbah was returned to office after nearly ten months in exile.

MARCH

16 The Vatican issued a landmark document examining the role of the Roman Catholic Church during the Holocaust—the mass murder by Nazi Germany of six million European Jews during World War II. In the document, the Vatican repented the failure of Roman Catholics to take strong action that might have prevented the killings. The document also expressed the Church's resolve to "build a new future in which there will be no more anti-Judaism among Christians or anti-Christian sentiment among Jews."

26 Scientists reported that the fossil of a baby dinosaur found in Italy about ten years earlier contained the preserved remains of its internal organs—large portions of intestines, muscles, liver, and windpipe. It's extremely rare to find a dinosaur's fossilized internal organs because this soft tissue decays easily. The dinosaur, a previously unknown species, was named *Scipionyx samniticus.* It lived about 113 million years ago and was distantly related to *Tryannosaurus rex.* Scientists hoped that the discovery would give them more information about the anatomy of dinosaurs, and help to confirm or disprove the theory that dinosaurs were the ancestors of modern birds.

The model (*below*) of a baby dinosaur named *Scipionyx samniticus* was constructed using the fossil remains (*left*) as a guide. Many of the dinosaur's internal organs were still intact.

The Bug Is Back!

People flocked to automobile showrooms in March to see the New Beetle, an updated version of a German Volkswagen that first sold in the United States in 1949 and went on to become one of the top-selling cars in the country.

When the original Beetle appeared on the scene about 50 years ago, American automakers were producing big, expensive cars. The Beetle, on the other hand, was small and inexpensive. For many Americans, especially students, it was their first car, and they were crazy about it. Because it was shaped somewhat like a ladybug, it was nicknamed the Bug.

Drivers didn't care that the design of the car stayed the same over the years. They were even proud of the advertising slogan, "It's ugly but it gets you there." By the time "Beetlemania" ended in the late 1970s, 21 million of the cars had been sold worldwide—more than any other single car in history.

The New Beetle resembles the Old Bug, but it's slightly bigger and the design is more modern. The engine is in the front, not in the back. The car has airbags, air-conditioning, cruise control, and other items that today's drivers expect. It even has a small bud vase on the dashboard, so drivers can enjoy their favorite flower along with the ride.

Government changes in March: In national elections in **Armenia,** Robert Kocharyan was elected president. He succeeded Levon Ter-Petrosyan, who had led the country since 1991.... In **China,** Zhu Rongji was named premier. He succeeded Li Peng, who had been premier since 1987.... Following national elections in **India,** Atal Bihari Vajpayee became prime minister. He succeeded Inder Kumar Gujral, who had been in office less than a year.... In **South Korea,** Kim Jong Pil became premier. He succeeded Koh Kun, who had been premier for one year.

APRIL

2 U.S. President Bill Clinton and First Lady Hillary Rodham Clinton completed an eleven-day trip to sub-Saharan Africa. It was the first time a U.S. president had visited the region in more than twenty years. He visited Ghana, Uganda, Rwanda, South Africa, Botswana, and Senegal. In meetings with national leaders and in speeches before huge crowds, Clinton called for a new partnership between the United States and Africa.

Scientists reported the discovery of an ancient complex of huge stones and slabs in the Sahara Desert in southern Egypt. Like England's famous Stonehenge, it seems to have been designed along astronomical principles. The Sahara complex was built about 7,000 years ago—2,000 years before Stonehenge. Thus it may be the oldest known monument of its kind.

10 In Northern Ireland, leaders of Great Britain and Ireland, and Protestant and Catholic groups, reached an agreement designed to bring peace to the region. Since the 1960s, Northern Ireland, a part of Great Britain, has been plagued by violence between Protestants and Catholics. (On May 22, voters in Northern Ireland and Ireland approved the agreement.)

President Bill Clinton visits with a group of schoolchildren in Uganda. Also shown are the First Lady and, next to her, Ugandan President Yoweri Museveni.

A Record-Breaking Bridge

On April 5, the world's longest suspension bridge, the Akashi Kaikyo Bridge, opened in Japan. The bridge, which is 2.4 miles (3.9 kilometers) long, crosses the Akashi Strait and connects the city of Kobe with Awaji Island. It has a center span of 6,532 feet (1,991 meters), which makes it longer than the main span of Britain's Humber Estuary Bridge—the previous record holder.

Like all suspension bridges, the Akashi Kaikyo Bridge has tall support towers built on firm foundations in the water. Two thick cables, made of thousands of steel wires bound together, swoop between the towers and down to each end of the bridge, where the cables are secured in huge blocks of concrete. Thinner vertical cables—called suspenders—hang from the main cables and hold up the road. If all the steel wire used to make the bridge were laid end to end, it would circle the Earth seven times!

Because Japan is often battered by violent weather, the bridge was built to withstand winds of up to 180 miles (300 kilometers) per hour and earthquakes of magnitude 8.5 on the Richter scale.

28 The U.S. Senate confirmed the nomination of Togo D. West, Jr., as Secretary of Veterans Affairs. He succeeded Jesse Brown, who had resigned in 1997.

Government changes in April: In **Romania,** Radu Vasile was named premier. He succeeded Victor Ciorbea, who had been premier since 1996.

MAY

3 The U.S. space shuttle *Columbia* completed a sixteen-day mission. Some 2,000 creatures were aboard the shuttle, including rats, mice, fish, snails, and crickets. The mission focused on studies of the nervous system, and included the first surgery performed in space on live animals. The crew consisted of Scott Altman, Jay Buckey, Jr., Kathryn Hire, Richard Linnehan, James Pawelczyk, Richard Searfoss, and Dafydd Williams of Canada.

11–13 India detonated five underground nuclear devices. It was the first time since 1974 that India conducted a nuclear test. (On May 28–30, Pakistan—India's neighbor and rival—carried out its first-ever nuclear tests, a series of six underground explosions.)

17 In Birmingham, England, the leaders of the major industrial nations ("the Group of Eight") ended their 24th annual summit meeting on world economic issues. The countries represented were Canada, France, Germany, Great Britain, Italy, Japan, Russia, and the United States. The meeting marked the first time that Russia was given full membership status. Among the issues discussed were the financial problems of the world's poorest nations and global warming.

Government changes in May: Following national elections in **Hungary,** Viktor Orbán became premier. He succeeded Gyula Horn, who had been

On May 26, the *Grand Princess*—the largest cruise ship in the world—embarked on its twelve-day maiden voyage. Twice the size of the *Titanic,* the ship contains five swimming pools, three theaters, several tennis courts, a nine-hole putting golf course, and a virtual-reality entertainment center.

Tornado Warning!

From February through May, the southeastern United States was battered by severe tornadoes, making the spring of 1998 one of the most deadly tornado seasons ever. The violent twisters, with their spinning funnel-shaped clouds, caused more than 100 deaths and millions of dollars in property damage.

On February 22–23, at least seven tornadoes hit central Florida, killing 42 people. Considered the worst tornadoes ever to hit the state, they unleashed winds of up to 206 miles (332 kilometers) per hour. In March through May, similar storms struck parts of Alabama, Arkansas, Georgia, Kentucky, Mississippi, North Carolina, South Carolina, Tennessee, and Virginia.

Most meteorologists said that the storms in the Southeast were caused by El Niño, a Pacific Ocean climate disturbance. Usually, late winter and early spring is tornado season in the south-central states of Texas, Oklahoma, and Kansas. But El Niño apparently caused a shift in the swift westerly winds called jet streams. This, in turn, pushed the tornado-producing storms eastward, over the southeastern states.

A homeowner folds a flag recovered from his tornado-ravaged house in Alabama.

premier since 1994. . . .In **Indonesia,** President Suharto resigned, after weeks of widespread unrest and rioting. Suharto, who had been president since 1967, was succeeded by Bacharuddin Jusuf Habibie. . . .In national elections in **Paraguay,** Raúl Cubas Grau was elected president. He succeeded Juan Carlos Wasmosy, who had been president since 1993. . . .In national elections in the **Philippines,** Joseph Estrada was elected president. He succeeded Fidel Ramos, who had been president since 1992. . . .In **Yugoslavia,** Momir Bulatovic was named premier. He succeeded Radoje Kontic, who had been premier since 1992.

JUNE

3 A high-speed passenger train traveling 125 miles (200 kilometers) per hour derailed and slammed into a concrete bridge near the town of Eschede in northern Germany. The accident killed 102 people and injured about 300 others. It was Germany's worst railroad crash in more than fifty years.

12 The U.S. space shuttle *Discovery* completed a ten-day mission. It was the ninth and final U.S. mission to the Russian space station *Mir*. The crew consisted of Franklin Chang-Diaz, Dominic Gorie, Janet Kavandi, Wendy Lawrence, Charles Precourt, and Valery Ryumin of Russia. U.S. astronaut Andrew Thomas, who had been on *Mir* for four and a half months, returned to Earth.

18 U.S. President Bill Clinton nominated Bill Richardson to succeed Federico Peña as Secretary of Energy. He named Richard C. Holbrooke to succeed Richardson as U.S. Ambassador to the United Nations. (On July 31, the Senate confirmed Richardson's nomination; by the end of the year, Holbrooke's nomination had not been confirmed.)

25 Scientists reported that dinosaur fossils found in northeastern China had feathers. It was the strongest evidence yet found that birds are directly descended from dinosaurs. The fossils were of turkey-sized dinosaurs that lived more than 120 million years ago. There were two species. One had a cluster of feathers at the end of its tail. The other

Firefighters search the wreckage of a high-speed German train that crashed in June, killing 102 people.

Crazy Horse Returns in Stone

On June 3, thousands of people attended the dedication of the Crazy Horse Memorial in the Black Hills of South Dakota. The mountain carving shows the face of Crazy Horse—the famous 19th-century Sioux chief who resisted American occupation of the northern Plains, and who led the attack on George Armstrong Custer's cavalry in the Battle of the Little Bighorn in 1876. He surrendered in 1877 and died several months later after being stabbed by an American soldier. Following his death, a medicine man said that Crazy Horse had told the Sioux, "I will return to you in stone."

The sculptured head of Crazy Horse is 90 feet (27 meters) tall—30 feet (9 meters) taller than the heads of the four U.S. presidents on nearby Mount Rushmore. When the memorial is completed, in about 50 years, it will depict Crazy Horse seated on his horse, pointing over the Black Hills. It will be the largest sculpture on Earth: 563 feet (172 meters) high and 641 feet (195 meters) long.

Sculptor Korczak Ziolkowski began the project on June 3, 1948, at the request of Native American leaders who wanted a monument to honor their heritage. Ziolkowski spent 35 years sculpting the mountain, until his death in 1982. His family is carrying on with his work.

had feathers covering much of its body. Neither dinosaur could fly; the scientists suggested that the feathers may have been used for insulation, camouflage, or mating displays.

Government changes in June: In national elections in **Colombia,** Andrés Pastrana Arango was elected president. He succeeded Ernesto Samper Pizano, who had been president since 1994.…In **Nigeria,** Sani Abacha, who had led the nation since 1993, died. He was succeeded by Abdulsalam Abubakar.

JULY

3 U.S. President Bill Clinton completed a nine-day trip to China. It was the first visit by a U.S. president to China since 1989, when Chinese troops crushed a student-led democracy movement. A highlight of Clinton's trip was a summit meeting with Chinese President Jiang Zemin. This was followed by a news conference, broadcast live on Chinese television, during which the two leaders discussed human rights.

5 In Florida, the worst outbreak of wildfires in more than 50 years was gradually being brought under control. The fires, which had begun in late May, burned more than 450,000 acres (182,000 hectares) and injured about 95 people.

17 A tsunami, a series of giant ocean waves, crashed onto the coast of Papua New Guinea, killing some 2,000 people and leaving 4,500 homeless. The largest wave was 30 feet (9 meters) high. The tsunami was triggered by an undersea earthquake measuring 7.0 on the Richter scale of ground motion.

23 U.S. scientists reported that they had produced more than 50 cloned mice, including clones of some of the clones. It was the first time that three generations of clones had been created from adult cells. Unlike other creatures, which result from the mating of a male and a female, a clone has only one parent. It's grown from a single cell taken from an adult animal. Thus, a clone is an exact copy of its parent.

24 In Washington, D. C., a gunman broke into the Capitol and exchanged fire with police officers. Two officers—Jacob Chestnut and John Gibson—were killed; the gunman, Russell Weston, was wounded.

Scientists announced that they had created more than 50 cloned mice. A clone is an exact copy of an adult animal. Two of the genetically identical mice are shown here.

First Lady Hillary Rodham Clinton visits the Thomas Edison National Historic Site in West Orange, New Jersey.

Saving America's Treasures

From July 13 through July 16, First Lady Hillary Rodham Clinton toured neglected historical sites in four states and Washington, D.C. Her tour launched a campaign called "Save America's Treasures." Its purpose was to call attention to the deteriorating condition of many significant historical and cultural sites, and to the importance of preserving them.

One of the first stops on the tour was the Francis Scott Key Monument in Baltimore, Maryland, which honors Key's writing of "The Star Spangled Banner." In New Jersey, she visited Thomas Alva Edison's laboratory, where he created hundreds of inventions. Stops in New York and Massachusetts included an Indian archeological site, a theater built in 1903, and the home of abolitionist Harriet Tubman.

The First Lady's final stop was Seneca Falls, New York, where she joined in celebrating the 150th anniversary of the first Women's Rights Convention. The women who gathered in Seneca Falls in 1848 to proclaim that "all men and women are created equal" started the women's rights movement—at a time when women were forbidden to vote or even to own property. The 1998 celebration included re-enactments of the convention, museum tours, and concerts by women performers.

Government changes in July: Following national elections in the **Czech Republic,** Milos Zemin was named premier. He succeeded Josef Tosovsky, who had been premier since December 1997. . . . In national elections in **Ecuador,** Jamil Mahuad Witt was elected president. He succeeded Fabián Alarcón, who had been in office since early 1997. . . . In **Japan,** Keizo Obuchi was named premier. He succeeded Ryutaro Hashimoto, who had been premier since 1996.

AUGUST

7 Two bombs exploded within minutes of each other outside the U.S. embassies in Nairobi, Kenya, and Dar es Salaam, Tanzania. The Nairobi blast killed at least 247 people, including 12 Americans, and injured thousands more. In Dar es Salaam, 10 people were killed and about 75 were injured. Within days, the U.S. government linked the coordinated attacks to a secretive Islamic terrorist group headed by Osama bin Laden, a Saudi-born millionaire living in Afghanistan.

15 In Northern Ireland, a car bomb exploded in the town of Omagh, killing 28 people and injuring another 220. It was the deadliest bombing since 1969, when the Irish Republican Army (IRA) began a terrorist campaign to rid the province of British rule. The Real IRA, a splinter group of the IRA, claimed responsibility for the bombing.

16 American balloonist Steve Fossett was forced to end his fourth attempt to become the first person to fly nonstop around the world in a hot-air balloon when his craft, *Solo Spirit,* plunged into the Coral Sea east of Australia. Although Fossett didn't reach his goal, he traveled 15,200 miles (24,462 kilometers), breaking the former distance record of 10,360 miles (16,673 kilometers), which he had set in January 1997.

20 Retaliating against the U.S. embassy bombings earlier in the month, U.S. Navy ships in the Arabian and Red Seas launched about 75 cruise missiles at two targets. One target was terrorist training camps in eastern

The American embassy in Nairobi, Kenya, shown moments after a terrorist bomb exploded. Here, a U.S. Marine guard instructs a cameraman to move away from the wreckage.

Chinese villagers make their way through the floodwaters that devastated their town.

Floods Devastate Asia

As August ended, millions of people in large areas of China, India, and Bangladesh were homeless, as floodwaters covered the land. The disaster was caused by a summer of torrential rains. But added to this were the harmful effects of years of poor environmental practices. In many places, loggers had stripped trees from the land. Elsewhere, people had drained wetlands to create farms. As a result, the land had lost its ability to absorb large amounts of water during flood periods.

In China, flooding along the Yangtze River and smaller rivers in the northeast was described as the worst in at least 44 years. The floods killed over 3,000 people, destroyed eight million homes, and ruined crops.

In northern and eastern India, heavy rains caused landslides and flash flooding that killed nearly 1,000 people. Rains in Uttar Pradesh, India's most populous state, left millions homeless and swelled the Ganges River.

The flooded Ganges rose to record levels as it flowed through Bangladesh, which had already been hit by unusually heavy monsoon rains. Higher-than-normal sea levels trapped the floodwaters in the country. In addition to killing hundreds of people and marooning many people on the roofs of their homes, the waters became polluted and stagnant, causing epidemics of malaria and other diseases.

Afghanistan. The second target was a chemical plant in Sudan that U.S. officials said was producing ingredients used in the production of deadly nerve gas.

Government changes in August: In **Jordan,** Fayez al-Tarawnah was appointed prime minister. He succeeded Abdel Salem al-Majali, who had been prime minister since early 1997.

SEPTEMBER

15 In southern Mexico, torrential rains caused the country's worst floods of the century. At least 185 people died, and several hundred others were missing and feared dead.

21 The 53rd annual session of the United Nations General Assembly opened at U.N. headquarters in New York City. Didier Opertti of Uruguay was elected to serve as assembly president for one year.

11–28 Hurricane Georges carved a path of destruction through the Caribbean Sea and the Gulf of Mexico before dying down as it drifted into Mississippi and Alabama. Hardest hit was the Dominican Republic, where at least 125 people were killed. In the United States, Georges was blamed for three deaths. The powerful storm caused extensive property damage in the Florida Keys and along the Gulf coast from New Orleans, Louisiana, to Pensacola, Florida.

30 U.S. President Bill Clinton announced that the federal budget had a surplus of about $70 billion for the fiscal, or financial, year. (A fiscal year runs from October 1 to September 30.) It was the first time since 1969 that the government took in more money than it spent.

Government changes in September: In **Albania,** Pandeli Majko became premier. He succeeded Fatos Nano, who had been premier since 1997. . . . In national elections in **Germany,** Gerhard Schröder of the Social Democratic Party was

Key West, Florida, residents hold on tightly to each other as they battle Hurricane Georges's fierce winds.

Above: Inside Expo's Pavilion of the Future.
Right: Fish-gazing in the Ocean Pavilion.

Portugal's Expo '98

"The Oceans: A Heritage for the Future" was the theme of Expo '98, the first world's fair ever held in Portugal. The festival opened on May 22 and ended on September 30. It celebrated both the International Year of the Ocean and Portugal's historical role as a seafaring nation.

One of the fair's most popular buildings was the Ocean Pavilion. Visitors to this giant aquarium felt they were actually in the sea, as they walked among walls of water filled with fish and other marine life. The aquarium showcased some 10,000 creatures, representing 250 species from around the world.

Most of the 146 nations that participated in Expo '98 built pavilions with an oceans theme. Germany created an imaginary underwater research station. Finland let people use a simulator to try to steer an icebreaking ship. In the United States Pavilion, visitors were able to handle sea slugs; touch an iceberg; and, with the help of a satellite connection to the North Atlantic Ocean, follow a whale-tagging exercise.

elected chancellor. He defeated Helmut Kohl of the more conservative Christian Democratic Union, who had been chancellor since 1982. . . . Following national elections in **Malta,** Eddie Fenech Adami became prime minister. He succeeded Alfred Sant. Fenech Adami had previously served as prime minister from 1987 to 1996.

OCTOBER

1 In New York City, hundreds of people packed the main concourse, or hall, of Grand Central Terminal to celebrate a $200-million project that restored the great train station to its former glory. Grand Central first opened in 1913 and quickly became one of the nation's busiest train stations. In the 1970s, it almost fell victim to the wrecking ball. But a group of people, led by former First Lady Jacqueline Kennedy Onassis, launched a campaign to save the terminal.

17 In Nigeria, about 700 people were killed by a gasoline fire. The fire occurred after vandals, hoping to collect and sell fuel, broke into a pipeline near the town of Warri. Officials believed that the fire erupted when sparks from tools used by the vandals caused the fuel to explode into a ball of flames that raced through nearby farms and villages.

23 After intense negotiations, Israeli Prime Minister Benjamin Netanyahu and Palestinian leader Yasir Arafat signed a peace agreement in Washington, D.C. Israel agreed to give the Palestinians authority over an additional 13 percent of the West Bank and agreed to free scores of Arab

New York City threw a party to celebrate the restoration of one of its most famous buildings—Grand Central Terminal, a train station with breathtaking architecture. Especially dramatic was the vaulted ceiling, its constellations twinkling with tiny lights like stars in the sky.

The 1998 Nobel Prizes

Chemistry: Walter Kohn, an Austrian-born American and John A. Pople, a Briton working in the United States, for developing methods to predict how atoms link up to form molecules and how various molecules behave.

Economics: Amartya Sen, an Indian working in England, for his work in an area known as welfare economics. Sen showed that famines in which thousands of people die don't occur because of a lack of food. Rather, people starve because they don't have the money to buy the food.

Literature: José Saramago of Portugal, for his imaginative novels. Saramago used irony, supernatural events, and inventive techniques to create an atmosphere of unreality, in order to comment on important issues of life.

Peace: John Hume and David Trimble of Northern Ireland, for their efforts to end the violence between Protestants and Catholics that had plagued their land since the 1960s. The two men played key roles in formulating the peace agreement that was signed on April 10, 1998.

Physics: Daniel C. Tsui, a Chinese-born American; and Robert B. Laughlin and Horst L. Störmer of the United States (working together), for their work in the field of quantum physics. They showed that when subatomic particles called electrons are placed in a strong magnetic field, they behave as if they were a fluid.

Physiology or Medicine: Robert F. Furchgott, Louis J. Ignarro, and Ferid Murad of the United States, for discovering that the gas nitric oxide plays an important role in the human body. For example, nitric oxide causes the walls of blood vessels to relax, increasing blood flow.

prisoners. The Palestinians agreed to arrest terrorists and seize weapons, and to remove the part of their government charter that calls for the destruction of Israel.

27–31 More than 11,000 people were killed and one million were left homeless after Hurricane Mitch battered Central America with torrential rains. Hardest hit were Nicaragua and Honduras, where entire villages were engulfed by floods and mud slides. It was one of the biggest and deadliest hurricanes ever to strike the region.

Government changes in October: In **Italy,** Massimo D'Alema was named premier. D'Alema was the first former Communist to become premier of Italy. He succeeded Romano Prodi, who had been premier since 1996. . . . In **Lebanon,** Emile Lahoud became president. He succeeded Elias Hrawi, who had been president since 1989.

NOVEMBER

1 More than three dozen television stations across the United States officially introduced digital high-definition television (HDTV). This new system produces super-sharp wide-screen pictures with movie-quality sound. But few people in the United States owned the digital TV sets needed to view HDTV, and very little programming was available. However, all commercial broadcast stations will have to send out digital signals by the year 2002.

7 The U.S. space shuttle *Discovery* completed a nine-day mission. The mission's highlight was the return to space of U.S. Senator John Glenn, who in 1962 became the first American to orbit Earth. The 77-year-old Glenn was the oldest person ever to go into space. The mission also included the release and retrieval of a satellite that photographed the sun's outer atmosphere. In addition to Glenn, the crew consisted of Curtis Brown, Jr., Steven Lindsey, Scott Parazynski, Stephen Robinson, Pedro Duque of Spain and Chiaki Mukai of Japan.

17-18 Thousands of meteors—commonly called shooting stars—flashed through the night sky as the Leonid meteor shower bombarded Earth. The Leonid meteors are debris left behind by Comet Tempel-Tuttle as it orbits the sun. This meteor shower occurs every year in November, but the intensity of the shower varies from year to year—depending on what part of the comet's trail Earth crosses. The 1998 Leonids were the most dazzling in more than 30 years.

Skywatchers in Asia had the best "seats" to view the dazzling Leonid meteor shower.

The Republican Bush brothers, Jeb and George, won the governorships of Florida and Texas—two of the nation's most populous states.

America Votes!

U.S. voters went to the polls on November 3. Democrats won victories in some important Congressional races, as well as key governorships. But Republicans kept control of Congress. Although they lost five seats in the House of Representatives, they still held a 223 to 211 majority (with one independent). In the Senate, Republicans kept their 55-45 advantage.

In some ways, the election was considered a victory for Democrats. For one thing, it was a midterm election, coming in the middle of a four-year presidential term. Historically, the party that holds the presidency—in this case, the Democrats—loses Congressional seats in midterm elections. The 1998 vote was the first midterm election since 1924 in which the party holding the presidency gained so many seats in Congress.

Many people thought the Democrats would do poorly because President Bill Clinton was at the center of a scandal. Republicans predicted that public outrage over the scandal would lead to big electoral gains for their party. However, surveys showed that most voters approved of the way Clinton was doing his job, but were disappointed in Congress's performance. Education, taxes, Social Security, and jobs were the issues most on peoples' minds.

Many Republicans soon realized that these issues should have been the focus of their campaigns. They blamed Newt Gingrich, the powerful Speaker of the House, for not seeing that and for making the presidential scandal the major issue. As a result, under pressure from fellow Republicans, Gingrich resigned as Speaker and said he would be leaving Congress.

Government changes in November: In **Cambodia,** Hun Sen was named prime minister, following disputed national elections in July. Hun Sen succeeded Ung Huot, who had been in office since 1997.

DECEMBER

1 The two largest U.S. oil companies, Exxon and Mobil, agreed to merge, forming a new company called Exxon Mobil. The company would be the biggest in the world, with annual sales of $204 billion. Before the merger can take effect, it must be approved by the Federal Trade Commission, to make sure that it won't harm consumers by controlling the supply or price of gasoline.

15 The U.S. space shuttle *Endeavour* completed a twelve-day mission, with a crew that consisted of Robert Cabana, Nancy Jane Currie, James Newman, Jerry Ross, Frederick "Rick" Sturckow, and Sergei Krikalev of Russia. The objective of the mission was to connect and make functional the first two sections of the new *International Space Station.* During activities that included three space walks, the *Endeavour* crew hoisted the U.S.-built module *Unity* from the shuttle's cargo bay and attached it to the Russian-built *Zarya* module, which had been placed in orbit on November 20.

16–19 The United States and Great Britain launched a series of air strikes against military targets in Iraq. The attacks followed the refusal by Iraqi President Saddam Hussein to cooperate with United Nations weapons

On December 19, the U.S. House of Representatives voted to impeach President Bill Clinton. Clinton thus faced a trial in the Senate in 1999.

Furby: The "Must-Have" Holiday Toy

As 1998 drew to an end, the toy on everyone's holiday wishlist was a fur-covered, big-eyed, floppy-eared, talking-singing, gremlinlike critter named Furby. Stuffed with a microprocessor and electronic sensors, Furby can respond to touch, light, and noise. It even talks. At first, it speaks only its own language—Furbish. But it soon "learns" to speak English, too! It has a total vocabulary of about 100 words of English and 100 words of Furbish, which it can combine into about 800 phrases. Pet a Furby and it purrs. Turn the lights out and it croons "Sing me to sleep." Put on a CD and it begins to dance. It wiggles and giggles, sneezes and burps—and delights kids of all ages.

inspectors. The inspectors have been searching for evidence of weapons of mass destruction: chemical, biological, and nuclear weapons. These inspections were mandated by the agreement that ended the 1991 Persian Gulf War, when Iraq invaded neighboring Kuwait. The aim of the air strikes was to weaken Iraq's weapons program and lessen its ability to threaten other nations in the Persian Gulf region.

19 The U.S. House of Representatives voted to impeach President Bill Clinton. It was only the second time in American history that a president was impeached. The House approved two articles of impeachment, charging Clinton with lying under oath and obstructing justice to conceal an improper relationship with a former White House intern. The vote was almost entirely along party lines, with Republicans voting for the articles and Democrats voting against them. Clinton faced a trial in the Senate in 1999; if convicted, he would be automatically removed from office.

Government changes in December: In national elections in **Venezuela,** Hugo Chávez was elected president, to take office in 1999. He would succeed Rafael Caldera Rodriguez, who had been president since 1994.

President Bill Clinton was impeached by the House of Representatives on December 19. He was the first elected president ever to be impeached.

CRISIS IN THE WHITE HOUSE

On December 19, 1998, the U.S. House of Representatives impeached President Bill Clinton, voting to send formal charges of wrongdoing against him to the Senate. Clinton thus became only the second president in American history to be impeached. He faced the prospect of a trial in the Senate in 1999—and if he were to be convicted at that trial, he would be the first U.S. president ever removed from office.

This stunning event grew out of charges that the president had lied about an improper personal relationship with a young woman who had worked at the White House. It divided the country along political lines. And it seemed likely to have lasting effects on the office of the presidency.

THE INVESTIGATION

The charges against Clinton stemmed from a four-year investigation conducted by an independent counsel, Kenneth W. Starr. The job of an independent counsel is to make sure that high-level government officials, such as the president, are not above the law. When there's evidence that a crime may have been committed by someone high in government, a federal court appoints an independent counsel to find out if there's anything to it. Because the counsel is appointed by a court and not by the president, the reasoning is, he or she can investigate fairly and thoroughly.

Starr, a judge and prosecutor, was appointed in 1994 to examine business dealings that Bill and Hillary Clinton had during the 1980s, when Clinton was governor of Arkansas. Starr was specifically asked to investigate the Clintons' involvement in Whitewater, an Arkansas real estate venture. In the four years that followed, he expanded the scope of his investigation. He pursued rumors that the Clintons had hidden records and urged associates to keep silent about Whitewater, received illegal campaign contributions during their years in Arkansas, and improperly obtained FBI files at the White House.

None of these investigations turned up any evidence of wrongdoing on the part of the President or the First Lady. The issue that sparked the impeachment proceedings was something entirely different.

While Starr was investigating Clinton, the president was also facing a civil lawsuit filed by Paula Jones, an Arkansas woman. Jones claimed he had made an unwelcome advance to her in 1991, when he was governor. The suit was thrown out of court, but not before Clinton gave a deposition—a formal statement, given under oath. In his deposition he denied not only Jones's charge but also rumors of an affair with Monica Lewinsky, a 21-year-old former White House intern. Lewinsky also denied the rumors under oath. But she said otherwise to friends—and one, Linda Tripp, taped her conversations. Based on that, Starr launched an investigation to learn if Clinton had lied under oath and urged Lewinsky to do the same.

For months, Clinton continued to deny having had an improper relationship with Lewinsky. But on August 17, in testimony taped for Starr's grand jury and in a televised address to the nation, he acknowledged the relationship. He asked for the forgiveness of the country and his family. He continued to state that he had not lied under oath and had not encouraged anyone else to do so.

Three weeks later, Starr delivered the results of his investigation to Congress. Two vans pulled up to the Capitol and unloaded box after box of transcripts, depositions, and other documents. Starr's report accused the president of perjury (lying under oath), encouraging others to lie, and trying to hinder his investigation.

The Road to Impeachment

Impeachment is a way in which Congress can remove the president (and certain other officials) from office. This is the procedure:

- A special investigator, such as the independent counsel, brings evidence of wrongdoing to the House of Representatives.
- The House votes to send the evidence to its Judiciary Committee for review.
- The Judiciary Committee reviews the evidence. If the committee finds the accusations serious enough, it draws up a list of charges—called articles of impeachment—against the president.
- The full House reviews the articles and votes on whether to impeach the president, or formally bring charges against him.
- If the House votes to impeach, the Senate then conducts a trial on the charges. The Chief Justice of the Supreme Court presides as judge, and the president is allowed to present a defense.
- If two thirds of the senators vote for conviction, the president is removed from office. Then the vice-president is sworn in as president.

Independent counsel Kenneth Starr (*below*) presented Congress with box after box of documents in his report.

This, Starr said, was enough for Congress to consider one of the most serious actions it can take: removing a president from office. That action begins with impeachment, which is the act of bringing charges against the president.

President Clinton's involvement with former White House intern Monica Lewinsky sparked the crisis.

THE REACTION

Starr's investigation was in the news constantly in 1998. Television and newspapers reported every new rumor and twist as the tale unfolded. But news of the scandal didn't hurt Clinton's popularity. Polls showed his approval rating rising to new heights. Even after the Starr report came out, polls showed that a majority of Americans wanted Clinton to stay in office. Americans were disappointed in Clinton and thought less of him as a person, but they still approved of the job he was doing as president.

Some people felt that Starr's investigation had probed too deeply into Clinton's personal life. Presidents have had improper or inappropriate relationships in the past, they said, but those relationships weren't exposed by a prosecutor. Other people said investigating the president's personal life was right, because a president should follow the highest standards of behavior. Not surprisingly, opinions about the president often split along political lines. Clinton's political opponents, especially conservative Republicans, were especially harsh in attacking his conduct. His Democratic supporters said that Starr, a conservative Republican, was politically motivated and had set out to trap the president.

On October 8, the House of Representatives voted to start an impeachment inquiry against Clinton, and the House Judiciary Committee began to review the charges. Meanwhile, many observers expected the Clinton scandal to affect the 1998 election. This was a midterm election (midway through a four-year presidential term), and the party that holds the presidency historically loses seats in Congress in midterm years. Republicans predicted that public outrage over the scandal would lead to big gains for their party in 1998.

But on Election Day, the Republicans lost five seats in the House of Representatives and just kept their 55–45 majority in the Senate. Surveys taken as voters left the polls showed that most didn't want Clinton to be impeached. Education, taxes, Social Security, and jobs were the issues most on people's minds.

THE INQUIRY AND VOTE

The election had no effect on the work of the House Judiciary Committee, which was already underway. The committee had to answer two questions: Was there evidence to back up the charges? And were the charges grounds for impeachment? The committee called Starr to testify, and he repeated the allegations made in his report. Clinton responded to a list of written questions, giving the same information he had previously given to Starr. There was no new information from either side to help the committee make its decision.

The committee also heard from experts on constitutional law. The Constitution permits impeachment for "Treason, Bribery, or other High Crimes and Misdemeanors." Were the charges against the president as serious as treason and bribery? The answer wasn't clear. Republicans said that perjury was a very serious offense, even when committed in a civil lawsuit that was thrown out of court.

Presidents in Trouble

Besides Clinton, only two other presidents have faced impeachment. They were Andrew Johnson and Richard M. Nixon.

- Andrew Johnson became president after Abraham Lincoln was assassinated in 1865. He battled with Congress over Reconstruction, the plan to rebuild the South after the Civil War. When he installed governments in Southern states, Congress removed them and put the army in control. The dispute grew so intense that the House voted to impeach Johnson in 1868, charging him with misusing his powers. He was acquitted in the Senate—by one vote—and finished his term.

- Richard Nixon resigned in 1974 to avoid almost certain impeachment. His trouble began in the 1972 campaign, when workers for his re-election committee broke into Democratic Party headquarters at the Watergate apartments in Washington, D.C. Nixon and his aides tried to cover up their links to the burglary. Nixon won re-election, but his role in the cover-up and other campaign irregularities was discovered. When the House Judiciary Committee voted to send articles of impeachment to the full House, he resigned.

Democrats said that the president's offenses weren't "high crimes" and not grounds for impeachment because they involved his personal life, not his job as president.

After the November elections and polls showed support for the president, many people expected Republicans to drop their demands for impeachment. Some people suggested that Congress should instead censure Clinton, or vote to condemn his behavior. They pointed out that Clinton could always answer to charges of perjury in court after his term ended. But Republicans in the House refused to consider censure and pressed on.

On December 11–12, the House Judiciary Committee voted along party lines to send four articles of impeachment to the full House for a vote. On December 19, after a day of bitter debate, the House passed two of the four articles. Those articles charged Clinton with perjury before Starr's grand jury and obstructing justice by encouraging others to lie. The House divided sharply in its vote. Nearly all Republicans voted for the articles, and nearly all Democrats voted against them. Republicans had a majority in the House, so the articles passed.

That historic vote set the stage for a presidential impeachment trial in the Senate in 1999—only the second such trial in U.S. history. But it seemed unlikely that two thirds of the senators would vote to turn the president out of office. Most people hoped that Democrats and Republicans would find a way to compromise. They worried about the effects a trial would have on the nation, which was already bitterly divided on the issue, and on the presidency, which seemed certain to be weakened.

Traders at the Tokyo Stock Exchange watch stock prices plummet.

THE ASIAN "FINANCIAL FLU"

Banks and businesses closed. People lost their jobs. Stock prices plummeted, and people lost their savings. For many people in East Asia, 1998 was a very hard year, as the region struggled with an economic crisis. And there was growing concern that the Asian "financial flu" might spread. Some experts thought that if the crisis couldn't be stopped, it might trigger a worldwide economic slump.

BOOM AND BUST

East Asia's economic troubles took many people by surprise because, until recently, the region had been booming. Beginning in the 1960s, the nations of East Asia enjoyed spectacular economic growth. Japan led the way. Fueled by exports of cars and high-tech products, its economy grew to be the second largest in the world, after that of the United States. Hong Kong, Singapore, Taiwan, and South Korea were quick to follow Japan's lead. Other nations, including Thailand, Indonesia, Malaysia, and the Philippines, weren't far behind. Foreign investors poured money into the region, financing everything from airports to skyscrapers. But by 1997, the effects of too much building, too much spending, and especially too much borrowing began to hit home.

The trouble started in Thailand in July 1997. Thailand had borrowed heavily abroad, and its lax regulations allowed banks to finance all sorts of uncreditworthy projects. The country was awash in half-empty office buildings and unprofitable shopping centers, built with borrowed funds. When the loans weren't repaid, the banks were stuck. The Thai stock market headed down.

Currency traders sensed that the Thai economy was headed for trouble and began to sell off their holdings of Thai currency. That forced the value of the currency down. The fall in currency values made it even harder for Thailand to repay loans it had obtained in dollars and other foreign currencies. Foreign investors were alarmed and began to pull out. More Thai businesses closed their doors, putting two million workers on the streets.

One by one, other East Asian countries went into the same tailspin. South Korea was hit next. Its industries, guided and protected by the government, had grown into huge conglomerates. But as in Thailand, banks and businesses had borrowed huge amounts from foreign investors. Now those investors began to pull out. Stock prices fell, and the value of South Korean currency was nearly cut in half.

Investors also took another look at Indonesia, where favoritism and corruption helped bring on a crisis. Indonesian President Suharto had been in power for more than 30 years. His children and supporters had built up huge business empires, based on government concessions. Indonesian banks and businesses had borrowed heavily abroad, and much of the money wasn't well managed. Now currency and stock market values plunged, and the economic troubles fueled political unrest. In May 1998, after riots broke out, Suharto was forced to resign.

Stock Market Jitters: The faltering economies in East Asia and Russia affected the United States, too. The U.S. economy had been booming for six years, but stock prices fell sharply in the summer.

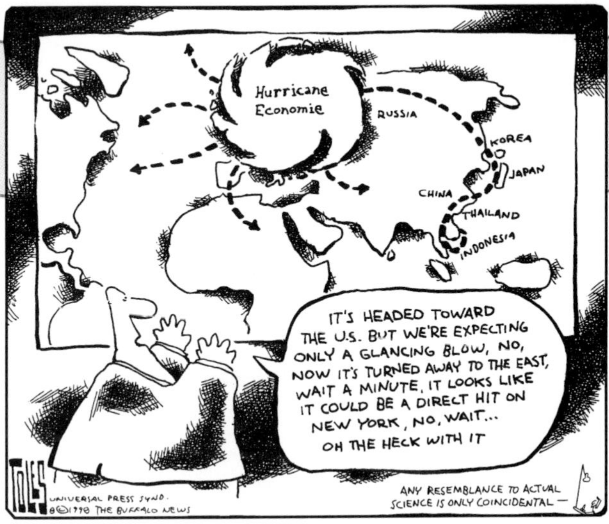

THE "FLU" SPREADS

Many people expected the worst of the economic "Asian flu" to be quickly over. But by mid-1998, Indonesia, South Korea, and Thailand were still suffering, and they had been joined by Malaysia. Hong Kong was in a slump.

So was Japan, the region's leading trading nation. As other East Asian economies staggered, the market for Japanese goods shrank. Unemployment and business bankruptcies, once rare in Japan, became real worries. Loaded with bad debts, banks stopped lending, putting more pressure on businesses and consumers. In the spring of 1998, the Japanese government announced a $128 billion program of government spending, tax cuts, and other measures designed to revive the economy. But it didn't seem to be enough.

As Japan faced a deepening recession, even Asian countries whose economies had managed to keep growing—China, the Philippines, Singapore, and Taiwan—were slowing down. And effects of the regional slump were felt worldwide.

One result was growth in the U.S. trade deficit. The United States annually imports more from Asian nations than it exports to them. By spending more on imports than it earns on exports, the United States has built up huge trade deficits. When Asian currencies tumbled, Asian imports—from cars to clothing to television sets—dropped in price, so Americans could afford even more imports. At the same time, hard-pressed consumers in Asia could no longer buy American goods.

A WORLDWIDE CRISIS?

The International Monetary Fund (IMF) is an organization consisting of 182 member nations. Members contribute money to the Fund, according to their financial strength. That money is used to help other members in times of economic crisis.

Because East Asia is so important in the world economy, the area received record amounts of aid from the IMF. But the aid came with conditions: The IMF asked these countries to cut public spending, limit credit, lower barriers to foreign trade and investment, end subsidies for inefficient industries, break up monopolies, and take action against corruption. These steps were meant to help bring the countries onto firmer economic footing. However, the conditions were also likely to make life harder, by increasing bankruptcies and unemployment.

Meanwhile, concern grew that the economic "flu" would spread worldwide, as nervous investors pulled out of other countries. That happened in Russia in the summer of 1998. Russia's currency collapsed in value, and the country's economy all but collapsed with it.

Brazil, with the largest economy in Latin America, seemed next in line. Latin America buys nearly 20 percent of America's exports and is home to thousands of American-owned factories. If this region were to join Asia in recession, the U.S. economy would be badly hurt.

The U.S. economy had been booming for six years. People who held stock in U.S. corporations had watched their investments grow, as stock prices hit record highs. But now they began to worry. Concern about the world financial crisis sent stock prices down sharply in the summer of 1998.

In the fall, U.S. President Bill Clinton called on world leaders to cut interest rates and take other steps to spur economic growth. But no one could tell whether that would be enough to stop the spreading economic woes.

The world was alarmed when India and Pakistan conducted underground nuclear tests in May. Many people in India (*above*) and Pakistan celebrated their countries' nuclear weapons tests. Others, like this Indian boy (*right*), protested the nuclear explosions.

A NEW NUCLEAR THREAT

In May 1998, India and Pakistan set off a series of explosions that caused alarm around the world. The explosions were underground tests of nuclear weapons—weapons that neither country had previously admitted to having.

Nuclear weapons are among the most powerful and feared weapons in the world. They have tremendous destructive power, and they poison air, soil, and water with radioactive wastes. These weapons have been used in war only once, when the United States dropped two atomic bombs on Japan at the end of World War II. During the Cold War, the period after World War II, the United States and the Soviet Union built up huge nuclear arsenals. Their arms race produced enough nuclear weapons to destroy the world many times over.

The Cold War ended with the collapse of Communism in 1990. The Soviet Union fell apart. Since then, the United States and Russia (which inherited the Soviet arsenal) have been trying to reduce the number of nuclear weapons. Along with France, Britain, and China, they agreed in 1996 to ban nuclear weapons tests. (The United States signed the test-ban treaty, but the Senate has yet to approve it.) Above-ground nuclear weapons tests had already been stopped because of the danger of radioactive wastes. Now underground tests were banned as well.

The United States, Russia, France, Britain, and China were the only countries that agreed to this ban—because they were the only countries that acknowledged having nuclear weapons. India and Pakistan were thought to be among a handful of other nations developing the weapons, but they didn't talk about it. All the same, it was a shock when India set off a series of underground nuclear tests on May 11–13, 1998.

A NEW ARMS RACE?

India and Pakistan have a long history of conflict. Both countries were ruled as a single British colony until 1947. When they won independence, the former colonial territory was divided. Ethnic and religious differences caused violence and played a major part in the division. India is mostly Hindu; Pakistan is mostly Muslim. And since independence, India and Pakistan have fought three wars—in 1947, 1965, and 1971.

In addition, the countries have a running dispute over Kashmir, a region on the border between them. India governs Kashmir as a state. But Pakistan wants the people of Kashmir, who are mostly Muslim, to decide for themselves which country to belong to. India has agreed to allow a vote on the issue; but the vote has never been held. Meanwhile, Pakistan has armed and financed Muslim rebels in Kashmir. At least 30,000 people have been killed in fighting there in the past ten years.

Were the tests the beginning of an arms race between the two countries? The answer came at the end of May, when Pakistan started its own series of test explosions. Since both countries were thought to be developing nuclear weapons, the 1998 tests weren't a complete surprise. But now, it seemed, there was a real possibility of nuclear war along the India-Pakistan border.

The United States and other nations condemned the tests and imposed economic sanctions on both countries. On June 11, Pakistan declared that it would stop testing and would be willing to start talks with India and other nations on nuclear matters. India also said it wanted to end testing and was willing to talk.

Pakistanis read newspaper headlines announcing Pakistan's nuclear bomb tests. The tests raised concern over the possibility of a nuclear war along the India-Pakistan border.

The two countries didn't really seem ready to drop bombs on each other. In fact, their tests seemed mostly to be a way of asserting national pride. Neither country could afford to build a huge arsenal of nuclear bombs and missiles to carry them. As the crisis cooled, the United States lifted the severest economic sanctions against them.

But there was still a risk that, in a dispute, one or both countries might reach for its

A nuclear missile in Kazakhstan—a former Soviet republic. Since the end of the Cold War, the United States and Russia have been trying to reduce the number of nuclear weapons. But the Indian and Pakistani tests have raised fears of a new arms race.

nuclear weapons—and start a nuclear war. And if the two countries didn't lay down strict procedures for use of the weapons, a careless or hot-headed soldier could even start a nuclear war by accident. It was hoped that both nations would set up emergency communications systems and take other steps to prevent this. Such measures had helped keep the United States and the Soviet Union from pressing the nuclear button through the long years of the Cold War.

People hoped that India and Pakistan would abandon their nuclear programs—before they could build up stockpiles of the dangerous weapons and be tempted to use them. That didn't happen. But in the fall, both countries announced that they were willing to sign the test-ban treaty—as long as the other did. They also resumed peace talks that had been broken off a year before, after an argument over Kashmir.

THE NUCLEAR DANGER

The tests conducted by India and Pakistan put a spotlight on a serious international problem—the spread, or proliferation, of nuclear weapons. Many nations have agreed not to develop nuclear arms, in the hope that the world will never have to face a nuclear war. Since 1968, more than 120 countries have signed an international agreement on nuclear nonproliferation. Under this agreement, they have agreed to work to halt the spread of nuclear weapons.

The United States and other Western countries are strong supporters of the treaty. Limiting nuclear proliferation, they say, is the only way to limit the enormous danger of these weapons. But less developed countries don't all share this view. They point out that the nuclear powers haven't agreed to give up their weapons or even, despite lots of talk, significantly reduce their own stockpiles. As long as some powers have nuclear weapons, they say, others will want them too. India, for example, began to develop nuclear weapons because it felt threatened by China's nuclear weapons. Then Pakistan felt threatened by India, so it began its own program.

But as more countries get these weapons, the danger that they will be used increases. A country might turn to nuclear weapons for defense and unleash a nuclear war. An unscrupulous ruler might use the weapons to wage aggressive war. Or terrorists might obtain a nuclear device. A small nuclear weapon would be easy to conceal but powerful enough to do tremendous damage.

Countries that have nuclear weapons closely guard the secrets of how they are made, and the materials and systems used to make the weapons are tightly controlled. The International Atomic Energy Agency monitors the shipping of nuclear materials, to make sure that nothing falls into the wrong hands. But countries that want the weapons have found ways to get around the controls.

How Nuclear Weapons Work

Nuclear weapons get their tremendous destructive power by unlocking the energy in the center, or nucleus, of atoms. The energy may be released in two ways: fission or fusion.

- In fission, an atomic nucleus is split, giving off energy and subatomic particles called neutrons. The neutrons strike other nuclei and split them, releasing more energy and neutrons. This process is called a chain reaction. It requires a material that undergoes fission easily, such as uranium or plutonium.

A fission bomb contains separate pieces of fissionable material. Each is too small to support a chain reaction. But the bomb also contains a conventional explosive, such as TNT. When the explosive goes off, it forces the fissionable material together and starts the chain reaction. A huge amount of energy is released all at once.

- In fusion, atomic nuclei are forced together. This releases even more energy than fission. Fusion weapons use deuterium and tritium, which are forms of hydrogen. Conventional explosives aren't powerful enough to fuse the nuclei of these materials. Instead, a fusion weapon contains a fission device that's set off to trigger the massive fusion explosion.

One of the weapons tested by India in 1998 was a hydrogen fusion device powerful enough to destroy a city.

Israel and South Africa have both been rumored to have some nuclear weapons, although neither will say so. A few other countries are thought to be secretly trying to build the weapons. Among them are Iran, Iraq, and North Korea—three nations commonly thought of as "rogue" states. They are ruled by repressive governments, and they have been linked to international terrorism.

Iraq's ruler, Saddam Hussein, has long hoped to dominate the Middle East. In the 1980s, Iraq fought a long war with Iran, and in 1990 it invaded Kuwait—an action that sparked the Persian Gulf War. All that time, Iraq was trying to develop nuclear weapons. It hired Western experts and bought equipment and even some bomb supplies abroad, despite controls meant to prevent such sales. Since Iraq's defeat in the Persian Gulf War, teams of United Nations inspectors have been combing the country, looking for the chemical, biological, and nuclear weapons that the Iraqis were known to be developing. But Iraq hasn't cooperated with the inspectors, and no one knows what it might be hiding.

North Korea agreed in 1994 to give up attempts to build nuclear weapons, in exchange for large amounts of aid from the United States and other Western countries. But in 1998, spy satellites revealed that the North Koreans might simply have moved their nuclear program to an underground site, deep within a mountain. No one knew for sure what was going on inside the mountain, or how close the North Koreans might be to developing nuclear weapons.

The nuclear tests conducted by India and Pakistan were worrying. The idea of nuclear weapons in the hands of states such as Iraq and North Korea was truly chilling. But convincing these nations to give up their nuclear weapons programs would be an enormous challenge.

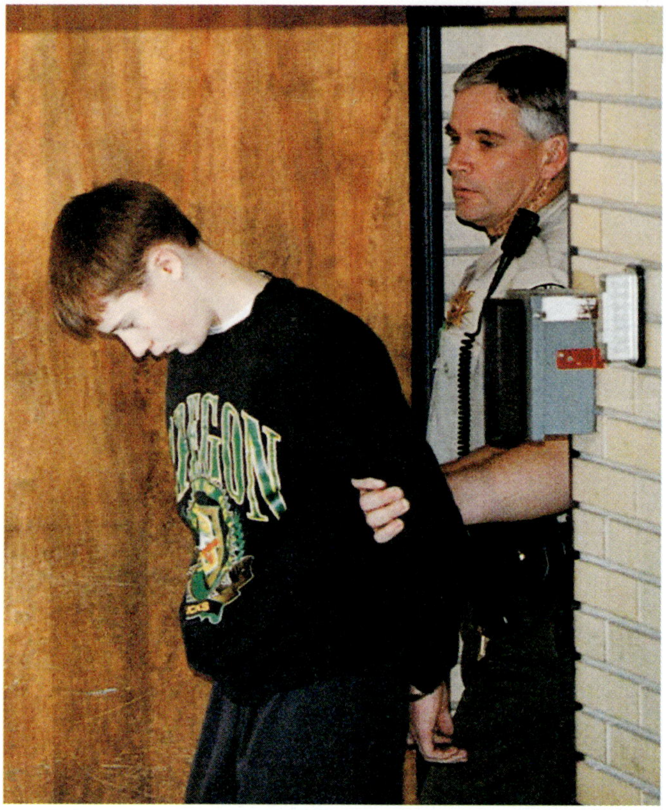

Fifteen-year-old Kipland Kinkel is arrested after having killed two high school classmates and his parents in Springfield, Oregon. He was one of many kids involved in "schoolyard killings" during the 1997–98 school year.

SCHOOLYARD KILLINGS

A series of deadly shootings shocked Americans in 1997 and 1998. The shootings weren't connected, but they had something in common—the very thing that made them so shocking. It was this: All the shootings involved kids who opened fire on classmates in school.

The United States has more than its share of violence, including violence carried out by young people. City schools have been especially troubled by gang violence. But violent crimes by people under 18 actually declined by more than a third from 1990 to 1998. The wave of schoolyard killings was doubly disturbing because it ran against this trend and because the shootings took place in rural and suburban areas that weren't used to such crimes.

In all, fifteen people died in four school shooting incidents during the 1997–98 school year.

- **Pearl, Mississippi:** On October 1, 1997, Luke Woodham, 16, fired on students at Pearl High School, killing two people and wounding seven. Just before that, he had stabbed his mother to death.
- **West Paducah, Kentucky:** On December 1, 1997, Michael Adam Carneal, 14, opened fire in the lobby of Heath High School. A before-school prayer meeting was just ending. Three girls were killed; bullets left a third paralyzed from the waist down.
- **Jonesboro, Arkansas:** On March 24, 1998, Andrew Golden, 11, and Mitchell Johnson, 13, set off a false fire alarm at Westside Middle School. Then, when students and teachers left the building, the two boys opened fire with high-powered rifles. A teacher and four girls were killed; another teacher and nine students were wounded.
- **Springfield, Oregon:** On May 21, 1998, Kipland Kinkel, 15, walked into the cafeteria at Thurston High School and began firing randomly, killing two students and wounding 22 others. Police later found his parents murdered at home, and the house booby-trapped with explosives.

WHY DID THEY DO IT?

What led these kids to commit such terrible crimes? People looked for common threads that might provide an answer.

- **Troubled kids:** All the kids who carried out the crimes were smart but troubled. Some had difficult family lives and had been in trouble with authorities. They felt inferior and believed that other students had picked on them. Former girlfriends of the shooters were victims in Pearl, Mississippi, and Jonesboro, Arkansas. Some of the kids were described as filled with resentment against their parents. Many young people have similar feelings but never become violent. However, these students all gave warning signs of the trouble to come. Some brought guns to school before the shooting. All made dark threats, and several of them wrote about their plans. No one took them seriously.
- **Pop culture:** The students who carried out the shootings were obsessed with violent pop

culture. They were fans of violent movies and video games and rock or rap music that celebrated violence. Woodham belonged to a cultlike group and was fascinated with the occult. Several other members of the group were later charged with plotting other murders. Psychologists don't agree about how strongly movies and other forms of entertainment influence behavior. But most agree that exposure to violent pop culture can make people insensitive to violence in real life. Brought up on make-believe violence in video games, television, and movies, kids may not fully realize that real bullets really kill. At his court hearing in Jonesboro, Mitchell Johnson said, "I thought we were going to shoot over their heads. We didn't think anybody was going to get hurt."

• **Guns:** All the kids were able to obtain high-powered, rapid-fire weapons, and they knew how to use them. Andrew Golden stole guns, including one with a telescopic sight, from his grandfather to use in the Jonesboro shooting. Kipland Kinkel used his own gun—a .22-caliber semiautomatic that his father had bought him. The easy availability of guns is a major issue. Guns have even turned up in grade schools. Many people believe that controls on gun ownership should be much stricter. Opponents of stricter controls argue that the real problem isn't the availability of guns but the fact that kids aren't taught to respect and use them properly. However, all the shooters in the schoolyard killing cases had been trained in gun use. Golden had been to a militia camp and had won awards for marksmanship.

Mourners of the students who were killed console each other and place flowers outside Thurston High School in Springfield.

THE AFTERMATH

Most of the youths involved in the 1997–98 killings were old enough to be tried as adults on charges of murder and other crimes. They faced life in prison. In Jonesboro, Golden and Johnson were placed in juvenile detention. An Arkansas state law provides special treatment for anyone who commits a crime before turning 14, so they couldn't be tried or punished as adults. They will be held in a juvenile detention center until they turn 21.

Shootings in school are very rare. In fact, most of the time, school is a very safe place to be. But, following the motto "better safe than sorry," many schools are taking steps to improve security. In some, security officers routinely screen students for weapons, using metal detectors to find knives and guns. Instead of just suspending kids who bring weapons to school, some schools require them to attend counseling sessions.

Teachers and school administrators are also dealing strictly with students who talk about violence. Students who threaten classmates or teachers may find themselves suspended from school or even arrested. At the least, they will be interviewed by psychologists trained to assess their potential for violence.

Kids are also being urged to speak up when one of their classmates threatens violence. After the 1997–98 shootings, everyone realizes how important it is to take these threats seriously.

The U.S. embassies in Kenya (*left*) and Tanzania were bombed in coordinated terrorist attacks in August.

THE TERRORIST WAR

On August 7, 1998, the United States was suddenly plunged into a strange sort of war. In a pair of carefully planned terrorist attacks, bombs exploded just minutes apart at the United States embassies in Nairobi, Kenya, and Dar es Salaam, Tanzania. The explosions in these two African nations weren't the work of any army or country. Instead, the United States was up against a secret Islamic terrorist group.

The embassy bombings were among the most serious acts of terrorism ever directed against the United States. Twelve Americans and nearly 300 Africans were killed, and thousands of other people were injured. Americans now faced the problem of finding and stopping the terrorists before they struck again.

ATTACK AND COUNTERATTACK

Within days of the bombings, the United States had evidence linking the attacks to a terrorist organization led by Osama bin Laden, a wealthy Saudi Arabian exile and the sworn enemy of the United States. Bin Laden, who was living in Afghanistan, was well known for his anti-American views. The son of a Saudi builder, he had inherited a fortune thought to be worth $250 million. His wealth was so great that he could easily fund terrorist operations, and he had supported terrorist groups in several countries. He had been linked to the terrorists who set off a bomb in the World Trade Center, in New York City, in 1993. The Saudi government had exiled him in 1994 for his terrorist activities, and his family had disowned him. But that hadn't stopped him.

Bin Laden was especially angered by the presence of U.S. troops in Saudi Arabia. The troops were there to provide security, with the Saudi government's permission. But Bin Laden condemned what he termed the American "occupation" of Saudi Arabia, which is home to several of Islam's holiest sites. He called on Muslims to launch a religious war and attack American targets. Bin Laden was thought to have been behind two bombings of American military facilities in Saudi Arabia, in 1995 and 1996. The Egyptian and Saudi governments were also among his targets.

The United States was already investigating Bin Laden when the two 1998 bombings occurred. In fact, charges had been filed against him for his earlier terrorist acts. Now witnesses put members of Bin Laden's organization on the scene, and other evidence pointed to the Saudi exile as well.

U.S. officials were convinced that Bin Laden's organization, Al-Qaeda, was behind the embassy bombings. But taking action against the terrorists wasn't as easy as identifying them. Al-Qaeda is a loose alliance of Islamic terrorist groups, operating secretly in several countries. Its headquarters are wherever Bin Laden happens to be.

In August 1998, Bin Laden was in Afghanistan. The Afghan government is controlled by extreme Muslim fundamentalists, and it wasn't likely to turn him over to the United States. So the United States counterattacked on August 20. U.S. Navy ships in the Arabian and Red Seas launched about 75 cruise missiles at two targets. One target was a terrorist training complex in Afghanistan, near the Pakistani border. The missiles inflicted heavy damage and caused an unknown number of casualties. Bin Laden was thought to be at the complex, meeting with other leaders of his group, at the time of the attack. But he wasn't among those killed.

The second target was a chemical plant in Sudan that U.S. officials said was producing ingredients for chemical weapons. Sudan protested the attack strongly. Sudanese officials said the plant, which was destroyed by the missiles, had produced only medicines. But the United States insisted that evidence, mainly soil samples taken just outside the plant, showed that dangerous chemicals were produced there. The plant had financial links to Bin Laden.

INVESTIGATING THE PLOT

The missile strikes showed that the United States was ready to act quickly and forcefully against terrorism. Meanwhile, the investigation into the U.S. embassy bombings continued. Several people were arrested for playing a direct role in the attacks. One was a passenger in the truck that carried the Nairobi bomb. He had been trained at Al-Qaeda's Afghanistan camp. Another, a member of Al-Qaeda, admitted a role in plotting the twin bombings. Other Al-Qaeda members were arrested in Tanzania, Germany, and Great Britain.

U.S. authorities issued a warrant for Haroun Fazil, an explosives expert from Comoros who worked for Bin Laden. He was said to have orchestrated the Nairobi bombing and perhaps built the bomb. Fazil was on the run, and a $2 million reward was offered for information leading to his capture. U.S. authorities also arrested an American citizen, Wadih el Hage of Arlington, Texas, who had once served as Bin Laden's personal secretary. He was charged with lying about his connections to members of Al-Qaeda.

Even after these arrests, American facilities around the world remained on alert. Airport security was beefed up. Bin Laden promised to attack again, and he made it clear that all Americans were his targets.

Osama bin Laden, a wealthy Saudi Arabian exile, was formally charged in November for his role in the bomb attacks on the U.S. embassies.

In November, a U.S. grand jury formally charged Bin Laden in the embassy bombings. Yet his whereabouts remained unknown, and it was uncertain if he would ever stand trial in the United States.

Fighting terrorism presents many difficulties. One is finding the enemy. It's hard to fight an organization that works in secret and has no address. That's one reason why many people believe this strange war against terrorism will be a long one.

In December, Iraqi leader Saddam Hussein once again interfered with United Nations weapons inspections. The United States and Great Britain responded by launching a series of air strikes against Iraq.

AROUND THE WORLD

A confrontation between the United States and Iraq, progress toward peace in Northern Ireland, and a devastating famine in Sudan were in the news in 1998. Following is an overview of these and other events.

IRAQ: A YEAR-END ATTACK

Three times during 1998, the United States and Iraq were close to war. Twice the crisis eased at the last minute. But the threat of war became a reality in December, when the United States and Great Britain launched air strikes against military targets in Iraq.

The trigger for the crises was a program of United Nations weapons inspections, dating back to the 1991 Persian Gulf War. That war was fought after Iraq invaded the neighboring nation of Kuwait. With the support of the United Nations, the United States and almost 40 other countries banded together to drive the Iraqis out of Kuwait.

At the time, people were very concerned that Saddam Hussein, Iraq's leader, was developing "weapons of mass destruction"—nuclear, chemical, and biological (germ) weapons. So under the treaty ending the war, Iraq agreed to let teams of U.N. inspectors search for such weapons. The United Nations placed tight restrictions, or sanctions, on Iraq's trade, to make sure the Iraqis lived up to the agreement. The sanctions were to remain until the inspectors finished their work.

Almost from the beginning, Saddam put many obstacles in the path of the inspectors. That delayed the inspectors' work, so the inspections dragged on for years—and increased suspicions that Iraq had something to hide. In November 1997, Iraq ordered the inspectors to leave the country. They were allowed to return only after Russia stepped in to negotiate. But in January 1998, Saddam refused to let inspectors into sites where they suspected weapons might be. That brought a threat of military action from the United States. U.S. President Bill Clinton ordered troops, ships, and planes to the Persian Gulf. But just when fighting seemed certain, U.N. Secretary General Kofi Annan went to Iraq and convinced Saddam to let the inspections continue.

However, many people suspected that this wouldn't be the end of the matter. They were right. In August, Iraq again balked at the inspections and demanded that the sanctions be ended. The United Nations agreed to review the situation, but the sanctions weren't lifted. In the fall, Saddam stopped cooperating with the inspectors. The U.N. Security Council called that a "flagrant violation" of Iraq's earlier agreements. And President Clinton once again ordered troops, planes, and ships to the Persian Gulf.

The United States was within minutes of launching missile strikes on November 14 when Saddam Hussein backed down again, promising full cooperation. The U.N. inspectors returned to Iraq. But on December 15, the inspectors submitted a report stating that once again, Saddam had broken his word and blocked the inspections. About 24 hours later, without any further negotiations, U.S. and British forces began their attack.

The goal of the attack was to set back the weapons program and reduce Iraq's ability to threaten other nations in the Persian Gulf region, which is one of the world's most important sources of oil. For four nights, bombs and missiles rained down on strategic targets. Then the bombing stopped, and U.S. officials said that the goals had been achieved. But they acknowledged that Iraq could rebuild its weapons of mass destruction. It seemed likely that the United Statses would need to keep forces in the Gulf region for at least several years.

THE MIDEAST: SLOW PROGRESS

On October 23, 1998, Israeli Prime Minister Benjamin Netanyahu and Palestinian leader Yasir Arafat signed an important agreement at the White House in Washington, D.C. The purpose of the agreement was to get the on-again, off-again Mideast peace process back on track. But almost before the ink was dry on the new agreement, terrorism and mistrust threatened to undo it.

Palestinian Arabs, many of whom were displaced when Israel was created as a Jewish homeland in 1948, have long demanded a country of their own. Because of this, several wars between Israel and Arab countries have kept the region in turmoil. In a 1967 war, Israel occupied the West Bank and Gaza Strip—two areas that were supposed to form the Palestinian state. Palestinians have struggled to end the Israeli occupation of those regions, often using terrorism to achieve their goal.

In 1993, Israel and the Palestinians signed an agreement called the Oslo accords. It gave the Palestinians control over most of the Gaza Strip and about 3 percent of the West Bank. They were allowed to set up their own government, the Palestinian Authority. Another 27 percent of the West Bank was put under joint Palestinian-Israeli control. The Oslo accords also called for negotiations on the question of a Palestinian state.

Those talks were to have been finished by May 4, 1999. Instead, they ground to a halt in 1996, after Netanyahu, leader of the conservative Likud bloc, was elected Israeli prime minister. For a year and a half, the gulf between the two sides grew wider. Palestinian leader Yasir Arafat warned that if negotiations didn't bring progress by the May 1999 deadline, he would simply declare an independent Palestinian state. People began to worry that the deadline would bring a new war instead of peace to the Middle East.

In October 1998, the United States mounted a last-ditch effort to bring the two sides together. Arafat and Netanyahu met at a secluded spot on the Maryland shore. U.S. President Bill Clinton and King Hussein of Jordan acted as

Left to right: Palestinian leader Yasir Arafat, Jordan's King Hussein, U.S. President Bill Clinton, and Israeli Prime Minister Benjamin Netanyahu at the White House in October.

mediators. After nine long days of intense negotiations, they had an agreement. It wasn't the final accord, but it was a big step forward.

Israel agreed to withdraw its troops from another 13 percent of the West Bank, putting those areas under joint Israeli-Palestinian control. In addition, another 14 percent would be transferred to sole Palestinian control. Israel also agreed to free scores of Arab prisoners. The Palestinians agreed to change the charter that established their government—to remove the part that called for the destruction of Israel. They also agreed to arrest alleged terrorists and confiscate weapons.

Many Israelis and Palestinians supported the new agreement. But others didn't. Conservative members of the Israeli government mistrusted the Palestinians and wanted to set stricter conditions for the troop pullback. Meanwhile, Palestinian terrorists staged several bombings that were clearly meant to destroy the accord. The attacks were spearheaded by Hamas and Islamic Holy War, two militant Arab groups that oppose any peace with Israel. Palestinian leader Yasir Arafat denounced the violence, but Israeli officials said that the Palestinians should do more to bring the terrorists to justice.

Israel Celebrates 50 Years

The state of Israel was born on May 14, 1948, when the Israeli leader David Ben-Gurion declared its independence. In 1998, celebrations and special events marked the country's first 50 years—years that have seen enormous progress and bitter struggles.

Long before Israel was founded, many people dreamed of founding a Jewish state in Palestine, the biblical homeland of the Jews. The dream began to take shape after World War II, when thousands of Jewish refugees from Europe were homeless. In 1947, the United Nations passed a plan that would have set up both a Jewish state and an Arab state in Palestine, which was then controlled by Great Britain. But the Arabs rejected the plan. Thus only Israel was founded.

The United States was among the first countries to recognize the new nation. But Arab countries denied that Israel had a right to exist and immediately declared war. In the following years, Israel fought a series of wars to defend its borders—and, in the course of those wars, took control of some former Arab lands. Since 1979, when Israel and Egypt agreed to a formal peace, relations with Arab countries have improved. But Israelis still face terrorist threats from outside and inside their borders.

Israel faces many other challenges. People have come to live in Israel from all over the world—from the United States, Russia, Africa, and other regions. They don't always get along. Nor do they always agree about the role religion should play in the government. And Israel's many Arabs, who make up a sixth of the population, are treated like outsiders.

Despite these problems, the country has thrived, becoming a modern and powerful nation. So Israelis turned out in force to celebrate their country's birthday. The highlight came on April 30, the official holiday. A nationally televised, three-hour gala traced the nation's history in song and dance. And millions of people marked the holiday with barbecues and other events. Israelis were proud of their country, and they had much to celebrate.

A youngster in Northern Ireland jumps for joy to show his support of the Good Friday Agreement. It was hoped that the peace pact marked the end of the "Troubles."

Despite the opposition, the Israeli parliament approved the accord. In November, Palestinians celebrated the opening of their own international airport, in Gaza—a moment of great national pride. But the two sides remained far apart on major issues. Among them were the status of East Jerusalem, which Arabs and Israelis alike claim, and the future of Israeli settlements in the West Bank.

In December, President Bill Clinton traveled to the Middle East to help move the process along. But by that time, the peace agreement was breaking down. Netanyahu said he wouldn't turn over any more West Bank land until the Palestinians met a series of conditions and gave up the idea of declaring an independent state in 1999. Netanyahu himself was in political trouble—conservative Israelis opposed any land transfer, while liberals wanted the peace process to go ahead. Unable to get the Israeli parliament to support his tough stand toward the Palestinians, he called for new elections early in 1999.

NORTHERN IRELAND: A FRAGILE PEACE

In April 1998, a formal peace agreement hopefully marked the end of the "Troubles"—almost 30 years of fighting between Roman Catholics and Protestants in Northern Ireland.

The causes of Northern Ireland's long conflict go way back in history. For centuries, Great Britain (a Protestant country) controlled all of Ireland (a Roman Catholic country). The Irish struggled for independence and, with the exception of Northern Ireland, won it in 1921, when the Republic of Ireland was formed. The people of Northern Ireland, which is also called Ulster, chose to stay under British rule because most of them were Protestants.

But Northern Ireland's Catholics were unhappy. They were a minority, and they were discriminated against. They wanted fairness in jobs and housing, and they wanted stronger ties with Ireland. In the 1960s, violence flared up between Catholics and Protestants. Then, in 1969, a Catholic group called the Irish Republican Army (IRA) started a terrorist campaign. Its goal was to force the British out and unite Northern Ireland with Ireland.

For 24 years, terrorist bombings and other acts kept the province in turmoil. Great Britain sent troops, but they couldn't stop the fighting. The IRA also staged terrorist attacks in Britain. Some Ulster Protestants formed terrorist groups of their own, striking at Catholics.

Many people spoke out against the violence. One of them was John Hume, the leader of the largest Catholic political party in Northern Ireland. In 1993, Hume took a bold step. He met secretly with representatives of the IRA, and those talks led to a temporary cease-fire in 1994.

Hume and many others continued their work, trying to forge a permanent peace. Many Protestants were bitterly opposed to negotiating with Catholic groups. But they began to come around after David Trimble, leader of Northern Ireland's largest Protestant party, announced his support of the peace talks.

The peace talks went forward. Former senator George Mitchell of the United States played an important role in leading the negotiations. Leaders of Ireland and Great Britain were involved as well. And on April 10, 1998, the Catholic and Protestant representatives signed a peace pact, the Good Friday Agreement. The agreement led to the election, in June, of a new assembly in which Catholics and Protestants share power.

The 1998 Nobel Peace Prize was awarded to Hume and Trimble for their work. But Catholics and Protestants still have many problems to settle. Although the IRA and major Protestant groups have promised to keep the cease-fire, splinter groups staged scattered bombings throughout the year.

KOSOVO: ETHNIC CONFLICT

Since early 1998, hundreds of people have been killed in Kosovo, a province in Yugoslavia. They were the victims of a military crackdown launched by the Yugoslav government. In the fall, thanks to pressure from countries around the world, a cease-fire brought the fighting to a halt.

Yugoslavia is in the Balkans, a part of Europe that has long been torn by fighting among ethnic groups. Until 1991, Yugoslavia covered much more territory than it does today. But the country fell apart as Serbs, Croats, Muslims, and other ethnic groups began to fight. One by one, the republics of Slovenia, Croatia, and Bosnia-Herzegovina broke away. Each was the scene of fighting. The conflict was especially intense in Bosnia, where Serbs battled Bosnian Muslims and Croats. Fighting there ended with a peace agreement in December 1995. But during 1998, U.S. troops continued to be stationed in Bosnia, as part of a North Atlantic Treaty Organization (NATO) peacekeeping force.

What is now left of Yugoslavia consists of two republics, Serbia and its small neighbor Montenegro. Ethnic conflicts were behind the 1998 problems in Kosovo, which is a part of Serbia. Kosovo lies just north of the border with Albania. Most of the people in Serbia are Serbs, while most of the people in Kosovo are ethnic Albanians. There are great differences between them in culture and in religion—most Serbs are Christians, while most Kosovans are Muslims.

Kosovo once enjoyed a great deal of autonomy, or self-government. But in 1989, Serbia took the province's privileges away. As a result, Kosovans began to demand freedom. They formed their own "shadow" government. Some of them took up arms, fighting for independence.

In February 1998, Yugoslav president Slobodan Milosevic cracked down on the rebellion. Soldiers scoured villages looking for rebels. Entire families were rounded up, and there were reports of massacres. More than 250,000 Kosovans fled their homes to escape the military. With Serb military units prowling their villages, they were afraid to return.

Alarmed by the bloodshed—and by the risk that the conflict might spread to neighboring regions—countries around the world called on Milosevic to stop. He ignored them. The United Nations passed a resolution demanding that he withdraw his troops from Kosovo. He didn't. Then NATO, the

Ethnic Albanian children make their way through wreckage in their war-torn village in Kosovo, Yugoslavia.

In 1998, Russia's currency became almost worthless. Here, Russians mob a bank to withdraw their money while it still has some value. And as the crisis deepened, the power of Russian President Boris Yeltsin (*above*) declined.

Western military alliance, stepped in to put pressure on Milosevic. In October, the allies announced that they would begin bombing Serbia if the troops weren't pulled out.

To find a way out of the crisis, Richard Holbrooke, a U.S. envoy, flew to Yugoslavia to talk with Milosevic. The result was a peace accord, announced on October 13. Yugoslav soldiers would leave. A group of 2,000 unarmed observers would roam Kosovo to make sure the violence stopped. And talks would start on restoring self-rule in Kosovo.

The first step toward peace was taken when Milosevic completed a troop pullback by October 27. Soon after that, NATO planes began flying over the region to monitor troop positions, and the first of the observers arrived. But permanent peace was a long way off. The Kosovan rebels still wanted independence—and Yugoslavia still wasn't willing to grant the rebellious province more freedom.

RUSSIA: BIG TROUBLE

Russia, the world's biggest country, was in big trouble in 1998. Its currency, the ruble, was almost worthless. Businesses were out of cash. Many workers hadn't been paid for months. And as Russian leaders debated what to do, the economic crisis was matched by a political crisis.

Russians have been divided over politics and economics since 1991, when the Soviet Union fell apart. Under the Soviet Communist system, the government controlled the economy. That system led to widespread shortages and hardships. In the early 1990s, Russia's first elected president, Boris Yeltsin, promised to change the country quickly to a Western-style free-market system. In this system, the economy is determined by individuals and businesses, and not controlled by the government.

Russians welcomed the change at first. But changing the system was harder than they expected. People lost their jobs. Prices went up. Corruption was rampant. And Russians grew more and more dissatisfied.

To make ends meet—and soothe the growing anger in the country—the Russian government took out huge loans from Western banks. But it didn't raise taxes or find other ways to get money to repay those loans. Then came a drop in the world price of oil, a big source of income for Russia. Soon the government had to borrow more money just to make loan payments. By mid-1998, foreign investors were worried that Russia would never dig its way out of debt, so they stopped lending. The Russian government, running out of cash, stopped making loan payments.

The Western banks and the other organizations that had invested money in Russia began to sell off the rubles they had, sending the value of the currency down. Russians who had money in banks saw the value of their savings shrinking. They rushed to get their rubles out and buy goods, while the money still had some value. As the ruble's value went down, prices went up, doubling and doubling again in just a few weeks. Many Russians gave up on currency and began to barter, trading goods for goods.

Meanwhile, the Russian government was in turmoil. Yeltsin dismissed Prime Minister Viktor Chernomyrdin in March 1998, blaming him for the economic troubles. But just five months later, in August, he fired Chernomyrdin's replacement and tried to bring the old prime minister back. The Russian parliament refused to go along. In September, Yeltsin was forced to name Yevgeny Primakov, a former Communist, as prime minister.

Primakov seemed likely to place more government controls on the economy. He also promised to resume payments to workers and lenders. Financial experts worried that Primakov would do that by simply

The Taliban's Rules

After nearly 25 years of rebellion and civil war, Afghanistan was close to peace in 1998. But peace came at a price. The nation's rulers, an Islamic fundamentalist group called the Taliban, imposed strict rules that many Afghans found hard to follow.

The Taliban won control of much of Afghanistan in 1996, but opposition groups still controlled large parts of the north. In the summer of 1998, Taliban forces pushed the opposition back. By fall they were in firm control of 90 percent of the country.

After many years of fighting and suffering, Afghans were ready for peace. But the Taliban's restrictions on almost every aspect of life weren't so welcome. Television, movies, and popular music were banned. So were dancing and pastimes such as kite flying and bird keeping. Men weren't allowed to trim their beards—a man could be arrested on the street if his beard was too short.

The harshest restrictions were imposed on women. Women were forbidden to hold jobs or receive education. They were not allowed to go out without a male relative, and then they had to be completely covered, from head to toe, in a long garment called a *burka.* The Taliban said these rules were necessary to restore order. But even Muslim religious leaders said the rules went too far.

In the fall, Afghanistan faced a new threat from Iran, its neighbor to the west. Although Iran is also ruled by strict Muslim fundamentalists, its rulers follow a different branch of Islam. They supported the Afghan opposition. In September, after several Iranians were killed by Taliban troops in northern Afghanistan, Iranian troops staged war games near the border between the two countries. The message was clear: Afghanistan's peace might be short-lived.

printing more rubles—which would drive the value of the currency down even further.

Problems piled on top of problems. The 1998 harvest was the worst in 45 years, and by fall there were shortages of food and heating oil. Thousands of workers staged a one-day strike on October 7 to protest the situation. Many denounced Yeltsin for failing to solve the crisis. Meanwhile, both Yeltsin's health and his political power were declining. Russia seemed to be caught in a downward spiral, and no one had a solution.

A mother and child in Sudan search for food in their famine-torn country.

SUDAN: FAMINE AND WAR

As many as 2.6 million people faced starvation in Sudan during 1998, despite a massive international relief program. Famine has gripped this African nation for more than ten years. Drought and crop failures, the common causes of famine, aren't the biggest problems. The main cause of Sudan's famine is civil war.

The Sudanese government has been fighting a rebellion in the southern part of the country for fifteen years. The government is controlled by Muslim Arabs, who mostly live in the north. The people of the south are Africans, mostly Christians and followers of tribal religions. They want a greater say in the government and a greater share of the country's wealth. But the government wants greater control over the south, which is thought to have rich oil reserves.

In 1983, the government tried to impose Muslim religious law on the entire country. The southerners rebelled. Government soldiers retaliated by burning crops and killing livestock in the south. Many people had to leave their homes to find food, so they couldn't plant new crops on their land. Even if they had stayed home, they didn't have the seeds and equipment they needed to start again. That's how the famine began. Since that time, about 1.5 million people have been killed in the fighting or have died from starvation.

By 1989, Sudan's famine was so severe that the United Nations declared it an international emergency. Almost $2 billion in food and other aid has poured into Sudan since then. But distributing food is a big problem. There are few roads and even fewer aircraft landing strips in the south. As a result, food is airlifted to remote areas and dropped from planes. Most of the aid goes to a handful of relief centers. Thousands of people, mostly women and children, have come to the centers from the countryside, where they wait in line every day for food. The aid has helped many Sudanese survive. But many others have died of starvation because aid couldn't reach them in time.

Some people fear that aid may actually add to Sudan's problems. For example, the Sudanese government has used the aid program to try to weaken the rebels. At times it has stopped aid flights and banned deliveries of aid in rebel-held areas. The government hopes that this will force people to move away from rebel-held areas and into towns that government soldiers can more easily control.

After so many years of suffering, Sudan's famine was worse than ever. In August 1998 the United Nations World Food Program stepped up its aid to Sudan. With almost 15,000 tons of food being sent each month, the agency's Sudan program became its biggest aid effort ever, costing more than $1 million a day. But ending the civil war seemed to be the only way to truly end the famine.

ELAINE PASCOE
Author, *South Africa: Troubled Land*

NEWSMAKERS

A former professional wrestler as governor of Minnesota? Political experts thought it was a joke. But on Election Day 1998, **Jesse Ventura** (born James Janos) flattened his opponents and won, staging the year's biggest political surprise.

From 1975 to 1986, Ventura was Jesse "The Body" on the pro wrestling tour, where wrestling is more stunt than sport. He paraded into the ring wearing a pink feather boa and dispatched his opponents with body slams and boot stomps—without hurting them. Later, he had small roles in action movies and hosted a radio talk show in Minnesota. His only political experience was as mayor of Brooklyn Park, from 1991 to 1995. So when the Reform Party nominated "The Body" for governor, few people thought he would do well. The Democratic and Republican candidates were much more experienced.

But Ventura was serious, and he ran a colorful campaign on a shoe-string budget. One ad showed a Jesse Ventura action-figure battling "evil special interest man." Voters liked his sense of humor and his straight answers to the state's problems. On Election Day he won more votes than either major party candidate. After his stunning victory, the governor-elect announced that he would take a new nickname: Jesse "The Mind."

Shirley and Frank Capaci gave new meaning to the word "lucky" in 1998. In May, the Streamwood, Illinois, couple won $104.3 million in the multistate Powerball lottery. It was the largest single lottery payment in U.S. history. Frank, 67, is a retired electrician, and Shirley, 63, is a retired secretary. They planned some purchases, but they said they would go on living the way they always had—despite being new millionaires. Could it happen to you? That's very unlikely. The Capacis held five $1 tickets, out of 138 million tickets sold. The odds against their big win were a whopping 80 million to one.

In October 1998, Pope John Paul II pronounced **Edith Stein** a saint of the Roman Catholic Church. Stein was a victim of the Holocaust—the Nazi campaign against the Jews. She was born in Germany in 1891 and was a well-known Jewish teacher and philosopher. In the 1920s she converted to Christianity. After the Nazis came to power in Germany in 1933, she was forced to give up her job by a Nazi decree that barred Jews from teaching. She became a Roman Catholic nun, taking the name Sister Teresia Benedicta of the Cross. As the Nazis' persecution of the Jews increased, she fled to the Netherlands to escape. But she was arrested there in 1942 and sent to a Nazi death camp, where she was killed. Although she died because she was Jewish, the Church considers her a martyr for the Roman Catholic faith.

Anne Frank was just 15 years old when she died in 1945, a victim of the Holocaust. In her last years, she kept a diary that told how her family lived in hiding, in constant fear of the Nazis. Today her diary is famous. And in 1998, five previously unknown pages were discovered. Torn from the original, they had been kept secret for more than 50 years.

Anne's parents, Otto and Edith Frank, were German Jews. When the Nazis came to power in 1933 and began to persecute the Jews, the Franks left Germany for Amsterdam, in the Netherlands. But World War II began, and the Nazis occupied the Netherlands in May 1940. They began arresting Jews and sending them to death camps. Hoping to avoid this fate, in 1942 the Franks went into hiding, moving into a secret attic apartment. Anne was 13. In her diary, she wrote about their life and her secret thoughts and dreams.

On August 4, 1944, Nazi police raided the apartment and arrested the Franks. Anne and her sister died of typhus in March 1945 at a Nazi death camp. Otto Frank found Anne's diary after the war. It was so moving that he decided to publish it, first removing the most personal sections. After he died in 1980, those sections were put back—except for five pages in which Anne wrote about the problems in her parents' marriage and her sometimes strained relationship with her mother. Otto Frank gave those pages to a friend. And in 1998, they were finally made public. The diary was complete at last.

When she turned 98 on August 4, 1998, **Britain's Queen Mother** became the longest-living royal in her nation's history. Born Elizabeth Bowes-Lyon, the popular "Queen Mum" is the mother of Queen Elizabeth II and the widow of King George VI.

Gerhard Schröder, 54, launched Germany into a new era when his party won national elections in September 1998. Schröder thus replaced Helmut Kohl as chancellor—becoming the first German chancellor too young to remember World War II.

ANIMALS

These glitzy insects seem to have been rolled in glitter. They are imperial weevils, and their shining, jewel-studded coats are completely natural. Like all its insect relatives, the imperial weevil has an exoskeleton—a hard outer shell—in place of a bony skeleton inside its body. An insect's exoskeleton is like a suit of armor, protecting the animal's soft internal organs. And in the case of the imperial weevil, that suit of armor is also extremely beautiful.

In April 1998, Koko the gorilla went on the Internet for an online chat. Koko, who uses American Sign Language, answered questions from computer users with the help of her human tutor. But does Koko really understand language? Scientists disagree over whether animals can use language to communicate.

CAN WE TALK?

Wouldn't it be wonderful to talk with animals? Most people think that happens only in stories, like the famous children's book, *The Story of Dr. Dolittle.* But if you were at a computer and logged onto the Internet on April 27, 1998, you would have had a chance to chat with a gorilla.

Koko, a 26-year-old gorilla who has learned American Sign Language, was on line that day to answer questions. Her human tutor, Francine Patterson, was with her to translate the questions from computer users into sign language. When Koko signaled her answers, Patterson relayed them to a typist sitting at a computer keyboard. It was the first-ever interspecies Internet chat, and it was held as part of an Earth Day celebration.

Koko and animals like her have caused many people to question a long-held idea. That idea is that only humans are smart enough to communicate with language. Scientists disagree about this. Some think that animals like Koko don't really understand and use language—they've just been taught to perform a trick. But others think animals may be saying much more than we know. Perhaps we just don't know how to listen.

SEARCHING FOR SIGNS

For many years, people pointed to the ability to use language as one of the greatest differences between humans and animals. Animals communicate in simple ways, it was thought, while only people use symbols. Words, signs, and pictures are all symbols. They are used to represent other things—physical things, like a chair or an orange, and complicated concepts, like love and death. It was believed that animals were not only incapable of using symbols, they also couldn't understand such complicated ideas.

Now scientists aren't so sure. Research with intelligent animals such as dolphins and members of the ape family has cast doubt on those beliefs. In particular, studies with gorillas and bonobos—also known as pygmy chimpanzees—has caused many scientists to rethink ideas about language. The apes can't speak words because their mouths and vocal cords aren't designed for human speech. But in several studies, scientists have taught apes to communicate with signs and symbols.

Koko, a western lowland gorilla, is the star of the longest-running ape language study. Since she was 1 year old, she has been tutored in American Sign Language, the hand language used by deaf people. Her teachers say that she regularly uses more than 500 different signs and understands more than 2,000 words of spoken English.

Koko, who lives at a research center near San Francisco, can identify many objects and name many activities. She uses signs to ask her human teachers to give her favorite foods and play her favorite games. When she comes across something new, she makes up a sign for it. To describe a ring, for example, she used signs for "finger" and "bracelet."

Language experts question whether Koko's skills show that she can really use language. In experiments done in the late 1970s, common chimpanzees also seemed to learn sign language and even use it to form sentences. But it turned out that they didn't really understand the hand signs. Eager to please their human teachers, they twisted their hands in all sorts of configurations. The teachers, eager to see the chimps succeed, thought they recognized hand signs.

CHATTING WITH CHIMPS

At the University of Georgia, Sue Savage-Rumbaugh and other researchers have taken a different approach. They are working with bonobos, which are thought to be the closest to humans of all the apes, and with com-

Kanzi, a bonobo, "talks" by pressing geometric symbols on a keyboard. Researchers say that Kanzi's language skills are very humanlike. Here Kanzi, shown wearing headphones, is taking a vocabulary test.

mon chimpanzees. And they have taught several of these animals to communicate with a special keyboard. The keyboard has 250 different symbols, each representing a different object or action.

Two bonobos—Kanzi, a male, and Panbanisha, a female—are the stars of the program. Kanzi is especially good at the symbol keyboard. He began to use it on his own, at age 2½, after watching researchers use it in their work with other bonobos. Now he and the others use it all the time. They ask to go places, play games, and watch their favorite television shows and videos. Movies that feature apes are especially popular with the bonobos. Kanzi presses the symbols for "ice" and "TV" to see his favorite, *Iceman*.

The bonobos use the keyboard to tell their teachers all sorts of things. For example, one day Panbanisha took one of the researchers aside and pressed the keys for "fight," "mad," and "Austin." She was

Animal Think Tank

Do animals think? Not long ago, most scientists would have answered "no." Animals, they believed, act out of instinct—they don't plan or think about what they do. Now scientists aren't so sure.

At the National Zoo in Washington, D.C., researchers are looking for answers in a building called Think Tank. The building houses a number of exhibits, but its main attraction is a group of orangutans. Most of the orangs "commute" to Think Tank from the zoo's Great Ape House by way of cables strung high in the air—a special orangutan highway that the zoo calls the O-Line.

At Think Tank visitors can watch the orangutans and staff members interact in staged events, to find out if the animals are thinking in various situations. How do you know an animal is thinking? Researchers look for three qualities. The first is the ability to form a mental image. The second is intention—that is, the animal acts deliberately, to reach a goal. The third is flexibility, or the ability to try different techniques and adapt to new situations.

By these standards, orangutans and other apes seem to think a lot of the time. When food is out of reach, for example, they'll stack boxes or hunt around for a stick or some other tool, so they can get to it. If one method doesn't work, they'll try another.

"What is it?" A researcher asks Indah, an orangutan, to identify an apple by pressing the correct symbol.

The orangutans at Think Tank also take "language" lessons. They're learning to associate symbols on a computer screen with objects and actions. That's another indication of animal brain power.

telling her teacher that two other bonobos, one of which was named Austin, had been in a fight.

The bonobos seem to understand what the symbols mean, and they can use the board to answer questions put to them in spoken English. They also put symbols together in ways that suggest they understand a little grammar—the rules that govern how words and phrases are arranged.

Some other scientists still aren't convinced. The bonobos, they suggest, are skilled mimics. The apes guess what their human teachers want, and perform to get a treat. They also point out that even the cleverest bonobos demonstrate fewer language skills than most 3-year-old children.

The Georgia researchers have tested the bonobos by asking questions from behind a barrier, so they won't cue the animals with gestures or facial expressions. They believe their work proves that at least some of these animals can use language. Recently, their view has been supported by two remarkable discoveries.

First, researchers in Africa found that wild bonobos use a complicated system of trail markings to communicate with each other. In African forests, bonobos live in bands of 100 or more. During the day, the band breaks up into small groups, and the bonobos forage for food in the forest.

The groups cannot see or hear each other, but at night they come together in a new location. How do they know where to go? Researchers noticed that whenever the lead group crosses a new trail, the bonobos trample vegetation or tear off large leaves and place them on the ground. These markings, they think, are signposts for the other groups to follow.

The second discovery was made by medical researchers in New York City. They discovered a striking similarity between the brains of chimpanzees and people. A part of the human brain called the *planum temporale* (PT) is generally larger on the left side of the brain than the right side. Scientists have long believed that this enlargement allows people to use and understand language. They also believed that only people had it. But medical researchers examined eighteen chimpanzee brains and found that seventeen of them had enlarged left-side PT's.

Do apes use this part of the brain as people do—to communicate with language? Perhaps, for example, chimps "talk" to each other with gestures that are more meaningful than people realize. Researchers are trying to find out. Learning the answer, they believe, will help us understand more about our own language abilities, as well as those of animals.

Are apes just skillful mimics, or can they truly communicate with us through their gestures? What do you think this chimp is trying to tell us?

A giant green grasshopper (*above*) is one of the residents of the Robot Zoo. The mechanical animals in this traveling exhibit are designed to show how the bodies of real animals work. Visitors are welcomed by a robot giraffe (*right*), poking its head through a window at the exhibit entrance.

THE ROBOT ZOO

Did you ever wonder how a grasshopper can hop so far, or how a giraffe balances its long neck? Then you'll want to take a trip to the Robot Zoo. This is a zoo unlike any other zoo you've ever visited. It has no live animals! All the animals in the Robot Zoo are mechanical, designed to show how the body parts of living animals work.

The Robot Zoo is a traveling exhibit that will tour many cities in North America for five years. Stops are scheduled at major science and natural history museums through the year 2002.

The exhibit is based on the popular children's book *The Robot Zoo,* by John Kelly. The idea behind the book and the exhibit is simple:

Animals are so well suited to their surroundings and way of life that they almost seem to have been designed by a master engineer. Every body part is perfect for its special function. By turning eight animals into robots and replacing body parts with mechanical devices, the Robot Zoo helps people discover how real animals work.

Giraffe. Giraffes are the world's tallest animals. They roam the African plains, nibbling leaves from treetops. The larger-than-life Robot Zoo giraffe consists only of the shoulders, head and neck—and it's 9 feet (2.7 meters) tall! A powerful piston attaches the giraffe's neck to the shoulder. It acts like the real animal's neck muscles, allowing the robot to raise and lower its head. The robot blinks its eyes (visual receptors) and turns its ears (microphones) to follow sounds. In place of teeth, it has sharp blades and files. A pump pushes "blood" up the long neck through flexible tubing that takes the place of blood vessels.

Rhinoceros. The white rhino is the second largest land animal, after the elephant. It's an awesome animal, too, with a tough hide, sharp horns, and a reputation for being hot tempered. The Robot Zoo rhino has a suit of armor and a pair of wicked-looking spikes. But it's shown just partly constructed, as a way to introduce visitors to the workings of the mechanical animals. Wall panels illustrate some of the basic robot parts that are used throughout the exhibit. "Brains" are computers that control the other parts. Pistons take the place of muscles, and filtering pipes are intestines.

Chameleon. In nature, chameleons are tree-dwelling lizards that catch insects with their long sticky tongues. In the Robot Zoo, the chameleon is a 9-foot monster. It grips a branch with its feet (clamps) and tail (flexible tubing). Like a real chameleon, it rocks back and forth and nods its head. It also rolls its eyes (visual receptors wired to the computer brain) in all directions. Its insect-snatching tongue is a spring coil—with a piece of flypaper at the end.

One of the most remarkable traits of real chameleons is their ability to change color, to blend in with their surroundings. The robot

The robot rhinoceros is shown in a "body shop"—a factory setting. The rhino is only partly constructed, to help people understand how the mechanical animals in the exhibit are made.

Using computer workstations, visitors can explore the chameleon's ability to change color. They "paint" colors and patterns at the computer, and their choices are displayed almost instantly on the video monitors that cover the robot chameleon's body.

chameleon can do that, too. Its "skin" is made up of video screens. Visitors use computer "paint" stations to create colored patterns that are instantly displayed on the screens. As the screens change, the model changes color—showing how quickly real chameleons can change.

Bat. Most bats roost in caves or hollow trees during the day and hunt for food at night. They can find flying insects in total darkness with a unique system called echolocation. The bat sends out ultrasonic sound waves, and its super-sensitive ears pick up the echoes that result when the sound waves bounce off insects or other objects. To mimic this system, the robot bat has a loudspeaker on its nose that's similar to the sonar transmitters used on submarines. Its ears are sonar receptors. The robot bat's wings are made of flexible material stretched over struts, powered by pistons instead of muscles.

Housefly. You've never seen a housefly like the Robot Zoo version. It's 6 feet (1.8 meters) long, with a 10-foot (3-meter) wingspan! Apart from its size, the mechanical fly's eyes are its most striking feature. They're made up of clusters of visual receptors, like the compound eyes of a real fly. The robot has a hard outer shell, like the exoskeleton of an insect. Its

The robot bat is shown at twilight, just as it's getting ready to go out hunting. It's still in its roosting position—hanging upside down from a branch. A real bat's feet are designed to lock in a gripped position, so the bat can hang while it sleeps. The robot feet lock, too—they're clamps.

The Robot Zoo platypus is doing what all platypuses do—foraging for food underwater. As the mechanical animal "swims" along, its front legs move in a sort of breaststroke, and its tail moves up and down.

wings are made of flexible material stretched over struts and powered by pistons. Its mouth looks suspiciously like a vacuum-cleaner nozzle. And its feet are equipped with grippers and sensory pads—because real flies taste with their feet.

In part of the exhibit, visitors can play "Swat the Fly"—trying to swat "flies" that light up briefly on a screen. Few people score well at the game. The reaction time of a typical housefly is twelve times as fast as a person's!

Grasshopper. The grasshopper is a champion jumper in the insect world. It's also a champion eater, with strong jaws that gobble up leaves. The Robot Zoo grasshopper is a whopping 9 feet long. Its jointed legs are equipped with powerful springs that compress and release to launch it. The springs stand in for the muscles that allow real grasshoppers to jump.

Grasshoppers don't have true brains. Instead, they have nerve centers called ganglia. Several minicomputers take the place of ganglia in the robot, gathering sensory information.

Platypus. With webbed feet and a bill, like a duck, and fur and a flat tail, like a beaver, the platypus is one of the strangest animals on Earth. Even stranger is the fact that the platypus lays eggs, like a bird, but feeds its young milk, like a mammal (which it is). The Robot Zoo platypus shows how this odd collection of features works.

The robot has a computer for a brain, flippers for feet, pistons for muscles, and a food processor for a stomach. It mimics some special platypus features, too. The real platypus finds food in murky stream bottoms with the help of sensitive nerves. The model's mechanical snout is equipped with electromagnetic sensors. The male platypus has a poison spur, which he uses in fights with other males. The robot version has a "poison injector."

Giant squid. Giant squid live in the deepest parts of the ocean. They are truly giant—up to 60 feet (18 meters) long. Unlike the other robot models, the robot squid is smaller than its real-life counterpart—24 feet (7 meters), including body and flexible tentacles. A real squid travels by jet propulsion, sucking in water and squirting it out to push itself forward. The robot has a nozzle that does the same. Like a real squid, it also squirts out eggs, waste, and a dark ink, which squids release to confuse predators.

No one has ever seen a giant squid alive. But if you visit the Robot Zoo, you'll find out just how the squid and the other animals get along in their natural homes.

When Spaniards first came to the Americas and saw a mammal covered with bony plates, they named it the ARMADILLO, or "little armored one." Most armadillos have a solid shield over the shoulders, and another one over the rear part of the body. Between the two shields are crosswise bands, which allow for easier movement.

The SNAIL travels here and there with a hard coiled shell on its back. The shell is attached to the rest of the body by a muscle. When danger threatens, the snail pulls itself into the shell. The oldest part of the shell is the smallest whorl, at the top. As the snail grows, glands in its body secrete material to make the shell larger.

ANIMAL ARMOR

Managing to stay alive isn't easy in the animal world. Enemies lurk around every root, rock, and reef. But all creatures, from tiny sponges to giant rhinos, have ways to defend themselves. One of the most effective defenses is a tough protective covering that in some ways resembles the armor worn by a medieval knight. This "armor" can take various forms, but its purpose is always the same: to protect against attacks by predators.

One form of animal armor is an exoskeleton. Your skeleton is inside your body; but some animals wear their skeletons on the outside, as a hard covering for their soft internal organs. Scorpions, spiders, insects, centipedes, and shrimps all have exoskeletons.

Most mollusks also wear their skeletons on the outside. But this type of skeleton is called a shell. The shell is made of limestone secreted from special glands. Some mollusks, such as snails, have a one-part shell. Clams, oysters, and other bivalves have a shell formed of two parts (or valves). Some

As it swims through a coral reef in a tropical sea, the PARROT FISH is protected—from head to tail—by a suit of hard overlapping scales. The scales, which act like a flexible suit of armor, are thin and transparent. They protect the parrot fish without interfering with its ability to dart away from a predator.

The SPINY LIZARD loves to crawl onto a rock, fence, or tree stump and lazily bask in the sun. Even though predators may see the reptile, they keep their distance—because the spiny lizard is well named. Its body is protected by large, overlapping scales that end in sharp points. The scales are separated from one another by flexible skin.

shells have protuberances that offer extra protection. For example, the spiny cockle's shell is covered with spikes.

Another type of shell protects the turtle. This reptile has two halves—a top and a bottom—joined on each side by a bony bridge. Some turtles, such as box turtles, can pull their entire bodies into their shells and then close up tight.

Turtles—like all reptiles and many fish—also have a protective armor of scales on their skin. Sometimes, the scales are fantastically modified. The horned lizard has enlarged, pointed scales that form "horns" on its head. The porcupine fish has scales with pointed spines. When threatened, it inflates itself, puffing up like a living pincushion.

Another pincushion is the porcupine, whose body is covered with needle-sharp quills. When attacked, the porcupine raises its quills and spears the attacker. The quills are loosely attached in the porcupine's skin and easily break off—enabling the porcupine to shuffle off while the attacker, pierced by stinging quills, tends to its wounds.

For all these animals, their suit of armor enables them to stay alive another day.

Animal noses do more than just sniff. The proboscis monkey, for example, uses its huge, drooping nose to magnify its calls.

WHO NOSE?

Animal noses come in hundreds of different sizes and shapes, from a pig's stubby snout to an elephant's huge trunk. But animal noses aren't just for sniffing. They're designed to perform a wide variety of jobs.

Noses serve as hands, arms, tools, and weapons. They're used to dig, probe, spear, cut, tear, drill, crack, spray, strain, snorkel, and net. Some animals fight with their noses. Some rely on their noses to greet friends, warn enemies, spank youngsters, capture prey, or find their way home in the dark.

Super Sniffers. The human nose can distinguish thousands of different odors. That's good, but lots of animals can do better. Mammals like dogs, cats, pigs, and rats are much more sensitive to odors than we are. Smells guide these animals to their mates, warn them of their enemies, and help them find food.

A dog's cool, moist nose may not seem large, but it's crammed with smell-sensitive tissue. Inside the nose, this tissue is arranged in many wrinkles and folds. Stretched out flat, it would be 40 times the size of the smell-sensitive tissue in a human nose. A dog can sense odors that escape us. And it can analyze a complex mixture of many odors and concentrate on one of them. Sniffing through the woods, a hunting dog will pick up the scent of a rabbit that may have hopped by an hour earlier. The dog can tell which way the rabbit was going, then follow the scent.

Compared to a dog, an anteater has a highly specialized nose: Its nose is meant to sniff out termites and ants. In South America, the giant anteater shuffles along with its long snout close to the ground. When it sniffs an ant or termite mound, it scratches and digs with its claws, tearing away huge chunks of earth. Then the anteater's long sticky tongue flicks into the inside of the mound and laps up hundreds of insects and their eggs.

Another extra-long nose belongs to the little elephant shrew, which has a trunk like an elephant and long hind legs like a kangaroo, but is no bigger than a rat. The elephant shrew twitches and turns its trunklike nose as it sniffs for insects on the forest floor.

Like many mammals, fish also have a powerful sense of smell. Since they breathe with their gills, they use the nostrils on their snouts strictly for smelling.

A shark has one of the keenest noses of any animal. It can sniff one ounce of fish blood in a million ounces of sea water. It can pick up this scent from more than a quarter mile away. And once it smells blood, it swims to the source like a guided missile.

Salmon use their noses as amazingly accurate direction finders. When they return from their ocean migrations, they locate their home stream from among hundreds of others by nosing in on its special smell.

Elephants' Trunks. No nose is more useful than an elephant's talented trunk. And no nose is bigger. The trunk of a full-grown elephant can be up to 6 feet (2 meters) long! water 3 miles (5 kilometers) away. They can sniff a person several miles downwind. By smelling a bush or tree, an elephant can tell instantly if the leaves or fruit are good to eat.

Along with its two nostrils, an elephant also has one or two small fleshy "fingers" at the tip of its trunk. The African elephant has two of these fingerlike projections; the Indian elephant has only one. With these projections, an elephant can reach down to pull grass, or reach up to pluck leaves or fruit. The "fingers" are so sensitive and their touch is so delicate that they can pick up an object as small as a peanut and carry it to their mouth.

When friendly elephants meet, they twist their trunks together in an affectionate greeting—one of the many uses of an elephant's talented nose.

Since it's shaped like a rubber hose, a trunk can bend in almost any direction. When testing for smells, the trunk weaves through the air like a cobra and bends toward the source of every interesting odor. An elephant can check for the smell of food, water, friends, or enemies without even moving its head. The nostrils at the tip of the trunk can pick up the scent of

While the tip of the trunk is sensitive, the trunk itself has plenty of muscle power. Reaching high into a tree, an elephant can rip off a big leafy branch and bring it down to earth. Its trunk has more than 40,000 muscles and is powerful enough to lift a ton of logs.

When an elephant visits a water hole, it draws the water into its trunk. Then it puts the

The little elephant shrew's trunklike snout is a powerful insect-sniffer.

trunk deep into its mouth and squirts the water down its throat. It takes 20 or 30 squirts to satisfy an elephant-sized thirst.

On hot days, elephants use their trunks to spray cooling water across their ears and backs. They're good swimmers, and in deep water they may hold their trunks above the surface and use them as snorkels. After a swim, an elephant likes to roll in the mud and finish its grooming session with a nice dust bath. It sucks up sand or dirt with its trunk and blows it over its body to help keep biting insects away.

An elephant also "talks" through its trunk, using it to scream with rage or squeal with pleasure. Male elephants, or bulls, test each other's strength by locking trunks in a giant-sized tug-of-war. Mother elephants caress their babies with a soft touch of their trunks. They punish them with a swift, hard whack. When a herd is on the move, the baby follows along by gripping its mother's tail with its trunk. And when friendly elephants meet, they twist their trunks together in an affectionate elephant greeting.

Beaks and Bills. A bird's nose is where its mouth is. Its beak or bill is actually a combination of nostrils and lips. Beaks are made of hardened epidermis, or skin, attached to the bird's jaws.

The beak is important to a bird because it serves as both a hand and a tool. Birds use their beaks to find, catch, kill, and eat their food. Simply by looking at a beak, you can often tell what kind of food the bird likes to eat.

Among birds of prey, the beak is a sharp-edged meat hook. An owl or hawk uses its hooked beak to tear a freshly killed mouse or rabbit into convenient bite-sized pieces.

Seed-eating birds like sparrows or cardinals have short, fat nutcracker beaks that are strong enough to crush a cherry pit. And a woodpecker has a pointed chisel of a beak that's

A spoonbill's beak resembles a long serving spoon, and it's used to sift for food in shallow waters.

The toucan's fabulous beak is perfect for picking and slicing fruit.

made for drilling holes in tree trunks. The woodpecker then laps up grubs and insects with a long, barbed, sticky tongue.

Some beaks are designed for probing, poking, or pulling. A curlew uses its long curved beak to pull crabs out of deep mud and crickets out of tall grass. A hummingbird pokes its slim beak into flowers, then flicks out its long tongue and sips up the sweet nectar. And an oystercatcher jabs its pointed beak into partly open oyster shells, paralyzing the oyster before it can snap shut.

The spoonbill's beak resembles a long serving spoon. When feeding, the bird moves its slightly open beak from side to side in wide arcs, sifting the shallow waters for small fish, insects, and other food.

The spoonbill also uses its beak to make loud clapping noises when it returns to the nest and greets its mate.

The long hooked beak of a pelican, with its big flabby pouch, makes an excellent fishing net. White pelicans often fish in groups. They form a semicircle offshore and beat the water with their wings, driving fish into the shallows, then scooping them up with a dipnet motion of their gaping pouches.

Before swallowing a fish, a pelican raises its beak to drain water out of the pouch. That's the moment when a bold seagull may swoop down to snatch the fish from the pelican's pouch. And it's true that a pelican's beak holds more than its "bellican"—a white pelican has a pouch capacity of 3 gallons (11 liters), and a stomach capacity of only half that much.

The spectacular, brightly colored beak of the South American toucan is useful too. Notice the saw-tooth edges of the beak. They are designed to slice and dice fruits, insects, lizards, and small snakes in the woodlands where the toucan lives.

With a giant beak like that, a toucan can reach for fruit that might be hard to get otherwise. This bird will often pick a small fruit, toss it into the air, then catch it with its open beak. Toucans also like to duel with their beaks. Two rival birds will knock beaks together like a couple of practiced swordsmen.

In some toucans, the beak is as long and bulky as the rest of the body, giving the bird a rather top-heavy appearance. Luckily, the beak is honeycombed with air pockets and is almost as light as foam rubber. If it were much heavier, the big-beaked toucan would fall on its nose.

Noses That Sound Off. A proboscis monkey is born with a cute turned-up nose. But as the monkey grows up, its nose gets larger and grows downward. By the time a monkey is fully grown, its nose may hang down over its mouth.

Even with its baby sitting atop its head, the Jackson's chameleon appears ready to defend its territory by mounting a three-pronged attack with its nose.

It may be so long that the monkey has to push it aside to eat. That's why these animals are called proboscis monkeys. *Proboscis* means "long snout."

These monkeys live along rivers and swamps on the island of Borneo in Southeast Asia. And they use their drooping noses to magnify their calls and cries. When a male honks to call his mate or to warn a rival away from his territory, his long nose fills with sound and acts as an echo chamber. The nose makes the sound of the call louder.

The male elephant seal also has a noisy proboscis. During the mating season, he uses his trunklike nose to make long trumpeting sounds, warning rival males to stay away.

Bats use their noses in a form of sonar. As they fly through the night, they blow great bursts of supersonic sound through their nostrils. The sounds bounce back from any object in the bat's path, and its sensitive ears pick up the echoes. These echoes keep the bat from flying into

The spatulate-nosed tree frog can use its spatula-shaped nose to protect itself in hot, dry weather.

obstacles and help it find food. With its nose as a navigational guide, a bat can fly through a dense forest in total darkness without touching a tree. Listening to echoes, it can nose in on a flying insect 15 feet (4.5 meters) away.

Dangerous Noses. The Jackson's chameleon of Africa uses its nose as a weapon. It has a pointed horn at the tip of its snout, with two other horns just above it. It can mount a three-pronged attack when it defends its territory from rivals, charging headlong with its nose.

Among certain kinds of tropical termites, the soldier termites have heads shaped like squirt guns, with snouts like nozzles. When ants or other enemies invade the termites' nest, these soldiers rush forward and squirt a sticky substance from their snouts, trapping the ants or driving them away.

Noses to Hide Behind. The spatulate-nosed tree frog has a nose shaped like a flat spoon, or spatula. When the weather is hot and dry, the frog finds a hole in some rocks and crawls inside. Then it plugs up the entrance with its flat nose. Protected from the sun and wind, the frog can keep its body cool and moist.

The rhinoceros viper has "horns" that jut up from the tip of its snout. This 4-foot (1.2-meter) poisonous African snake lives among thorny, spiky plants. As it lies in ambush, waiting to strike out at passing prey, its horny snout helps it blend into the background.

A Star Among Noses. The prize for the strangest-looking nose of all should probably be awarded to the star-nosed mole. This animal has 22 fleshy feelers forming a ring around its nostrils. The two top feelers are held rigidly forward. The rest wiggle constantly as the mole searches for worms and insects to eat.

With 22 fleshy feelers circling its nostrils, the star-nosed mole takes top prize for the strangest-looking nose!

Moles live in dark underground burrows. The star-nosed mole is nearly blind. It finds its way and its food with the twitching feelers that fringe its nostrils. While its nose may look odd, it really works. A star-nosed mole finds and eats half its weight in insects and grubs every day.

On the beach with Buddy: President Bill Clinton plays with the new First Dog.

BUDDY: FIRST DOG

The White House went to the dogs in 1998, and Americans were doggone happy about it! They were delighted to see a pooch in the official presidential residence—a chocolate Labrador retriever named Buddy, who was the newest member of the First Family.

President Bill Clinton and First Lady Hillary Rodham Clinton decided to get a dog after their daughter Chelsea went off to college, leaving them feeling lonely. The First Family already had a First Pet—Socks, a black and white cat that came with them from Arkansas when Clinton was elected president in 1992. But Socks had never been much of a companion for the president—because Clinton is allergic to cats. So, on December 5, 1997, a three-month-old puppy moved into the White House.

This wasn't the first time the White House had become a dog house. A long list of presidents have had dogs. Warren G. Harding's Airedale Laddie Boy had his own seat at Cabinet meetings. Franklin D. Roosevelt's Scottie Fala went everywhere with him. John F. Kennedy's mutt Pushinka, Gerald Ford's golden retriever Liberty, and George Bush's spaniel Millie all gave birth to litters of puppies in the White House.

The Clintons' new puppy was a gift from a friend. Everyone wanted to know what the dog's name was. When the president said he hadn't decided, suggestions poured in. "Fudge" would match the dog's color. "Boots" would fit well with Socks. "Barkansas" would remind Clinton of his home state. In the end, Clinton named the dog after a great-uncle of his who had raised dogs.

At first, rumor had it that the puppy was keeping the president up at night—something lots of puppies do to their owners. But before long Buddy was fitting in well at the White House. He went to work with the president in the Oval Office, rode along in the official limousine when the president went to meetings, and went on vacation with the Clintons. Photographers loved to take pictures of the president and his dog together.

One member of the First Family clearly wasn't happy about the new arrival, however. That was Socks. In fact, Socks didn't think much of Buddy, and Buddy didn't care for Socks. In January, a photographer caught the First Cat and First Dog in a face-off on the

When Buddy was introduced to Socks, it clearly wasn't love at first sight—prompting this humorous cartoon.

White House lawn. Socks arched his back and hissed, while Buddy barked furiously—and the president kept a firm hand on the dog's leash. Along with improving relations between countries, President Clinton now had a new priority—improving relations between Socks and Buddy. But he was confident that the two would learn to get along.

Like the pets of earlier First Families, Socks and Buddy have lots of fans. And they receive lots of mail, much of it from children. In November 1998, samples of those letters were published in a book, *Dear Socks, Dear Buddy.* The book included candid photographs of the First Pets at home, along with an introduction by the First Lady. Profits went to the National Park Foundation, which helps support the U.S. national parks.

MAKE WAY FOR THE BOOBY!

Attention, please: The blue-footed booby would like some respect. After all, this is an impressive bird, about the size of a goose. It's an expert flier, performing spectacular ocean dives to catch fish in its long, tapering beak. So why do people laugh at the blue-footed booby? They can't help it—the sight of the bird waddling along on its big bright blue feet is just too funny.

The name doesn't help either—it's hard *not* to laugh at something called a "booby." How did the bird get the name? No one is sure, but it probably comes from *bobo,* a Spanish word that means "stupid fellow." To early sailors, the booby was a *bobo* because it was so easy to catch. Boobies would land on ships and let sailors walk right up and snatch them.

The blue-footed booby is one of six kinds of boobies, and the others are nearly as comical. They're fascinating birds, related to gannets, pelicans, and cormorants—all ocean birds that dive for food. And they're wonderfully adapted to their way of life.

This blue-footed booby (*left*) wants you to take a closer look at him and his comical cousins. Boobies may look clownish, but they are really daring divers, dazzling dancers, and devoted parents (*below*).

BIGFOOT

Boobies are big birds, as much as 3 feet (1 meter) long, depending on the species. Their graceful, tapered wings stretch up to 5 feet (1.5 meters) from tip to tip. Streamlined from beak to tail, boobies are perfectly designed for flying and diving.

A booby cruises through the air as high as 100 feet (30 meters) over the ocean surface. It keeps its head cocked, on the lookout for signs of fish or other prey. When it sees a possible meal, it goes into dive mode. Flapping its wings to build speed, the bird turns and plummets straight down into the ocean, beak first. Just before it reaches the surface, its wings fold back, so it enters the water like a guided missile. Its nostrils close, and air sacs in its head cushion the tremendous impact.

Sometimes a booby makes a shallow horizontal dive. It speeds along close to the water, skims under the surface for a few feet, and pops out in full flight with a fish in its beak. The beak has serrated (jagged) edges to hold the prey tight. The booby gulps down what it catches on the spot.

However, all the booby's skills seem to disappear when it's on land. It touches down with the grace of a hippopotamus. Its big webbed feet, which are ideal for swimming in the ocean, aren't very good for walking. The bird waddles around comically, trying hard not to step on its own feet. But those big feet come in handy at nesting time.

A blue-footed booby begins its courtship dance by pointing its bill upward and rocking from side to side.

Most birds sit on their nests. A bald spot on the belly, called a brooding patch, allows the bird's skin to come in contact with the eggs and keep them at a constant temperature. A booby doesn't have a brooding patch—its belly is completely covered with feathers. So it stands on its eggs, keeping them warm with its big feet. And for about a week after they hatch, the chicks sit on their parents' feet, where they're sheltered from cold winds and the hot sun.

People in the United States and Canada don't often have a chance to see these wonderful birds in the wild. Various kinds of boobies are found worldwide, but only in tropical and semitropical regions. They raise their young on rocky seacoasts and islands. Red-footed boobies and brown boobies nest in Hawaii. Blue-footed boobies sometimes visit southern California. But when researchers want to study these birds, they usually head for the Galápagos Islands, in the Pacific Ocean off the coast of South America.

Three kinds of boobies—blue-footed, red-footed, and masked—nest in large numbers on these remote islands. And because no people live there, the boobies aren't afraid when people come close. Scientists have been able to learn a great deal about the Galápagos boobies, and they've discovered that each species has its own way of life.

TRUE BLUE

About 30 percent of the world's blue-footed boobies nest in crowded colonies on the Galápagos Islands. Watching these brown and white birds perform their courtship dance is something no one forgets. The male blue-foot starts the performance by pointing his bill and tail straight up, partly unfurling his wings, and whistling. He rocks from side to side, picking up one blue foot and then the other. The female joins, honking and dancing. They bow, nod, touch bills, and then turn away shyly. Then they offer presents—twigs and pebbles—to each other.

The birds clear an area to be their nesting site, and the female lays two or three eggs on the rocky ground. Both parents help raise the chicks, taking turns bringing fish to them. The adult bird swallows the fish and carries it in its crop, a sort of pouch in the throat. It regurgitates the fish at the nest. If food is plentiful, all the chicks get some. But if food is in short supply, the strongest chick pushes the others aside. Often the strongest is the only one to survive.

Besides being outstanding dancers, blue-footed boobies are daredevil divers. Females, which are larger and heavier than males, dive in open water. Males hunt in the shallows along the shore. A blue-foot can dive full speed into water less than 3 feet (1 meter) deep and then maneuver, using its tail like a rudder, so that it doesn't hit the bottom. Sometimes flocks of the birds team up to hunt, driving fish into the shallows and diving in turns.

MASKED ATTACKER

The masked booby is a striking bird, with trim black and white plumage, an orange beak, and a black mask. It's the largest of all the boobies, and the most aggressive. Masked boobies are constantly squabbling in their huge nesting colonies. Even their courtship dances are aggressive—the birds jab at each other in a mock fight.

Like blue-footed boobies, masked boobies nest on the ground. The female lays one or two eggs. If there are two eggs, they hatch several days apart—and then a strange thing happens. The older chick turns on the younger chick and

A pair of masked boobies preen each other while courting. These striking birds are very aggressive—they may even jab at each other in a mock fight during their courtship dance.

Red-footed boobies are the only boobies on the Galápagos Islands that nest in trees. The red-foots do this to protect their chicks from being attacked by adult masked boobies.

drives it out of the nest, where it dies of starvation or exposure or is attacked by other adults in the colony. Researchers don't fully understand why this happens, but it always does.

The parents share the duties of raising the remaining chick, which now gets all the fish they bring. One bird stays at the nest to guard the chick while the other hunts. Masked boobies fly farther out to sea to hunt than blue-footed boobies do, and they dive deeper. They can nearly always find food, even when other boobies can't. Sardines are their favorite fish.

Adult masked boobies will attack the chicks of other booby species—so blue-footed and red-footed boobies are careful to build their nests away from masked booby colonies.

A LITTLE RED

Red-footed boobies safeguard their eggs by building nests in trees. They're the only boobies in the Galápagos Islands that do so. They're also the smallest boobies on the islands. But they're still good-sized birds, measuring 2 to 2 ½ feet (60 to 75 centimeters) long. With their drab feathers, these birds blend in well with the island vegetation—except for their screaming red feet.

Red-footed boobies gather in huge nesting colonies in the brush. They build nests out of twigs, and some of these constructions are more than 3 feet (1 meter) tall. Masked boobies nest in some of the same areas, but the big birds don't bother their red-footed cousins as long as they're in the trees.

A red-foot female lays a single egg, and the parents work together to raise their chick. These birds fly far out over the ocean to find food in places where other boobies don't hunt. Their favorite foods are flying fish and squid. Red-footed boobies may be smaller than other types, but they are quick and agile. They are excellent hunters and can snap up a flying fish "on the fly." Still, a red-foot may be away from the nest as long as six days when it's hunting for food.

All that time, its partner waits patiently at the nest, protecting the chick. Red-footed boobies are excellent parents. They continue to feed their chick even after it fledges, or leaves the nest, and begins to hunt on its own. That usually happens when the young bird is about four and a half months old.

Good parents, daredevil divers, dynamite dancers—it's clear that boobies of all colors deserve some respect!

Visitors to the Computer Museum in Boston can have some fishy fun at the **Virtual Fish Tank,** which opened in June 1998. There's no water in this aquarium—it's a simulated underwater world, created by computers. Comical cartoon fish swim around the "tank," which is made up of twelve large projection screens. At three "Build Your Own Fish" stations, visitors can assemble the virtual fish of their dreams by choosing various behavioral traits. Is the fish friendly or shy? A predator? A deep-sea species? The traits they select determine the shape and color of the fish, as well as how it reacts to people, other fish, food, and water depth. Then they "launch" their fish and watch it interact with the other fish in the tank. The exhibit shows how a few simple rules of behavior lead to complex patterns in groups, even when there's no leader of the group. People can change the undersea environment or the fish's traits to see how that affects the group. Other parts of the exhibit show how the same types of behavioral patterns develop in insect colonies and even in highway traffic.

A rare sight, these **twin albino white-tailed deer fawns** were born in the Michigan woods in 1998. White-tailed deer fawns are usually brown with white spots. Their colors are created by pigments—color-producing chemicals—in their fur, skin, and eyes. Albinos have no pigments, so they're snowy white. Albinism occurs in many kinds of animals. It's inherited; that is, it's passed from parents to offspring by the genes inside cells. The mother of these fawns was brown, but she carried an albino gene that showed up in the twins. Albino fawns like these are at a disadvantage—they are easy for predators to spot.

A pint-sized pup took top honors at America's most prestigious dog show, the Westminster Kennel Club Show, held in February 1998 in New York City. **Champion Fairewood Frolic,** better known as Rocki, was a female Norwich terrier, a breed known for its spirited, friendly temperament. She was small enough to fit inside her silver trophy!

Abandoned as a newborn, a gray whale named **J.J.** was rescued off the coast of Los Angeles and brought to Sea World, in San Diego. And in March 1998, she was returned to the ocean. Workers maneuvered the 10–ton whale onto a sling (above) and hoisted her onto a truck that took her to a waiting Coast Guard cutter. The cutter carried her out to sea, where she was hoisted overboard and released.

Another famous whale began a journey to freedom in 1998. **Keiko,** the orca (killer whale) that starred in the movie *Free Willy,* had fallen on hard times after his 1993 film role. He was living in a cramped tank in Mexico City, suffering from lung and skin infections. In 1996 fans raised money to bring him to Oregon, where he spent more than two years recovering in a spacious tank. In September 1998, he was loaded onto an Air Force cargo plane and flown to Iceland, where he had been captured almost 20 years earlier. Keiko will spend at least two years in a sea pen there. He must get used to the chilly North Atlantic waters and remember how to catch fish on his own. If he does that, and shows that he can get along with other orcas, he'll be set free.

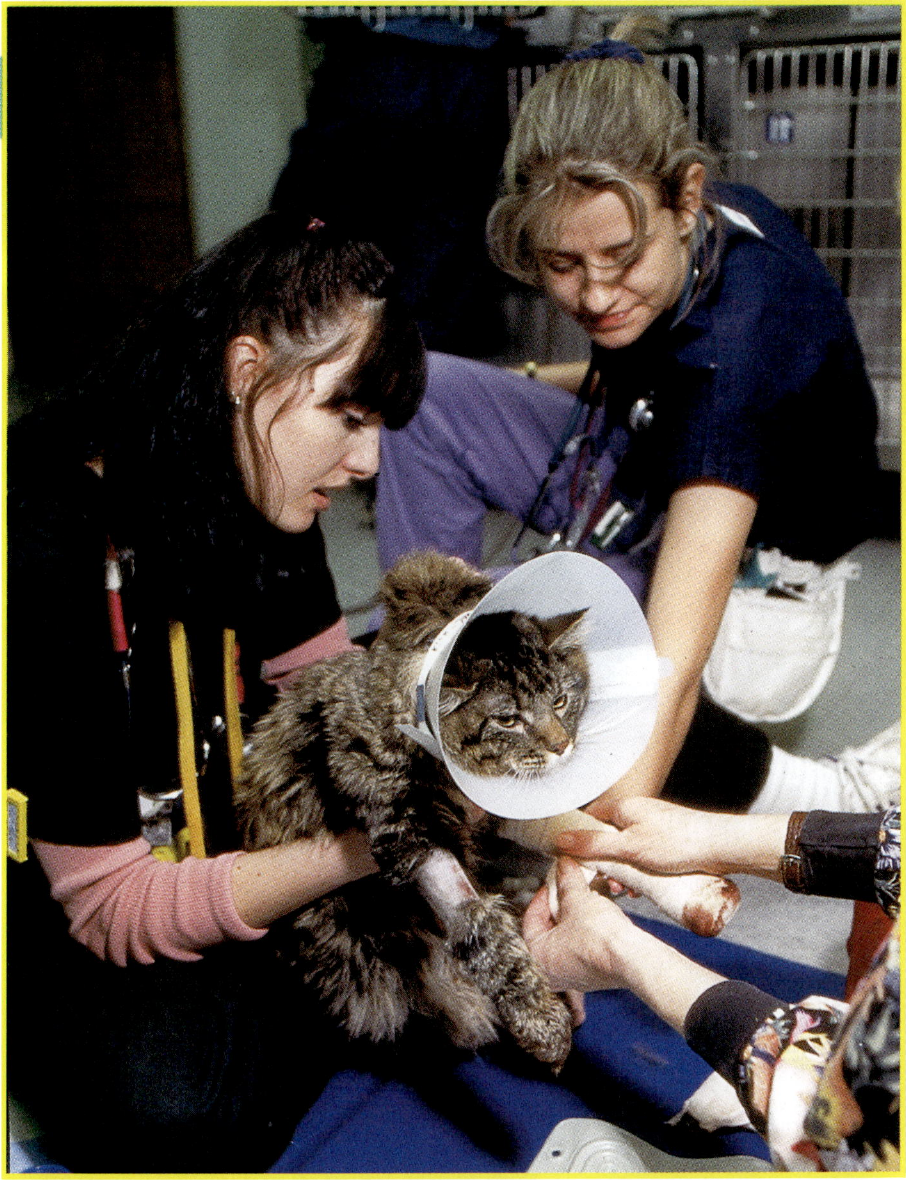

One of 1998's most unusual new television shows was a fast-paced, suspenseful series in the tradition of the hospital drama *E.R.* The twist that set this show apart was the fact that all the patients being rushed in for treatment were animals. *Emergency Vets* (above) was one of the prime-time offerings on a new cable network, **Animal Planet.** The network is designed for big-time animal lovers who want more from television than nature documentaries, and it's one of the fastest-growing theme cable channels. Besides *Emergency Vets,* Animal Planet offers *The Pet Shop,* a talk show with animal guests; *Pet Line,* with advice for pet problems; *Wild Rescues,* about people saving animals from danger; *Amazing Tails,* incredible real-life animal stories; and reruns of classic animal shows like *Lassie* and *Flipper.* In the works are a biography series profiling famous animals and sports coverage of dog shows and other events. With programs like these, the Animal Planet network promises to live up to its slogan: "All animals, all the time."

SCIENCE

In 1962, John Glenn captured America's imagination by becoming the first U.S. astronaut to orbit Earth. In 1998, 36 years later, he did it again, by becoming the oldest person ever to go into space. On his first space trip, Glenn circled Earth three times in a tiny one-man space capsule called Friendship 7. *The flight lasted less than five hours, but it made him an American hero. Later, he turned to politics and served four terms as a U.S. senator from Ohio. And on October 29, 1998, at age 77, he fulfilled a lifelong dream by returning to space aboard the shuttle* Discovery. *On the mission, he served as sort of a medical guinea pig, to see how space flight would affect older people. When* Discovery *returned to Earth safely on November 7, Glenn once again received a hero's welcome.*

From space, Earth looks like a big blue ball—because 70 percent of Earth's surface is covered with water. To make people more aware of the importance of these waters, 1998 was declared the International Year of the Ocean.

YEAR OF THE OCEAN

If aliens on some distant planet turn their telescopes on Earth, they might name our world the Water Planet. Water covers more than 70 percent of Earth's surface. And 97 percent of this water makes up Earth's oceans—the Atlantic, Pacific, Indian, Arctic, and Antarctic Oceans. From space, the ocean makes our planet seem like a shiny blue ball.

But the ocean is much more than Earth's most notable feature. It's essential for life. It's a major source of food. It helps create climate patterns around the world. And it's Earth's last great frontier, filled with unknowns.

People enjoy and benefit from the ocean—but they have sometimes harmed it, too. Today the ocean and the life it contains are in danger from pollution and other threats. To draw attention to the ocean's importance and the dangers it faces, the United Nations declared 1998 the International Year of the Ocean. During the year, scientists focused their research on the seas. Governments, organizations, and individuals worked to educate people about the ocean. And people everywhere stepped up their efforts to protect this wonderful resource.

PEOPLE AND THE OCEAN

From icy Arctic waters to tropical coral reefs, from shallow coastal bays to deep trenches on the sea floor, the ocean world is very different from the world on land. It's home to more different kinds of living things than any other habitat. An amazing variety of plants and animals—from tiny one-celled organisms to huge whales—dwell in the ocean depths. They are linked in an intricate web of life, in which each creature is important to the whole.

The animals and plants of the sea are important in many ways. For people all over the world, fish and shellfish are food staples. If you're like most people in North America, you ate 15 pounds (7 kilograms) of seafood last year. Marine life provides many other products, too. For example, a substance called carrageenan, which is produced by red algae, is used to add smoothness to toothpaste, peanut butter, and other products. A compound derived from sea sponges may one day be used to fight cancer. Other marine substances may be useful as medicines, too. The ocean world also contains useful minerals—sand and gravel, calcium carbonate, tin, and sulfur. Because undersea mining is difficult, most of these reserves are untouched.

Ever since people first took to the sea in boats, the world's oceans have been important transportation routes. Even today, crude oil, new cars, clothing, television sets—all sorts of products—are transported by ship. In coastal areas, the ocean is a place for fun. Swimming, sailing, fishing, scuba diving, and other water sports draw people to the sea. So does the beauty of the seacoast. Perhaps that's why so many people choose to live in coastal regions.

OCEAN AND AIR

The ocean is also important in ways we may rarely think of. For example, the ocean is a major force behind the weather.

Most of the moisture that falls as precipitation begins as water vapor that has evaporated from the vast ocean surface. The vapor condenses into rain or snow and falls back to the surface, in an endless cycle. The ocean also drives weather patterns around the

The Coral Reefs

Perhaps you've heard this advice: If you want to really get to know a place, live there. That's what at least one group of scientists did to find out more about coral reefs during the International Year of the Ocean.

Coral reefs are among the most delicate ocean habitats. The reefs are formed by tiny organisms called coral polyps, which live in huge colonies in warm waters. The polyps form protective shells of calcium carbonate. When they die, their shells remain, and the next generation builds on top of the old shells. Over centuries, a coral reef can grow until it stretches for miles. Reefs form a habitat for many kinds of fish and other animals that are found nowhere else. But in recent years reefs have been dying, and scientists have been trying to find out why.

In 1998, a group of scientists set up shop in an underwater lab on Conch Reef, off the coast of Key Largo, Florida. The pressurized lab, *Aquarius 2000,* had all the comforts of home—bunk beds, a shower and toilet, a microwave oven. The researchers could stay on board for a week at a time, collecting video images and data about the reef.

The scientists hoped to find out if the reef was being affected by pollution or ultraviolet radiation from the sun. They also gathered information on chemicals produced by coral polyps to ward off predators. Some of these chemicals may be used to develop cancer-fighting medicines and other drugs.

The ocean is essential for life on Earth. It affects the weather. It provides us with food. And it's a great place for having fun!

world. Droughts, floods, hurricanes and tornadoes—the ocean gives rise to all these, through changes in temperature and currents.

Ocean currents are determined by many factors—winds, water temperatures and salt content, the mountains and valleys on the seafloor, and Earth's rotation. Warm currents like the Gulf Stream, which crosses the Atlantic Ocean from the Caribbean Sea to Europe, help create mild climates in lands along their paths. Cold currents like the Humboldt Current, which sweeps up from Antarctica along the western coast of South America, have a cooling effect.

The world had an excellent example of the ocean's affect on weather in 1997 and 1998: El Niño, a climate disturbance caused by warming ocean currents in the Pacific, played havoc with weather. For example, storms caused by El Niño resulted in widespread damage to property and crops.

During the International Year of the Ocean, scientists studied how changes in the atmosphere affect the oceans. They are concerned about two developments, both of which result from air pollution. The first is global warming. A worldwide warming trend has already caused some melting of polar glaciers. As glaciers melt into the ocean, the sea level rises. Glacial melt also dilutes the salt content of the ocean, and that may cause changes in ocean currents.

Ozone depletion is the other concern. High in the atmosphere, a layer of ozone gas protects Earth's surface from the sun's harmful ultraviolet radiation. But certain pollutants destroy ozone, and they have caused the layer to thin. The thinning is greatest over the polar regions. These regions are also home to a rich variety of algae and zooplankton—tiny organisms that are the first link in the ocean food chain. If these organisms are lost, the entire web of ocean life would be in danger.

ALL THE FISH IN THE SEA

The ocean's many plants and animals face other dangers, too—and many of those dangers are the result of things people do.

The Grand Banks, off the eastern coast of Canada, was once one of the world's great fishing grounds. In the 1400s the explorer John Cabot found so many fish in these waters that his crew just scooped them up in baskets. The supply seemed endless—but it wasn't. In the early 1990s, the Canadian government had to halt commercial fishing in the Grand Banks, for fear that the remaining fish would be wiped out.

Overfishing has created similar problems in many other places. As the world's population has grown, so has demand for fish. At the same time, new methods have made it possible to catch fish by the ton. Commercial fishing fleets use sonar, aircraft, and satellite positioning systems to track down schools of fish. Huge "factory" trawlers set out nets that stretch for miles and can pull in up to 300,000 pounds (136,000 kilograms) of fish at a time.

When modern trawlers go after a particular type of fish, they can have a terrible impact. Species such as bluefin tuna, once common, are now rare. Populations of cod, flounder, herring, salmon, king crab, and shrimp have decreased. The fishing methods are wasteful, too. Everything that swims into the net is caught and killed—crabs, sharks, starfish, squid—along with food fish. Some 27 million tons of unwanted "bycatch"—about a fourth of the total commercial catch—are tossed out each year.

One focus of the International Year of the Ocean was to find less damaging fishing methods. There have been successes in the past. Bans on certain types of nets, changes in fishing techniques, and limits on fishing in sensitive areas have already helped cut waste. More steps like these may help preserve marine life—and the fishing industry itself.

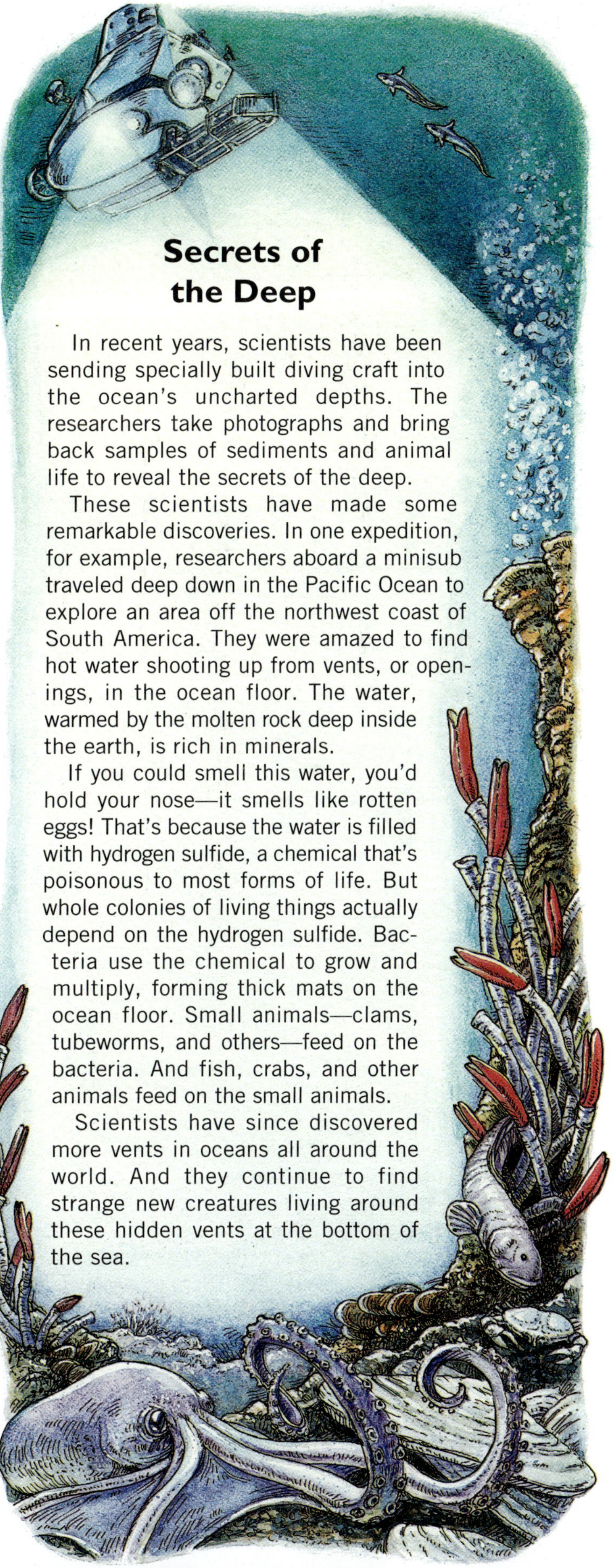

Secrets of the Deep

In recent years, scientists have been sending specially built diving craft into the ocean's uncharted depths. The researchers take photographs and bring back samples of sediments and animal life to reveal the secrets of the deep.

These scientists have made some remarkable discoveries. In one expedition, for example, researchers aboard a minisub traveled deep down in the Pacific Ocean to explore an area off the northwest coast of South America. They were amazed to find hot water shooting up from vents, or openings, in the ocean floor. The water, warmed by the molten rock deep inside the earth, is rich in minerals.

If you could smell this water, you'd hold your nose—it smells like rotten eggs! That's because the water is filled with hydrogen sulfide, a chemical that's poisonous to most forms of life. But whole colonies of living things actually depend on the hydrogen sulfide. Bacteria use the chemical to grow and multiply, forming thick mats on the ocean floor. Small animals—clams, tubeworms, and others—feed on the bacteria. And fish, crabs, and other animals feed on the small animals.

Scientists have since discovered more vents in oceans all around the world. And they continue to find strange new creatures living around these hidden vents at the bottom of the sea.

As the world's population has grown, so has the demand for fish. At the same time, new methods have made it possible to catch fish by the ton. Today, overfishing is a serious threat to marine life.

DIRTY WATER

Overfishing is only one threat to marine life. Pollution also poses grave dangers. Major oil spills make headlines, but there are countless small spills every year. Industrial wastes—including harmful mercury and PCB's—are discharged or dumped at sea. Tin compounds leach from the paint used on ships. Rain washes pesticides off farmland, and the pesticides travel down streams and rivers to the ocean. And fertilizers wash into the sea, causing algae to grow out of control. Debris—torn nylon fishing nets, plastic soda-can rings, and other discarded items—entangles or chokes marine animals.

Many pollutants stay in the water for years, and they build up. In some areas, the damage is serious. A section of water off the U.S. Gulf Coast is so empty of life that scientists call it the "dead zone." Pollution has been blamed for falling birth rates and increasing illness among dolphins and whales, as well as the deaths of many marine animals. It may also contribute to the deadly events called red tides. In a red tide, billions of one-celled organisms overspread the ocean surface, producing toxins that kill marine animals.

Tighter controls on pollutants will help. Several groups are working to identify and ban the most harmful chemicals. There are also ways to reduce the runoff of pesticides and fertilizers from farmland—for example, by planting bands of trees and grasses that would absorb the polluted rainwater.

MARINE MAMMALS

Whales, dolphins, seals, sea lions—marine mammals are highly appealing ocean animals. People are fascinated by them. Scientists have devoted a great deal of research time to dolphins, in the wild and in captivity, because these animals are so intelligent. But the ways of some marine mammals are still mysterious.

The mammoth sperm whale, for example, dives to depths of more than 9,000 feet (2,740 meters). During the International Year of the Ocean, a research expedition explored one of the sperm whale's favorite haunts, deep Kaikoura Canyon, in the ocean off New Zealand. Using special cameras that could be lowered to great depths, the scientists hoped to see sperm whales encountering their favorite prey—the giant squid, an animal that grows up to 60 feet (18 meters) long and has never been seen in its deep ocean habitat.

Let's Help!

• **Learn:** Read about the ocean, and visit it if you can.

• **Reduce pollution:** Disposing of trash in the ocean has become a major problem. And if plastic items are tossed in the ocean and wash up to shore, seals and other animals can get tangled up in the plastic and be harmed (as shown here).

• **Preserve ocean habitats:** Be aware of wildlife when you go fishing, boating, or swimming. If you dive, look, but don't touch. Leave shoreline areas undisturbed—and don't leave trash behind, in the water or on the beach.

• **Be a smart shopper:** Don't buy types of fish that are overfished or caught with equipment that endangers ocean life.

• **"Think globally, act locally."** Follow this slogan, and learn what you can do in your area to help protect the ocean.

Whales and other marine mammals have been victims of overhunting in the past. They have also felt the effects of pollution. And because many of these animals, especially seals and sea lions, live in coastal waters, they have been pushed aside by shoreline development. As a result, many marine mammals are endangered today. Only about 300 northern right whales remain off the eastern coast of North America. Hawaiian monk seals have been reduced in number to about 1,300.

But there are also success stories. For example, in the 1800s gray whales were hunted almost to extinction. But after laws were passed to protect this and other whales, their numbers grew. In 1994, the gray whale became the first marine mammal to be removed from the endangered species list, which names animals in direct danger of dying out. The gray whale's story stands as an example of what can be done when people take action to preserve wildlife.

Overfishing, development in coastal regions, dumping refuse at sea—these and other damaging activities can be controlled. The message of the International Year of the Ocean was this: The ocean is essential for life on Earth. The more we know about it, and the more we understand how our activities affect it, the better we'll be able to protect it.

FEARFUL PHOBIAS

Darkness. Bridges. Flying in airplanes. Thunder and lightning. Riding in elevators. Snakes. Spiders. A visit to the dentist.

You may consider these things unpleasant, or you may think nothing of them at all. You may think some of them—an airplane trip or a window-rattling thunderstorm—are fun and exciting. On the other hand, you may turn pale and start to shake at the mere thought of one of these objects or situations. For some people, they're sources of deep, overwhelming fear.

These are people who suffer from phobias, or intense, irrational fears. People may develop phobias toward almost anything—even objects, situations, and activities that other people consider pleasant. A person may be terribly afraid of cats or dogs, for example. People have even been reported to panic at the sight of such everyday objects as eyeglasses, clocks, and three-legged stools.

These fears may sound silly to people who don't share them. But to people who have them, phobias are no joke. Phobias can disrupt people's lives, causing them to drive miles out of their way to avoid crossing a bridge, to give up a vacation to avoid getting on an airplane, or even to stay home all the time.

Phobias are far from rare. Many people have them—an estimated thirteen million in the United States alone. Psychologists who have studied these fears aren't sure what causes them. But they have learned one thing: With proper treatment, most phobias can be cured.

FEARS OF ALL KINDS

The term "phobia" comes from the Greek and Latin words for fear. Dozens of specific phobias have been given Greek and Latin names, too. Claustrophobia, for example, is

the fear of being trapped or confined. The name comes from the Latin word *claustrum,* meaning "confined place."

Psychologists divide phobias into five major groups. A **simple phobia** is a fear of a specific object or situation. Fear of heights is a common example of a simple phobia. Other simple phobias include fear of elevators, tunnels, driving, flying, crossing water, swimming, darkness, crowds, strangers, and drafts.

Social phobias are fears of public embarrassment. A person with a social phobia may panic at the thought of speaking before a group, for instance. The fears of eating in public and of signing one's name in front of others are also examples of social phobias.

Some people suffer from **animal phobias**—fear of dogs, cats, birds, or other animals. Fear of snakes is common, and so is the fear of spiders and certain insects, even moths and other innocent-looking bugs. There are also **injury phobias,** in which the person panics at the sight of blood or the thought of injury. People who suffer from injury phobias are often terrified by the thought of a visit to the doctor or the dentist.

Agoraphobia is the most complex form of phobia. This is the fear of being in open spaces or away from a safe person or place. A person with agoraphobia may start to panic anytime he or she is in an open, public place, like a shopping mall or theater. People with severe agoraphobia may be terrified to leave their homes at all or to be left alone for even a few minutes.

People who suffer from phobias don't simply shy away when they're confronted with the objects or situations they fear. They experience what psychologists call a panic reaction. They may shake or sweat and feel dizzy. Their hearts race, they become short of breath, and they may feel as if they were choking or smothering. Worst of all, they're overwhelmed by fears that they'll do something uncontrollable, faint, or even die. A person who is afraid of driving across bridges, for example, may think, "What if I lose control of the car?" A person who is afraid of heights may think, "What if I faint—and fall?"

Most people who have phobias realize that their fears don't make sense. But the panic reaction is so unpleasant that they go out of their way to avoid the situations that produce it. They may even start to panic at the thought of having the reaction. Then they develop phobophobia—the fear of fear itself.

FINDING CAUSES AND CURES

Psychologists who have studied phobias say that the people who suffer from them are perfectly normal in all other ways. They are good family members, good workers, and good friends. Often, they're warm, sensitive, and imaginative people. Why, then, do the phobias develop?

Many researchers believe that most animal phobias stem from frightening experiences in childhood. Events that older children and adults take in stride—an insect bite, a barking dog, a scratching cat—can make a big impression on a small child. This theory is supported by the fact that animal phobias often begin in childhood, while other phobias usually emerge between the ages of 15 and 30.

The other phobias are generally more difficult to explain. Frightening experiences may play a part, but heredity and upbringing have also been blamed. Stress may be a factor too. Many phobias seem to begin or worsen when people experience some stressful event, such as the death of a loved one or a move to a new city.

Regardless of their cause, phobias create more than inconvenience for the people who suffer from them. They can also disrupt family life. And they can affect business—by some estimates, the fear of flying costs the airline industry as much as $1.5 billion a year.

Phobia Frenzy

Acrophobia: fear of heights
Agoraphobia: fear of open spaces or being away from a safe place or person
Ailurophobia: fear of cats
Amaxophobia: fear of vehicles or driving
Aquaphobia: fear of water or swimming
Arachnophobia: fear of spiders
Astraphobia and **tonitrophobia:** fear of thunder and lightning
Aviophobia (or **pterygophobia**): fear of flying
Blennophobia: fear of slime
Cathisophobia: fear of sitting down
Claustrophobia: fear of confinement
Cynophobia: fear of dogs
Entomophobia: fear of insects
Gephyrophobia: fear of crossing a bridge or large body of water
Musophobia: fear of mice
Nyctophobia: fear of darkness
Ochlophobia: fear of crowds
Odontiatophobia: fear of dentists
Ophiophobia: fear of snakes
Panophobia: fear of everything
Phobophobia: fear of fears
Selenophobia: fear of the moon
Tropophobia: fear of moving
Xenophobia: fear of strangers
Zoophobia: fear of animals in general

The Top Ten

1. Spiders, bugs, mice, and snakes
2. Heights
3. Being on public transportation
4. Being in water
5. Being in crowds
6. Being in a closed place
7. Storms
8. Tunnels or bridges
9. Speaking in front of a small group of acquaintances
10. Speaking to strangers or meeting new people

Unlucky Thirteen

The year 1998 was a dreadful one for people who suffer from **triskaidekaphobia**— fear of the number thirteen. The thirteenth day of the month fell on a Friday three times, in February, March, and November. And as triskaidekaphobes know, that's an especially unlucky combination.

More a superstition than a true, panic-inducing phobia, triskaidekaphobia has a long history. The idea that thirteen is an unlucky number reaches back to ancient Greece and to Biblical times. In the Middle Ages, witches were thought to gather in covens of thirteen members.

The fear of thirteen is still with us today. Most high-rise buildings are built without a thirteenth floor—the actual thirteenth floor is numbered fourteen. And most airplanes don't have a thirteenth row. Some people still believe that it's unlucky to travel on the thirteenth day of the month or to have thirteen people at dinner.

Combining thirteen with Friday makes matters even worse. Friday has long been considered an unlucky day—right through the 1800s, executions were held on that day, which was called Hangman's Day.

Every year has at least one Friday the Thirteenth. No year has more than three, so 1998 had the maximum. But, fortunately for triskaidekaphobes, this won't happen again until 2004!

But as research has led to better understanding of phobias in recent years, new methods of treatment have been developed. In the United States and Canada, there are hundreds of clinics and specialists who treat phobias. They are able to cure the problem 70 to 80 percent of the time. There are also special programs for specific phobias. Some airlines, for example, sponsor programs for people who are afraid to fly, helping thousands of people with this fear.

Several different techniques, including psychotherapy and the short-term use of drugs that can block panic attacks, are used. One popular treatment technique is called exposure therapy. In this technique, a group of people who suffer from the same phobia meet with a therapist and learn how to deal with their fear. They also learn ways to reduce panic and stay in control, such as counting backward by threes from 100 or reciting a poem or the words of a song. Deep breathing and other relaxation techniques are also taught.

Then they begin to confront the real situation. People who are afraid to fly, for example, may just sit in a parked airliner and practice relaxation techniques. The exposure is gradually increased until, finally, they're able to take long airplane trips without fear. A person who's afraid to drive across bridges may start with dozens of trips across short spans and gradually work up to longer, higher bridges.

Most of the time, people in these programs find that they can control their fears and end the panic attacks—and resume normal, happy lives.

THE Y2K BUG

Airplanes will be grounded. Traffic lights will go out. Financial markets will crash. Home appliances won't work. Neither will factory machinery. Huge areas will go dark as electrical power is cut off.

Those disasters may happen at the stroke of midnight on December 31, 1999—or they may not. People who are looking ahead to that date are worried about a big computer glitch called the millennium problem, or the Y2K (for Year 2000) bug. Experts agree that the Y2K bug is a real threat, but they don't agree about just how big a threat it is.

WHAT COULD HAPPEN

Here's the problem: Dates play a part in the operation of nearly all computers, but most computers won't be able to recognize any year after 1999. That's because computers use only the last two digits to identify years—1998 was just "98." So when "19" rolls into "20" on January 1, 2000, computers will read the date as "00." Some won't recognize that as a date. Some will think it's 1900. And then they'll crash or begin to make mistakes.

Although the Y2K bug seems simple, its effects will be anything but. Here are some of the disruptions that could occur:

- City traffic control systems, which are run by computers, could go haywire. Other local services—from water distribution to emergency services—could be disrupted too.
- The computers that control air traffic might shut down, grounding planes and forcing long delays at airports.
- In hospitals, medical equipment could fail. Hospital records and billing systems could also be affected.
- Banks may lose track of accounts. When checks are presented for payment, banks may reject them—because the accounts the checks are drawn on didn't exist in 1900.
- Financial markets, which rely heavily on computers, could be disrupted. People won't be able to track their investments or buy and sell stocks and bonds, because their investment accounts and the securities they own weren't around in 1900.
- In factories, automated machinery may go haywire. Assembly lines could shut down. Companies would lose track of inventories and production deadlines.
- Goods may not be shipped—because computers can't process the orders and tell the trucks to roll. Everything from food to furniture could be affected.
- Stores may reject credit cards. The electronic equipment used to "swipe" cards and detect coded information on them won't recognize expiration dates after 1999. Automated teller machines may swallow bank cards, thinking they've expired.

• Cars, clock radios, VCR's, and any other machine that relies on computer chips to track dates may stop operating.

• Electric utilities, which rely on computers to regulate power flow, could shut down. This could be the worst disaster of all because electrical generation and transmission facilities are linked in networks, or power grids. Many facilities are designed to shut down if a problem is sensed in a neighboring sector. So a Y2K problem in one sector could have a "cascade" effect, causing many more sectors to shut down.

Some people are so worried about the Y2K bug that they're predicting that just about everything will grind to a halt. Most experts don't foresee anything so disastrous. But they agree that the problem must be taken seriously.

FIXING THE GLITCH

The Y2K bug is a software problem: It's a glitch in the programs, or coded instructions, that tell computers what to do. To fix it, programmers need to rewrite the sections of software that contain information about dates. That sounds simple—and if all computers were the same, it would be simple. Programmers could just write a universal correction, and it could be copied by every computer.

Unfortunately, there's no universal correction. There are many kinds of computers, from big mainframes to palm-sized portables to tiny chips that make household appliances "smart." There are even more kinds of programs running in those computers. Programs are written in several computer languages and customized for different uses. That means corrections must be tailored to the situation. Programs contained in tiny chips generally can't be changed; instead, the chip must be replaced.

The Y2K bug has sent businesses and governments scurrying to find and fix all date fields in computer programs. That can mean scanning millions of lines of computer code. The Internal Revenue Service (IRS), for example, has 50 different computer systems, running 19,000 different programs—more than 62 million lines of code in all. It's a time-consuming job, and a costly one. Getting rid of the bug in federal computers could cost anywhere from $4.7 billion to $30 billion.

Financial firms have been working especially hard to correct the problem. In July 1998, major U.S. brokerages and exchanges tested their computers to see if the fixes would work. To everyone's relief, the computers handled transactions dated 2000 without a hitch.

It's unlikely that every computer system will be fixed by December 31, 1999. But if the most important systems are corrected, the Y2K bug may turn out to be just a minor annoyance.

Back to the Future...

Here's how your day could start on January 1, 2000, if the Y2K bug isn't fixed.

10:00 A.M. You overslept! Your clock radio thinks that today is January 1, 1900, and it doesn't come on.

10:15 You pop a frozen bagel in the microwave. But the microwave won't work—its computer chip has crashed. You settle for cold cereal.

10:25 You turn on the television to check the weather report. There's no weather report—National Weather Service computers are down. But the TV news tells you that traffic is snarled all over town because traffic lights are out.

10:40 The late-night movie your VCR was set to record while you slept isn't on tape. When midnight struck, the VCR couldn't figure out the date. You decide to read a book.

10:45 The phone rings. It's your Aunt Margaret, who was flying in for a visit. Her plane was due in at 11, but it hasn't even left yet because air traffic computers are down.

10:46 The phone line goes dead. Service has been cut off because phone company computers miscalculated the date.

11:00 It's a holiday, so you don't know about your problems at school. Your records have been lost—it's 1900, according to the school's computer, and you haven't been born yet!

This is what the *International Space Station* will look like when completed in 2004. Huge solar panels will provide the station with power. Inside the station, there will be as much room as in two jumbo jets.

THE INTERNATIONAL SPACE STATION

Get ready for a new era in space travel at the start of the 21st century: That's when the *International Space Station* (*ISS*) is scheduled to be completed. The *ISS* will be an orbiting lab where scientists and astronauts will live and work year-round. Sixteen countries, including the United States and Russia, have joined forces to build the station. It will be assembled in space, 220 miles (354 kilometers) above Earth, and will cost more than $30 billion.

The *ISS* won't be the first space station. The United States had a space station, *Skylab,* in the 1970s. And a Russian space station, *Mir,* has been orbiting Earth since February 1986. But the aging *Mir* has been experiencing many problems, and the Russians plan to retire it in 1999. The *ISS* will not only be brand new, it will be much larger than the earlier stations, with room for a crew of seven.

The *ISS* is also the first project of its kind to be jointly built and used by so many countries. Besides the United States and Russia, the partners include Japan, Canada, and members of the European Space Agency. The station won't be finished until the year 2004, at the earliest. But when it's done, the hope is that it will stand as a model, showing how nations can work together for the benefit of all. One day the *ISS*, or a space station like it, may serve as the jumping-off point for long space missions... to the moon, to Mars, or beyond.

BUILDING IN ORBIT

The *ISS* will consist of several pressurized units, or modules, where the crew will live and work. In all, it will have about as much room inside as two jumbo jets. External platforms and unpressurized areas will carry instruments and additional equipment for research. Almost an acre of solar panels will draw energy from the sun to provide the station with power.

The United States and Russia are the world leaders in space exploration, and they are taking the lead in building the *ISS.* Completing the job will take at least 43 space flights. On the first flight, on November 20, 1998, a Russian rocket, carried a pressurized module—called *Zarya,* for the Russian word meaning "sunrise"—into orbit. A cylinder more than 41 feet (12.5 meters) long, it will provide power, communications, and navigational control for the *ISS* in the early stages of construction. Later, it will be used mainly for storage. *Zarya* has ports where spacecraft can dock and other components of the *ISS* can attach.

In this drawing, the space shuttle *Endeavour* prepares to use its robot arm to capture the Russian-built *Zarya* module and attach it to *Unity.*

Just a few weeks after *Zarya's* launch, the U.S. space shuttle *Endeavour* carried the first American-built part of the *ISS* aloft. Called *Unity,* it's the main point of attachment for additional U.S. space station modules. The *Endeavour* astronauts—five Americans and a Russian—used the shuttle's robot arm to grab *Zarya* from the cargo bay and maneuver it into position. The robot arm was then used to link *Zarya* and *Unity.* After that, the astronauts made several space walks to hook up power and data-transmission cables. The mission was a complete success.

A Russian-built service module, with life-support systems for astronauts, will be added in 1999, and a crew of three could be on board a few months after that. Other pieces of the station—including a robot arm and hand built in Canada, an experiment module from Japan, and laboratory units from the United States and the Europeans—will make the station a working research center. The final piece will be a U.S.-built habitation ("hab") module with living quarters for crew members.

WORKING IN SPACE

Once the *ISS* is up and running, space shuttles and Russian *Soyuz* spacecraft will continue to visit, ferrying supplies and carrying crews back and forth. A *Soyuz* will stay attached to the station, in case the crew has to evacuate suddenly. The U.S. National Aeronautics and Space Administration (NASA) is developing a new space vehicle, the X-38, that will eventually take over that role. Crew members will also be able to use the X-38 to make short trips away from the station—for example, to pick up supplies launched from Earth in unmanned spacecraft.

On board the station, scientists will be able to perform a wide range of experiments in the gravity-free environment of space. They'll research protein crystals, polymers, semiconductors, and other materials that behave differently when there's no gravity. Their findings may lead to better ways of

Weightless Woes

Weightlessness can do funny things to people. For example, gravity normally draws body fluids down into your legs. In space, fluids are distributed evenly—so your face is puffier and your legs are thinner than they are on Earth. Your heart doesn't have to work so hard to pump blood throughout your body, either. And without the pull of gravity on your spine, you may "grow" an inch or two.

When you return to Earth, all these changes are reversed. Back in gravity, you feel as if you weigh a ton. It's hard to keep your balance. Your body fluids rush back to your legs, and you may even faint. Returning astronauts wear special suits with pants that keep pressure on their legs, so fluids won't rush down too fast.

The space station will have an exercise machine to help crew members stay in shape and to counter some of the physical effects of weightlessness. Muscles and bones don't work hard in space because they don't have to push against gravity. They lose strength, and bones can lose calcium. Exercise can help prevent that.

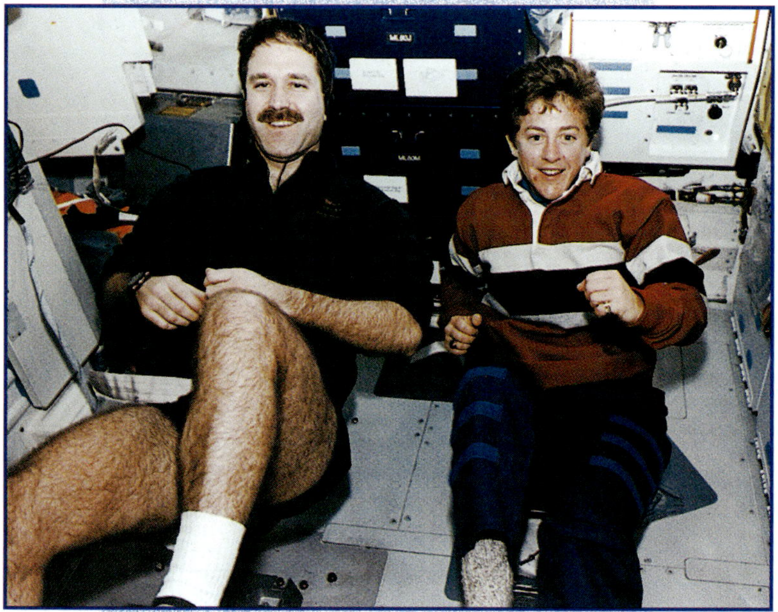

producing everything from medicines and computer chips to contact lenses and house paint.

Scientists will study the effects of weightlessness on humans and animals, too. What they learn may help them plan for future space missions and find treatments for health problems such as heart disease and osteoporosis (bone loss).

In a way, the space station crews will be part of their own research. They'll be learning firsthand what it's like to live and work in space for months at a time. And life in space is nothing like life on Earth. If you had a chance to spend some time on the *ISS,* here's what you could expect.

UP IS DOWN

Orbiting 220 miles (354 kilometers) up, the station won't be completely free of Earth's gravity. A very slight pull—microgravity—will keep it in orbit. But microgravity won't be strong enough to keep anything that's not tied down from floating, including you. Drop a pencil, and it will just drift around in the air. Stand up from your seat, and you'll vault across the compartment. You'll need to wear a seat belt or slip your feet into holders attached to the floor if you want to stay in one spot.

Without gravity, there's no difference between up and down. That sometimes makes a floating astronaut feel space-sick. To help crews feel at home, the space station will have visual ups and downs. Light fixtures will run along "ceilings," and tables will be attached to "floors."

Hard jobs are easy in this weightless world. You can lift heavy objects, even another crew member, with a fingertip. But easy jobs can be hard because nothing stays where you put it. If you want to make a peanut-butter sandwich, you'll need to ask someone to hold the jar while you spread the peanut butter on the bread.

FLOATING FOOD

Peanut butter is on the menu in space. But mealtimes are different than they are on

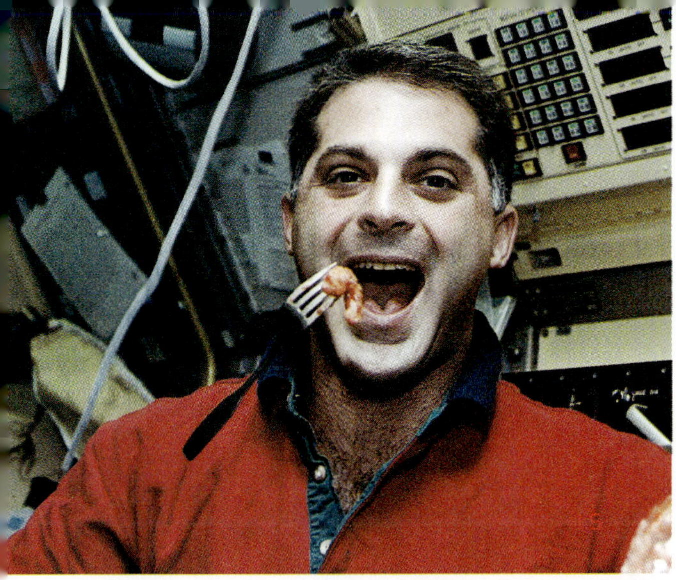

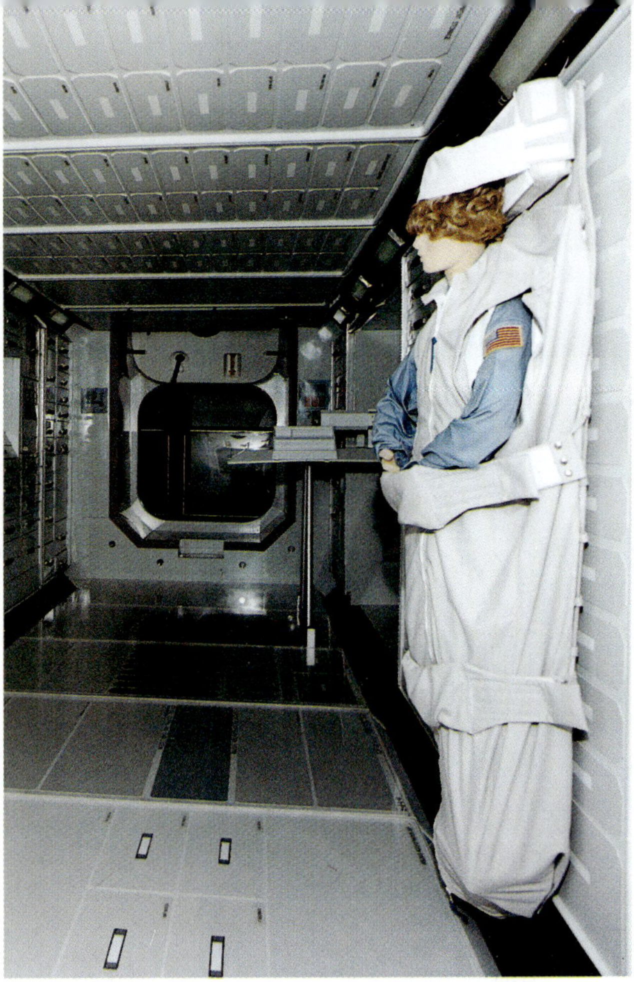

Life aboard the space station will be an adventure in more ways than one for astronauts. Performing everyday activities like eating, sleeping, and bathing is a real challenge when there's no gravity and no up or down!

Earth. Most food is precooked, packed in pouches, and freeze-dried—frozen and dried—so it will weigh less. It's a lot like the food that backpackers take on camping trips. Equipment on board adds water and warms the food before you eat. Drinks can't be poured into cups; instead, you use straws to drink beverages from the pouch.

NASA has already developed 70 foods and 20 drinks for shuttle flights. But researchers know that on long missions, space crews will want more variety. They're developing recipes for dishes that might one day be prepared in space, using vegetables grown in space. Meanwhile, space station crews will have a refrigerator and a microwave oven, so they can enjoy some fresh foods.

Playing with your food takes on a new meaning in space. Lift your fork toward your mouth, and then let go—and the fork keeps coming. If your drink spills, the liquid forms a perfect sphere that floats in the air, waiting for you to suck it up with your straw.

OFF DUTY IN ORBIT

There will be no lounge chairs on the space station. When astronauts want to relax, all they have to do is float for a while. Without gravity, staying in a chair is work! The "hab" module will have a table where the crew members can share meals, and a window where they can watch space and Earth roll by.

There will be no beds, either. When there's no up or down, you really don't need to lie down to sleep. But you do need to be tied down—or else you would simply float! Space station astronauts will tuck themselves into sleeping pods that look something like hanging sleeping bags.

The "hab" module will have a space toilet, which uses air suction to pull waste into a tank. Solid waste will be freeze-dried and then shipped back to Earth. Liquid waste will be purified. In the shower compartment, airflow will keep water moving down and out the drain. Plans call for the station to have a specially designed clothes washer and dryer, too. Since water will be in short supply, it will be recycled as much as possible—purified and used again for laundry and bathing.

Life on the space station will be challenging in many ways. Imagine spending months in a room with the same few people. You can't leave, and you have no private place where you can go to be alone. Crew members will need to find ways to combat boredom and homesickness, and they'll need to get along.

Astronauts will make a total of 144 space walks—suited up in complex gear—to assemble the space station.

DRESSED FOR WORK

Working on the *ISS* will call for lots of space walks. Astronauts will often have to leave the safety of the pressurized modules and go outside—and for that, they'll need space suits. NASA's term for a space suit is Extravehicular Mobility Unit (EMU), and the gear is almost as complicated as the name. Here's how U.S. astronauts get dressed for outdoor work:

- Underneath the suit, the astronaut wears a urine collection device and a stretchy mesh garment. Water circulates through plastic tubes woven into the garment, to keep the astronaut cool. The cooling system can be shut off when the station is on the dark side of the Earth and temperatures plunge.
- Next, the space suit bottom—the lower torso assembly—goes on. It's made of eleven layers of high-tech materials that protect against extremes of heat and cold, radiation, and micrometeors. The materials are tough—a tear or a leak in the pressurized suit could be deadly.
- Under the layers of the upper torso section is a rigid frame with an aluminum chest. Ring joints connect the upper torso to the lower torso and the sleeves, forming an airtight seal.
- Gloves, like all the space suit parts, attach with an airtight ring joint. They have molded rubber finger caps to help astronauts perform delicate work.
- A close-fitting cap carries communications equipment, linking the space walker to other crew members.

Skylab: The First U.S. Space Station

The year 1998 marked the 25th anniversary of the first U.S. space station, *Skylab,* which was launched on May 14, 1973. Plagued by problems from the start, *Skylab* was in use for less than a year. But researchers learned a lot about space travel during that time.

Skylab's problems began with its launch, when its two main solar panels were damaged by vibrations. Once it was in orbit, temperatures inside the crew cabin soared to 126°F (52°C). Engineers on Earth scrambled to make the station livable before the three-man crew arrived in late May. That crew stayed a little less than a month. After installing a sunshade to keep the temperature down, they conducted several experiments. Two more *Skylab* missions followed, the first lasting 59 days and the second 84 days—a record at that time.

The 84-day mission didn't begin well. The crew suffered first from motion sickness and then from overwork, so their schedule was adjusted to allow more time off. In the end, they completed more experiments and observations than had been scheduled. They took photographs of Earth, collected X-ray and ultraviolet images of the sun, and made observations of a passing comet.

That was the last *Skylab* mission. After the astronauts left in February 1974, the empty space station began to slowly lose altitude. Officials at NASA developed a plan: They would send up a space shuttle, to boost it into a higher orbit. There was just one catch—the space shuttle wasn't ready to fly.

Skylab slipped lower and lower, and in July 1979 it made a fiery trail in the sky as it re-entered Earth's atmosphere. It crashed in Australia, scattering debris over a 2,000-mile (3,218-kilometer) path in Australia. Luckily, no one was hurt.

Ever since then, most U.S. astronauts have had to be content with short space missions. A few have stayed longer as guests aboard *Mir,* the Russian space station. With *ISS,* that will change.

- A helmet goes over the cap. The helmet has a reflective gold visor to screen out the sun's rays, and a clear visor and two spotlights for working in the dark. Inside is a drinking bag with a mouthpiece that the crew member can reach with simply a turn of the head.
- A backpack contains the suit's portable life-support system. It carries enough oxygen, water, and electrical power for six to seven hours. A microcomputer monitors the space suit constantly and sounds a warning if anything goes wrong.

As you can see, it will take a special kind of person to live and work in space. But the people who crew the space station will have the satisfaction of knowing that they are pioneers. Their experiences, and the knowledge they gain, will help guide future space travelers and may even lead to the founding of space colonies far from Earth.

The October 1998 space shuttle mission was the most celebrated in many years because John Glenn was aboard. At age 77, the former astronaut became the oldest person ever to go into space—an American hero once again.

SPACE BRIEFS

The return to space of John Glenn, the first American to orbit Earth, was a highlight of 1998, thrilling millions of viewers around the world and showing that older people have the "right stuff." Other exciting news from space during the year included discoveries about the moon and Jupiter, observing a new kind of star, and the first photograph of a planet outside the solar system.

SHUTTLE MISSIONS

John Glenn first made headlines at the dawn of the Space Age. On February 20, 1962, he circled Earth three times aboard a tiny craft called *Friendship 7.* Not wanting to risk the life of a hero, then-President John F. Kennedy told the National Aeronautics and Space Administration (NASA) that it wouldn't send Glenn into space again. Glenn left the space program, and in 1974 he was elected to the U.S. Senate. But his desire to return to space never faded, and he kept pestering NASA to let him fly aboard a space shuttle. On October 29, 1998, his wish came true as he and six other astronauts were launched aboard *Discovery.* At age 77, Glenn set a new record: He became the oldest person to travel in outer space.

An important part of Glenn's mission aboard *Discovery* was to take part in medical experiments. He was poked and prodded, gave blood, and saved urine—all to help scientists better understand how people change as they age, and how outer space can affect older people. Glenn had a fabulous time in space, and his ability to withstand the rigors of the journey delighted everyone. After nine days of living in a weightless environment, he was able to walk out of *Discovery* when it returned to Earth. And after a good night's sleep, he looked and sounded as fit as ever.

The *Discovery* mission was the final space shuttle mission before the building of the new

International Space Station, which will take more than five years to complete. During many of the space shuttle missions, astronauts practiced techniques that would be needed for assembling the space station. For example, Glenn's fellow astronauts tested a laser tracking system. On shuttle missions to the Russian space station *Mir,* astronauts had practiced rendezvous and docking techniques. On the January 1998 flight of *Endeavour,* they tested a virtual-reality medical unit that allows anyone—even someone who isn't a doctor—to conduct a complete physical examination, with the data then sent to a physician on Earth.

Expanding our knowledge about the solar system was another central objective of shuttle missions. For example, the mission that carried Glenn aloft also carried *Spartan,* a satellite that was released and, two days later, retrieved after it took hundreds of photographs of the sun's outer atmosphere and the particles that stream outward from the sun's surface.

Learning more about living things was still another important goal. In April, *Columbia* was launched as the first mission devoted entirely to studies of the nervous system, particularly the brain—in humans as well as animals. Astronauts monitored their own sleeping patterns and studied the effects of weightlessness on eye-hand coordination. There were also some 2,000 animals on board. Astronauts performed the first surgery in space on animals meant to survive. Infant rats were observed to determine how they learned to walk, and the balance mechanisms of snails and fish were studied.

PLANET AND ASTEROID NEWS

Mars. Back in 1976, the unmanned *Viking 1* spacecraft visited Mars and beamed back some of the first detailed pictures of the planet's surface. In one photo, taken of the region called Cydonia, a blurry oval image appeared. Some people believed they saw the ghostly image of a human face—because shadows seemed to outline eyes, nose, lips, and a chin. In fact, there were those who thought the image was proof that there was intelligent life on Mars. In 1998, NASA scientists maneuvered the *Mars Global Surveyor* to take new, sharper pictures of the region. These pictures showed that the image was no more than a trick of light and shadow. The "face" was nothing but a hill with a lot of bumps and hillocks on top.

Jupiter. *Galileo,* the first spacecraft ever to orbit Jupiter, sent data showing how the giant planet's rings were formed. Debris from comets and asteroids slammed into Jupiter's moons at speeds 100 times faster than that of a speeding

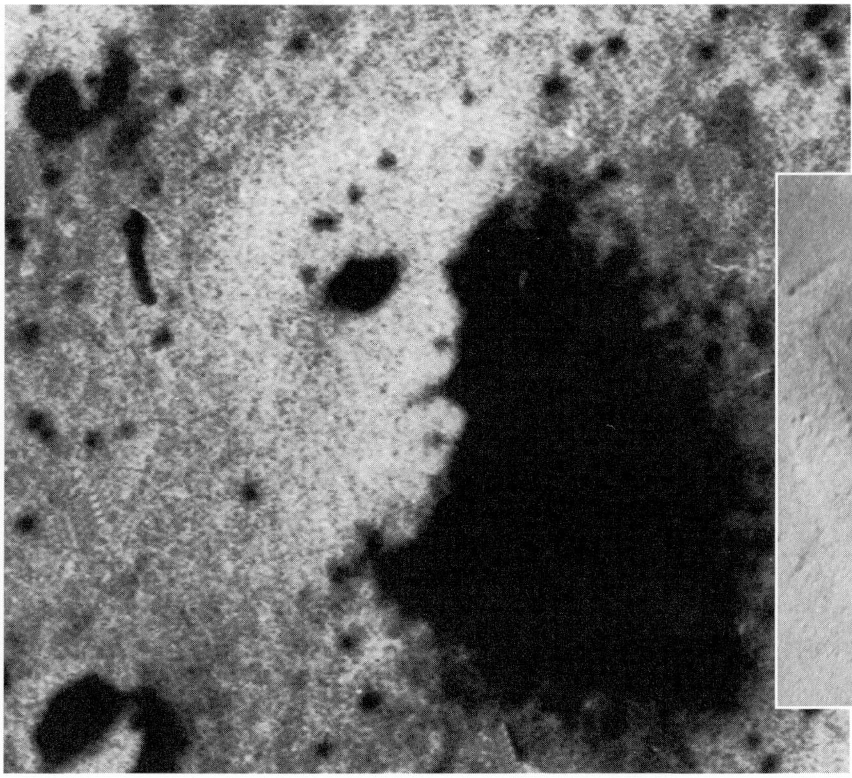

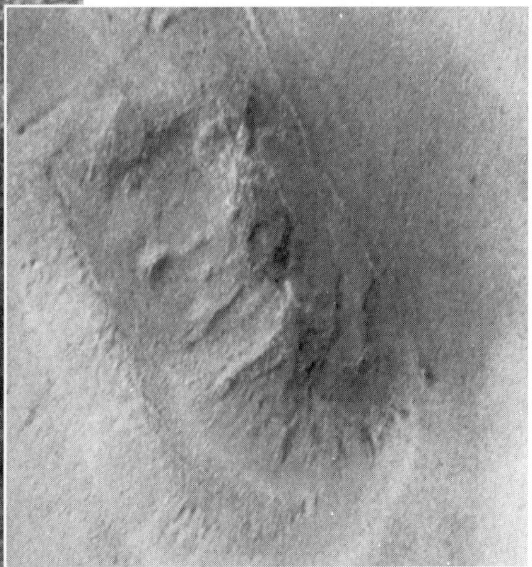

Left: Do you see a face in this 1976 *Viking 1* photo of the surface of Mars? Inset: Photos taken in 1998 by the *Mars Global Surveyor* of the same area showed that the "face" is just a bumpy hill.

Water on the Moon

The moon was dry when it was formed four billion years ago. But in 1998, scientists made an astonishing discovery. *Lunar Prospector*—a spacecraft that was launched in January—found signs of ice on the moon.

The ice was brought from far out in the solar system by comets, heavenly bodies made up of material that was left over when the planets were formed. Comets are nothing more than large, dirty snowballs—dark chunks of ice, rock, and dust.

Over the years, millions of comets crashed onto the moon's surface, creating huge craters. On most parts of the moon, sunlight caused the ice in those craters to evaporate. But this didn't happen at the north and south poles. At the poles, sunlight never reaches the bottoms of some deep craters. And that's where the ice was found. Scientists say that there's so much ice in those craters that if it could be melted, it would make more than a trillion gallons of water—enough to fill a lake 25 miles square and 300 feet deep.

Why are scientists so excited about finding water on the moon? Well, life as we know it can't exist without water. So it's possible that some day the water could be used to support an astronaut base on the moon. But it won't be easy to "mine" the water. For one thing, the ice is mixed in with moon soil and would have to be separated out. And the temperature is about 300 degrees below zero. We don't know if astronauts could work for long periods of time in such cold, or even if mining machinery would operate.

If scientists solve these problems, there could be enough water to support a moon colony for a hundred years. The water could be used for drinking and washing. It could also be broken up into its two parts, oxygen and hydrogen. The oxygen could be used for breathing, adding to the astronauts' regular oxygen supplies. And the hydrogen could be made into fuel for rockets that would power spaceships traveling to the far reaches of the solar system.

bullet. This kicked up dust clouds from the moons' surfaces. Gradually, the clouds spread out, turning into thin rings.

Galileo also found super-hot lava spewing from more than 30 volcanoes on one of Jupiter's moons, Io. In fact, the lava is the hottest material ever found in the solar system other than on the sun. And the amount of lava flowing from the volcanoes every year is enormous—enough to cover Io's entire surface with a layer almost 1/2 inch (1 centimeter) deep.

1992 KD. In October, NASA launched *Deep Space 1* (*DS1*) on a journey to an asteroid called 1992 KD. The space probe is expected to fly past 1992 KD in July 1999. But *DS1* is also on a mission that could open new chapters in space exploration. It's the first mission in NASA's "New Millennium" program, which is designed to test some exciting new technologies. If these technologies are successful, they will be used in spacecraft of the 21st century. The most talked-about technology on *DS1* is its ion propulsion engine—which uses the gas xenon and is ten times more efficient than chemical fuel.

STAR NEWS

A New Kind of Star. Light and other radiation travels a distance of about 5.9 trillion miles (9.5 trillion kilometers) a year. At this speed, it takes sunlight about 4.3 years to reach Earth from Alpha Centauri, the nearest star to the sun. Imagine how far away from Earth an object must be if its radiation takes 20,000 years to reach us!

Just such a blast-from-the-past slammed into the Earth's atmosphere in August. The radiation—a mix of deadly X-rays and gamma radiation—came from a newly discovered kind of star called a magnetar. A magnetar is believed to be an extremely small, dense star formed after a large star collapses and explodes. Its magnetic field is so powerful that it can cause the star's crust to crack, causing a starquake. When this happens, radiation flies outward in all directions.

Fortunately, the magnetar's radiation that hit Earth didn't cause a health hazard. But it did briefly disrupt radio transmissions and caused temporary shutdowns of several spacecraft orbiting Earth.

A New Planet. In May, California astronomers produced what appeared to be the first image ever of a planet outside the solar system. The astronomers did this by reconstructing pictures made by the Hubble Space Telescope, which orbits high above Earth. The planet, about 450 light-years from Earth, is much bigger than Jupiter and is unusual because it doesn't orbit a star. Rather, it appears to have been ejected from a binary star system (a system of two stars that circle each other). It's rapidly traveling away from the binary stars—much as if it had been pushed out from a powerful slingshot!

***Deep Space 1*, a spacecraft that sounds like something straight out of a science-fiction movie, was launched on October 24, 1998. It's the first mission in NASA's "New Millennium" program, which is designed to test some exciting new technologies that may be used in future spacecraft.**

New Galaxies. Scientists think the universe began about 13 billion years ago. Thanks to ever-stronger telescopes, they have been able to look further and further back into time, closer to the dawn of the universe. In 1998, they detected at least one galaxy, or cluster of stars, that was more than 12 billion light-years from Earth. It was the most distant object—and the oldest—ever seen. Scientists hope that by finding the very oldest galaxies they will be able to learn how galaxies first formed.

Are you a couch potato? Well then, get up, get moving, and get fit! It's the healthy thing to do.

KEEP FIT!

"I Was a Teenage Couch Potato!" That's the title of a horror movie that could be coming soon to your television screen. You know couch potatoes—they spend all their free time sitting in front of the television. Are you one? The "couch potato" label fits many kids—too many, experts say.

This has health professionals worried. Studies show that couch-potato kids are setting themselves up for serious health problems later in life. They are missing out on some immediate benefits of fitness, too. When you're fit, you feel good and look good. You have more energy, and you're less likely to get sick. You may even do better in school.

Why are so many kids out of shape? And what can you do to get in shape?

FIT OR FLABBY?

The links between good health, exercise, and diet are clear. Even moderate exercise, such as a brisk daily walk, can reduce the risk of heart disease, cancer, diabetes, and other serious illnesses. So can a healthy diet—one that includes plenty of nutritious foods, which provide the body with the chemicals (or nutrients) it needs.

In the 1980s, as researchers piled up more and more evidence of the benefits of exercise and diet, adults jumped on a fitness bandwagon. They took up walking, running, and other forms of exercise. Salad bars and low-fat, low-salt foods were "in." But in the end, most adults didn't shape up very much. Many didn't stick with their exercise programs, and their eating habits didn't change enough—they still loved fatty burgers and fries. The average weight for men and women actually rose.

For young people, the statistics have been even worse. Many young people skipped the 1980s fitness craze completely. While adults were out jogging, they were watching television and snacking. In fact, the percentage of kids age 6 to 17 who were overweight more than doubled from the mid-1960s to the early 1990s.

The trend has continued, and the reasons aren't hard to find. Kids are less active in school because many school systems have cut back on physical education and sports programs in an effort to save money. Young people are less active after school, too. Video games have replaced outdoor games as a top after-school activity. And when kids are hungry, many reach for chips, candy, and other junk foods.

Because most young people are healthy and seem to have plenty of energy, it's often assumed that they're getting all the nutrition and exercise they need. The sad fact is that many young people, from elementary-school to high-school age, are overweight and out of shape. Most kids perform poorly in basic fitness tests. Many can't run a mile in thirteen minutes—a speed that health experts suggest adults *walk* to promote fitness. Eleven out of every 100 school-age children are seriously overweight. As many as 40 percent of children 5 to 8 years old show at least one sign of heart-disease risk.

Fitness can benefit kids as much as adults, and maybe more. Being fit boosts energy levels and increases self-esteem. Several studies have shown that kids who exercise regularly do better in school and miss fewer days due to illness. And exercise and eating habits that are developed in childhood can stay with a person throughout life, warding off heart disease and other illnesses that usually don't develop until adulthood.

GET MOVING!

You want to start exercising. But what, exactly, should you do? To turn a flabby body into a fit one, you need the right kind and the right amount of exercise.

The best type of exercise for overall fitness is aerobic exercise—activities that involve steady, sustained movement, such as jogging and jumping rope. The word "aerobic" means "with oxygen." Your muscles use oxy-

Burn It Off

Studies show that even moderate amounts of exercise can improve health. Just burning an extra 150 calories a day may help prevent serious illnesses such as heart disease. What does it take to do that? Here are a few ways:

- Spend 45 minutes to an hour washing a car or a floor.
- Play volleyball or touch football for 45 minutes.
- Walk 2 miles (3 kilometers) or bicycle 3 miles (4 kilometers) in 30 minutes.
- Rake leaves for 30 minutes.
- Swim laps for 20 minutes.
- Play basketball for 15 to 20 minutes.
- Run 1.5 miles (2 kilometers) in 15 minutes.
- Shovel snow for 15 minutes.
- Spend 15 minutes walking up and down stairs.

Shape Up Safely

Follow these tips to avoid injury when you exercise.

- Warm up before you work out or play sports. Do stretching exercises, or walk briskly for three to five minutes. These easy activities get blood flowing to your muscles, and you'll be less likely to pull or strain a muscle as a result.
- Finish your workout with a few minutes of easy activity, too. For example, if you run, walk for a few minutes. This keeps your blood circulating smoothly as your heart rate gradually returns to normal.
- Wear protective equipment in activities that call for it—a helmet for bicycling, for example, and a helmet, wrist guards, and knee and elbow pads for in-line skating.
- Drink plenty of water before exercise, and during if your workout lasts longer than 20 to 30 minutes.
- Don't push yourself too hard. Do the amount of exercise that's comfortable for you. Always increase your workload gradually, as your muscles grow stronger. Any time you feel pain, stop what you're doing.
- Many experts advise children under 15 to avoid very strenuous forms of exercise, such as long-distance running and weightlifting. The reason is that their bones aren't fully developed and may be damaged by too much stress.

gen during this type of exercise. The oxygen is taken in by your lungs and carried to the muscles by your blood, and your heart and lungs have to work hard to supply the muscles with the oxygen they need. But the muscles' demand for oxygen never exceeds the ability of the heart and lungs to supply it.

Aerobic exercise improves general muscle tone, makes you more flexible, and burns up calories, helping to control your weight. It also strengthens the heart, helping to prevent heart disease. The heart is made of muscle, and like any other muscle it grows stronger with use.

A second type of exercise consists of short bursts of very strenuous activity, such as sprinting or lifting heavy weights. The heart and lungs can't supply the muscles with enough oxygen for such strenuous work. Instead, the muscles rely on their own stores of energy for this anaerobic (without oxygen) exercise. Those stores are quickly used up. You can actually feel this happening—you feel pain or a burning sensation in the muscles as they "run out of gas." Thus you can't continue the activity very long. Anaerobic exercise builds up individual muscles, but it won't promote general fitness or burn up calories the way aerobic exercise does.

The great thing about aerobic exercise is that there are so many ways to do it. If the thought of jogging makes you yawn, try bicycling, in-line skating, rowing, or swimming. They all give your heart and lungs a good workout. So do sports like basketball, cross-country skiing, and tennis. You can get fit and have fun at the same time.

Many schools have caught on to this idea. They're changing physical education programs to include fitness-building activities that kids actually want to do, and letting students pick and choose from a variety of activities. Along with kickball and other traditional gym sports, some schools are offering offbeat activities such as unicyling, juggling, step aerobics, karate, and line dancing.

Switching from one activity to another has advantages. It helps you stay interested in your workouts, so you'll be less likely to become a "fitness dropout." And cross-training, as this approach is called, lets you focus on different aspects of fitness. For example, aerobic dancing improves flexibility and coordination, while rowing builds upper-body strength.

The key in all these activities is to work hard enough to make your heart beat faster for at least fifteen minutes. But don't do so much that your muscles start to hurt and you get out of breath. If you're out of shape, start with short workouts and easy activities. A brisk fifteen- or twenty-minute walk may be enough at first. As your fitness improves, you can make your workouts longer and add more strenuous activities. And always follow safety guidelines.

HEALTHY EATING

Exercise is an important part of fitness, but it's only part. A good diet is essential, too.

A bacon cheeseburger, fries, and a shake—that fast-food meal is a North American favorite. But if good health is your goal, fast food's a poor choice, for several reasons:

A hamburger, fries, and a shake is the meal of choice for many kids—but it's loaded with salt, fat, and calories. A steady diet of fast food can lead to health problems later in life. A balanced diet that includes plenty of fruits and vegetables has more of the nutrients you need to stay healthy now—and later. Plus it tastes good too!

• It's high in calories. A calorie is a unit of measure for the amount of energy that can be obtained from food. If you consume the proper number of calories, you'll stay at a healthy weight. If you eat more calories than your body can use, you'll store the excess as fat—and gain weight.

• It's high in fat and salt. Fat and salt are necessary parts of the diet, but only in small amounts. Diets that are high in fat and salt have been linked to heart disease, strokes, and other health problems. Even though these problems usually affect older adults, the conditions that cause them begin early in life.

• It's high in sugar. Sugary foods like that shake fill you up without providing the nutrients that your body needs. Then you aren't hungry for the foods that could provide those nutrients.

Nutrients are substances that your body gets from food and uses for growth, for energy, and for all body processes. You need about 50 different nutrients to stay healthy. These nutrients are usually divided into six main groups: proteins, carbohydrates (starches and sugars), fats, vitamins, minerals, and water. One way to be sure of getting all you need is to eat a variety of foods every day—because different foods contain different types of nutrients.

Fruits and vegetables provide carbohydrates—your main source of energy. They also provide vitamins, especially vitamins A and C. And they contain fiber, which helps move food and waste through the digestive system. One guideline is to eat four servings of fruits and vegetables a day. You could have an orange at breakfast, a salad at lunch, an apple after school, and green beans with dinner. By varying the fruits and vegetables, you'll get the vitamins you need.

Bread and cereal are another good source of carbohydrates. They're made from grain, which is rich in B vitamins and iron. However, many cereals and breads are made from grain that has been processed, or refined, and has lost a lot of its nutritional value. Whole-grain breads and cereals contain important nutrients that aren't found in refined products, and they have more fiber, too. Try to have four servings of bread or cereal a day.

Milk, cheese, and yogurt are rich in calcium, a mineral that's especially important while you're growing. These dairy foods also contain protein, which is needed to build body tissues, and important vitamins. Experts in nutrition recommend three servings a day for children. But choose low-fat dairy foods, such as low-fat milk and yogurt, over cheese and other fatty foods.

Meat, poultry, fish, eggs, and dried beans and peas are all good sources of protein. Many also provide minerals and B vitamins.

Fake Fat

Potato chips like these are among our favorite snacks. But they have way too much fat and too many calories. So what's a chip lover to do? How about fat-free potato chips! Sounds like a dream come true. In 1998, North American supermarkets began to carry chips made with olestra, a fat substitute made of vegetable oil and sugar. Olestra passes right through the digestive system without being broken down, so it provides no calories. That means chips made with olestra have less than half the calories of regular chips—and no fat.

Does that mean you can munch mindlessly? Not exactly. Some people have developed digestive problems—gas, bloating, and diarrhea—from olestra. Some scientists worry that the fake fat may latch onto vitamins and other nutrients in the digestive system and prevent them from being absorbed. Although olestra is generally considered safe, it's still smart to limit the amount of chips you eat.

Experts suggest two servings a day and recommend low-fat choices, such as fish, over fatty meats such as beef. Ideally, less than 30 percent of the calories in your daily diet should come from fat.

If you follow the guidelines that nutritional experts recommend, you won't have a problem getting the nutrients you need. People run into trouble when they fill up on junk food and then skip nutritious meals. Eating too much can lead to trouble, too—those calories can add up and make you overweight.

How many calories do you need? That depends on several factors, including your age and how active you are. An active 12-year-old needs between 2,200 and 2,800 calories a day. Teenagers who play active sports may need 4,000 calories a day. But that's way too many for a couch potato. And it's easy to eat too many calories. A fast-food cheeseburger, fries, a soda, and an apple turnover can add up to 1,200 calories—in just one meal.

Experts in nutrition generally don't recommend that children diet to lose weight. Cutting calories too much can mean cutting out nutrients that are important for growth. The best way to lose weight, and to stay in shape once the weight is off, is to exercise and eat a healthy diet. That makes good sense for anyone, overweight or not.

Because so many people today are concerned about what they eat, it's easy to find healthy foods. Low-fat milk, whole-grain bread, and cereals that are low in sugar and salt are available everywhere. You can substitute veggie burgers for hamburgers, or make a delicious shake from yogurt and fresh fruit. Snack on carrots or fruit instead of cookies, and nibble plain popcorn instead of chips. If it's close to dinner time, skip the snack and save your appetite. When you stick to a healthy diet most of the time, you'll be able to enjoy an occasional cheeseburger and fries or a candy bar without worrying.

Eating wisely and exercising can only do you good. So what are you waiting for? Put down the potato chips. Get off the couch. Shape up!

EARTH WATCH

Humans interact with the natural world in many ways. Sometimes, as when natural forces disrupt weather patterns, we have little control over events. But often our actions have dramatic consequences on the world around us. This was evident during 1998, when human activities contributed to global warming; harmed fish and orangutans; and threatened thousands of kinds of plants, including the trees that produce chocolate.

Going to Extremes. Two climate disturbances have been playing havoc with the weather in many parts of the world. The two are called El Niño and La Niña, and both start far out in the Pacific Ocean.

El Niño is a climate disturbance that appears from time to time. It occurs when the ocean waters in the eastern Pacific Ocean, near the equator, suddenly warm up. The abnormal temperature change upsets weather patterns around the world. Places that usually get heavy winter rains, such as Indonesia and Australia, experience drought. Places that are normally dry in winter, including parts of North and South America, get soaked. Severe storms, including tornadoes, strike in places that aren't used to them.

In the past, El Niño appeared about every seven years. But recently, it has shown up more often—every two to five years. The 1997–98 El Niño was an exceptionally strong disturbance. Violent storms pounded southern California. The U.S. South was hard hit by floods, while Hawaii suffered a drought. The winter was unusually mild in much of eastern North America, but Canadians coped with severe ice storms. Other areas of the world were hard hit, too. For example, severe floods in Peru, Ecuador, and Brazil ruined crops and left thousands of people homeless.

Humans weren't the only ones hurt by El Niño. Sea lions and other fish-eating animals off the coast of California went hungry because the warm Pacific waters chased away the fish that were a main part of their diet. And winds blew migrating birds and butterflies off course, sending some thousands of miles from their usual homes.

El Niño faded in the spring. But by summer it was clear that another climate disturbance—La Niña—would most probably take its place. La Niña is the exact opposite of El Niño. It develops when the Pacific waters near the equator suddenly cool, again upsetting weather patterns around the world. Weather scientists were predicting that La Niña would mean more wacky weather for the winter of 1998–1999.

Plants in Danger. When many people think of endangered and threatened species, they think of animals—especially furry mam-

El Niño was blamed for severe winter weather in 1998. It lashed southern California with powerful storms, like this furious February squall, and left the U.S. South drenched in deep floods.

Might beautiful meadow flowers like these one day disappear? In 1998, it was reported that a worldwide survey of plants had found that nearly 34,000 species were in danger of extinction.

A baby orangutan is rescued from a forest fire in Indonesia. The vast forest fires in that country are pushing these magnificent red apes toward extinction.

mals. But a worldwide survey of plants, conducted by the World Conservation Union, produced a list of nearly 34,000 types that are in danger of becoming extinct. The plants range from fragile alpine wildflowers to tropical palm trees. Many grow only in certain countries or regions—on a particular island or mountain, for example.

Plants are in trouble because people have destroyed wild areas by logging forests and clearing land for farming and development. In addition, people often carry plants from other parts of the world to new areas. Sometimes, these "foreign" plants grow so well in their new homes that they drive out native species.

One way to help save plants is to preserve their natural homes, or habitats. Another is to educate people about endangered plants, so that they won't harm these plants out of ignorance. In some places, botanists are growing endangered plants in nurseries and transplanting them as seedlings to the wild.

Fires Threaten Orangutans. In Indonesia, people purposely destroy thousands of acres of forests each year. Trees are logged, or simply burned, to clear the land for farms and plantations. In 1998, this practice, along with a severe drought, fueled vast forest fires. The fires killed thousands of forest animals. One of the animals that's being pushed toward extinction as a result of this catastrophe is the orangutan. This animal faces another threat, too. Hunters capture baby orangutans and sell them to people who want pets. Often, the hunters kill the mothers in order to get the babies.

Orangutans now survive only on Borneo—an island that's divided among Indonesia, Malaysia, and Brunei; and on the Indonesian island of Sumatra. Conservation groups have been able to rescue some of the orangutans that have been injured or orphaned by the fires. And they have recovered some animals kept as pets. But the number of orangutans they save and return to the wild are few, and the world's population of these magnificent red apes is falling rapidly.

Chipping Away at Chocolate. Are you a chocolate lover? Well here's some really bad news. In five to ten years, a chocolate bar may be a rare, expensive treat. Scientists are predicting that chocolate will be in short supply because pests and diseases are attacking cacao trees, the source of this delicious food.

In the wild, cacao trees grow in tropical forests, where they are shaded by taller trees. But today, most of the world's cacao crop is grown on big plantations that have been carved out of the tropical forests. Rows of cacao trees stretch for acres on the plantations. They aren't shaded, so the trees are easy victims for diseases and pests—which can sweep through a plantation quickly.

In the past, cacao growers moved on when this happened. They cleared more land, planted young cacao trees, and started again. However, growers are running out of forests to clear. The cacao crop is smaller—but people are still eating just as much chocolate. That's why experts are predicting shortages.

What can be done? One solution is to plant cacao trees in small groves tucked into the tropical forests, instead of on big plantations. In small groves, cacao trees can be shaded by larger trees. They'll get more individual attention from growers, and they'll stay healthier.

Global Warming. Early in 1998, scientists reported that 1997 was the warmest year on record. This record may soon be broken—

In a few years, chocolate candy may be a rare and expensive treat. That's because pests and diseases are attacking cacao trees (*left*), the source of this yummy food.

global temperatures reached new highs during the first eight months of 1998.

Global warming is the gradual warming of Earth's climate. There has been a rise in the average surface temperature of the Earth over the past century of about 1°F (0.5°C). Scientists predict that a further increase of a few degrees will occur during the coming century. The higher temperatures could cause an increase in extreme weather, the spread of tropical diseases into now-temperate areas, droughts, wildfires, and a rise in sea levels.

Most scientists believe that human activities are a major cause of global warming. They say that carbon dioxide and other gases that are produced by the burning of coal, oil, and other fossil fuels are to blame. In November, delegates from more than 150 nations attended a global warming conference in Buenos Aires, Argentina. They agreed to adopt a set of rules for reducing the emission of these gases by the end of the year 2000.

Disappearing Ice. Are parts of Antarctica melting away? In 1998, scientists reported that the West Antarctic ice sheet—a part of the icy mantle that covers the continent—is shrinking. Every year, about 212 square miles (550 square kilometers) of West Antarctic ice tumbles into the sea. But in the past ten years, that amount has been increasing. Huge icebergs are also breaking off other Antarctic ice shelves.

If the ice that covers Antarctica melts, sea levels around the world would rise dramatically. For example, if the West Antarctic ice shelf melted away, all the world's oceans

Scientists say there's an increase in the number of icebergs that are breaking off Antarctic ice shelves and tumbling into the sea. This could lead to a dangerous rise in sea levels around the world.

would rise by 20 feet (6 meters). Cities such as Miami and New York—plus all your favorite beaches—would be underwater.

Scientists are blaming global warming for the disintegrating ice, and for similar melting in the Arctic. In Alaska, glaciers are shrinking, or retreating, too. For example, the front of the Columbia Glacier retreated 8 miles (13 kilometers) between 1983 and 1998. Even sub-Arctic areas are affected. One team of geologists predicted that all the glaciers in Montana's Glacier National Park might vanish in the next 50 to 70 years!

Death by Poison. In early August, tens of thousands of fish—including striped bass and menhaden—died in the Neuse River of North Carolina. The culprit was a one-celled algae called *Pfiesteria piscicida*. This algae has probably been around for thousands of years without causing much harm. In recent years, however, it's become a killer in river mouths and coastal waters of the eastern United States.

Pfiesteria normally exists in nontoxic forms, feeding on algae and bacteria. But sometimes it shifts to a toxic form and begins giving off poisons that are deadly to fish. People exposed to waters in which toxic forms of *Pfiesteria* are active can also get very sick.

These striped bass escaped harm from a poisonous algae that has been killing thousands of fish along the coastal waters of the eastern United States.

Exactly what causes toxic outbreaks of *Pfiesteria* isn't fully understood. One factor may be a high level of nutrients such as nitrogen and phosphorus in the water. These nutrients are thought to encourage the growth of *Pfiesteria* populations. Excess nutrients are common pollutants in rivers and coastal waters. Major sources of nutrient pollution include sewage treatment plants, septic tanks, and runoff from lawns, farms, and mining operations.

In recent decades, there's also been an increase in hog and poultry farms in the region. Some fifteen million pigs are now raised in North Carolina, and about 600 million chickens are raised in the Chesapeake Bay area. Lots of pigs and chickens means lots of manure, which is extremely rich in nitrogen and phosphorus. Environmentalists have called for measures to prevent the manure from being washed into the water by rainfall.

JENNY TESAR
Author, *Endangered Habitats*

MAKE AND DO

These critters are made from strips of construction paper. Tape two different colored strips together at one end, forming a right angle. Fold one strip over the other, forming a right angle in the opposite direction. Keep folding (and taping on more strips) until the body is nice and long. Add a funny face. Now squeeze the critter into a decorated can and cover with the lid. Ask a friend to remove the lid—and watch things POP!

PAPER
STAINED GLASS

Stained-glass windows consist of pieces of colored glass held together by strips of black lead, to form a picture or design. They are among the most beautiful and dramatic of all arts and crafts. Paper versions of these windows are fun to create, and they can be used in a variety of ways: as pictures, greeting cards, bookmarks, even tree ornaments.

A paper stained-glass window is made by cutting out a design from a sheet of black paper, and then placing colored paper behind each cutout area. You'll need the following materials: black paper, colored papers, graph paper, a glue stick, and scissors.

Begin by creating your design on graph paper that's the same size as the black paper. Working on graph paper makes it easier to draw symmetrical and uniformly thick black strips. As you draw the design, make certain that every black strip connects to at least one other black strip.

When your design is completed, place the graph paper on the black paper. Use the glue stick to lightly attach them around the edges. Then carefully cut out the design. When you are finished, gently remove the bits of graph paper still attached to the black paper. What you are looking at will be the back of your picture. Continue working on the back.

Next, cut pieces of colored paper to fit each cutout area of the design; each piece should be a bit larger than the cutout, so that it slightly overlaps the black strips. Glue the edges of each color piece onto the black strips. Keep working until all the cutout areas have been filled. Then cover the back of the picture with a sheet of paper to protect it. Finally, turn your creation over—and enjoy your eye-catching version of a stained-glass window!

If you'd like to hang your pictures in a window, use colored cellophane instead of colored paper in the cutouts. Experiment with layering one color of cellophane atop another to create a new color.

STAMP COLLECTING

The Winter Olympic Games, holidays, and the approach of the year 2000 were among the occasions that prompted new stamp issues in 1998. Cartoon characters, works of art, and all sorts of animals were featured on postal items from many nations. All in all, collectors had plenty of interesting new items to choose from.

U.S. STAMPS

The U.S. Postal Service is marking the end of the 20th century in a big way—with a pane of stamps for every decade in the century. Each pane will bear fifteen stamps portraying people and events associated with that decade. Taken together, the 150 stamps in the "Celebrate the Century" series will depict a panorama of American history and culture. The Postal Service plans to complete the series by the year 2000.

The first pane of 32-cent stamps showed subjects chosen for the years 1901 to 1910. They included the first baseball World Series, Crayola crayons, and the Model-T Ford. For 1911 to 1920, crossword puzzles, the Panama Canal, comedian Charlie Chaplin, and scientist George Washington Carver were among the fifteen subjects.

One of the stamps for the 1920s marked the 19th Amendment to the Constitution, which granted women the vote. Subjects for the 1930s ranged from President Franklin D. Roosevelt to the cartoon character Superman, who first appeared in that decade. These subjects, like all the subjects for the five panes covering 1901 to 1950, were chosen by a special committee. Subjects for the remaining panes are being chosen by vote—starting in September 1998, people could cast ballots for their favorites at post offices.

Two popular cartoon characters popped up on a 32-cent stamp in 1998. They were Sylvester and Tweety, the cartoon cat and bird whose antics have been making people laugh for 50 years. Another lighthearted issue was a group of five vividly colored 32-cent stamps called "Bright Eyes." The stamps featured cartoonlike

1998 STAMPS FROM AROUND THE WORLD

pictures of popular pets—a dog, a cat, a goldfish, a parrot, and a hamster.

In a more serious vein, the Postal Service released a sheet of 20 stamps celebrating American art from the 1600s to the 1960s. The sheet, titled "Four Centuries of American Art," included portraits from the country's early days, one of John James Audubon's famous bird pictures, landscapes of the American West, and abstract modern works.

Long before there were nightmares on Elm Street, the director Alfred Hitchcock kept movie audiences on pins and needles. He was featured on a new stamp in the "Legends of Hollywood" series in 1998. Hitchcock's films ranged from classic suspense dramas like *The 39 Steps* (1935) to thrillers like *Psycho* (1960). Besides his photograph, the stamp carried a profile that Hitchcock drew himself and used as his trademark.

Among the year's other U.S. issues were stamps honoring alpine skiing, gospel singing, and ballet. A colorful stamp marked the Chinese New Year—the Year of the Tiger in the Chinese calendar. The stamp showed a stylized tiger against a bright blue background.

Late in the year the Postal Service released a first-class stamp bearing the letter H in place of a denomination, with a picture of an "Uncle Sam" hat. The stamp heralded an increase in postage rates set for January 10, 1999.

STAMPS AROUND THE WORLD

The circus was the theme for one of the year's most colorful stamp issues, released by Canada in October in honor of Stamp Collecting Month. The four 45-cent stamps featured an inventive design that combined photographs of clowns with illustrations of acrobats and animal acts. The stamps were produced in both booklet and souvenir sheet forms.

The famous Royal Canadian Mounted Police—the Mounties—marked their 125th anniversary in 1998, and the event was honored with a pair of stamps. One showed the Mounties of old in their original job, which was to police Canada's western frontier. The other showed the Mounties today, a modern crime-fighting force.

In June 1998, the Canadian city of Vancouver was the site of the first sumo wrestling championship ever held outside Japan. Two

Canadian commemoratives marked the event and celebrated Canadian-Japanese relations. Figures of sumo wrestlers in traditional costumes were superimposed on symbols of the two nations—Canada's maple leaf, and Japan's rising sun.

Britain honored Diana, Princess of Wales, with a group of five stamps. The death of the popular princess in August 1997 caused a worldwide outpouring of grief. Several other countries issued stamps honoring her soon after her death. The British stamps, issued in February 1998, showed five different portraits of her, and demand for them was huge. Profits from sales of the stamps went to Diana's favorite charities.

Valentine's Day stamps are an annual tradition in several countries. For 1998, Ireland featured cartoon characters. The four stamps carried the words "Love is…"; but the phrase was completed differently on each—"from my heart," "a birthday wish," "keeping in touch," and "thinking of you." Finland's six Valentine's Day stamps had heart-shaped scratch-off panels that concealed secret messages. France featured a little angel dressed as a postal carrier, carrying a bouquet of flowers.

Imagination ran riot on a group of stamps issued especially for children by the Czech Republic. The inventive designs featured a water sprite riding a catfish and comical devils playing musical instruments. Britain honored classics of children's literature with a group of five stamps called "Magical Worlds." The stamps showed scenes from J.R.R. Tolkein's *The Hobbit,* E. Nesbit's *The Phoenix and the Carpet,* Lewis Carroll's *Through the Looking Glass,* Mary Norton's *The Borrowers,* and C. S. Lewis's *The Lion, the Witch and the Wardrobe.* Also popular with young collectors were stamps showing Mickey Mouse and other Disney characters, issued by several other nations.

Festivals and holidays were featured on the 1998 Europa stamps, produced by many European countries. A Swedish stamp showed children celebrating Midsummer Day (observed on June 24) by dancing around a Midsummer pole. Music festivals, parades, boat races, and food festivals were among the events honored on Europa stamps from other countries.

A TOPICAL COLLECTION OF BIRDS

Nations that weren't part of the Europa group also celebrated holidays on stamps. For example, the Caribbean nation of Netherlands Antilles kicked off the year with a stamp marking New Year's Day.

Japan hosted the 1998 Winter Olympic Games, and it released a set of ten stamps to mark the event. Five of the stamps showed winter sports—curling, speed skating, cross-country skiing, Alpine skiing, and snowboarding, which became an Olympic sport in 1998. The other five featured flowers, along with the Olympic symbol of five rings. Among the many other countries that honored the Winter Games with stamps was Hungary, which was the first to release a snowboarding stamp.

Adorable pigs posed on a group of three stamps from Finland. The stamps, part of a series portraying domestic animals, showed young pigs, a boar, and a sow and her litter. Each carried a red cross in one corner, indicating that profits from sales of the stamps would go to the Finnish Red Cross.

Many other countries issued stamps featuring animals. Zimbabwe released a set depicting some little known beasts, such as the clawless otter. Each stamp showed a picture of the animal and its paw print. The Solomon Islands showed four deep-sea bill fish—the swordfish, shortbill swordfish, black marlin, and sailfish.

Deep-sea fish, along with other ocean life, were featured on three sheets of stamps issued by the United Nations Postal Administration to honor the International Year of the Ocean. Each sheet carried twelve stamps in a se-tenant design; that is, the individual stamps formed a complete picture. The sheets showed a cross-section of ocean life in tropical regions, temperate regions, and polar regions.

A TOPICAL COLLECTION OF BIRDS

Birds are colorful and fascinating, and that makes them a wonderful subject for a topical collection—a collection built around a single theme. There's an enormous range to choose from. You might begin with a set of four U.S. stamps showing tropical birds, which was issued in 1998. And stamps from countries around the world show everything from common birds, like the European robin, to exotic species like the keel-billed toucan. Collecting bird stamps is a great way to let your imagination take flight.

IT'S GAME TIME...

LOOKIN' FOR THE GOLD

"Is that gold?" wondered James Marshall. On January 24, 1848, Marshall was inspecting a newly dug water channel along the banks of the American River in California. He noticed some small yellow objects glittering in the shallow stream. He picked them up and had them tested. Sure enough, he had discovered gold! When word of Marshall's discovery spread, thousands of people rushed to California. They, too, hoped to find gold and strike it rich.

The site where Marshall discovered the gold has become famous as the place where the California gold rush began. To learn its name, you need a pencil and a sheet of paper. Carefully follow the directions given below. Hint: It will be easier if you rewrite the complete words at each step. (The solution is on page 414.)

1. Print the words CALIFORNIA GOLD. Leave the words separated.
2. Remove the first letter of the first word.
3. Replace every A with an S.
4. Put a U after the first vowel from the left.
5. Remove the two O's.
6. Add an E between the F–R combination.
7. Change the D to an M.
8. Remove the fifth consonant from the left.
9. Find the F. Replace it with two T's.
10. Find the L–I combination. Move it between the L–M combination.
11. Insert an apostrophe after the last vowel in the first word.
12. Remove the letter that comes after F in the alphabet.
13. Remove the second vowel from the right.
14. Reverse the order of the letters of the second word.

The first large group of gold hunters to reach California in response to Marshall's discovery arrived in 1849, which is why they came to be called "forty-niners."

MEET THE EXPERTS

Imagine going to a party where everyone is an expert. One is a conchologist. Another is a genealogist. Still another is an oologist. If you know what subject each person is an expert on, you'll be able to have some pretty interesting conversations.

All the experts at the party are listed below, in the left column. Match them with their subjects, which are listed in the right column.

The Experts	**Their Subjects**
1. biologist	**a.** ancient animal life
2. conchologist	**b.** animals
3. cosmetologist	**c.** birds
4. cosmologist	**d.** birds' eggs
5. dermatologist	**e.** blood
6. entomologist	**f.** cosmetics
7. genealogist	**g.** diseases
8. geologist	**h.** drugs
9. hematologist	**i.** ears, nose, and throat
10. herpetologist	**j.** earth
11. ichthyologist	**k.** family histories
12. meteorologist	**l.** fish
13. oologist	**m.** fossils
14. ornithologist	**n.** insects
15. otorhinolaryngologist	**o.** living things
16. paleontologist	**p.** moon
17. paleozoologist	**q.** poisons
18. pathologist	**r.** reptiles and amphibians
19. pharmacologist	**s.** shells
20. selenologist	**t.** skin
21. toxicologist	**u.** universe
22. virologist	**v.** viruses
23. volcanologist	**w.** volcanoes
24. zoologist	**x.** weather

ANSWERS: 1,o; 2,s; 3,f; 4,u; 5,t; 6,n; 7,k; 8,j; 9,e; 10,r; 11,l; 12,x; 13,d; 14,c; 15,i; 16,m; 17,a; 18,g; 19,h; 20,p; 21,q; 22,v; 23,w; 24,b.

PAPER STUFFINGS

Making big sculptures has never been more fun. In an afternoon you can turn large sheets of paper into models of spaceships, animals—and even your best friend!

Start with two big sheets of paper, such as kraft paper or butcher paper. Place one sheet on top of the other. Draw or trace an outline of your sculpture on the top sheet. Use paints or markers to color your drawing.

When the paint is dry, cut out the sculpture, both sheets at the same time. Staple together the edges of the sheets, working one section at a time. As you staple a section,

WHAT YOU NEED TO MAKE "SOCCER BOY":

- Large sheets of paper
- Paper scraps for stuffing
- Paints and brushes
- Stick
- Markers
- Scissors
- Stapler
- Glue and clear tape
- Decorations, such as yarn and a bandage

1. Place two big sheets of paper on the floor. Have a friend lie down on the paper. Then trace around him.

2. Color the tracing—skin, hair, clothing, shoes and socks, and soccer ball. Add lots of details to make it look like a real person.

3. Staple together the two sheets of paper in four or five places. Carefully cut out the "person," both sheets at once. Save the scraps.

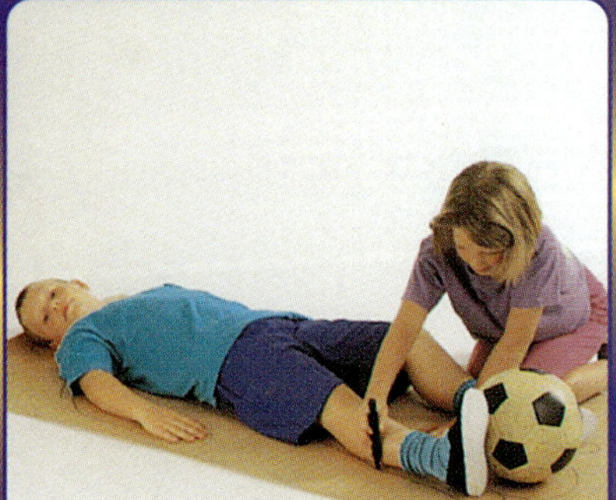

SPACESHIP

FAT CAT

SMILING FISH

stuff it with paper. Repeat this process until the entire sculpture is stapled and stuffed. Then give the sculpture some special finishing touches. If your sculpture is a person, glue paper fringes around the eyes for eyelashes. Hang a real bracelet around the wrist. Put a baseball cap on the head.

Once you've made one sculpture, you'll want to make more. Let your imagination run wild! Create a sculpture of your favorite movie star...mom's favorite flower...dad's dream car...or a gigantic space alien!

4. Staple around the edges of the head. Put the staples very close together. Stuff the head with paper scraps. Then staple and stuff another small area.

5. Use a stick to gently push scraps into hard-to-reach places. Use tape to patch rips. When the paper person is stuffed, staple the last opening.

6. Add lots of fun details and decorations—yarn on the hair, fringed paper eyelashes, a bandage, perhaps real shoelaces.

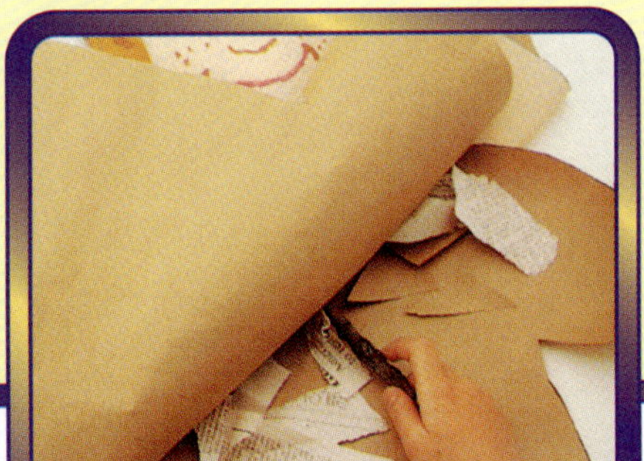

GO FLY A KITE

People have enjoyed making and flying kites for at least 2,000 years. It's fun to watch a kite lift in the breeze and rise until it's just a speck of color in the sky. The word "kite" is the name of a bird of the hawk family, known for its grace in the air.

A kite may be a simple arrangement of two sticks, crossed and covered with paper or cloth and flown at the end of a string, also known as a **flying line**. Or the kite may be a more elaborate shape, such as a box or a pyramid. Kites may be made of paper, light plastic, or cloth. Sticks may be made of wood, plastic, or fiberglass.

In Asia, kites are made in the shapes of birds, fish, and butterflies. Many are beautifully decorated. One of the largest kites is the Chinese dragon kite. It's a long train of individual kites connected by lines. The first kite represents the dragon's head, and a number of circular kites behind it represent the dragon's body. This kite is so long that it must be launched by several people.

TYPES OF KITES

Kites come in an enormous number of colors and styles. Some of the most common kites include the flat kite, the bowed kite, and the box kite.

The Flat Kite. The flat kite with a tail is the oldest and most familiar kind of kite. The weight of the tail helps keep the bottom of the kite down and the nose tilted up. The tail also steadies the position of the kite in the air. It acts somewhat like the rudder of a ship. When the wind pushes the kite too hard in one direction, the surfaces of the tail act as an opposing force to the wind, so the kite can remain steady.

The Bowed Kite. One of the best fliers, this kite is built on a framework of two sticks crossed in a T, with the cross stick bent like an archer's bow. This creates an angle to the wind, so that the kite doesn't need a tail. One kind of bowed kite was invented in 1898 by an American, William A. Eddy, which is why this type of kite is also called the Eddy kite.

The Box Kite. This type of kite is shaped like a long box with open ends. The sides are covered except for an open section in the center. This kite was invented by Lawrence Hargrave, an Australian, about 1892.

Other Types of Kites. The delta kite is shaped roughly like a triangle. This type of kite has wide wings and is supported by a flap of material called a keel underneath the wings. The keel guides the kite and steadies it. Another type is the flexible kite, which has no supporting rods. These kites form dif-

Beautifully decorated kites fly at a kite festival in Mitsuke, a city on the island of Honshu in Japan. Although no one is sure who invented the kite, we do know that making and flying kites have been popular pastimes in many Asian countries for hundreds of years.

ferent shapes—an airplane, for example—when they are filled with wind. Another example is the parafoil, which looks somewhat like a parachute. Stunt kites are able to dip, spin, loop, and twirl in the sky with the operator manipulating one or more strings. Some kites look like dragons or other animals. Others may have various geometric shapes.

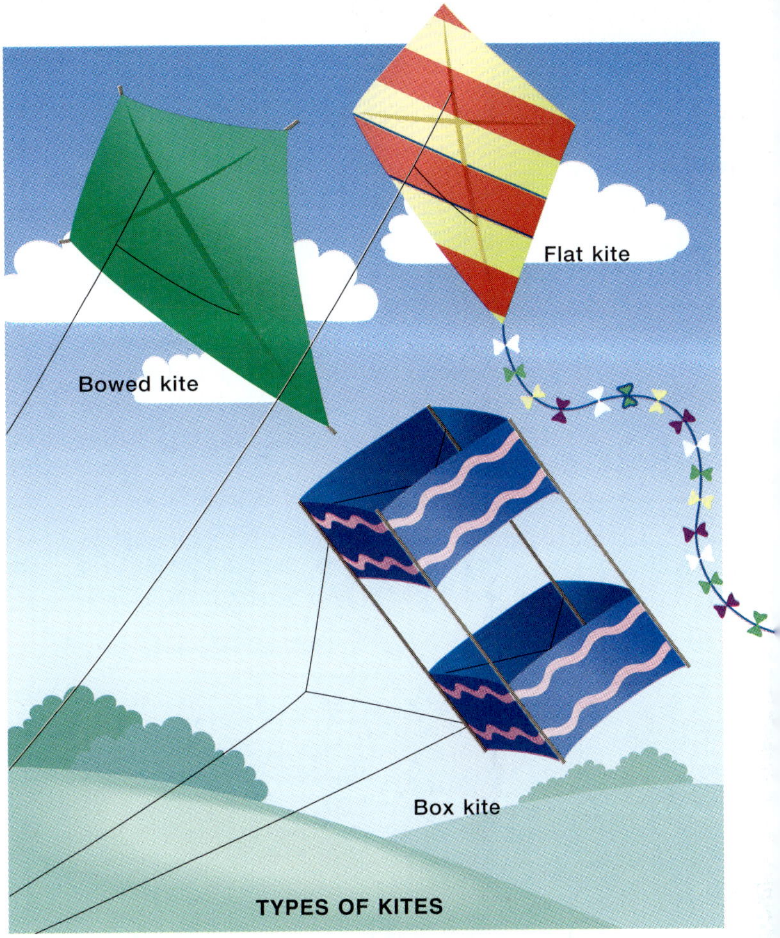

TYPES OF KITES

HISTORY

No one is sure who invented the kite. Some historians believe it was invented by a Greek named Archytas about 400 B.C. Other people believe it was invented 200 years later by Han-Sin, a Chinese general. But we do know that making and flying kites have been popular pastimes in China, Japan, Korea, and other countries of the Far East for many hundreds of years. And they are still popular pastimes today.

In China, the ninth day of the ninth month is known as Kites' Day, or the Festival of Ascending on High. It's

How Does a Kite Fly?

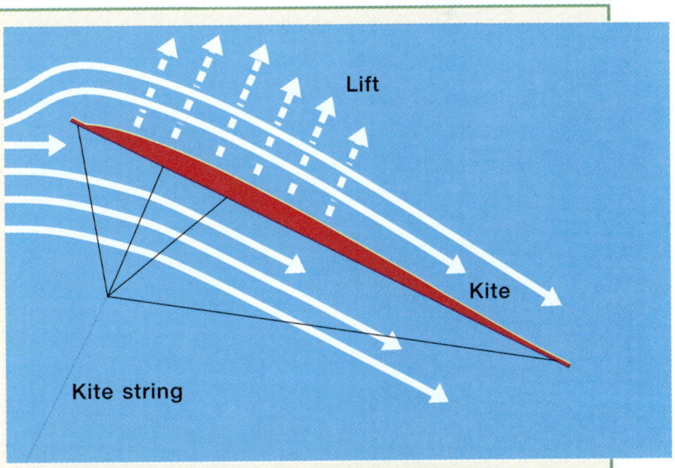

Two opposing forces act on a kite. One is the lifting force of the wind. The other is the pull of the kite string back to the ground. When these two forces are balanced or nearly equal, a kite remains in the air.

The force of the wind on a kite is similar to the force of the wind on a sail. When a kite is launched correctly, it should be at an angle to the horizontal movement of the air. This angle, called the angle of attack, forces the air to strike the underside of the kite and be deflected downward. In reaction to this downward force, the air pushes back up on the underside of the kite. This upward force is a kite's main source of lift.

In some designs, such as those of bowed kites, the kite billows slightly upward, in much the same way that an airplane's wings are curved on top. The wind blowing over this curved surface travels faster than the wind blowing underneath, creating a lower pressure above the kite than below it. This difference in pressure produces an upward force, which is a second source of lift.

the tradition for people of all ages to fly kites on that day.

In Japan, Children's Day is celebrated on May 5. Each family flies a fish kite from a bamboo pole in front of the house for each boy in the family. The Japanese and other Asians also enjoy a sport known as kite fighting. Large numbers of people play at one time. Each kite flier coats a portion of his kite string near the kite with a mixture of powdered glass and glue. When all the kites are in the air, a player tries to cross and cut the string of another kite with the sharp, glass-coated part of his own string.

Kites have also been used in scientific experiments. In 1749 two Scottish scientists, Alexander Wilson and Thomas Melville, sent up a train, or connected series, of kites with a thermometer attached to each in order to find out the temperature of different altitudes.

In 1752, Benjamin Franklin used a kite in his famous experiment with lightning. He wanted to prove that it was a form of electricity. To do this, he had to find a way to attract lightning. He decided to fly a kite into a thundercloud during a storm. Franklin had attached a metal key on the flying line. He hoped the lightning flashing in the thundercloud would travel along the kite string to the key. This happened, and Franklin got an electric shock. We realize

A clear day with light winds is best for kite flying. Look for a level, open area such as a field or stretch of beach.

How to Fly Your Kite

A day of clear skies and winds of 8 to 15 miles (13 to 24 kilometers) per hour is ideal for kite flying. The best place to launch a kite is a level field with no trees.

Stand with your back to the wind. With one arm raised, hold your kite upright by the lower corner. The cover of the kite should be facing the wind, and the nose should be tilted slightly toward you. This is the angle at which the kite will fly. With your other hand, hold the reel of string. When the wind blows steadily, let go of the kite, giving it a little push into the stream of air. Then move backward and start to let out the line.

You can also launch your kite with the help of a friend. Have your friend face the wind and hold the kite while you walk backward into the wind, letting out string as you walk. Let out about 75 feet (23 meters) of string. Don't let any of it rest on the ground. Now have your friend lift the kite and hold it in the launching position described above. When the wind tugs at the kite, your helper will feel the kite string tighten and should then release the kite gently. As it begins to rise, walk backward, letting out more line.

To bring your kite down, walk toward the kite, in the direction in which the wind is blowing, and reel in line as you walk.

today that Franklin's experiment was extremely dangerous. A person who comes into contact with electricity while he or she is wet could be killed.

Many years later, kites also played a part in the development of the airplane. Before they built and flew the first airplane in 1903, Wilbur and Orville Wright experimented with huge box kites strong enough to lift an adult into the air.

Kites have also been used for other purposes. They have been equipped with cameras in order to take pictures from the air. During the Spanish-American War (1898), a kite was used when a photographer stood on the ground and clicked the shutter of the camera by pulling a string that was attached to it.

In the early part of the 1900s, the United States Weather Bureau (now the National Weather Service) used box kites that were equipped with instruments to obtain various information for weather forecasts.

During the Boer War in South Africa (1899–1902), large kites carried British soldiers over enemy territory so that

Kites of all shapes and sizes can be seen at kite festivals. Above: A lizard-shaped kite soars in the air in Rome, Italy. Below: Onlookers surround a huge fish kite in Castiglione de Lago, Italy.

How to Make a Flat Kite

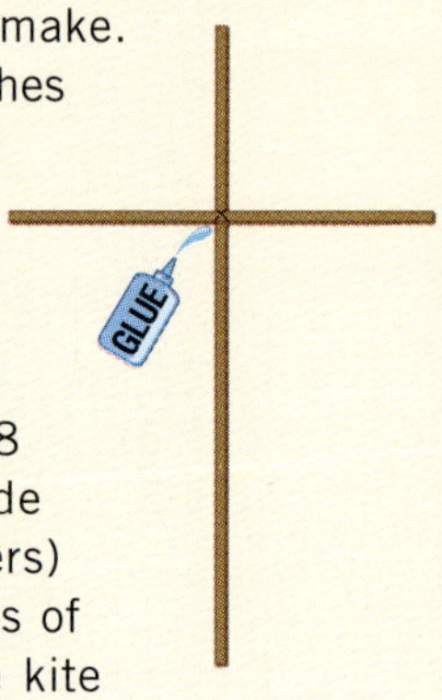

The flat kite is easy to make. You'll need one stick 36 inches (91 centimeters) long and one 30 inches (76 centimeters) long. The sticks may be round dowel sticks 1/4 inch (6 millimeters) thick, or strips of wood 3/8 inch (10 millimeters) wide and 1/4 inch (6 millimeters) thick. It's best to use sticks of pine or spruce to keep the kite lightweight.

Using a pencil, mark the center of the smaller stick and a point 9 inches (23 centimeters) from one end of the longer stick. The longer stick will be the upright, or **spine.** Place the two sticks in a t-shape so that the two pencil marks meet. Wind string tightly around them, then coat the string with glue. (You can use special kite string, fishing line, or cotton twine both in making the kite and in flying it later.)

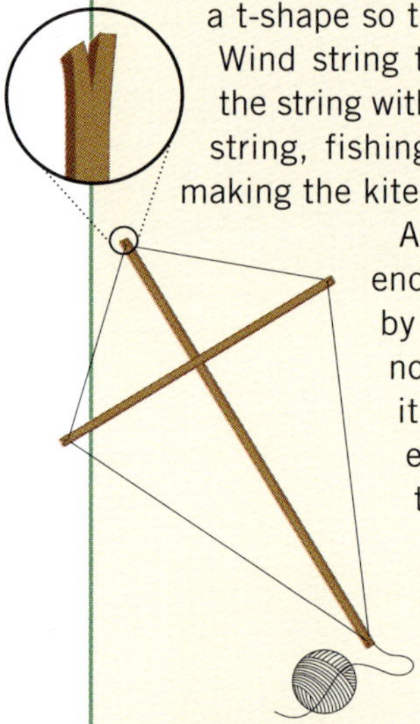

Ask an adult to cut a notch in the end of each stick. Outline the kite by slotting the string into the notches and pulling it tight. Knot it firmly. Put a drop of glue in each notch. This will help keep the string in place.

Place the framework of the kite on a large piece of tissue paper, gift wrap paper, newspaper, or thin plastic. Cut the covering so that it's 2 inches (5 centimeters) larger than the framework. Fold the margin of the covering over the string and glue or tape it down. Trim the corners of the kite.

To decorate a paper kite, paint it with poster paints or watercolors. Be careful not to tear the paper.

Now you are ready to attach the kite to the string. The string isn't fastened directly to the kite, but to two slack strings called the **bridle**, which helps keep the kite tilted upward at a good flying angle. To make the bridle, put the kite on the floor with the paper covering facing you. Tie one end of a piece of string 42 inches (107 centimeters) long to the top and the other end to the bottom of the upright kite stick. Tie a second piece of string 36 inches (91 centimeters) long to the two ends of the cross stick.

A flat kite is fun to make. After you finish, take it outside for a test flight. Be sure to hang on tightly to the string!

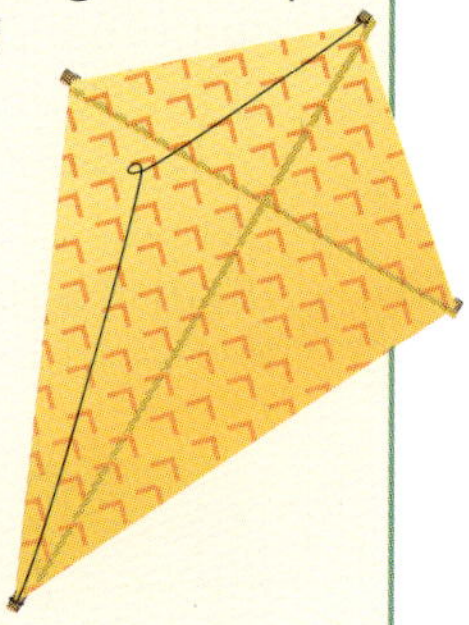

Pick up the two strings of the bridle where they cross, and attach the end of your reel of kite string at this point. After trying out your kite, you may find that you need to adjust the length of the bridle string so that the kite flies well.

To make a tail for your kite, you will need a piece of string at least 8 feet (2.4 meters) long. (After you have flown the kite, you can adjust the length of the tail if necessary.) Cut some cloth into 6- by 2-inch (15- by 5-centimeter) pieces. Attach each piece of cloth, at its center, to the tail string. Leave 6 inches (15 centimeters) between pieces. Tie the tail to the bottom of your kite.

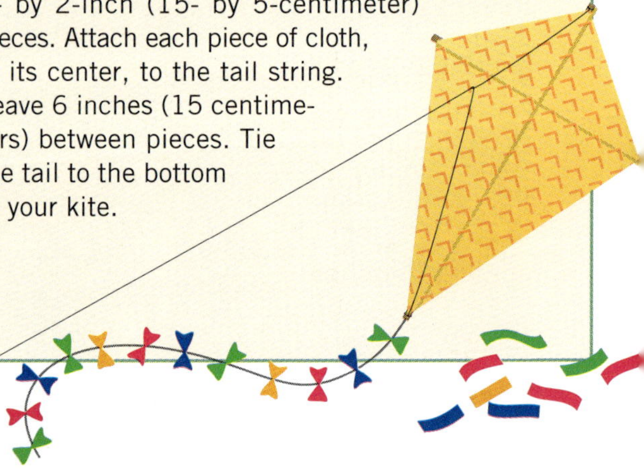

Kites can take many forms. Right: A complex geometric box kite requires many strings to be flown properly. Below: A bird kite and flower kite are examples of creative kite design. Below, right: This whimsical "airplane" is a type of flexible kite, which takes shape when filled with wind.

the soldiers could report on the movements of the enemy. In World War I (1914–18), the Germans developed a kite that could be used to fly people from a submarine.

Kites were used as targets in gunnery practice by the United States military during World War II (1939–45). Life rafts were also equipped with kites. These kites were used to fly wire radio antennae into the air. In this way radio signals could easily be transmitted long distances.

Today kites are flown mostly for enjoyment and recreation. Kite festivals are held in a number of cities and towns around the world. In the United States, popular kiting events include the annual Smithsonian Kite Festival in Washington, D.C. At a kite festival, you can see kites of all shapes and sizes flying in the air, many of them handmade. Games and contests offer something of interest for every kite flier.

LARRY KETTELKAMP
Author, *Kites*

Safety Rules

Certain safety rules should be carefully observed by all kite fliers.

◆ Don't use any metal materials in a kite. Don't use wire as a kite string.

◆ Never fly a kite in the rain. Remember that metal attracts electricity, and that electricity will travel along a wet kite string.

◆ Don't fly a kite near electric wires or poles.

◆ Never try to rescue a kite if it's caught on a wire or pole.

◆ Don't fly a kite near the edge of a steep slope.

STAR SEARCH

Annie Mae Bullock and David Kotkin are well-known entertainers. Never heard of them? Sure you have! But you know them as Tina Turner and David Copperfield. Like many other entertainers, these two people took new names on their road to stardom.

Entertainers have many reasons for changing their names. Some want names that are easier to pronounce. Others choose names that they believe sound more attractive to audiences. And then there are people like Michael Keaton. He was born Michael Douglas, and he would have used that name professionally. But there already was a well-known actor named Michael Douglas, and so he changed his name to avoid confusion.

Of course, not all entertainers change their names. Matt Damon, Drew Barrymore, and Paul Newman are among those who kept their original names.

The names of 20 famous entertainers are listed below (in the left column). Match each to his or her birth name (in the right column).

1. Woody Allen
2. Babyface
3. Nicolas Cage
4. Cher
5. Tom Cruise
6. Danny DeVito
7. Kirk Douglas
8. Judy Garland
9. Whoopi Goldberg
10. Cary Grant
11. Elton John
12. Don Johnson
13. Diane Keaton
14. Marilyn Monroe
15. Demi Moore
16. Winona Ryder
17. Susan Sarandon
18. Ringo Starr
19. Sting
20. Stevie Wonder

a. Nicholas Coppola
b. Winona Horowitz
c. Norma Jean Baker
d. Frances Gumm
e. Stevland Morris
f. Richard Starkey
g. Gordon Sumner
h. Kenneth Edmonds
i. Reginald Dwight
j. Demetria Guynes
k. Allen Konigsberg
l. Cherilyn Sarkisian
m. Daniel Michaeli
n. Donald Wayne
o. Susan Tomaling
p. Archibald Leach
q. Diane Hall
r. Thomas Mapother
s. Issur Danielovitch
t. Caryn Johnson

ANSWERS: 1,k; 2,h; 3,a; 4,l; 5,r; 6,m; 7,s; 8,d; 9,t; 10,p; 11,i; 12,n; 13,q; 14,c; 15,j; 16,b; 17,o; 18,f; 19,g; 20,e.

Next, go on a hunt. The first and last names of all 20 people are hidden in this word-search puzzle. Try to find them. Cover the puzzle with a sheet of tracing paper. Read forward, backward, up, down, and diagonally. Then draw a neat line through each name as you find it.

W	S	N	S	T	E	V	I	E	W	O	N	D	E	R
I	H	A	E	N	O	S	N	H	O	J	N	O	D	I
N	E	O	N	L	E	N	I	Y	A	J	C	K	R	R
O	R	S	O	O	L	W	O	U	U	A	I	I	I	A
N	O	T	R	P	T	A	X	D	R	R	L	M	N	M
A	T	I	N	A	I	A	Y	L	K	C	A	R	G	A
R	I	N	E	D	W	G	E	D	A	I	M	A	O	R
Y	V	G	A	E	A	D	O	K	O	W	R	O	S	I
D	E	H	R	R	C	U	E	L	E	O	R	L	T	L
E	D	O	L	I	G	A	R	I	D	N	W	E	A	Y
R	Y	A	H	L	S	Y	F	S	R	B	A	M	R	N
O	N	F	A	C	H	E	R	Y	U	O	E	I	R	M
D	N	S	A	C	R	U	B	A	B	L	D	R	D	O
A	A	N	I	C	O	L	A	S	C	A	G	E	G	N
N	D	E	L	T	O	N	J	O	H	N	B	I	D	R
N	O	D	N	A	R	A	S	N	A	S	U	S	U	O
A	M	O	P	M	W	D	E	M	I	M	O	O	R	E

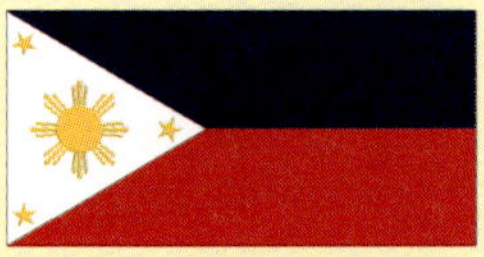

BANANA NIBBLES
from the Philippines

Time for a snack. Have a fried banana, Philippine style. These banana chips are often dipped in batter and then fried. Or you can simply slice and fry them quickly in oil. Bananas thrive in tropical climates, so it's no wonder they crop up in Philippine foods as often as they do—in soups, stews, desserts, and snacks. (Have an adult help you with this recipe.)

INGREDIENTS

6 bananas
oil for deep frying
salt

EQUIPMENT

knife
high-sided frying pan
slotted spoon
oven mitts
paper towels

HOW TO MAKE

1. Peel bananas and cut into ½-inch slices.
2. Heat the oil until it bubbles.
3. Carefully drop several slices at a time into the hot oil and fry until golden brown. Use oven mitts to protect your hands.
4. Remove bananas with slotted spoon and drain on paper towels.
5. Sprinkle with salt and serve hot.

This recipe serves 6 people.

Note: *This recipe works best with plantains, which are green and less sweet than yellow bananas.*

GAZPACHO
from Spain

Cool off in hot summer weather. The Spanish know how, with a cold soup-salad—gazpacho. Chop and mix fresh tomato, cucumber, and green pepper. Season and chill. You're set for a drinkable feast. In Spain, different towns make different versions of this soup. After you make this one, invent your own gazpacho by adding any of your favorite vegetables.

INGREDIENTS

- 2 cucumbers
- 5 medium tomatoes
- 1 onion
- 1 green pepper
- 2 cloves garlic
- 2 cups cold water
- 2 cups tomato juice
- ¼ cup olive oil
- 1 tablespoon salt

EQUIPMENT

- paring knife
- large mixing bowl
- mixing spoon
- measuring cups
- blender or food mill
- fork

HOW TO MAKE

1. Peel cucumbers and cut into pieces. Peel tomatoes and onion and chop coarsely. Cut green pepper into small pieces. Chop garlic fine.
2. In a large mixing bowl combine chopped cucumbers, tomatoes, onion, green pepper, and garlic. Mix well.
3. Stir in water and tomato juice.
4. Pour mixture into a blender 2 cups at a time and blend at high speed for 1 minute. If using a food mill, pour mixture in small amounts and purée.
5. Pour the puréed mixture into a mixing bowl. Beat in the olive oil with a fork. Add salt.
6. Cover the bowl and refrigerate. Chill and serve very cold.

This recipe serves 6 people.

Each of these handmade mini-pets has a personality all its own.

POPULAR CRAFTS

When you turn your hand to crafts, there's no end to the things you can do. Couple your imagination with some of the ideas on these pages and you'll have lots of fun as you create items that are both decorative and useful.

PERKY PETS

Bring a smile to people's faces with a menagerie of cheerful little pets.

To make one of these animals, you'll need a small plastic-foam ball (1 inch, or 2.5 centimeters, in diameter), one skein of embroidery floss, dimensional paints, glue, felt scraps, chenille stems, small blue feathers, and fishing line.

Gently press one side of the ball to create a flat bottom. Using craft glue, glue one end of the floss to the flat bottom. Then wrap the floss around the ball, crisscrossing as necessary, until the ball is evenly covered with the entire skein. Glue the remaining floss end to the bottom of the ball.

Now give the mini-critter some character. Use dimensional paints to create eyes, nose, and smiling mouth. Divide a green chenille stem to make a frog's long legs. Use scraps of felt to give a fish its fins and a puppy its droopy ears. Cut up a blue feather for a bird's wings, and some fishing line for a cat's whiskers.

When you've finished, show off your animals on your desk, or glue a magnet to the back of each one and decorate your refrigerator with a zoo of perky pets!

PICTURE PERFECT

Take an ordinary frame and turn it into a three-dimensional work of art that will add pizzazz to one of your favorite photos.

To make the frame shown here, you'll need a wide wood frame, a wood bird, four wood

Blue Bird Picture Frame

hearts, wire, and a twig. You'll also need acrylic paints, a black fine-line permanent marker, all-purpose primer, clear matte varnish, paintbrushes, a drill, craft glue, sandpaper, and tack cloth. If you'd like to give the bird a checkerboard design, you'll need a checkerboard stencil and stencil brush.

Have an adult help you drill a hole into the center top of each heart. Drill three holes into the side edge of the frame's top right corner. Drill a hole near the frame's lower left corner.

Apply primer to all sides of the frame, the hearts, and the bird. When the primer is dry, lightly sand each item, then wipe it clean with tack cloth.

Now paint the frame white. When dry, use medium blue paint to make a wiggly line around the frame opening and to spatter the front and sides of the frame with small specks. Paint the wood hearts green, to make the leaves. Use the permanent marker for accent lines on each leaf and around the outside edge of the bird. When all surfaces are dry, apply a coat of varnish.

Cut four lengths of wire. Create spirals by wrapping each length around a paintbrush handle. Glue one end of each wire and insert the end into a leaf. Glue and insert the other end of three wires into the holes at the upper corner of the frame. Spiral wrap the end of the fourth leaf wire several times around the twig. Then glue the wire end into the hole at the lower left of the frame. Finally, glue the bird to the front of the frame so that it sits on the branch.

BAH, BAH BAG

A fluffy sheep sporting a pink calico ribbon adds a playful look to an ordinary white bag.

To create your own unique sheep, you'll need a white gift bag, pink and tan acrylic paints, a stencil brush, craft glue, white buttons, a black fine-line permanent marker, and a pink calico bow.

Sweet Sheep Gift Bag

Warren the Wind Chime

Begin by drawing a design on the bag, working with very light lines. To paint the sheep, use just a bit of acrylic paint on your brush, and work with a circular motion. Paint pink cheeks, then give the sheep tan curls and ears. Using a black fine-line marker, make small, evenly spaced dots over the design lines. Add a pair of black eyes. Glue a white button to each curl and a pink calico bow to the sheep's head. Make a sheep card to match your sheep bag—and you'll have an enchanting gift package.

WARREN THE WIND CHIME

Here's the perfect craft for people who believe in recycling. "Warren" is a wind chime, with an old clay flowerpot for his body and hair made from a plastic bag!

To make Warren, you'll also need two wooden beads, outdoor paints and brushes, jute twine, jingle bells, small bows, a black fine-line permanent marker, and cotton fabric to make a scarf. You can also purchase a miniature straw hat, basket, and pitchfork at a craft store.

Give the flowerpot two coats of blue paint. Then choose contrasting colors to paint several raglike patches with horizontal and vertical stripes.

For the head, use a wooden bead that's about the same diameter as the bottom of the flowerpot. Paint it a flesh color. Keeping the bead's holes at the top and bottom of the head, add blushing cheeks and other facial features. For the hair, cut out a flat sheet from a plastic grocery bag. Paint both sides of the sheet yellow.

Use jute twine for the legs, arms, and hanger. Cut three pieces of twine in the following lengths: 22 inches (55 centimeters), 18 inches (45 centimeters), and 16 inches (40 centimeters). Thread the three pieces of twine through the second bead—a 14-millimeter bead—so that the bead is centered on the pieces. Tie the twine together in a knot around the bead, giving you six segments of twine.

Place the bead inside the flowerpot. Thread the two short and two medium segments of twine up through the hole in the pot. Pull one short segment to each side of the pot, to form the arms. Thread the two medium segments through the hole in the head and tie together at the top of the head; this is the hanger. Let the two long segments of twine hang down, to form the legs.

Tie jingle bells to each arm and leg. Glue small bows atop each bell. Cut strips of "hair" from the painted plastic bag, and glue them onto the top of the head. Make a small hole in the top of a little straw hat, and thread the two hanger segments through the hat. Glue the hat to the head. Tie together the ends of the two hanger segments.

Birdhouse Visor

Finally, tie a scarf around his neck and give him a miniature pitchfork and basket. Now hang him up outdoors and listen to Warren the wind chime's jingly melody.

VISOR VISION

Instead of wearing a plain visor to protect your eyes against the sun's glare, you can use paints and buttons to create a visor that expresses your interests or hobby. Craft stores carry colorful buttons in a wide variety of shapes—everything from birds and cows to cars and footballs.

To make this birdhouse visor, start with a white visor. You'll also need a sponge, a paintbrush, fabric paint, buttons, and glue.

Sponge paint a grassy green background on the visor. Using a darker green, paint flower stems and birdhouse poles. Glue a birdhouse button onto each pole, a bird button atop one of the flower stems, and colorful round buttons atop the remaining stems. Finish by adding random dots of contrasting paints to the grassy background.

Now wear your visor the next time you head outdoors!

NONA PIORKOWSKI
Crafts 'n Things magazine

COIN COLLECTING

Heroes—real, mythical, and biblical—shared the spotlight on United States, Canadian, and world coins during 1998.

U.S. COINS

The U.S. Mint honored two of the country's most famous fallen leaders on one popular set of coins. The 1998 Kennedy Collector's Set featured a new commemorative silver dollar marking the 30th anniversary of the assassination of Robert F. Kennedy in 1968. It showed a full-face view of the former U.S. attorney general, who was President John F. Kennedy's younger brother, with the seal of the U.S. Department of Justice on the reverse. In the set, the new coin was teamed with a special John F. Kennedy silver half dollar in a matte finish.

U.S. silver dollar coins honoring Robert F. Kennedy and Revolutionary War patriot Crispus Attucks.

A new Black Patriots silver dollar depicted Crispus Attucks, slain by the British in the infamous Boston Massacre of 1770. The coin's reverse featured the Black Patriots Revolutionary War Memorial planned for the National Mall in Washington, D.C. Collectors could purchase proof or uncirculated silver dollars and a special coin and stamp set honoring African-American patriots.

A majestic eagle flying along the northeastern seaboard of the United States at moonrise served as a new reverse for the annual platinum American Eagle bullion coins. The 1998 coins were the first in a five-year series planned to portray the eagle in regional American landscapes.

The U.S. Mint was also gearing up for the 50 States Quarter Program. Beginning in 1999, this ten-year series will honor each state with its own special coin. It should send collectors hunting through their pocket change for five new U.S. quarter designs every year. Preliminary designs were released in 1998 for the first five states to be honored—Delaware, Pennsylvania, New Jersey, Georgia, and Connecticut.

WORLD COINS

The Royal Canadian Mint celebrated its 90th birthday in 1998. Not surprisingly, it did so with coins. An anniversary set of five coins, ranging from a large cent to a 50-cent piece, combined designs from 1908 with the portrait of Queen Elizabeth II carried on today's Canadian coins. The set raised a stir when it was realized that the large cent didn't display the name "Canada" on either side. The design was quickly revised, but not before collectors scrambled to get the Canada-less sets.

Another special Canadian issue was a $350 gold coin showing the flowers on the Canadian Coat of Arms: a French fleur de lis, an English rose, a Scottish thistle, and an Irish shamrock. This coin was produced in "five nines" gold—gold that's .99999 pure. The legend of the white buffalo was portrayed on a $200 gold coin, the second in a set honoring Canada's native cultures. According to the Chipewyan people of western Canada, the birth of a white buffalo calf signals renewal for people and the land.

Canada's gold coins featuring the flowers on the Canadian Coat of Arms and a white buffalo.

Macao's Year of the Tiger silver coin, and the Isle of Man's coin featuring an Egyptian mau cat.

The gray wolf was honored on Canada's annual platinum proof sets. A $300 coin showed a female wolf with cubs, a $150 coin had two wolf cubs at play, a $75 coin showed a lone wolf, and a $30 coin carried the profile of a wolf. The 125th anniversary of the Royal Canadian Mounted Police was the subject of Canada's annual silver dollar. And Canada's 1998 gold cameo aviation coins featured unusual aircraft—an Argus anti-submarine plane, used from 1957 to 1981, and a Waterbomber, which fights forest fires by scooping water from lakes and dumping it on the fires.

It was the Year of the Tiger in the Chinese lunar calendar, and many nations celebrated with coins. Among them were Macao, Canada, China, Myanmar, Nepal, and North Korea. Cats of many kinds appeared on other coins. South Africa showed leopards on its gold Natura series. The Isle of Man's 1998 cat coins featured Birman and Egyptian mau cats, two ancient breeds.

The United Nations designated 1998 as the Year of the Ocean, and several countries produced coins on ocean themes. Canada issued a set of four silver 50-cent coins showing whales and dolphins. Gibraltar's Year of the Ocean series included gold and silver one-crown coins showing everything from fish to a polar bear—even a surfer.

One of Gibraltar's coins in its Year of the Ocean series, and Liberia's coin depicting the *Titanic.*

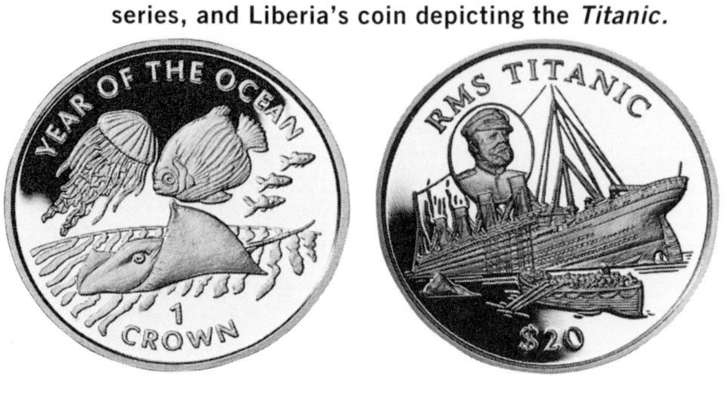

Some of the year's coins held special appeal for children. Peter Rabbit and Paddington Bear were shown on one-crown coins from Gibraltar. The Isle of Man released flower-fairy coins featuring Lavender, Sweet Pea, White Bindweed, and Daffodil.

With the huge success of the movie *Titanic,* that ill-fated ship surfaced on several coins. Liberia and Somalia issued coins showing

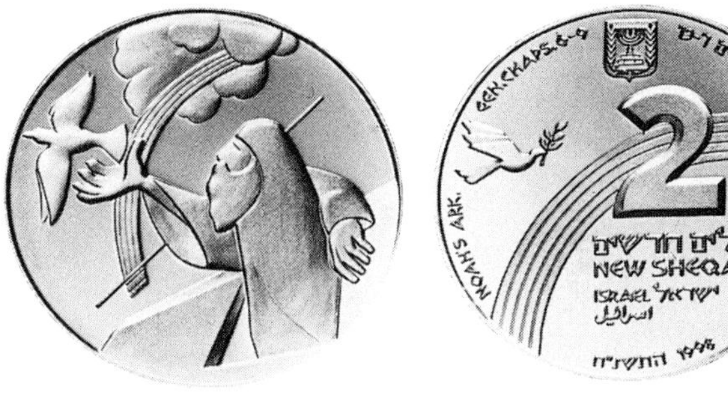

Israel's silver coin showing Noah releasing a dove from the Ark.

the dramatic final moments of the ship, which went down in the Atlantic Ocean in 1912. A ship with a happier fate—Noah's Ark—was the subject for 1998 coins in Israel's Biblical Arts series. Noah was shown sending a dove to find land on gold and silver coins in three denominations.

Jamaica's silver coin commemorating the Soccer World Cup, and Armenia's silver coin marking the Olympics.

As always, sports provided a popular theme for coins. The 1998 Winter Olympic Games, held in Nagano, Japan, and the 1998 Soccer World Cup, held in France, were spotlighted on coins from many nations.

Bob Van Ryzin
Editor, *Coins* magazine

LEAGUE BASEBALL

SPORTS

On September 7, 1998, St. Louis Cardinal first baseman Mark McGwire slugged his way into the baseball record books—he hit his 61st home run of the season. This tied the single-season home-run record set in 1961 by New York Yankee Roger Maris. The very next day, McGwire set a new record of 62 home runs. As the ball cleared the left-field fence, the fans at St. Louis's Busch Stadium burst into cheers. McGwire, raising his hands in victory, rounded the bases, touched home plate, and picked up and hugged his 10-year-old son Matthew. After being mobbed by his teammates, he jumped into the stands and embraced the six daughters and sons of Roger Maris. McGwire was even hugged by Sammy Sosa, the right fielder for the opposing team—the Chicago Cubs. These two were good friends—and good sports—and Sosa was right behind McGwire in the home-run race. In fact, Sosa hit his 62nd homer just days later. But at the end of the season, McGwire had 70 home runs, and Sosa 66.

The 18th Winter Olympic Games were held in Nagano, Japan, in February. As part of the opening ceremonies, performers joined hands around a huge balloon representing Earth (*above*); and 1992 Japanese Olympic silver medalist Midori Ito lit the Olympic flame (*right*).

THE 1998 WINTER OLYMPIC GAMES

Japan was the host of the 18th Winter Olympic Games, which lasted from February 7 through February 22, 1998. The official site of the Games was the city of Nagano, which is on Honshu, Japan's main island, about 110 miles (177 kilometers) northwest of the Japanese capital of Tokyo. Ceremonies marking the opening and closing of the Olympics were held there, as were numerous sports events. But other competitions took place in four nearby towns and on the slopes of the majestic snow-covered Japanese Alps that surround Nagano.

THE OPENING CEREMONIES

The Games officially opened in Minami Stadium. With Japanese Emperor Akihito and Empress Michiko looking on, Japan's best sumo wrestlers performed a special purification ceremony—to stamp out evil spirits. Leading the wrestlers was grand champion Akebono, a native of Hawaii, who stood 6 feet, 8 inches (203 centimeters) tall and weighed 516 pounds (234 kilograms).

Young people also played a role in the opening ceremonies, as 150 Nagano schoolchildren dressed as cherry blossoms danced to the Olympic theme song, "When Children Rule the World." Another highlight was the lighting of the Olympic torch—by Japanese figure skater Midori Ito, who won the silver medal at the 1992 Winter Games.

Tradition and technology combined to bring the ceremonies to a breathtaking close with the singing of the "Ode to Joy," the finale of Beethoven's Ninth Symphony. This piece is performed at every Olympics. The voices of the singers—five giant choral groups from Japan and around the world—were linked simultaneously by satellite for the Nagano and worldwide television audiences.

When the Nagano Games ended fifteen days later, most people agreed that they were among the best Winter Olympics ever. In addition to the thrilling sports events, the Japanese were gracious hosts who made everyone feel welcome. It seemed fitting that Japanese athletes would win 5 gold medals, 2 more than they had won in all previous Winter Olympics combined.

THE CHAMPIONS

Some 2,450 athletes from 72 nations competed in 68 events, including three new ones—women's ice hockey, snowboarding, and curling. Germany won the most medals, 29, and the most gold medals, 12. Norway was just behind, with 25 medals, 10 of them gold. Behind Norway were Russia (18 medals, 9 gold), Austria (17, 3), Canada (15, 6), and the United States (13, 6). Canadian and American female athletes performed extremely well. Women won 7 of the 15 Canadian medals and 3 of the 6 golds. And women won 8 of the 13 American medals and 4 of the 6 golds.

Beauty on Ice. When the figure skaters took to the ice in the Olympic rink, all eyes were focused on the two Americans—Tara Lipinski and Michelle Kwan—who were the top competitors for the women's figure-skating gold medal. In 1997, Lipinski had dethroned Kwan as the top American skater by winning both the U.S. women's figure-skating championship and the world championship. In January 1998, however, Kwan reclaimed the national title, and Lipinski went into the Olympics as the underdog.

When Kwan placed first in the Olympic short program, Lipinski seemed even more of an underdog. But in the free-skating program, Kwan fell short of the near perfection she had exhibited at the nationals. Lipinski, on the other hand, was a marvel to behold. She landed seven perfect triple jumps, including her signature triple-loop, triple-loop combination. And her leaps and pivots and landings had a new level of grace and fluidity. As a result, six of the judges gave Lipinski first-place votes, compared to three first-place votes for Kwan.

Tara Lipinski of the United States delivered an exuberant performance—and became the youngest Olympic figure skater ever to win a gold medal.

At age 15, Lipinski became the youngest person ever to win the gold medal in Olympic figure skating. Kwan took the silver medal, while Lu Chen of China took the bronze.

In men's figure skating, Russia's Ilya Kulik won the gold, Canada's Elvis Stojko won the silver (despite a torn groin muscle), and France's Philippe Candeloro won the bronze. Kulik's outstanding performance included a perfect quadruple toe loop as well as eight triple jumps. Kulik was the first Olympic champion to land a quadruple. A disappointed Todd Eldredge, five-time U.S. national champion, placed out of the medals. Russians also won the gold and silver medals in ice dancing and pairs. In dancing, Pasha Grishuk and Yevgeny Platov repeated their 1994 Olympic win with another of their breathtakingly fast routines, and Angelika Krylova and Oleg Ovsyannikov won the silver medal. In pairs, Oksana Kazakova and Artur Dmitriev won the gold medal, and Yelena Berezhnaya and Anton Sikharulidze won the silver.

Speed on Ice. In the 1998 Winter Olympics, speed skaters wore the new, technologically superior "clap skates." These skates allow the blades to stay on the ice longer than regular skates, thus enabling skaters to take longer, smoother strides. As a result, skaters broke five world records at the Olympics. Americans, however, weren't among them. The only medals for the United States were Chris Witty's silver in the women's 1,000-meter and her bronze in the 1,500-meter. Canadian skaters did better, with Catriona LeMay Doan taking the gold medal in the women's 500-meter event and the bronze in the 1,000. Susan Auch finished behind LeMay Doan for the silver in the 500, and Jeremy Wotherspoon and Kevin Overland won silver and bronze, respectively, in the men's 500 meters.

Speed skating, however, was dominated by the powerful team from the Netherlands. The Dutch speedsters won 11 of the 30 medals, including 5 of the 10 golds. The outstanding Marianne Timmer won gold in the women's 1,000- and 1,500-meter events, setting a world record in the 1,500. Ids Postma, in the men's 1,000- , and Gianni Romme, in the 5,000- and 10,000-meter events, also took home gold medals. Romme's paces in the 5,000 and 10,000 set world records. The Germans also did well, winning 6 medals, including 2 golds. One of the golds—Claudia Pechstein's in the women's 5,000-meter event—set a world record. Yet another world record was set by Norway's Adne Sondral in the men's 1,500 meters. Host country Japan picked up 3 medals, including a gold by Hiroyasu Shimizu in the men's 500, a feat that made him a national hero.

In short-track speed skating, South Korea skated away with 6 medals, including golds in the women's 1,000-meter and 3,000-meter

The Olympic Mascots

Sukki, Nokki, Lekki, and Tsukki—four owl-like characters—were the official mascots of the 1998 Winter Olympics. These colorful cuddly characters were called Snowlets. The name "Snowlets" is made up of "snow," of which there was plenty at Nagano; "let's," an invitation for all to take part in the Games; and "owlets," which are baby owls. And a variation of the name is formed from the first letters of their names—*S*ukki, *No*kki, *L*ekki and *Ts*ukki.

Images of the Snowlets appeared on toys, pins, dolls, and many other items. But the most popular souvenirs of the Games were stuffed Snowlets.

relay and the men's 1,000-meter. The women's relay team set a world record. China tied South Korea with a total of 6 medals, but none of them were gold. Canada's impressive showing included 4 medals, including golds by Annie Perreault in the women's 500-meter and by the men's 5,000-meter relay team. Host country Japan picked up 2 medals, including a gold in the men's 500.

Skiing. The U.S. alpine skiing team didn't do as well as it had in the 1994 Winter Games, when American skiers won 4 medals, 2 of them gold. But great excitement was generated by Picabo Street's daring and surprising super giant slalom run, which she won by 1/100 of a second. Other female stars were Germany's Katja Seizinger, who won the women's combined and downhill and also took a bronze in the giant slalom; Italy's Deborah Compagnoni, the giant slalom gold medalist; and Germany's Hilde Gerg, winner of the slalom.

Austrian Hermann Maier starred among the men. Just three days after crashing on the slopes, he took the gold medal in the super giant slalom, and three days after that, the giant slalom. Other gold medalists were Mario Reiter of Austria (men's combined), Jean-Luc Cretier of France (men's downhill), and Hans-Petter Buraas of Norway (men's slalom). Cross-country skiing is probably Norway's most popular sport, and in 1998 the Norwegian men proved it. They won 4 of the 5 gold medals—in the 10-, 15-, and 50-kilometer events and the 40-kilometer relay. Bjorn Dahlie won gold medals in the 10- and 50-kilometers events, as well as the 40-kilometer relay, boosting his total number of Olympic medals to 12, a new Winter Olympics record. His 8 gold

In alpine skiing, Picabo Street of the United States (*left*) captured the gold in the super giant slalom by only 1/100 of a second. In cross-country skiing, Norway's Bjorn Dahlie (*below*) took home 3 gold medals—and a new Winter Olympics record.

medals also set a record. And Norway won the individual and team golds in the Nordic combined, a sport that combines cross-country skiing and ski jumping.

In the biathlon, which combines cross-country skiing and target shooting, the women's gold medals were won by Russia in the women's 7.5-kilometer, Bulgaria in the 15-kilometer, and Germany in the 30-kilometer relay. The men's gold medals went to Norway in the 10- and 20-kilometer and Germany in the 30-kilometer relay.

In ski jumping, Jani Soininen of Finland won the gold medal in the 90-meter event, but the big story at Nagano involved the Japanese jumpers, who won 4 of the 9 medals. Outstanding was Kazuyoshi Funaki, who took the silver medal in the 90-meter, the gold in the 120-meter, and a share of the gold in the 120-meter team event. In the team event, Takanobu Okabe and Masahiko Harada thrilled the spectators with the longest ski jumps—137 meters—in Olympic history.

Freestyle skiing was where U.S. skiers finally made their mark, winning 3 of the 4 events. Gold medals went to Nikki Stone in women's aerials, Eric Bergoust in men's aerials, and Jonny Moseley in men's moguls. Tae Satoya of Japan was victorious in the women's moguls.

Ice Hockey Firsts. There were two important "firsts" in the Olympic ice hockey competitions: Professionals from the National Hockey League (NHL) played for the first time, competing for their native countries; and women competed for the first time.

To everyone's surprise, the United States men's team was knocked out of medal contention in the quarterfinals. Another surprise was the Czech Republic's upset of the favored Canadian team, 2–1, in the semifinals. The outcome of this game was decided by a sudden-death shoot-out, in which each team took one shot each until a goal was scored. In the other semifinal, Russia defeated Finland 7–4. In the gold-medal game between Russia and the Czech Republic, the Czechs scored a 1–0 victory on a 50-foot slapshot by Petr Svoboda in the third period. The Russian team was awarded the silver medal, and the bronze went to Finland after its 3–2 defeat of Canada.

Women's ice hockey isn't a competitive sport in most of the world, so there were only six teams competing in the sport's Olympic debut. Two of them—the American and Canadian teams—dominated from the beginning. When they met in a first-round match, Canada surged to a 4–1 lead, but the Americans scored six goals in 13 minutes to win 7–4. There was

Women competed in Olympic ice hockey for the first time at the Nagano Games. After an intense tournament, the American team defeated Canada 3–1 to win the gold medal.

Two New Events: Snowboarding and Curling

Of the three new events at the 1998 Winter Olympics, two of them—snowboarding and curling—couldn't be more different. Snowboarding involves high-speed, downhill racing and aerobatic, body-contorting maneuvers on a single wide ski that's ridden like a surfboard. Curling, on the other hand, is a slow-paced game that involves sliding large stones across the ice toward a bull's-eye-like target. Critics call curling "shuffleboard on ice," but its popularity has spread from Canada to many other countries.

Snowboarding. Snowboarding began more than 30 years ago, when surfers and skateboarders decided to try their skills on California's snowy mountain slopes. Today, it's a fast-growing winter sport. There were two Olympic snowboarding competitions: the giant slalom and the freestyle half-pipe. In the giant slalom, snowboarders threaded their way through gates at breakneck speed as they made their way down the 3,100-foot run. In the freestyle half-pipe, snowboarders did various flips and rotations while racing down a course shaped like a pipe cut lengthwise. Ross Rebagliati of Canada (left) won the gold medal in the men's giant slalom, and Gian Simmen of Switzerland won the men's half-pipe. In women's events, Karine Ruby of France won the giant slalom, and Nicola Thost of Germany won the half-pipe. American snowboarders had to settle for two bronzes—Shannon Dunn in the women's half-pipe, and Ross Powers in the men's half-pipe.

Curling. The only equipment used in curling are 44-pound stones—with handles on top—and brooms. There are two four-person teams. Players slide the stones across the ice to a marked target area, or "house." As the stone heads toward the house, two of the player's teammates use brooms to sweep the ice in front of the stone. This creates a thin film of water on the ice, which makes the stone slide easier and go farther. The team that gets the most stones closest to the center of the house wins the game. In women's curling, Canada won the gold medal (below), Denmark the silver, and Sweden the bronze. In men's curling, Switzerland won the gold, and the Canadians had to settle for the silver. Norway won the bronze.

Canada and Italy shared a gold medal in the two-man bobsled event after finishing with identical times.

less scoring and more tension in the gold-medal game. The Americans scored once in the second period and again in the third before Canada scored with just minutes left to make it 2–1. As the tension mounted in the last minute of play, the Canadians pulled their goalie and put in an offensive player in an effort to tie the score. But with the Canadian goal unattended, American Sandra Whyte scored an easy empty-net goal within seconds of the final buzzer, giving the U.S. squad a 3–1 victory and the gold medal. Goalie Sarah Tueting distinguished herself with 21 saves in the game. Canada was awarded the silver medal, and Finland the bronze.

FINAL MEDAL STANDINGS

Country	Gold	Silver	Bronze	Total
Germany	12	9	8	29
Norway	10	10	5	25
Russia	9	6	3	18
Austria	3	5	9	17
Canada	6	5	4	15
United States	6	3	4	13
Finland	2	4	6	12
Netherlands	5	4	2	11
Japan	5	1	4	10
Italy	2	6	2	10
France	2	1	5	8
China	0	6	2	8
Switzerland	2	2	3	7
South Korea	3	1	2	6
Czech Republic	1	1	1	3
Sweden	0	2	1	3
Belarus	0	0	2	2
Kazakhstan	0	0	2	2
Bulgaria	1	0	0	1
Denmark	0	1	0	1
Ukraine	0	1	0	1
Australia	0	0	1	1
Belgium	0	0	1	1
Britain	0	0	1	1

Shooting the Chute. Bobsledding and luge are two of the fastest, most dangerous winter sports. On their special sleds, bobsledders and lugers race down ice-covered chutes at breakneck speed—90 miles per hour for bobsledders, and more than 75 miles per hour for lugers. At Nagano, the Canadian team tied with Italy for the gold medal in the two-man bobsled competition. This was the first time ever in the Olympics that two teams shared the gold in this sport. Germany took the gold in the four-man competition. Germany also won all 3 gold medals in luge—men's singles, women's singles, and men's doubles. The U.S. teams took the silver and bronze medals in men's doubles. One luger didn't win any medals, but he won everyone's heart. Sixteen-year-old Shiva Keshavan, the only athlete to represent India at Nagano, didn't even know what a luge was until a year before the Olympics.

Onward to the Next Century. As the 1998 Games ended, and the athletes made their way home, everyone looked forward to more great competitions—at the 2000 Summer Olympics in Sydney, Australia, and the 2002 Winter Olympics at Salt Lake City, Utah.

GOLD MEDAL WINNERS

BIATHLON
Men
10–km: Ole Bjorndalen, Norway
20–km: Halvard Hanevold, Norway
30–km Relay: Germany
Women
7.5–km: Galina Kukleva, Russia
15–km: Yekaterina Dafovska, Bulgaria
30–km Relay: Germany

BOBSLEDDING
Two-Man: Canada, Italy (tied)
Four-Man: Germany

CURLING
Men: Switzerland
Women: Canada

FIGURE SKATING
Men's Singles: Ilya Kulik, Russia
Women's Singles: Tara Lipinski, United States
Pairs: Oksana Kazakova/Artur Dmitriev, Russia
Dance: Pasha Grishuk/Yevgeny Platov, Russia

ICE HOCKEY
Men: Czech Republic
Women: United States

LUGE
Men's Singles: Georg Hackl, Germany
Women's Singles: Silke Kraushaar, Germany
Men's Doubles: Germany

SKIING, ALPINE
Men
Downhill: Jean-Luc Cretier, France
Slalom: Hans-Petter Buraas, Norway
Giant Slalom: Hermann Maier, Austria
Combined: Mario Reiter, Austria
Super G: Hermann Maier, Austria
Women
Downhill: Katja Seizinger, Germany
Slalom: Hilde Gerg, Germany
Giant Slalom: Deborah Compagnoni, Italy
Combined: Katja Seizinger, Germany
Super G: Picabo Street, United States

SKIING, FREESTYLE
Men's Aerials: Eric Bergoust, United States
Women's Aerials: Nikki Stone, United States
Men's Moguls: Jonny Moseley, United States
Women's Moguls: Tae Satoya, Japan

SKIING, NORDIC
Men
10–km Cross-Country: Bjorn Dahlie, Norway
15–km Cross-Country: Thomas Alsgaard, Norway
30–km Cross-Country: Mika Myllylae, Finland
50–km Cross-Country: Bjorn Dahlie, Norway
40–km Cross-Country Relay: Norway
Normal Hill (90–m Jump): Jani Soininen, Finland
Large Hill (120–m Jump): Kazuyoshi Funaki, Japan
Team Jump: Japan
Combined: Bjarte Engen Vik, Norway
Team Combined: Norway
Women
5–km Cross-Country: Larissa Lazutina, Russia
10–km Cross-Country: Larissa Lazutina, Russia
15–km Cross-Country: Olga Danilova, Russia
30–km Cross-Country: Yuliya Tchepalova, Russia
20–km Cross-Country Relay: Russia

SNOWBOARDING
Men
Half-pipe: Gian Simmen, Switzerland
Giant Slalom: Ross Rebagliati, Canada
Women
Half-pipe: Nicola Thost, Germany
Giant Slalom: Karine Ruby, France

SPEED SKATING, LONG TRACK
Men
500–m: Hiroyasu Shimizu, Japan
1,000–m: Ids Postma, Netherlands
1,500–m: Adne Sondral, Norway
5,000–m: Gianni Romme, Netherlands
10,000–m: Gianni Romme, Netherlands
Women
500–m: Catriona LeMay Doan, Canada
1,000–m: Marianne Timmer, Netherlands
1,500–m: Marianne Timmer, Netherlands
3,000–m: Gunda Niemann-Stirnemann, Germany
5,000–m: Claudia Pechstein, Germany

SPEED SKATING, SHORT TRACK
Men
500–m: Takafumi Nishitani, Japan
1,000–m: Kim Dong Sung, South Korea
5,000–m Relay: Canada
Women
500–m: Annie Perreault, Canada
1,000–m: Chun Lee Kyung, South Korea
3,000–m Relay: South Korea

The New York Yankees celebrate their four-game sweep of the San Diego Padres in the 1998 World Series.

BASEBALL

Baseball fans will long remember 1998. Both Mark McGwire and Sammy Sosa broke the single-season home-run record. And the New York Yankees set a new American League mark with 114 victories in the regular season. They then soared through the playoffs, ultimately winning the World Series by sweeping the San Diego Padres in four games.

Manager Joe Torre's New Yorkers so dominated the American League (AL) that they were compared with the legendary 1927 Yankees of Babe Ruth and Lou Gehrig. The 1998 Yanks topped the AL Eastern Division by 22 games, finishing ahead of the Boston Red Sox, who qualified for the playoffs with the second-best record in the league. The Cleveland Indians led the Central Division, and the Texas Rangers were first in the Western Division.

In the division series (the first round of the playoffs), New York swept Texas in three games, while Cleveland dumped Boston, 3 games to 1. The Yankees then ousted the Indians, 4 games to 2, in the American League Championship Series (ALCS). New York lefty pitcher David Wells won twice and was named Most Valuable Player (MVP) of the ALCS.

San Diego finished atop the Western Division of the National League (NL). The Atlanta Braves won the East, and the Houston Astros took the Central title, while the Chicago Cubs captured the wild-card slot.

In the division series, the Padres eliminated the Astros, 3 games to 1, and the Braves swept the Cubs in 3 games. In the National League Championship Series (NLCS), San Diego upset Atlanta, 4 games to 2. Sterling Hitchcock pitched the Padres to two victories and was named MVP of the NLCS.

Game 1 of the World Series, played at Yankee Stadium in New York City, turned into a home-run derby. San Diego's Greg Vaughn launched a two-run shot in the third inning; and in the Padres' fifth, Tony Gwynn and Vaughn crashed back-to-back roundtrippers. Losing 5–2 entering the seventh inning, the Yankees came out slugging: Chuck Knoblauch cracked a three-run homer, and Tino Martinez clubbed a grand slammer. New York won 9–6, and led the Series 1 game to 0.

In Game 2, the Yanks tallied three runs in the first inning and three in the second, two of which came on a four-bagger by Bernie Williams. Meanwhile, pitcher Orlando Hernandez handcuffed the Padres, striking out seven and allowing only one run in seven innings before being relieved. His batterymate Jorge Posada contributed a two-run homer. The final score was 9–3, New York. The Padres were down two games, and the Series moved to San Diego's Qualcomm Stadium.

But the NL champs would have no better luck at home. The Padres took a 3–0 lead into the seventh inning of Game 3, but Yankee third baseman Scott Brosius cracked a solo homer, and New York got another run in the same

1998 WORLD SERIES RESULTS

		R	H	E	Winning/Losing Pitcher
1	San Diego	6	8	1	Donne Wall (L)
	New York	9	9	1	David Wells (W)
2	San Diego	3	10	1	Andy Ashby (L)
	New York	9	16	0	Orlando Hernandez (W)
3	New York	5	9	1	Ramiro Mendoza (W)
	San Diego	4	7	1	Trevor Hoffman (L)
4	New York	3	9	0	Andy Pettitte (W)
	San Diego	0	7	0	Kevin Brown (L)

Visiting team listed first, home team second

frame. An inning later, Brosius unloaded his second roundtripper, this time with two men on. New York went on to win, 5–4. The Yanks were up, 3 games to 0.

Game 4 was scoreless until the top of the sixth inning, when the Yanks' Derek Jeter singled, went to third base on a double by Paul O'Neill, and came home on an infield out by Bernie Williams. In the eighth, Brosius drove home New York's second run with a bases-loaded single; a sacrifice fly by Ricky Ledee completed the scoring. Southpaw hurler Andy Pettitte, meanwhile, shut out the Padres through 7⅓ innings; relievers Jeff Nelson and Mariano Rivera closed down San Diego the rest of the way. Final score: 3–0. The New York Yankees had won their second World Series in three years, and the 24th in their fabled history.

Brosius was named the Series' MVP. He batted .471, hit safely in all four games, slugged two home runs, and had six runs batted in (RBIs).

Sosa was named the NL regular-season MVP; in addition to his 66 homers, he recorded 158 RBIs and a .308 batting average. The AL MVP was Juan Gonzalez of Texas; he had 45 homers and 157 RBIs, and batted .318.

Pitcher Roger Clemens of the Toronto Blue Jays won his unprecedented fifth Cy Young Award; he tied for the AL lead in victories (20) and led in earned run average (ERA) (2.65) and strikeouts (271). The NL Cy Young Award went to Atlanta's Tom Glavine, who won 20 games and recorded a 2.47 ERA.

Cub hurler Kerry Wood was the NL Rookie-of-the-Year; he struck out 233 batters, including a record 20 in one game, while compiling a 13–6 won-lost mark. Named the AL's top rookie was Ben Grieve of the Oakland A's; he batted .288 with 18 homers and 89 RBIs.

A YEAR TO REMEMBER

A home-run record, a games-played record, a perfect game—the 1998 season had it all.

- The single-season home-run record of 61, set by Yankee Roger Maris in 1961, was shattered in 1998: St. Louis Cardinal first baseman Mark McGwire blasted 70, and Chicago Cub rightfielder Sammy Sosa bopped 66.
- Baltimore Oriole infielder Cal Ripken voluntarily ended his record streak of games played. From May 1982 to September 1998, he played in 2,632 consecutive games.
- Yankee David Wells pitched a perfect game against the Minnesota Twins on May 17 in Yankee Stadium, facing the minimum 27 batters and retiring every one.

Jubilant Yankee pitcher David Wells is carried triumphantly off the field after pitching a perfect game.

Michael Jordan (#23) led the Chicago Bulls to another NBA title in 1998. He won the Most Valuable Player award for both the regular season and the playoffs.

BASKETBALL

In 1998, the Chicago Bulls repeated as National Basketball Association (NBA) champions for the third year in a row. Led once again by guard Michael Jordan, Chicago defeated the Utah Jazz in six games in the playoff finals, duplicating exactly the finals results of the year before. Considered the outstanding team of the 1990s, the Bulls won their sixth NBA title in eight years.

Chicago's lineup also included forward Scottie Pippen, like Jordan one of the league's all-time greatest players; forward Toni Kukoc, a fine shooter and ball-handler; top rebounding forward Dennis Rodman; center Luc Longley; defensive specialist Ron Harper, a guard; and sharpshooter Steve Kerr, another guard.

Under coach Phil Jackson, the Bulls finished the regular season in first place in the Central Division of the NBA's Eastern Conference. The other Central Division teams reaching the playoffs were the Indiana Pacers, the Charlotte Hornets, the Atlanta Hawks, and the Cleveland Cavaliers. Qualifying for post-season competition from the Atlantic Division of the Eastern Conference were the Miami Heat, the New York Knickerbockers, and the New Jersey Nets.

The first round of the playoffs is a best-of-five series, and the Bulls wasted no time, sweeping New Jersey in three games. All subsequent series are best-of-seven. Chicago eliminated Charlotte in round two, four games to one. In the Eastern Conference finals, Chicago needed all seven games to defeat Indiana.

In the Western Conference, the Utah Jazz finished the regular season atop the Midwest Division. Also making the playoffs were the San Antonio Spurs, the Minnesota Timberwolves, and the Houston Rockets. Meanwhile, the Seattle SuperSonics took first in the Pacific Division, and they were joined in the playoffs by the Los Angeles Lakers, the Phoenix Suns, and the Portland Trail Blazers.

Utah's veteran team was sparked once again by power forward Karl Malone and point guard John Stockton, the NBA's all-time leader in assists. In the first round of the playoffs, the Jazz outlasted Houston, three games to two. Utah ousted San Antonio in five games in round two, and then swept the Lakers in four games, in the Conference finals.

Game 1 of the NBA finals, played at the Delta Center in Salt Lake City, Utah, resulted in a Jazz victory in overtime. It was a battle. Malone's shots were off the mark until the fourth quarter; he finally got going, finishing with 21 points and 14 rebounds. Stockton totaled 24, including 7 in the overtime period, and added 8 assists. Final score: 88–85.

NBA FINAL STANDINGS

EASTERN CONFERENCE

Atlantic Division

	W	L	Pct.
Miami	55	27	.671
New Jersey	43	39	.524
New York	43	39	.524
Washington	42	40	.512
Orlando	41	41	.500
Boston	36	46	.439
Philadelphia	31	51	.378

Central Division

	W	L	Pct.
Chicago	62	20	.756
Indiana	58	24	.707
Charlotte	51	31	.622
Atlanta	50	32	.610
Cleveland	47	35	.573
Detroit	37	45	.451
Milwaukee	36	46	.439
Toronto	16	66	.195

WESTERN CONFERENCE

Midwest Division

	W	L	Pct.
Utah	62	20	.756
San Antonio	56	26	.683
Minnesota	45	37	.549
Houston	41	41	.500
Dallas	20	62	.244
Vancouver	19	63	.232
Denver	11	71	.134

Pacific Division

	W	L	Pct.
Seattle	61	21	.744
L.A. Lakers	61	21	.744
Phoenix	56	26	.683
Portland	46	36	.561
Sacramento	27	55	.329
Golden State	19	63	.232
L.A. Clippers	17	65	.207

NBA Championship: Chicago Bulls

COLLEGE BASKETBALL

Conference	Winner
Atlantic Coast	Duke (regular season) North Carolina (tournament)
Atlantic Ten	Temple; Dayton, George Washington, Xavier, (tied, regular season) Xavier (tournament)
Big East	Connecticut; Syracuse (regular season) Connecticut (tournament)
Big Ten	Michigan State, Illinois (tied, regular season) Michigan (tournament)
Big Twelve	Kansas (regular season and tournament)
Big West	Utah State; Pacific (regular season) Utah State (tournament)
Ivy League	Princeton
Missouri Valley	Illinois State (regular season and tournament)
Pacific-10	Arizona
Southeastern	Kentucky; Mississippi (regular season) Kentucky (tournament)
Southwestern Athletic	Texas Southern (regular season) Prairie View A&M (tournament)
Western Athletic	Utah; Texas Christian (regular season) UNLV (tournament)

NCAA, men: Kentucky
women: Tennessee

NIT: Minnesota

In Game 2, also at the Delta Center, both Chicago's Jordan and Utah's Malone missed numerous shots. Malone went without a field goal for the whole second half; credit Dennis Rodman's defense for Malone's frustration. Jordan did score 37 points, and Pippen netted 21, as the Bulls won, 93–88. Jeff Hornacek tallied 20 for the Jazz.

Games 3, 4, and 5 were contested at the United Center in Chicago. And Game 3 was a blowout: Powered by their defense, the Bulls won, 96–54. Utah's total of 54 represented the fewest points scored in any NBA game—regular season or playoff—since the 24-second shot clock was introduced in 1954. The 42-point margin of victory was the largest in the history of the NBA playoff finals, and Utah set another record for futility by amassing only 23 points in the second half. Jordan had 24 for Chicago, and Kukoc contributed 16.

The Bulls took a lead of three games to one by winning Game 4, 86–82. The Jazz played much better than they did in their embarrassing defeat in game 3. Chicago's Rodman again tied up Utah's Malone, holding him to only 2 points in the final period. And Pippen and Harper combined to limit Stockton to a total of 7 points, although the Utah point guard dished off 13 assists. Jordan scored 34 points.

Cynthia Cooper (with ball) powered the Houston Comets to their second straight WNBA championship. She was MVP of the regular season and the playoffs.

Utah hung on to eke out one more victory in Game 5, as Antoine Carr, a 13-year NBA veteran, came off the bench to notch 12 points, including 8 in the crucial fourth quarter. Malone poured in 39, and Kukoc had 30 for Chicago. The final tally was 83–81.

In Game 6, Michael Jordan once again showed why he's basketball's reigning superstar—and maybe the greatest of all time. As he had countless times before, he came through with the game on the line in the final minute. The Jazz took an 86–83 lead with 42 seconds left. Jordan quickly scored to bring the Bulls within a point; a few ticks of the clock later, he stole the ball from Malone, raced downcourt, and sank a 20-foot jump shot with 5.2 seconds remaining. The final score was Chicago, 87–86. Jordan scored 45 points, and the Bulls had the NBA title. Only Jordan, Pippen, and coach Jackson have been members of all six Chicago championship teams (1991–93, 1996–98).

Michael Jordan was named Most Valuable Player (MVP) of the playoffs for the third straight year. He averaged 32.4 points per game in post-season play. For the regular season, Jordan led the NBA in scoring for the tenth time, averaging 28.7 points per game, and he won his fifth regular-season MVP award. Dennis Rodman topped the league in rebounds for the seventh time in a row, averaging 15.0 per game. Rookie of the Year was forward Tim Duncan of San Antonio, who averaged 21.1 points and 11.9 rebounds.

Women's Pro Leagues. The American Basketball League (ABL) finished its second season in 1998, and the defending champion Columbus Quest captured its second ABL crown, downing the Long Beach StingRays, three games to two, in the playoff finals. Valerie Still was the MVP of the final series.

The Women's National Basketball Association (WNBA) also had its second year of competition in 1998, and the Houston Comets successfully defended its league title. The Comets defeated the Phoenix Mercury, two games to one, in the final series. Cynthia Cooper of the Comets was the MVP of the playoffs; she was also named regular-season MVP for the second straight year.

College Play. The Lady Volunteers of the University of Tennessee set a record by winning the National Collegiate Athletic Association (NCAA) women's basketball championship for the third straight year. Coach Pat Summitt guided the team to an unbeaten season (39–0). In the final game of the NCAA tournament, Tennessee stomped Louisiana Tech, 93–75. Junior Chamique Holdsclaw scored 25 points and was named the tourney's outstanding player.

On the men's side, the University of Kentucky won its second NCAA title in three years, defeating Utah in the final by 78–69. Kentucky guard Jeff Sheppard was the tournament MVP; he sparked the Wildcats with 16 points in the final. Coach Orlando (Tubby) Smith was in his first year on the sidelines for Kentucky.

FOOTBALL

Prior to 1998, the Denver Broncos had never won a Super Bowl. But in 1998, on their fifth attempt at the grand prize, the Broncos captured the championship of the National Football League (NFL). In the Canadian Football League, the Calgary Stampeders won the Grey Cup. At the end of the regular season in college football, the University of Tennessee was ranked number one; and a record-breaking running back ran away with the Heisman Trophy.

The Minnesota Vikings, quarterbacked by Randall Cunningham, had the best regular-season record in the NFL in 1998, winning 15 games and losing only 1.

THE NFL PLAYOFFS AND SUPER BOWL XXXII

Playing in the Western Division of the American Conference of the National Football League (NFL), the Broncos took the long way to the Super Bowl: Denver reached the 1997–98 playoffs as a wild-card team. The division leaders in the conference were the Pittsburgh Steelers, the New England Patriots, and the Kansas City Chiefs; the other wild-card berths went to the Jacksonville Jaguars and the Miami Dolphins.

In the first round of the playoffs, Denver swamped Jacksonville, 42–17, while New England chilled Miami, 17–3. The Broncos had a tougher time the following week, but outlasted the Chiefs, 14–10. And the Steelers nipped the Patriots, 7–6.

Denver also had a hard fight in the American Conference title game, played in Pittsburgh. Quarterback John Elway threw two touchdown passes in the final two minutes of the first half to put the Broncos ahead, 24–14, and Denver held on to win 24–21. Bronco running back Terrell Davis contributed 138 yards on 26 carries. Denver thus became the first wild-card team to reach the Super Bowl since 1992.

The Green Bay Packers, the New York Giants, and the San Francisco 49ers finished first in their divisions in the National Conference in 1997; the wild-card teams were the Minnesota Vikings, the Detroit Lions, and the Tampa Bay Buccaneers.

Tampa Bay eliminated Detroit, 20–10, in the first round of the playoffs, while Minnesota edged New York, 23–22. In round two, though, both of the previous week's winners lost: The 49ers victimized the Vikings, 38–22, and the Packers scuttled the Buccaneers, 21–7.

A week later, the Packers shocked the 49ers in the National Conference title game, handing San Francisco its first loss at home all season. The final score was 23–10.

Super Bowl XXXII was played in San Diego, California, on January 25, 1998. Green Bay, the defending NFL champion, was heavily favored. And National Conference titlists had won 13 consecutive Super Bowls, a streak that began in 1985. But Denver quarterback Elway wasn't about to lose, especially not with Terrell Davis at his side.

Even so, the Packers scored first, and led 7–0 barely more than four minutes into the game. But just over five minutes later, Denver tied the score on a one-yard touchdown run by Davis. In the second period, Elway also ran the ball in from the one-yard line, and Bronco placekicker Jason Elam booted a 51-yard field goal. At halftime, the Broncos led, 17–14.

The Packers tied the score early in the second half, but Denver regained the lead, 24–17, as Davis ran for another one-yard touchdown in the last minute of the third period. The Pack recovered quickly, though, tying the game, 24–24, just 88 seconds into the fourth quarter. And the teams wrestled up and down the field, neither side scoring until the last two minutes of the game. Finally, with 1:45 remaining on the clock, it was Terrell Davis time again. His third touchdown of the game, yet again from the one-yard line, ended the day's scoring. The final tally was 31–24. And Denver finally won its first Super Bowl.

Davis's three rushing touchdowns were a Super Bowl record; he gained 157 yards on 30 carries, and was named Most Valuable Player (MVP) of Super Bowl XXXII.

THE 1998 REGULAR SEASON

Denver finished first in its division in 1998, losing only twice in the regular season. Terrell Davis had a spectacular year, rushing for 2,008 yards. The other American Conference division titlists were Jacksonville and the New York Jets; the wild-card teams were New England, Miami, and the Buffalo Bills.

Minnesota, the Dallas Cowboys, and the Atlanta Falcons topped their divisions in the National Conference; wild-card berths went to San Francisco, Green Bay, and the Arizona Cardinals.

THE CANADIAN FOOTBALL LEAGUE

The Calgary Stampeders won the CFL championship, besting the Hamilton Tiger-Cats, 26–24, in a thrilling Grey Cup game, played in Winnipeg, Manitoba, on November 22, 1998. Calgary's winning score came on a 35-yard field goal by placekicker Mark McLoughlin in the last second of the contest. Named the game's MVP was Stampeder quarterback Jeff Garcia, who completed 22 passes in 32 attempts for 260 yards. Calgary has appeared in four Grey Cup games since 1991, winning two; during the 1998 regular season, the "Stamps" finished first in the CFL Western Division with a 12–6 record.

COLLEGE FOOTBALL

Tennessee, rated number one in college football at the end of the regular season with a 12–0 record, topped second-ranked Florida State (11–1) in the Fiesta Bowl. Number-three Ohio State (10–1) beat Texas A&M (11–2) in the Sugar Bowl; Wisconsin (10–1) dropped UCLA (10–1) in the Rose Bowl; Texas (8–3) trounced Mississippi State (8–4) in the Cotton Bowl; Florida (8–3) whipped Syracuse (9–2) in the Orange Bowl; and Purdue (11–1) outlasted Kansas State (8–4) in the Alamo Bowl.

University of Texas running back Ricky Williams overwhelmed his rivals in the voting for the Heisman Trophy; the Longhorn senior set a slew of Division I rushing records, including 6,279 career yards.

Quarterback John Elway had another superb year in 1998, leading the Denver Broncos to a 14–2 regular-season record.

University of Texas running back Ricky Williams won the 1998 Heisman Trophy as the best college player.

COLLEGE FOOTBALL

Conference	Winner
Atlantic Coast	Florida State, Georgia Tech (tied)
Big Ten	Michigan, Ohio, Wisconsin (tied)
Big Twelve	Texas A&M; Kansas State
Big West	Idaho
Pacific-10	UCLA
Southeastern	Tennessee; Arkansas
Western Athletic	Air Force; San Diego State

Alamo Bowl: Purdue 37, Kansas State 34
Citrus Bowl: Michigan 45, Arkansas 31
Cotton Bowl: Texas 38, Mississippi State 11
Fiesta Bowl: Tennessee 23, Florida State 16
Orange Bowl: Florida 31, Syracuse 10
Rose Bowl: Wisconsin 38, UCLA 31
Sugar Bowl: Ohio State 24, Texas A&M 14

Heisman Trophy: Ricky Williams, Texas

1998 NFL FINAL STANDINGS

AMERICAN CONFERENCE

Eastern Division

	W	L	T	Pct.	PF	PA
N.Y. Jets	12	4	0	.750	416	266
Miami	10	6	0	.625	321	265
Buffalo	10	6	0	.625	400	333
New England	9	7	0	.563	337	329
Indianapolis	3	13	0	.188	310	444

Central Division

	W	L	T	Pct.	PF	PA
Jacksonville	11	5	0	.688	392	338
Tennessee	8	8	0	.500	330	320
Pittsburgh	7	9	0	.438	263	303
Baltimore	6	10	0	.375	269	335
Cincinnati	3	13	0	.188	268	452

Western Division

	W	L	T	Pct.	PF	PA
Denver	14	2	0	.875	501	309
Oakland	8	8	0	.500	288	356
Seattle	8	8	0	.500	372	310
Kansas City	7	9	0	.438	327	363
San Diego	5	11	0	.313	241	342

NATIONAL CONFERENCE

Eastern Division

	W	L	T	Pct.	PF	PA
Dallas	10	6	0	.625	381	275
Arizona	9	7	0	.563	325	378
N.Y. Giants	8	8	0	.500	287	309
Washington	6	10	0	.375	319	421
Philadelphia	3	13	0	.188	161	344

Central Division

	W	L	T	Pct.	PF	PA
Minnesota	15	1	0	.938	556	296
Green Bay	11	5	0	.688	408	319
Tampa Bay	8	8	0	.500	314	295
Detroit	5	11	0	.313	306	378
Chicago	4	12	0	.250	276	368

Western Division

	W	L	T	Pct.	PF	PA
Atlanta	14	2	0	.875	442	289
San Francisco	12	4	0	.750	479	328
New Orleans	6	10	0	.375	305	359
Carolina	4	12	0	.250	336	413
St. Louis	4	12	0	.250	285	378

GOLF

PROFESSIONAL	
	Individual
Masters	Mark O'Meara
U.S. Open	Lee Janzen
Canadian Open	Billy Andrade
British Open	Mark O'Meara
PGA	Vijay Singh
World Series of Golf	David Duval
U.S. Women's Open	Se Ri Pak
Ladies PGA	Se Ri Pak

AMATEUR	
	Individual
U.S. Amateur	Hank Kuehne
U.S. Women's Amateur	Grace Park
British Amateur	Sergio Garcia
British Ladies Amateur	Kin Rostron
Canadian Amateur	Craig Matthew
Canadian Ladies Amateur	Kareen Qually
	Team
Curtis Cup	United States

Pak Leads the Pack

In 1998, Se Ri Pak (suh-REE Pak) swung and putted her way to the top in women's golf. In her rookie year, the shy 20-year-old South Korean won four tournaments, two of them majors—the Ladies PGA and the U.S. Women's Open. A golfer since the age of 14, Pak had won 30 amateur and six of her fourteen professional tournaments in South Korea. After moving to Orlando, Florida, she began touring with the Ladies Professional Golf Association (LPGA) in January 1998. The rest is history. Her popularity in the United States was exceeded only by the "Pakmania" in her homeland, where millions of South Koreans stayed up all night to watch her in action on television.

Detroit Red Wing captain Steve Yzerman (*foreground*) led his teammates to the National Hockey League championship in 1998. The Red Wings defeated the Washington Capitals in the Stanley Cup finals.

HOCKEY

The Detroit Red Wings repeated as champions of the National Hockey League (NHL) in 1998, winning their second consecutive Stanley Cup. In doing so, they accomplished still another rare "double": Just as they had done in 1997, they swept their opponents in the playoff finals in four games. Only four other teams in NHL history had achieved two straight sweeps in the Cup finals. Detroit's victims in 1998 were the Washington Capitals.

Detroit coach Scotty Bowman captured his eighth NHL title as a coach. He thus equaled the record of Hector "Toe" Blake, former coach of the Montreal Canadiens.

Between their 1997 and 1998 titles, however, the Red Wings suffered a great loss. Shortly after the 1997 playoffs ended, Detroit's star defenseman Vladimir Konstantinov was severely injured in an automobile accident. Nevertheless, the Red Wings played well in the 1997–98 regular season. They finished second in the Central Division, with a record of 44 victories, 23 losses, and 15 ties, for 103 points.

Washington was third in the Atlantic Division (92 points), behind the New Jersey Devils (107 points) and the Philadelphia Flyers (95 points). Leading the Central Division were the Dallas Stars (109 points, best in the NHL). The Pittsburgh Penguins finished atop the Northeast Division (98 points), and the Colorado Avalanche totaled 95 points to lead the Pacific Division.

In the first round of the playoffs, Detroit eliminated the Phoenix Coyotes, four games to two. They then ousted the St. Louis Blues, also in six games. In the Western Conference finals, the Red Wings needed yet another six games to defeat Dallas.

The Capitals advanced through the playoffs by beating the Boston Bruins, four games to two, in round one, and the Ottawa Senators, four games to one, in round two. Washington then won the Eastern Conference finals by dispatching the Buffalo Sabres in six games. The Capitals, coached by Ron Wilson, thus earned a trip to the Stanley Cup finals for the first time in the team's history.

Buffalo Sabre goalie Dominik Hasek was the MVP of the NHL for the second consecutive year.

The "Caps" had some top players, such as Peter Bondra, who had tied for the NHL lead in goals scored, with 52, during the regular season, and goalie Olaf Kolzig. And in outdueling the Sabres in the Eastern Conference finals, Washington was able to defeat Buffalo goalie Dominik Hasek, who was perhaps the top goaltender in the world. Nevertheless, hockey experts gave the Capitals little hope of beating Detroit, and the experts were proven right.

Even without the injured Konstantinov, the Red Wings still had the superb defense that had taken them to the 1997 Stanley Cup. But a different goalie, Chris Osgood, was now in the Detroit nets. On offense, the Wings boasted a bevy of fine scorers, among them Steve Yzerman, the team's captain since 1986.

Games 1 and 2 of the Stanley Cup finals were contested on the Red Wings' home ice, at the Joe Louis Arena in Detroit. Playing tentatively, the teams got off to a sluggish start in Game 1. But with just under six minutes remaining in the first period, Red Wing Doug Brown slipped a pass to Joe Kocur, who deftly sent the puck past Washington goalie Kolzig for the game's first score. A little more than two minutes later, Detroit scored again, this time on a shot by Niklas Lidstrom. Washington responded late in the second period with a goal by Richard Zednik, but that was all the scoring this game would see. The final tally was 2–1.

Game 2 was more exciting. Washington twice had a two-goal lead, but Detroit finally won in overtime. The Red Wings were ahead 1–0 after the first period, thanks to a goal by Steve Yzerman. But the Caps countered with scores in the second by Peter Bondra, Chris Simon, and Adam Oates. Yzerman then netted a shorthanded goal to draw Detroit within one early in the third period, but Washington's Joe Juneau gave his team a 4–2 lead shortly thereafter on a power-play goal. The Capitals, however, couldn't hold the lead. Detroit tied the game on scores by Martin Lapointe and Doug Brown, and the contest went into overtime. More than fifteen minutes of extra play elapsed before Kris Draper's goal ended the game in a 5–4 victory for the Red Wings. Washington goalie Kolzig deflected 55 Red Wing shots, while Detroit's Osgood stopped 29 by the Capitals.

NHL FINAL STANDINGS

EASTERN CONFERENCE

Atlantic Division

	W	L	T	Pts.
New Jersey	48	23	11	107
Philadelphia	42	29	11	95
Washington	40	30	12	92
N.Y. Islanders	30	41	11	71
N.Y. Rangers	25	39	18	68
Florida	24	43	15	63
Tampa Bay	17	55	10	44

Northeast Division

	W	L	T	Pts.
Pittsburgh	40	24	18	98
Boston	39	30	13	91
Buffalo	36	29	17	89
Montreal	37	32	13	87
Ottawa	34	33	15	83
Carolina	33	41	8	74

WESTERN CONFERENCE

Central Division

	W	L	T	Pts.
Dallas	49	22	11	109
Detroit	44	23	15	103
St. Louis	45	29	8	98
Phoenix	35	35	12	82
Chicago	30	39	13	73
Toronto	30	43	9	69

Pacific Division

	W	L	T	Pts.
Colorado	39	26	17	95
Los Angeles	38	33	11	87
Edmonton	35	37	10	80
San Jose	34	38	10	78
Calgary	26	41	15	67
Anaheim	26	43	13	65
Vancouver	25	43	14	64

Stanley Cup: Detroit Red Wings

OUTSTANDING PLAYERS

Hart Trophy (most valuable player)	Dominik Hasek, Buffalo
Ross Trophy (scorer)	Jaromir Jagr, Pittsburgh
Vezina Trophy (goalie)	Dominik Hasek, Buffalo
Norris Trophy (defenseman)	Rob Blake, Los Angeles
Selke Trophy (defensive forward)	Jere Lehtinen, Dallas
Calder Trophy (rookie)	Sergei Samsonov, Boston
Lady Byng Trophy (sportsmanship)	Ron Francis, Pittsburgh
Conn Smythe Trophy (Stanley Cup play)	Steve Yzerman, Detroit

Games 3 and 4 were played in MCI Center in Washington, D.C. Detroit won Game 3 by the score of 2–1. The team took a 1–0 lead just 35 seconds after the opening face-off on a goal by Tomas Holmstrom. Brian Bellows evened things at 1–1 for Washington midway through the third period, but Detroit's Sergei Fedorov finished the scoring with slightly under five minutes remaining. The Red Wings were up, three games to none.

Detroit mounted a 2–0 lead in Game 4 on a power-play goal by Doug Brown in period one and a Martin Lapointe score early in period two. Bellows cashed in the Caps' lone goal of the contest in the second period; Detroit's Larry Murphy made the score 3–1 on a power play a few minutes later. Doug Brown notched his second goal of the day in period three, and the game ended with a 4–1 score. Goalie Osgood recorded 30 saves. And the Red Wings were champions again. Captain Steve Yzerman won the Conn Smythe Trophy as the most valuable player (MVP) of the playoffs.

During their victory celebration, the Red Wing players honored Vladimir Konstantinov; he circled the playing rink in a wheelchair while holding the Stanley Cup in his arms.

For the regular season, Buffalo's Dominik Hasek won the Hart Trophy as league MVP and the Vezina Trophy as the top goalie, both for the second year in a row. He led the NHL with 13 shutouts. Hasek also manned the nets on the gold-medal-winning Czech Republic hockey team in the 1998 Winter Olympics.

Pittsburgh's Jaromir Jagr led the NHL in scoring with 102 total points, and tied with the New York Rangers' Wayne Gretzky for the lead in assists, with 67.

College Play. The University of Michigan won the hockey championship of Division I of the National Collegiate Athletic Association (NCAA). In the title game of the NCAA tournament, played in April, the "Wolverines" bested Boston College in overtime by a 3–2 score. Michigan goalie Marty Turco was named the tournament's outstanding player. The winner of the Hobey Baker Memorial Award as the top U.S. college player was senior Chris Drury of Boston University.

Michelle Kwan: Artistry and Grace

For 17-year-old figure-skater Michelle Kwan, 1998 was a great year! In January, she won her second U.S. women's figure-skating championship. In February, she won the silver medal at the Winter Olympics. In April, she triumphed for the second time at the world figure-skating championships. She then went on a 59-city tour with Champions on Ice—and she graduated high school. And in August, she placed first at the Goodwill Games!

Kwan, known for her artistry and grace, "takes your breath away," said one figure-skating coach. That's certainly what she did to the judges at the U.S. championships. Seven out of nine awarded her 6.0s in the short program. And eight out of nine gave her 6.0s in the free-skating program. No other U.S. skater had ever won that many perfect scores. "She floated," said one of the judges.

ICE SKATING

FIGURE SKATING

World Championships

Men	Alexei Yagudin, Russia
Women	Michelle Kwan, U.S.
Pairs	Yelena Berezhnaya/Anton Sikharulidze, Russia
Dance	Anjelika Krylova/Oleg Ovsyannikov, Russia

United States Championships

Men	Todd Eldredge
Women	Michelle Kwan
Pairs	Kyoko Ina/Jason Dungjen
Dance	Elizabeth Punsalan/Jerod Swallow

SPEED SKATING

World Championships

Men	Ids Postma, Netherlands
Women	Gunda Niemann-Stirnemann, Germany

SKIING

WORLD CUP CHAMPIONSHIPS

Men	Hermann Maier, Austria
Women	Katja Seizinger, Germany

U. S. ALPINE CHAMPIONSHIPS

Men

Downhill	Ed Podivinsky, Canada
Slalom	Sacha Gros
Giant Slalom	Bode Miller
Super Giant Slalom	(canceled due to weather problems)
Combined	Dane Spencer

Women

Downhill	Kirsten Clark
Slalom	Kristina Koznick
Giant Slalom	Sarah Schleper
Super Giant Slalom	(canceled due to weather problems)
Combined	Julie Parisien

Marion Jones: A Need for Speed

Move over Michael Jordan. There's another M. J. on the sports scene—22-year-old Marion Jones. Yes, she was a basketball star, too. But that was in college. Now she's the hottest thing in track and field. In 1997, she was named Female Athlete of the year by the International Athletic Foundation. And in 1998, she won 37 consecutive championships in the 100- and 200-meter dashes, the long jump, and relays.

Jones's need for speed began in high school, where she broke the 100- and 200-meter records for high school meets. She switched to basketball in college, and helped the University of North Carolina Tar Heels win the 1994 NCAA title. In 1997, however, Jones was back at the track—and quickly made her mark. In 1998, she became the first woman in 50 years to win the 100-meter, 200-meter, and long jump at the U.S. outdoor championships. And at the Goodwill Games, she set a 10.90-second Games record in the 100-meter.

But Jones isn't through yet. The late Florence Griffith Joyner was one of her idols, and it's FloJo's world records in the 100- and 200-meters that Jones is chasing. "I want to go down in history as the fastest woman who's ever been on Earth," she says.

Australian Patrick Rafter won his second consecutive U.S. Open crown in 1998.

TENNIS

For most of 1998, Martina Hingis and Pete Sampras remained atop the tennis world. But neither was quite so dominant as they had been the previous year, and each won only one Grand Slam tournament. Challenging Hingis for supremacy on the women's side was Lindsay Davenport; among the men, Patrick Rafter had his sights on Sampras.

The 17-year-old Hingis, from Switzerland, captured the first Grand Slam event of the year, the **Australian Open,** played in Melbourne in January and February. She easily defeated Spain's Conchita Martinez in the final, by scores of 6–3, 6–3. Having won the same event in 1997, Hingis thus became the youngest player ever to successfully defend a Grand Slam title.

Petr Korda of the Czech Republic took the men's Australian title. Attacking throughout the final match, he overwhelmed Marcelo Rios of Chile in straight sets, 6–2, 6–2, 6–2. For the 30-year-old Korda, it was his first Grand Slam crown ever.

Both singles titles at the **French Open,** held in Paris in June, went to Spaniards. The men's champion was 21-year-old Carlos Moya. In the final, he outplayed his friend and countryman, Alex Corretja, by scores of 6–3, 7–5, 6–3. Moya celebrated his first title in a Grand Slam event.

The women's champ in Paris was Arantxa Sanchez Vicario. The 26-year-old needed all three sets to beat Monica Seles of the United States in the final, 7–6, 0–6, 6–2. Hustling all over the court, the tireless

TOURNAMENT TENNIS

	Australian Open	French Open	Wimbledon	U.S. Open
Men's Singles	Petr Korda, Czech Republic	Carlos Moya, Spain	Pete Sampras, U.S.	Patrick Rafter, Australia
Women's Singles	Martina Hingis, Switzerland	Arantxa Sanchez Vicario, Spain	Jana Novotna, Czech Republic	Lindsay Davenport, U.S.
Men's Doubles	Jacco Eltingh, Netherlands/ Jonas Bjorkman, Sweden	Jacco Eltingh, Netherlands/ Paul Haarhuis, Netherlands	Jacco Eltingh, Netherlands/ Paul Haarhuis, Netherlands	Sandon Stolle, Australia/ Cyril Suk, Czech Republic
Women's Doubles	Martina Hingis, Switzerland/ Mirjana Lucic, Croatia	Martina Hingis, Switzerland/ Jana Novotna, Czech Republic	Martina Hingis, Switzerland/ Jana Novotna, Czech Republic	Martina Hingis, Switzerland/ Jana Novotna, Czech Republic

Davis Cup Winner: Sweden

Sanchez Vicario just wore Seles down. After the match, the victor paid tribute to Seles, formerly the world's number-one-ranked woman player.

For Sanchez Vicario, the victory was especially sweet. She hadn't won a Grand Slam event in four years. Interestingly, her first-ever Grand Slam title came in this same event in 1989, when she was just 17; she won it again in 1994.

A number of the top women players in 1998 were teenagers, such as Hingis, and Venus Williams of the United States. But the women's final of the All-England Tennis Championship, held at **Wimbledon** in July, proved that a woman's pro tennis career can last well beyond adolescence. Twenty-nine-year-old Jana Novotna of the Czech Republic won her first-ever Grand Slam title. She defeated 30-year-old Nathalie Tauziat of France, 6–4, 7–6. It was Tauziat's first appearance in a Grand Slam final.

Pete Sampras, 26, of the United States, won the men's crown at Wimbledon, outlasting Goran Ivanisevic of Croatia in the final, 6–7, 7–6, 6–4, 3–6, 6–2. It was a tense, hard-fought match. The 26-year-old Ivanisevic battled fatigue throughout; he wasn't completely recovered after having won an equally tough semifinal match. The victory was Sampras's fifth at Wimbledon. It was also the 11th Grand Slam title of his career, tying him for second on the all-time list with Bjorn Borg and Rod Laver. Only Roy Emerson, with 12, has more.

But Sampras was upended by Australian Patrick Rafter in a semifinal at the **U.S. Open** in New York City in September. The 25-year-old Rafter then went on to win the final over fellow Australian Mark Philippoussis by scores of 6–3, 3–6, 6–2, 6–0. It was Rafter's second Grand Slam crown; he had won the same event the year before.

American Lindsay Davenport used her power to overwhelm Martina Hingis's finesse in the women's final of the U.S. Open. The scores were 6–3, 7–5. Hingis had been the defending U.S. Open champ.

Lindsay Davenport: A Will to Win

In 1998, 22-year-old Lindsay Davenport won the women's championship at the U.S. Open, powering her way past defending champion Martina Hingis of Switzerland.

A few years ago, such a victory wouldn't have seemed possible. The 6-foot 2½-inch Davenport weighed more than 200 pounds. Her weight made it difficult for her to run down balls and sapped her confidence. She won the gold medal at the 1996 Summer Olympic Games. But no one thought she could win a Grand Slam event—a much more difficult accomplishment because there are more top players competing.

Davenport, however, was determined to improve her game. She ran sprints, jumped rope, and lifted weights. She lost 30 pounds—and gained speed and confidence. It all came together in 1998. At the Open, she swept through her matches without losing a single set. Her groundstrokes were deep, her serve powerful. She hit the corners with consistency, and ran down balls that she could never have gotten to before.

Davenport was the first American-born woman to win the U.S. Open since Chris Evert captured the title in 1982. Even Martina Hingis was moved to say that "Lindsay just had an awesome tournament."

Zinedine Zidane (*center*) scored two outstanding goals, both headers, in France's 3–0 defeat of Brazil in the World Cup championship match.

SOCCER: THE 1998 WORLD CUP

Soccer is the most popular sport in the world, and the World Cup soccer tournament is the world's most-watched sporting event. Played every four years, the tournament had been won four times by Brazil, three times each by Italy and West Germany, twice each by Argentina and Uruguay, and once by England.

In 1998, France, the host country and underdog, became only the seventh nation to win the World Cup. After 64 games involving teams from 32 countries, it emerged as champion by defeating Brazil, the strong favorite, by a score of 3–0. This stunning upset was watched on television by 1.7 billion people around the globe.

THE SEMIFINALS

The French team played brilliantly throughout the entire tournament, outscoring its seven opponents 15 to 2. In its semifinal match, France faced Croatia, a hard-playing team that had never before played in the World Cup. After a scoreless first half, Croatia scored early in the second half. But France's Lilian Thuram, a defender, retaliated within minutes by stealing a pass and shooting the ball past the Croatian goalie. Thuram scored once again to give France a 2–1 victory and a shot at a World Cup championship.

When the French players advanced to the finals, they knew they would face Brazil in the championship match. A day earlier, Brazil had defeated the Netherlands in a hard-fought match that ended in a 1–1 tie after regulation play and two overtime periods. The game was decided by a shoot-out, in which five players from each side challenged the opposing goalie, one-on-one, with a penalty shot, taken from twelve yards in front of the goal. The Brazilians outshot the Dutchmen 4–2, advancing to the World Cup's final game for the sixth time.

FRANCE TAKES ON BRAZIL

On July 12, some 80,000 spectators crammed into the Stade de France in the Paris suburb of St.-Denis to watch the championship match. France had played excellent defense during the tournament. But Brazil, with its strong offense, was favored to win. That didn't happen.

From the start of the match, the Frenchmen moved the ball quickly, precisely, and aggressively. The Brazilians, on the other hand, were sluggish and disorganized, and the French team was able to stop every one of their attacks. In addition, Ronaldo, the Brazilian forward who was considered the best soccer player in the world, suffered from an ankle injury and a sore knee.

By the end of the first half, France was ahead 2–0, the result of midfielder Zinedine Zidane's two headers, both scored on corner kicks. The Brazilians displayed more aggressiveness in the second half, but the French defense easily contained them. When Emmanuel Petit added a third French goal with moments left to play, French fans at the stadium, including French President Jacques Chirac, roared their approval.

Croatia, a small European country, surprised everyone by making it to the semifinal round and then taking third place by defeating the Netherlands 2–1. Croatia's star forward, Davor Suker, scored his sixth goal in that game, making him the highest scoring player in the tournament.

ONWARD TO THE 17TH WORLD CUP

With France's victory, European teams and South American teams each had eight World Cup championships to their credit. The U.S. team had been eliminated in the first round of 1998 Soccer Cup play. American players scored only one goal while losing to Germany, Iran, and Yugoslavia. It became apparent once again that North American teams, as well as those from Asia and Africa, need to improve dramatically. Only if they do so will they be able to challenge the dominance of European and South American teams at the 17th World Cup, to be held jointly in Japan and South Korea in the year 2002.

Vive la France!

Its World Cup victory brought France more than just a sports trophy. It brought the country some cherished unity. France, which once ruled a vast empire, is home to people from many parts of the world, and

they are often in conflict. Yet they all rallied behind the French soccer team and rejoiced in its victory.

This unity occurred because the team itself reflected the ethnic diversity of the country. Zinedine Zidane, the hero of the championship game, had his roots in the North African country of Algeria. Lilian Thuram, who scored two goals against Croatia, was born in Guadeloupe, a French island in the Caribbean Sea. Marcell Desailly, a star defender, was born in the West African nation of Ghana. And other soccer players on the French team had their roots in Poland and Armenia.

Once again, it was shown that the competitive challenge of sports can promote ethnic harmony.

LIVING HISTORY

Hurtling through corkscrews and spirals, looping completely upside-down, and plunging down sheer drops at breakneck speed—what could possibly be more fun than that? Roller coasters have been among the featured attractions at amusement parks since the 1800s. But those early roller coasters were tame compared to today's monster rides. Today roller coasters are bigger, faster, and more popular than ever, and amusement parks are competing to provide the scariest coasters with the most terrifying thrills and chills. They want to keep roller-coaster fans screaming with excitement—and coming back to stand in line for another ride.

THE CALIFORNIA GOLD RUSH

"Gold!" It was a magic word. It made people leave their homes, their jobs, their families. With just a few belongings, they set out across North America. They endured desert heat, mountain snows, hunger, disease, and the threat of outlaws. Many of them died. But more kept coming, driven by the dream of finding gold.

In 1848, the discovery of this glittering yellow metal in California set off America's first gold rush. The next year, 80,000 people poured into the California gold fields, all hoping for a share of the wealth in the ground. The "forty-niners," as they were called, staked their claims and dug, mined, and panned for gold. Few struck it rich. But many settled in the region, and in 1850 California became a state.

The California gold rush reshaped the Far West, opening it to settlement almost overnight. That made it one of the most important events in U.S. history. It was also one of the most colorful periods in America's past. And in 1998, on the 150th anniversary of the discovery that started it all, Americans looked back and celebrated the time when gold fever swept the nation.

RUMORS OF GOLD

On January 24, 1848, a carpenter named James Marshall was at work building a sawmill on the south fork of the American River, northeast of Sacramento. The mill belonged to John Sutter, an adventurer who was trying to build a private empire of land and businesses at Sutter's Fort, in the Sacramento Valley. On this day, Marshall was inspecting the new mill's water channel, or millrace, when he saw something glittering in the stream. He stooped for a closer look. Could it be gold?

Marshall wrapped grains and flakes of the gleaming yellow stuff in a handkerchief and rode off to tell Sutter of his find. Sutter agreed that it was gold, but he was more worried than excited by the discovery. He had hoped to get rich by selling goods and land to settlers as they gradually came into the area. If word got out, prospectors would descend in droves, and that would upset his plans. So Sutter asked Marshall and the other workers at the site to keep the find secret for at least six weeks, while they completed the mill.

But rumors have a way of spreading, and this one was no exception. After some of Sutter's workers began offering gold dust instead of cash to buy goods, word of the discovery spread. The person who did most to set off the gold rush was Sam Brannan, a Mormon settler and businessman whose many enterprises included a general store near Sutter's Fort. When Brannan heard the rumors, he developed a plan that would make him wealthy—but not by digging for gold. First, he bought up every sort of supply that miners might need, from shovels to bedrolls, and stashed it all in a warehouse. Then, in May 1848, he rode through San Francisco waving a bottle of gold dust and crying "Gold! Gold from the American River!" The rush was on.

The California gold rush was a landmark event that changed the course of U.S. history. News of the discovery of gold in 1848 at Sutter's Mill (*opposite, bottom*) spread like wildfire. By the following year, tens of thousands of forty-niners were flocking to California to try their luck in the gold fields (*opposite, top*). Almost overnight, San Francisco grew from a quiet fishing village to a bustling boomtown (*above*).

Hopeful forty-niners posed with their equipment for this daguerreotype, an early type of photograph. The California gold rush was the first important event to be chronicled by the camera. Daguerreotypes, which captured images on sheets of silver-plated copper, were invented only ten years before the rush began. Many miners sent pictures like this one home to their families, so they wouldn't be forgotten. In 1998–99, an exhibit of gold-rush daguerreotypes toured U.S. museums.

HO! FOR CALIFORNIA

California had been under U.S. control for only a few months when the gold rush began. Mexico had ceded the territory to the United States after the Mexican War, and the Treaty of Guadalupe Hidalgo, which made the transfer official, was signed in February 1848. By the end of the year, 10,000 miners—some from other parts of California, some from as far away as Chile, in South America—were at the gold fields.

Back east, many people still thought the tales of gold were just a hoax. But then President James K. Polk mentioned California's "abundance of gold" in a speech to Congress in December 1848. If the president believed the stories, people thought, they must be true.

Gold fever swept the nation and the world. Workers quit their jobs. Soldiers deserted their posts. People sold their possessions to get money for the trip west. Nothing mattered except gold. In California, people believed, they were sure to get rich. Rumor had it that the gold was just lying around on the ground—all you had to do was pick it up.

But first, the would-be prospectors had to get there. There were three ways to reach California from the East, none of them easy. People could sail around Cape Horn, at the tip of South America, a risky voyage that could take more than five months. Rather than waiting to book passage on a ship scheduled to make the trip, many people pooled their resources, bought a ship, and hired a crew. But these ships were often old and barely seaworthy, and the crews were inexperienced. That made the voyage even more dangerous. When the ships reached San Francisco, crews and passengers alike took off for the gold region, leaving the vessels to rot in the harbor.

A second route took prospectors by steamship as far as the Isthmus of Panama. There was no canal across the isthmus then, so they crossed it by mule. Many were stricken by cholera and other diseases on their way through the jungle. On the western side, they waited—sometimes for months—for a steamship to take them to San Francisco.

The third choice was to head right across the continent—the fastest and most direct route, and in many ways the most dangerous one. Many forty-niners headed west by wagon on the Oregon Trail, turning off in Idaho or Utah to head for California. Miles of scorching desert and the peaks of the Sierra Nevada range lay between them and their goal. If their animals died or ran off, if they ran out of supplies, or if they were attacked by outlaws or disease, they faced death in the wilderness. The overland route was marked by the graves of travelers and the bleached bones of horses and oxen that had died on the journey.

None of that stopped the gold seekers. At the start of 1848, there were only about 15,000 settlers in California. By the end of 1849, there were nearly 100,000. San Francisco grew from a sleepy fishing village to a boomtown filled with tents and ramshackle wooden buildings. Fire destroyed the town several times, but the buildings sprang back up almost as fast as they burned down. And people kept coming—from Canada, Europe, South America, Australia, even China. To the Chinese, California became "Gold Mountain," a place where fortunes could be made. The California gold rush started the first big wave of immigration from China to America.

IN THE GOLD REGION

When gold seekers reached California, most quickly made their way to the foothills of the Sierra Nevada, east of Sacramento. Alone or in small groups, they loaded up their gear on pack mules and headed into the hills. Prospecting, they soon found, was hard work.

Most of California's gold was mixed in with sand and gravel that had washed down from the mountains. It could be found using placer, or surface, mining methods. Prospectors panned for it in mountain streams. The lucky ones found what they were after, quickly staked a claim to the site, and got to work extracting as much gold as they could. They shoveled mountains of dirt through cradles and sluices, devices that used water to wash heavy gold particles from soil.

Once the gold near the surface was taken, miners found that they then had to dig, attacking rocks with picks. It was backbreaking work, and many prospectors never found enough gold to cover their expenses. Still, fortunes were made. In 1849, the California gold fields produced $10 million worth of the yellow metal. In 1852, the peak year, they produced $81 million. One mine yielded a single nugget worth more than $40,000.

A Fool for Gold

A miner dips a flat pan in a mountain stream, swirling and tilting it to rinse away the silt. And there, in the bottom of the pan, is the gleaming yellow color he's been searching for. Pay dirt! Or is it?

Greenhorns—newcomers to the gold fields—were often misled by "fool's gold," which was actually iron pyrite. Iron pyrite is yellow and shiny, just like gold. But unlike gold, it's brittle and crumbly. Hit it gently with a hammer, and it breaks—while soft gold just flattens out. And iron pyrite isn't worth anything. The picture above is pyrite; below is a chunk of gold. Would *you* be fooled by fool's gold?

Digging for gold wasn't the only way to get rich in California. Sam Brannan and many others made their fortunes by selling supplies to miners. With so many people crowding into California at once, just about everything was in short supply, and people charged outrageous prices for goods. At one point, a single sheet of paper went for $150. Neither James Marshall nor John Sutter profited from their discovery, however. Just as he feared, Sutter was financially ruined after hordes of miners swarmed over his land and vandalized his mill.

Many of the forty-niners were Chinese. In fact, the California gold rush started the first big wave of immigration from China to America.

A DARKER SIDE

The mining camps and boomtowns of the gold regions were rough places, full of drinking, gambling, and all sorts of wild goings-on. A fair number of criminals came west with the forty-niners—and disappointed miners sometimes turned to crime, too. From fraud and claim-jumping (stealing another miner's claim) to robbery and murder, crime was widespread.

There were few laws and almost no law enforcement—not even a territorial government—when the gold rush began. The camps had to organize, elect leaders, and adopt their own regulations with regard to staking claims. Sometimes people formed vigilante bands to go after criminals. Offenders were rounded up, given a quick, informal trial, and punished—even executed—on the spot.

Crime and vigilante justice weren't the only dark aspects of the gold rush. American Indians were driven out of the gold region with a vengeance, even hunted down and killed. There were about 150,000 Indians in California in 1849. Over the next twenty years, the number dropped to 30,000. Asians, Mexicans, and African-Americans faced discrimination. Laws and regulations kept the mines in white hands.

Gold mining also did tremendous damage to the environment. Because mercury combines with gold, it was used in a method of separating gold from crushed rock. Mercury poisoned some miners, and thousands of pounds of mercury were dumped into California streams. And once the most easily found gold had been taken, miners turned to other methods to get at deep deposits. One of the most damaging was hydraulic mining, in which powerful jets of water from huge hoses blasted away entire hillsides. By the time hydraulic mining was stopped in 1884, some 12 billion tons of earth had been dug up or washed away in the search for gold. And mercury-contaminated sediments still lie under San Francisco Bay.

A GOLDEN LEGACY

Within a few years of the amazing discovery at Sutter's Mill, big mining companies had taken over the work of gold mining. Only they could afford to operate deep mines and use mechanical methods like hydraulic mining. Once they began to operate, California's gold rush faded.

Gold fever struck again—not once but several times—before the end of the 19th century. In 1859–60, miners rushed to Virginia City, Nevada, on the eastern side of the Sierras. The lure was the Comstock Lode, a deep, incredibly rich deposit of gold mixed with silver. Other prospectors headed for Pikes Peak in Colorado or to Idaho and then Montana, where gold could be found by placer mining. In 1876, gold was discovered in the Black Hills of South Dakota. That set off a conflict with the Sioux, who held the region sacred. Another gold rush erupted in 1892, when rich deposits were found at Cripple Creek, Colorado. And the century's last gold rush began in 1897, when word came of a huge gold strike on the Klondike River in Canada's Yukon Territory. More than 100,000 people headed north to the Klondike and Alaska, chasing the dream of gold.

Meanwhile, the gold rush that drew thousands of people west in 1849 had changed California forever. Thanks to the huge numbers of people who came searching for gold, California was admitted to the Union as a state on September 9, 1850. In the years after the Civil War, as more Americans moved west in search of open land and opportunity, California was most often their destination.

So, despite the darker effects of the gold rush, there was much to celebrate in 1998. On January 24, about 20,000 people marked the anniversary of James Marshall's discovery by visiting a reconstruction of Sutter's Mill at Coloma, a town at the site of the mill. Many other events were planned for the year. In one, paintings, photographs, and reminders of the gold rush—including a nugget from James Marshall's find—were on display in exhibits mounted by the Oakland Museum of California.

These and other events were reminders of a time when Americans dreamed of gold and believed that, with a pan and a little luck, anyone could strike it rich.

Yellow Gold. . . and Blue Jeans

You could be wearing a bit of history right now! Blue jeans go back to California gold rush days, when miners started wearing tough denim work pants reinforced with copper rivets.

Among those who went to California searching for riches was a German-born businessman named Levi Strauss. Strauss was a dry-goods merchant. He arrived in San Francisco in 1853 not to pan for gold but to sell supplies—work clothes, tents, and more—to the gold-hunting miners.

Strauss's business was a great success, and he soon had a reputation for selling quality goods. Then, in 1872, he got a letter from Jacob Davis, a tailor in Nevada. Davis had found a way to make extra-strong work pants—by putting copper rivets at stress points. Davis and Strauss agreed to patent the idea and join forces to produce riveted "waist-overalls" in both heavy brown cotton and blue denim.

The rest, as they say, is history. The Levi Strauss denim jeans became favorites not only with miners but with cowboys and workers everywhere. They made Strauss wealthy. Years later, in the 1960s, denim jeans became a fashion item—and they never went out of style.

Since ancient times, people have predicted weather by using weather vanes—often with whimsical designs. The horse was a popular figure because it was important for work and transportation.

BLOWING IN THE WIND

A wind from the west
Brings weather at its best;
A wind from the east
Brings rain to man and beast.

Will the weather be fair or foul? To learn the latest forecast, you can simply pick up a newspaper or switch on the radio or TV. But 100 years ago, farmers, sailors—in fact, anyone who wanted or needed to know what the next day's weather might be—had to make their own forecasts.

Since ancient times, one of the tools people have used to predict weather has been the weather vane—the familiar rooftop device that shows the direction of the wind. Knowing which way the wind is blowing is helpful in forecasting because certain kinds of weather tend to come along with winds from certain directions. But over the centuries, weather vanes have taken on other uses as well. They have become symbols of power and religion, signs for merchants and tradespeople, and a unique form of folk art.

THE VANES OF THE OLD WORLD

No one knows who made the first weather vane. But one of the most famous vanes of the ancient world was built in Athens, during the 1st century B.C., by the Greek astronomer Andronicus. Andronicus mounted his vane on an eight-sided structure called the Tower of the Winds. The vane itself was a figure of Triton (the half-man, half-fish god of the sea) carrying a wand in one hand. When the wind blew, the figure swung around so that the wand pointed in the direction from which the wind was coming. The Triton vane set the pattern for later vanes in two important ways—it pointed into the wind, and it was decorative as well as useful.

Like the Greeks, the Romans used weather vanes. And through their empire, vanes spread across Europe. Two designs that are still used on weather vanes today—the banner and the cock—developed in Europe during the Middle Ages. Nobles, who by law were the only people allowed to fly banners and pennants, adopted the banner design. Banner vanes showing heraldic devices were placed on castle turrets to advertise the owner's rank.

Weather vanes in the form of cocks (roosters), on the other hand, were connected with religion. In the 9th century, the Roman Catholic Church ordered that every church be topped with the figure of a cock, a symbol associated with Saint Peter. Medieval artisans combined the cocks with weather vanes. This design became so widespread that its name, the weathercock, was often used to refer to any weather vane.

Gradually cocks, banners, simple arrows, and more elaborate designs began to be seen

Above: Vanes in the design of cows were placed on barns. Below: This unusual barnyard motif of a farmer pumping water is from Virginia's Colonial Williamsburg.

The silvery figure of a locomotive might have served as a weather vane over a train station.

on the shops of merchants and homes of common people, as well as on churches and castles. But as a form of folk art, the weather vane reached its peak in North America—especially in the United States—during the 18th and 19th centuries.

THE VANES OF AMERICA

In America, blacksmiths and wood-carvers turned out finely crafted vanes with devices that ranged from cows and horses to mermaids and square-rigger ships. Many of the early vanes were one-of-a-kind designs. A gilded copper grasshopper, for example, was placed on Boston's Faneuil Hall in 1742. It was made by Shem Drowne, who is thought to have been the first American artisan to make a living by designing and building weather vanes.

Other early designs were only slightly less fanciful. Paul Revere topped his coppersmith shop with a wooden codfish. George Washington favored a dove, carrying an olive branch as a sign of peace, for his estate, Mount Vernon. Seafaring designs were seen in coastal towns. Vanes sporting cows, hogs, and sheep were placed on barns that housed these animals. And figures of American Indians were especially popular in western Pennsylvania and New York—perhaps to show that the settlers wanted to be on friendly terms with Indian tribes.

The grasshopper over Boston's Faneuil Hall is a landmark.

During the 19th century, when patriotic feeling was strong in the United States, eagles and figures of Columbia, the goddess of liberty, topped town halls everywhere. Another popular subject for 19th-century vanes was the horse, which was essential for work and transportation. Vanes patterned after workhorses, riding horses, and famous trotting horses raced the wind from the roofs of homes and barns.

In the 19th century, vanes also became trade signs. A mortar-and-pestle vane might be seen over an apothecary shop, where medicines were made and sold. A figure of a locomotive might mark a railroad station, and a fire-engine vane might swing in the breeze over a firehouse.

The cock has been a popular weather-vane design since the Middle Ages.

The artisans who made these vanes were often traveling carpenters and blacksmiths. They sold their handiwork door-to-door or at taverns along the road. Most of the vanes were flat, carved from wood or shaped from iron or sheet metal. But some were hollow, three-dimensional figures, made by hammering thin sheets of copper into molds for the various parts of the figure. The shaped copper pieces were then soldered together. Gold leaf or paint was often used to finish the figure.

By the 20th century, factory methods were used to make most weather vanes. These mass-produced vanes often lacked the originality and fine design of the earlier ones. Vanes remained popular, however. Today a few artisans still make them by hand. And scientists who study weather still use vanes, in combination with devices that measure and record wind speed.

Some of the old, handcrafted weather vanes can still be seen atop homes, churches, and town halls. But yet another use has been found for these vanes—they have become popular collector's items. Today many of the finest ones can be seen in museums of folk art.

Weather vanes are often used as trade signs—this lobster might swing over a seafood restaurant.

AMISTAD AND *TITANIC:* THE TRUE STORIES

History came to the movie screen in 1998. Two of the year's most acclaimed hit films were based on dramatic historical events. *Amistad* told the story of a group of Africans who were sold into slavery in 1839. *Titanic* was a love story set aboard the ocean liner of that name, which sank in 1912.

Each of these films played with history, to one degree or another. Fictional characters, dialogue, and plot twists helped bring the stories alive. But both films also tried to be as accurate as possible. And in both films, much of the drama and suspense came from history, not Hollywood. Here's what *really* happened.

THE AMISTAD MUTINY

In 1839, a Portuguese ship arrived in Spanish Cuba from West Africa. Its human cargo consisted of Africans—some kidnapped, some captured in war, and some sold to pay off debts. All were headed for a life of slavery. They had crossed the Atlantic Ocean chained together in the ship's cramped hold. Now they would be sold at Havana's slave market.

Two planters, Pedro Montes and José Ruiz, bought 53 of the slaves. The Africans were loaded onto a schooner, the *Amistad,* which set sail for plantations on the north coast of Cuba. But they never arrived. On the fourth night of the trip, the Africans escaped from their chains and took over the ship. Led by a man the Spanish called Cinque, they killed the captain and the cook and took Montes and Ruiz prisoner.

Since Montes knew how to sail the ship, the Africans ordered him to steer for Africa. But the Spanish planter tricked them. By day, he

The movie *Amistad* (left) was based on the true story of a mutiny that occurred in 1839 (artwork, above). The *Amistad* case was the talk of its day, and it made people aware of how unjust slavery was.

sailed east, as ordered. At night, he turned north. In this way the *Amistad* sailed a zigzag course up the coast of North America. By the time the ship was off Long Island, food and water had run out.

On August 26, a U.S. Navy ship came upon the *Amistad.* Navy sailors boarded the ship, disarmed the Africans, and took them to New London, Connecticut, where they were put in jail. By this time there were just 43—ten had died of thirst or starvation or had been killed in the mutiny. None spoke English, so they couldn't tell their story.

Montes and Ruiz, now free, demanded the return of their "property"—the slaves. But the *Amistad* case wouldn't be so simple. Slavery was still allowed in Connecticut and in many other U.S. states. However, while it was legal for people to own slaves, it wasn't legal to capture new slaves. Now a court would have to decide: Were the Africans aboard the *Amistad* the property of the planters? Or were they free people who had been kidnapped and had acted out of self-defense?

The *Amistad* case captured the attention of the country. It was the subject of a play, a wax-museum display, paintings and engravings, and countless articles and pamphlets. Abolitionists—people who wanted to abolish, or end, slavery—raised money to pay for the Africans' defense in court. Attorney Roger Baldwin agreed to represent them. The abolitionists also found a translator who spoke Mende, the West African language of the Amistad captives. For the first time, the public had a chance to hear the Africans' side of the story.

The case didn't go to trial until January 1840. At first, many people expected the decision to go against the Africans. But the court heard evidence about the brutal Cuban slave trade; and Cinque told, through the interpreter, how he and the others had been captured and sold. The judge ruled that the *Amistad* captives were "born free and ever since have been and still of right are free and not slaves." He ordered that they be turned over to U.S. officials and taken back to Africa.

But the U.S. government appealed the decision, siding with the Spanish planters. The Africans were kept in custody until the appeal could be heard by the Supreme Court. Many people were outraged by this turn of events. Among them was John Quincy Adams, former president of the United States. Adams, 73, was serving as a Congressman from Massachu-

The *Titanic* carried only enough lifeboats for about half the 2,207 passengers on board. (Above, a scene from the movie. Opposite, actual headlines of the 1912 disaster.)

setts. He was famous for his eloquence, and he agreed to argue for the Africans before the Supreme Court.

The case was heard in February 1841. Government lawyers argued that the Africans were just cargo on a Spanish ship and must be sent back to Cuba. Baldwin and Adams presented the Africans' case. In a moving summary, Adams heaped scorn on the government for its unjust treatment of the captives.

The Supreme Court ruled in favor of the Africans. They were set free at once, and abolitionists set about raising money for their trip home. In November 1841, after almost three years in captivity, Cinque and the others sailed for West Africa aboard the ship *Gentleman.*

The *Amistad* case didn't change the laws that permitted slavery in much of the United States. But it helped make people aware of just how great an injustice slavery was. In that way, it brought the country closer to the day when slavery would end.

THE "UNSINKABLE" TITANIC

When the *Titanic* was launched in 1912, it was hailed as the largest and most luxurious ocean liner ever built—882 feet (269 meters) long and equipped with every comfort. The White Star Line, the British steamship company that owned the ship, advertised that it was unsinkable. And company officials believed that this was true. The *Titanic* had been designed with all the latest technology, including a series of watertight compartments that were supposed to seal off any leak, preventing the ship from flooding.

The *Titanic* left England on April 10, 1912, bound for New York on its maiden voyage. More than 2,200 people were aboard. They ranged from wealthy passengers who had booked luxurious first-class staterooms for the trip to immigrants crossing the Atlantic Ocean in cramped third-class quarters. All were excited to be part of the great ship's first trip.

The *Titanic* steamed steadily across the North Atlantic for four days. At 11:00 P.M. on

April 14, the ship was several hundred miles south of Newfoundland, Canada, when its radio operator received a warning from another ship: An iceberg had been sighted in the vicinity. The operator ignored the warning—he was busy sending messages from passengers to friends and relatives on shore.

Forty minutes later, the ship's lookout spotted the looming shape of a huge iceberg straight ahead. He called down to the bridge, and the ship tried to turn. But it was too late. The ship shuddered as the iceberg raked its side, carving a gash in the hull near the bow.

Passengers and crew weren't worried at first. After all, this ship was supposed to be unsinkable. But it quickly became clear that the *Titanic* was in serious trouble. The watertight compartments failed to stop the flooding. As water rushed into the front of the ship, it began to sink bow first.

Passengers were told to prepare to abandon ship. But the *Titanic* didn't have enough lifeboats for everyone—lifeboats hadn't seemed important on an "unsinkable" ship. So, as the ship's band played, women and children boarded the boats first. Loading started with first-class passengers, then second-class, and then third. In the rush to get away, many boats were sent off before they were full.

At 2:20 A.M. on April 15, the *Titanic* slid nose first into the depths. More than 1,500 people went down with the great liner or died of exposure in the cold North Atlantic waters. The survivors were picked up by other ships, but it took the rescuers hours to reach the scene. The closest ship had turned off its radio just before the *Titanic* hit the iceberg, so it never received the distress call.

The sinking of the *Titanic* ranks as one of the worst disasters in the history of ocean travel. Since then, ships have been required to carry enough lifeboats for all the people on board and keep their radios on 24 hours a day. Ships today are also better able to locate—and avoid—icebergs.

The *Titanic* still lies on the bottom of the ocean, almost 3 miles (5 kilometers) down. It was undiscovered until 1985, when a team of American and French scientists found it. Robert Ballard and his crew used a minisub and a robot camera to explore the wreck. They found a perfectly preserved capsule of life in 1912. Books, dishes, and personal belongings are scattered all around. Debris brought up from the wreck has shed light on the disaster.

"All the News That's Fit to Print."

The New York Times.

NEW YORK, TUESDAY, APRIL 16, 1912—TWENTY-FOUR PAGES

TITANIC SINKS FOUR HOURS AFTER HITTING ICEBERG;
866 RESCUED BY CARPATHIA, PROBABLY 1250 PERISH;
ISMAY SAFE, MRS. ASTOR MAYBE, NOTED NAMES MISSING

Col. Astor and Bride, Isidor Straus and Wife, and Maj. Butt Aboard.

"RULE OF SEA" FOLLOWED

Women and Children Put Over in Lifeboats and Are Supposed to be Safe on Carpathia.

PICKED UP AFTER 8 HOURS

Vincent Astor Calls at White Star Office for News of His Father and Leaves Weeping.

FRANKLIN HOPEFUL ALL DAY

Manager of the Line Insisted Titanic Was Unsinkable Even After She Had Gone Down.

HEAD OF THE LINE ABOARD

J. Bruce Ismay Making First Trip on Gigantic Ship That Was to Surpass All Others.

Biggest Liner Plunges to the Bottom at 2:20 A.M.

RESCUERS THERE TOO LATE

Except to Pick Up the Few Hundreds Who Took to the Lifeboats.

WOMEN AND CHILDREN FIRST

Cunarder Carpathia Rushing to New York with the Survivors.

SEA SEARCH FOR OTHERS

The California Stands By on Chance of Picking Up Other Boats or Rafts.

OLYMPIC SENDS THE NEWS

Only Ship to Flash Wireless Messages to Shore After the Disaster.

LATER REPORT SAVES 866.

Researchers think that some of the rivets in the ship's hull may have been defective, so the hull split apart easily.

The movie *Titanic* focuses on a fictional romance between two young people who never existed. But the filmmakers were able to study the actual wreck, to make their film as realistic as possible. A handful of tourists have visited the wreck, too. But those who really want to experience the *Titanic* may want to wait for December 1999. That's when a working replica of the great ship is scheduled to make its maiden voyage from England to America—with passengers and plenty of lifeboats on board.

THE THRILL OF THE RIDE

Slowly, the car lurches higher and higher. It's above the treetops now. Your heart is beating faster, and your palms begin to sweat—something dreadful is about to happen.

Suddenly the car swings around a bend and takes you over the top, plunging down toward the ground at 60 miles (98 kilometers) an hour. The wind whips your hair back and brings tears to your eyes. Your stomach is in your throat and your heart is in your knees. Your mouth is wide open, and you're screaming for all you're worth.

And you love every minute of it!

For sheer thrills and terrifying chills, nothing beats a roller coaster. Variations of this exciting amusement-park ride have been around for about three hundred years. And while roller coasters have had their ups and downs over the years, today they are more popular than at any time since the 1920s. New coasters—ever higher and faster, with steeper drops and more devilish twists and turns—are opening all the time. People spend hours in line, waiting for a ride that lasts a couple of minutes. And when the ride is over, they rush back to the line to wait again.

Today's roller coasters have more spine-tingling thrills than ever. One new scream machine—Superman, the Escape (Six Flags Magic Mountain, California)—is part roller coaster and part tower ride.

SLIPPERY BEGINNINGS

It was the Russians who came up with the basic idea behind the roller coaster. The first coasters were actually ice slides built in St. Petersburg in the 1600s. The slides, supported by wooden frames and angled at about 50 degrees, provided a slick, fast surface for sleds. Riders climbed to a platform at the top and then shot straight down the slide at thrilling speeds.

The French adopted the concept but redesigned the rides. They added tiny wheels to the sleds, so that ice wasn't needed and the slides could be enjoyed year-round. The first of the French slides, which were called Russian Mountains, was introduced in Paris in the early 1800s.

In the 1870s, the popular rides spread to the United States. The first U.S. coaster was actually a converted railway, originally designed to carry coal down Mt. Pisgah in Pennsylvania. As a passenger ride, it carried people to the top of the mountain and then sent them down again. Traveling at just 5 miles (8 kilometers) an hour, the Mauch Chunk Railway was tame by the standards of today's coasters. But the scenery was beautiful, and the ride was an instant success.

Soon artificial coasting courses were being built. In these rides, the slides were made up of fat rollers placed one after another, conveyor-belt style. The coasting-course fad didn't last long—but the name "roller coaster" survived.

Like the earlier Russian Mountains, these roller coasters carried people straight down—there were no stomach-flipping ups and downs. The first ride that resembled a modern coaster, with artificial hills and valleys, appeared in 1884. It was the Switchback Gravity Pleasure Railway, built by LaMarcus A. Thompson at Coney Island in Brooklyn, New York. In it, riders boarded a ten-person wheeled car and were carried down an undulating (up-and-down) track at 6 miles (10 kilometers) an hour.

The 1884 Coney Island coaster. Passengers paid a nickel for the "scary" one-minute ride.

People lined up to take a five-cent ride on the new invention, and Thompson soon was taking in about $700 a day. It was clear that lots of people were willing to pay money to be scared. Soon other amusement park owners were clamoring for similar rides, and a roller-coaster boom began.

By 1920, most amusement parks had some kind of roller coaster. The designers of these coasters made many improvements on Thompson's first design. For example, the Switchback Railway track followed a straight course, and the cars had no power. That meant that the cars had to be pushed to the top of the track after each ride. Circular tracks and power lifts were among the first refinements made in roller-coaster design.

Then designers concentrated on making each new coaster bigger, steeper, faster—in other words, more terrifying—than the one before. The scarier a coaster was, it seemed, the more people it drew. An especially terrifying roller coaster was the Coney Island Cyclone, perhaps the most well-known coaster of all time. World-famous aviator Charles Lindbergh declared it to be "a greater thrill than flying an airplane at top speed."

During the Great Depression of the 1930s, many people lost their jobs. Fewer people went to amusement parks—they just didn't have the money for rides. As park attendance dropped, roller coasters stood idle. Many were torn down.

After the Depression and World War II, however, the situation began to change. A new kind of amusement park—the theme park—appeared. Disneyland, which opened in Anaheim, California, in 1955, was the first of these parks. Disneyland introduced its first roller coaster, the Matterhorn Bobsleds, in 1958, and the ride was instantly popular. Soon other theme parks were being built. And more often than not, roller coasters were the centerpieces of these parks. Just as in the 1920s, people wanted the thrills and excitement that only a roller coaster could provide.

TERRIFYING TWISTS

Like amusement parks of the past, parks of today are constantly competing to have the

Above: The Alpengeist (Busch Gardens, Williamsburg, Virginia) is an inverted roller coaster. Below: Kumba (Busch Gardens, Tampa Bay, Florida) has one of the tallest vertical loops in the world.

biggest, tallest, fastest, and scariest roller coaster. And today's roller coasters provide thrills that riders of the 1890s could never have imagined. For one thing, some travel at more than ten times the speed of the early coasters. They don't just send riders around curves and up and down a few hills, either. The cars hurtle through corkscrews and spirals, turn upside-down in complete loops, and plunge into total darkness. Here are a few of the most terrifying—that is, fun—new rides:

- The Alpengeist at Busch Gardens Williamsburg, in Virginia, is an inverted roller coaster. It carries riders chair-lift style—the track is overhead, so your legs dangle free, with nothing between your feet and the ground. The ride carries you 195 feet (60 meters) in the air and then hurls you through six spins and loops, at speeds up to 67 miles (108 kilometers) an hour.
- The Riddler's Revenge at Six Flags Magic Mountain, in California, is the tallest (156 feet, 48 meters), fastest (65 miles, 105 kilometers, per hour) stand-up roller coaster. Firmly locked in a rigid harness, you speed through six full loops.
- The Magnum XL-200 is a big draw at Cedar Point in Sandusky, Ohio—a park with

The Science of Thrills

A day at an amusement park doesn't seem like an educational activity. But at many parks, you may see science students scurrying from ride to ride with notebooks. That's because the rides—especially the big roller coasters—demonstrate some basic principles of physics.

Once the cars in a roller coaster reach the top of the first hill, for example, the force of gravity (which pulls downward) is all that sends them speeding along the tracks. That means that the speed of a coaster ride is closely related to the height of the first hill—the bigger the drop, the more speed the cars pick up as they plunge, and the bigger the thrill.

When the car levels out and starts up the next hill, you feel as if you weigh hundreds of pounds. You're feeling G's—the units scientists use to measure gravity. One G is the normal force that keeps your feet on the ground. When a coaster shoots up a hill, almost 4 G's push down on you. But when the car crests a hill and starts down, you may feel zero or even negative G's—you float, just like an astronaut in space.

Roller-coaster tracks are banked, or angled, on curves to take advantage of G-forces. If the tracks were level, fast-moving cars might fly off as they whipped around turns. When the tracks are banked, G-forces just push the cars against the track. G-forces also help the cars flip upside-down through corkscrews and loops. The big loops on coasters aren't perfect circles. They are teardrop shapes called *clothoid loops.* In a perfect circle, the cars would slow down too much at the top of the loop. Then the G-forces might not be strong enough to keep you glued to your seat.

Designers calculate these forces carefully when they build a new coaster. They know just how fast the cars will be traveling at each point and how much each turn must be banked. That, combined with rider harnesses and rigorous operating and inspection standards, makes roller coasters far safer than they look.

twelve roller coasters. This one, 205 feet (62 meters) high, features three tunnels and lots of sickening "air time"—that weightless feeling you get when the car crests a hill.

• Superman, the Escape, also at Six Flags Magic Mountain, is part roller coaster, part tower ride. Powered by electromagnets, cars travel straight up for 410 feet (125 meters). Then they plunge down, hitting 100 miles (160 kilometers) an hour and leaving you weightless for more than six seconds.

These new coasters have tubular steel rails, which make the ride smooth. The car wheels grip the rails above, below, and at the sides. Even if a car stops upside down in the middle of a loop, it won't leave the rails. And thanks to well-designed harnesses, riders won't fall out!

But for some roller-coaster enthusiasts, there's nothing like an old-fashioned wooden coaster, or "woody." Loops and corkscrews are fine, but the jolts, shakes, and roar of a woody add extra thrills. Many old woodies, including the Coney Island Cyclone, still run. And new ones have been built. The Texas Giant, at Six Flags Over Texas in Arlington, is typical of these. Its first drop is 137 feet (42 meters)—and there are 20 more plunges after that.

The Magnum XL-200 (Cedar Point Park, Sandusky, Ohio) carries riders more than 200 feet high and features lots of sickening "air time"—the weightless feeling people get when the car crests a hill.

• Kumba, at Busch Gardens Tampa Bay, in Florida, sends you spinning through a series of stomach-churning loops and rolls. It has one of the tallest vertical loops in the world, with a drop of 135 feet (41 meters).

• Steel Force, at Dorney Park in Pennsylvania, lifts you more than 200 feet (60 meters) in the air for a spine-tingling ride that tops 75 miles (120 kilometers) an hour. This coaster features a thrilling dive down its second hill into a lake.

Old or new, roller coasters have a special appeal. What heart-stopping twist will coaster designers think up next? Whatever it is, one thing is certain: People will line up for a chance to experience the thrill of the ride.

THE SPANISH-AMERICAN WAR

On February 15, 1898, a sudden explosion destroyed an American warship, the U.S.S. *Maine*, at its berth in Havana, Cuba (shown in the drawing above). The incident helped to spark the Spanish-American War, which led to the United States becoming a world power with a colonial empire in the Caribbean Sea and the Pacific Ocean. The 100th anniversary of this war was marked in 1998.

The underlying cause of the war was Spain's harsh rule over the island country of Cuba. When Cubans revolted against Spanish rule in 1895, many Americans wanted to help the Cuban people win independence. Other Americans wanted to acquire an overseas empire and saw Cuba as a beginning.

Because of the mysterious explosion that sank the *Maine* and Spain's refusal to grant full independence to Cuba, President William McKinley and the U.S. Congress were pushed by public opinion toward war. On April 19, 1898, Congress passed a resolution recognizing Cuban independence. Six days later, on April 25, the U.S. declared war on Spain—and the battle cry was "Remember the *Maine*!"

The first major battle of the war didn't take place in Cuban waters, but in the Philippine Islands, a Spanish possession in the Pacific Ocean. Acting under orders from Assistant Secretary of the Navy Theodore Roosevelt (later to become president of the United States), Commodore George Dewey attacked the Spanish naval squadron in the Philippines and destroyed the entire fleet in an hour and a half. Not a single American ship or sailor was lost.

Meanwhile, in Cuban waters, another American naval force chased a Spanish fleet into Santiago harbor, on Cuba's southeastern coast. In June, 18,000 U.S. troops invaded Cuba. Among these troops was a colorful outfit nicknamed the Rough Riders, because many of its troopers were cowboys. Its commander was Theodore Roosevelt, who had resigned his navy post so he could take an active part in the fighting.

Pushing inland, the U.S. troops attacked Kettle Hill and San Juan Hill, whose fortifi-

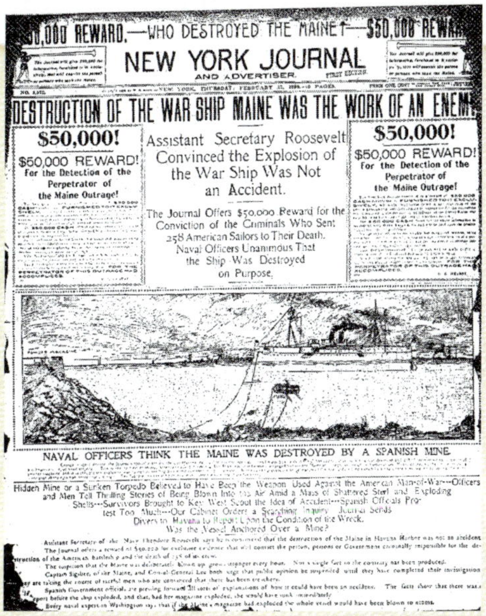

$50,000 REWARD.—WHO DESTROYED THE MAINE?—$50,000 REWARD.

NEW YORK JOURNAL
AND ADVERTISER.

DESTRUCTION OF THE WAR SHIP MAINE WAS THE WORK OF AN ENEMY

$50,000!
$50,000 REWARD!
For the Detection of the Perpetrator of the Maine Outrage!

Assistant Secretary Roosevelt Convinced the Explosion of the War Ship Was Not an Accident.

The Journal Offers $50,000 Reward for the Conviction of the Criminals Who Sent 258 American Sailors to Their Death. Naval Officers Unanimous That the Ship Was Destroyed on Purpose.

$50,000!
$50,000 REWARD!
For the Detection of the Perpetrator of the Maine Outrage!

NAVAL OFFICERS THINK THE MAINE WAS DESTROYED BY A SPANISH MINE.

Hidden Mine or a Sunken Torpedo Believed to Have Been the Weapon Used Against the American Man-of-War—Officers and Men Tell Thrilling Stories of Being Blown Into the Air Amid a Mass of Shattered Steel and Exploding Shells—Survivors Brought to Key West Scout the Idea of Accident—Spanish Officials Protest Too Much—Our Cabinet Orders a Searching Inquiry—Journal Sends Divers to Havana to Report Upon the Condition of the Wreck. Was the Vessel Anchored Over a Mine?

"Remember the *Maine!*"

By January 1898, tension between the United States and Spain over the issue of Cuban independence had reached the boiling point. Americans living and working in Cuba were thought to be in danger. So the U.S.S. *Maine,* a heavily armored battleship, was sent to Havana to protect American lives.

Arriving in Havana on January 25, the warship docked without incident. But shortly afterward, a handbill was distributed by Spanish supporters calling the arrival of the *Maine* a grave insult to Spain and concluding with the words "Death to the Americans!"

Despite the threats, no action was taken against the American ship during the next three weeks. Then at 9:40 P.M. on February 15, an enormous explosion shattered the evening's quiet and tore apart the steel-hulled battleship. In a matter of minutes the *Maine* sank. More than 260 members of the crew perished when the ship went down.

Americans were quick to blame the Spanish government for the explosion. Tabloid journalists used the incident to encourage war fever. The sinking of the *Maine* proved to be the spark that kindled the flames of war. Two months later the United States declared war on Spain.

At the time, U.S. naval experts believed that an underwater mine had caused the explosion. Spanish authorities claimed the blast was internal—possibly caused by a defective boiler. If it was external, they stated, it was probably the work of Cuban saboteurs who wanted to provoke a war between the United States and Spain. Years later, an American admiral offered the theory that spontaneous combustion in the ship's coal bins had started a fire that spread to the powder magazine.

To this day the explosion that destroyed the *Maine* remains an unsolved mystery. We may never know the truth.

cations protected Santiago. In one gallant charge, Colonel Roosevelt and his Rough Riders, aided by African-American soldiers from the Ninth and Tenth U.S. Cavalry regiments, defeated the Spanish in what became known as the Battle of San Juan Hill. A few days later, the Spanish fleet in Santiago attempted to slip past the blockading American ships. But in a four-hour battle, all the Spanish ships were sunk or run aground.

Cut off from reinforcements and supplies, Santiago's Spanish garrison surrendered on July 17, ending the war in Cuba. One week later U.S. troops invaded and occupied Puerto Rico, another Spanish Caribbean possession. In August, U.S. troops occupied Manila in the Philippines, and hostilities came to an end.

An armistice was signed in August, and a peace treaty was agreed to in December 1898. Under the terms of the treaty, the United States gained control over Puerto Rico, the Philippines, and the Pacific island of Guam. Cuba was placed under control of the U.S. military until 1902, when it became independent. The United States still maintains a naval base on the island at Guantánamo Bay. In order to connect the Caribbean and Pacific parts of the new American empire, the Panama Canal was built.

The Spanish-American War lasted just four months, prompting one American diplomat to call the conflict "a splendid little war."

HENRY I. KURTZ
Author, *John and Sebastian Cabot*

In 1590, Governor John White returned to Roanoke Island and found that the colony he had helped to establish had mysteriously disappeared. The only clue to the settlers' whereabouts was a single word carved on a tree.

THE MYSTERY OF THE LOST COLONY OF ROANOKE

On a balmy summer night in the year 1590, an English ship approached Roanoke Island, off the coast of present-day North Carolina. The ship carried fresh supplies for a group of settlers who had built a small fort on the island three years earlier, hoping to establish the first successful English colony in the New World. But at daybreak, when John White, the colony's governor, and a party of sailors landed on the island, not a single settler was to be found. The fort's log walls were crumbling, and the houses had been torn down. Smashed chests, a few cannons, a rusty suit of armor, and some personal possessions were all that remained of the Roanoke colony.

But what of the 117 settlers? What had become of them? They had mysteriously disappeared. Only one clue to their whereabouts was found—a single word carved in capital letters on the barkless trunk of a tree. The word was "Croatoan," a reference either to a neighboring island or to the tribe of Indians who had befriended the settlers when they first arrived.

During the more than 400 years since John White and his men discovered that single word chiseled into a tree, the fate of the Lost Colony of Roanoke has remained a mystery. Recently, however, new clues have surfaced that may help historians solve that mystery. But to fully understand that mystery, we must go back to those early colonial times, when England and Spain competed for territory and power in the newly discovered lands of the Americas.

SETTLING IN THE NEW WORLD

Five years after Christopher Columbus reached the New World in 1492, John Cabot planted England's flag on the coast of North America. The Cabot voyages (1497-98) gave England a claim to a portion of North America. But it wasn't until the 1580s that serious efforts were made to establish a permanent English colony there. In 1583, Sir Humphrey Gilbert landed on the coast of Newfoundland (in present-day Canada) with five ships and about 250 settlers. Gilbert's effort to establish a colony ended in failure. On the return voyage to England, he drowned when his ship sank in a storm.

One year later, in 1584, Gilbert's half brother Sir Walter Raleigh received permission from Queen Elizabeth I to start a colony. A soldier, adventurer, and poet, Raleigh was given a royal grant to search for lands "not actually possessed by any Christian princes, nor inhabited by Christian people."

Sir Walter Raleigh gave up his efforts to build an English empire in North America after the mysterious disappearance of the Lost Colony.

Soon after, Raleigh sent out ships to explore the North American coast for a good location to build a settlement. They found such a place along the coast of North Carolina. "The soil is the most sweet, fruitful and wholesome of all the world," they reported. They had equally glowing statements about the local Croatoan Indians, who were described as a "handsome and goodly people, and in their behavior as mannerly and civil as any in Europe." By way of proof they brought back two Indians, Manteo and Wanchese, along with such local products as tobacco and deer skins.

Raleigh named the new territory Virginia (covering present-day North Carolina and Virginia) in honor of England's Queen Elizabeth I, who was known as the "Virgin Queen." In return, the queen made Raleigh a knight and appointed him governor of the newly claimed region.

Raleigh quickly put together a larger expedition, and in April 1585, seven ships set sail from Plymouth carrying 108 colonists. Among them was John White, an artist who would make many fine drawings of Indian life. Landing on Roanoke Island, the settlers built a small fort, the first structure in what they hoped would be a permanent colony. They also had instructions to look for gold and silver.

But things didn't go well for them. The Indians, at first peaceful, turned hostile. And the settlers spent too much time gold hunting and too little on planting crops. By the middle of 1586, the shadow of starvation hung over the Roanoke colony. When Sir Francis Drake, fresh from plundering Spanish ships and settlements to the south, sailed in with his fleet, the colonists decided to return to England with him. So ended the second attempt to plant a permanent English colony in North America.

But Sir Walter Raleigh refused to give up his dream of an English empire in North America. One year later, in 1587, a new expedition put to sea. Among the 117 colonists were seventeen women and nine children. The artist John White was now the colony's governor, and his daughter Eleanor—the wife of a colonist named Ananias Dare—was one of the passengers. Also on board was Manteo, one of the Croatoan Indians who had been taken back to England three years earlier.

White and his colonists once again attempted to establish a permanent settle-

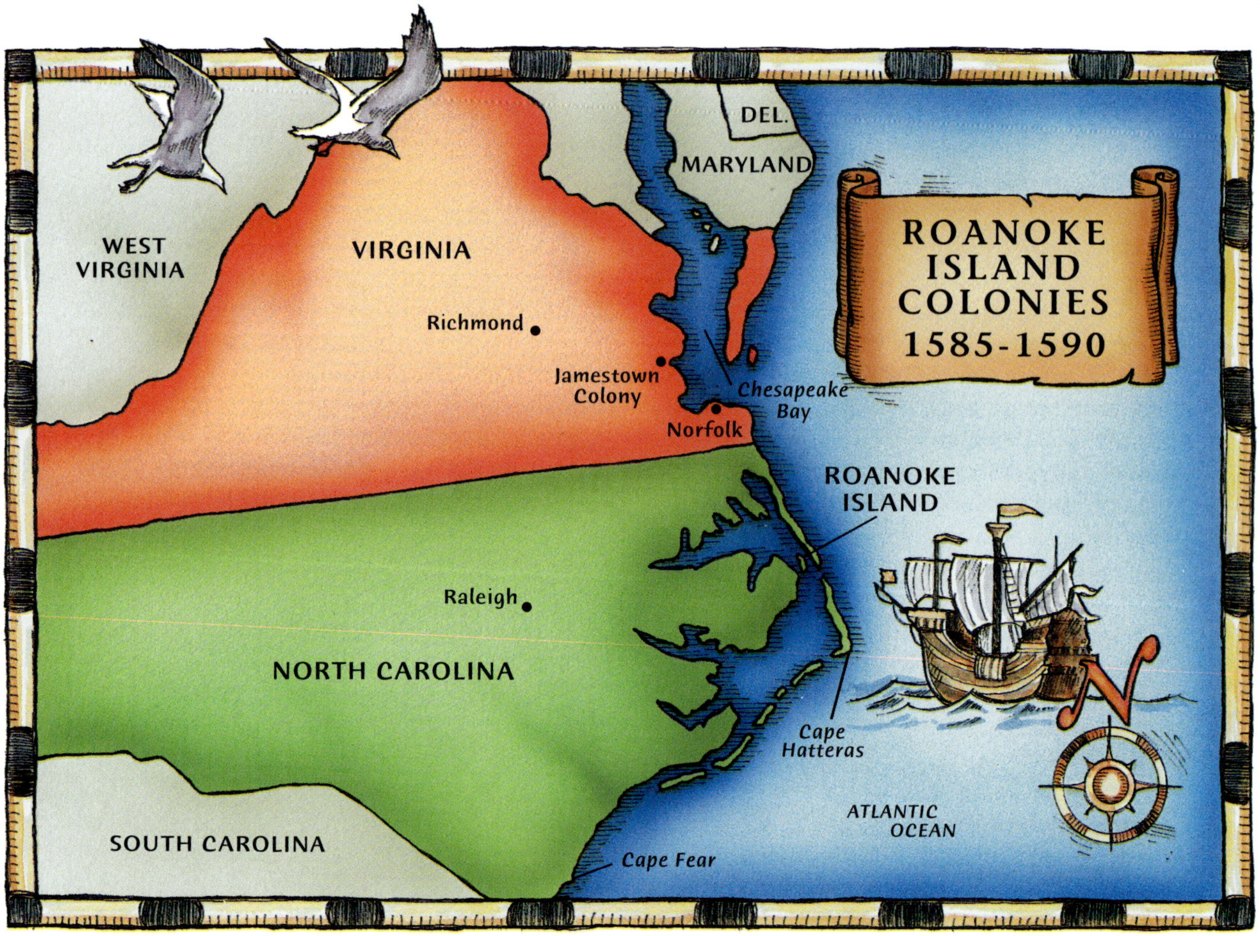

ment on Roanoke Island. But from the beginning, the colony faced serious problems. There weren't nearly enough settlers to build houses, plant crops, and also guard against Indian attacks. Because of these difficulties, Governor White decided to return to England to recruit additional settlers and get more supplies. Shortly before his departure, White's daughter Eleanor gave birth to a baby girl. The child was christened Virginia Dare, and she was the first child of English parents born in the New World.

Returning to England, White tried to outfit a relief expedition. But before he could sail again to North America, war broke out between Spain and England. A great Spanish Armada of more than 130 ships sailed for England in 1588, and all able-bodied English seamen were called upon to defend their country. Although the Spanish Armada was turned back by the English fleet, it would be two more years before White was able to assemble ships and provisions for a voyage back to Roanoke.

When he did return in 1590, he discovered that the colonists had vanished. For generations since, it has been widely believed that the settlers abandoned Roanoke and went to live with friendly Indians on Croatoan Island or other areas. Years later, when other settlers established the Jamestown colony, they were surprised to discover Indians with fair skin and gray-blue eyes. Even today the Lumbee Indians of North Carolina claim to be descendants of the Lost Colony's English settlers.

But in recent years, some new information has come to light. And this has led researchers to consider other possibilities about what became of at least some of the settlers of the Lost Colony.

A NEW CLUE

The most important new discovery involves a small 16th-century cannon, which weighed 300 pounds (136 kilograms) and measured 4½ feet (1.4 meters) in length. Fishermen found it in the waters off North Carolina in the early 1980s. Since then, it's been determined that the cannon was a British army field artillery gun known as a falcon. It was known that the Roanoke colonists had cannons of that type. But what was an army cannon, intended for use on land, doing on board a ship? The answer to this question led to a new theory about the Lost Colony.

The Roanoke colonists had a small ship called a pinnace. It may be that they gave up on their settlement and tried to sail back to England. It would have been logical to have taken along one or two cannons to protect their vessel from pirates or an attack by the ships of Spain, England's chief rival on the seas.

If that were the case, then perhaps the tiny ship ran into a storm and went to the bottom of the ocean with all its passengers. That would certainly explain how the cannon ended up on the ocean floor off the coast of North Carolina. Researchers are hoping that the site where the cannon was found may provide additional clues. They are now trying to raise money for an undersea research vessel. Such a craft was recently used to explore the wreck of the ocean liner *Titanic,* which sank in the Atlantic Ocean after hitting an iceberg in 1912.

Still, the question remains: *Why* did the colonists abandon Roanoke? There may now be an answer. Scientists who have been studying and analyzing the growth rings on 800-year-old bald cypress trees in the area concluded in 1998 that an extremely severe drought had struck Roanoke. This could have resulted in a number of scenarios:

First, the colonists could have been killed by Indians in a fight over scarce food supplies. Second, as has long been believed, they could have gone to live with friendly Indians farther south, away from the drought. Or, as the cannon suggests, they could have sailed north toward Chesapeake Bay or to England.

As exciting as this new research is, many more clues are needed before the mystery of the Lost Colony of Roanoke is completely solved. In the meantime, whatever became of Sir Walter Raleigh's dream of a permanent English colony in North America? Less than twenty years after the Roanoke colonists vanished, such a colony was established at Jamestown, Virginia—the first of the thirteen English colonies that eventually became the United States of America.

Governor John White was also an artist who drew many vivid watercolors of Indian life, including this one of an Indian man and woman eating.

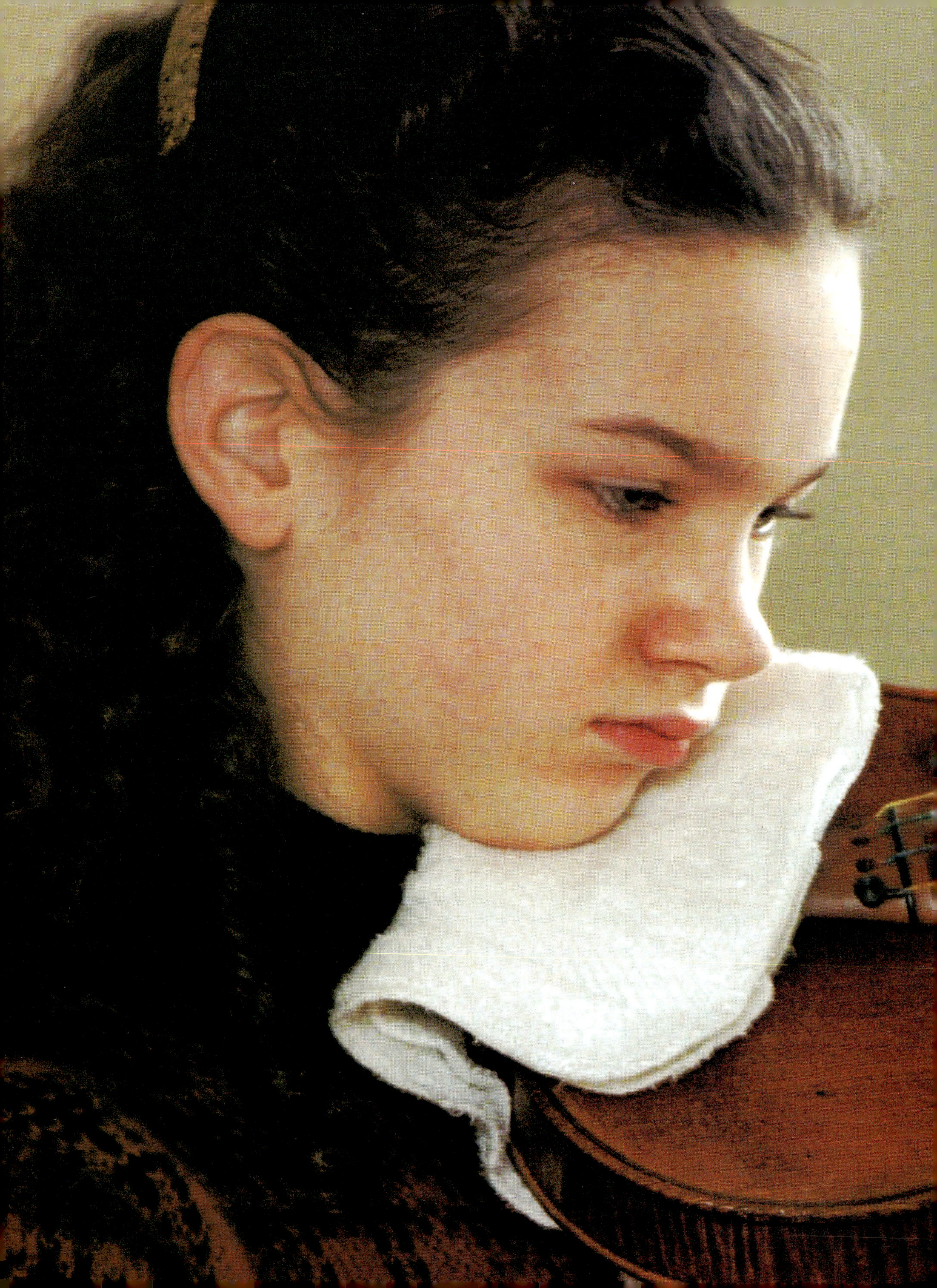

SPOTLIGHT ON YOUTH

Hilary Hahn began taking violin lessons when she was just four years old. She learned to play "Twinkle, Twinkle, Little Star," and she loved it. In 1998, the 17-year-old violinist was drawing attention with her first solo recording, featuring music by Bach. Hilary, who grew up in Baltimore, showed her talent early. She won a violin competition at age 9, was accepted by the Curtis Institute of Music in Philadelphia when she was just 10, and made her debut with the Baltimore Symphony Orchestra at 11. Home schooled, she commuted between Baltimore and the music school in Philadelphia at first. But by age 12, she was ready for college-level courses. Her family moved to Philadelphia so that she could attend Curtis full time, and she finished her bachelor's degree at age 16. But Hilary didn't rush her music career. Unlike many child music prodigies, who play hundreds of concerts and make recordings at a young age, she held to a limited schedule until 1997. Then, finished with school, she made her New York City recital debut at Lincoln Center and recorded her first CD.

WWW.COOLSITES

Stumped by a homework problem? Want to read a story from the land of your ancestors? Wonder where we are in the Milky Way? Eager to prepare a tasty dish for dinner? Find the answers on the Internet's World Wide Web—one of the coolest places to be these days. The Web is a huge community in cyberspace filled with thousands of sites that contain information on every subject imaginable. If your computer is connected to an on-line service, you can visit the four fun Web sites shown here. Each site has an address that begins with the letters http. Type in the address exactly as shown, and in seconds you'll be at the site.

The Curious Cat
http://www.wsu.edu/DrUniverse

Why does electricity shock? Do frogs sleep? What's a black hole? If you've got a question, ask Dr. W.S. Universe, the world's most curious cat. . .and a cat with connections! She'll go to a team of researchers at Washington State University for her information, and then give you the answer you're waiting for.

You also can read questions submitted by other kids. And if you'd like to contact a researcher who has answered a question for Dr. Universe, just send an e-mail to the doctor, and she'll put you in touch with the person behind the answer.

Tales From Around the World
http://storiestogrowby.com

Whootie Owl has a collection of folk and fairy tales that will delight readers of all ages. Select a category—perhaps magical creatures or tales from Spain—then choose a story. You can read the story on your computer screen or print it out to read later. You can let other readers know what you think of the story, and see what other kids have to say about it.

Know a good story that's not on this Web site? You can submit it to Whootie Owl. If he accepts it, it will be added to the site, your name will be featured beside the story, and you'll be entered in Whootie Owl's Hall of Fame!

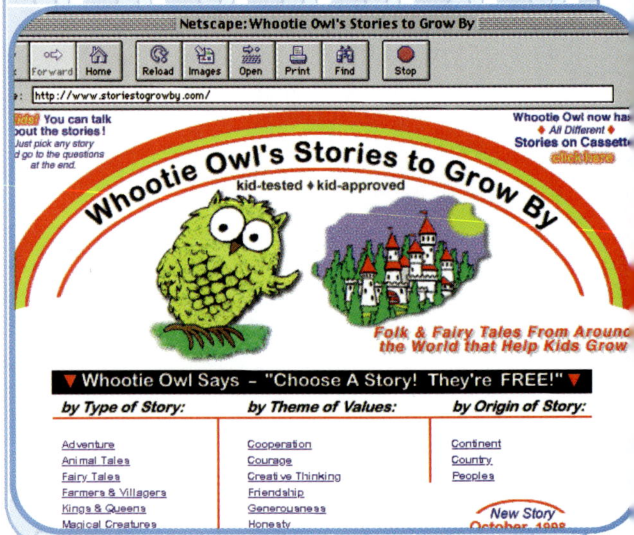

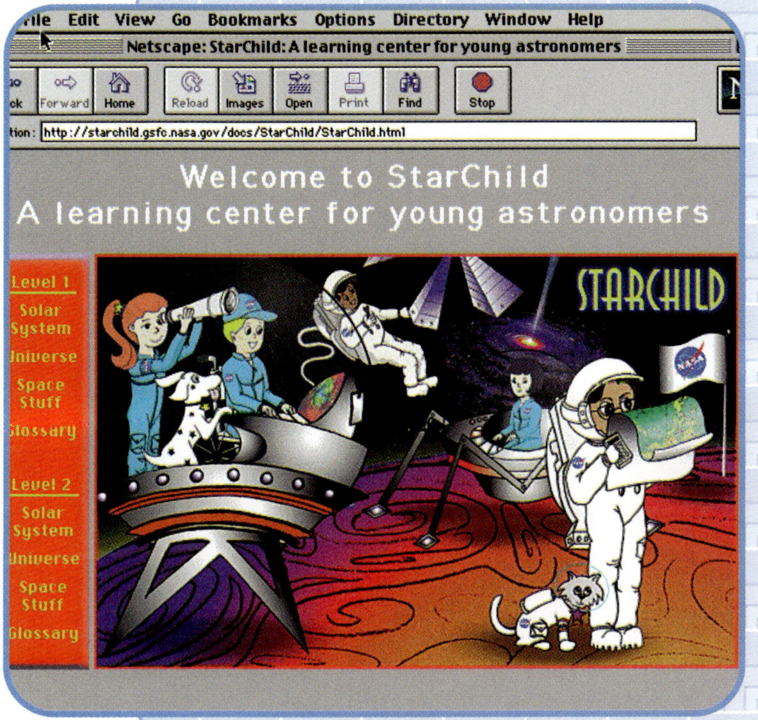

Calling Young Astronomers
http://starchild.gsfc.nasa.gov

Here's a wealth of information about stars, planets, comets, space travel, and other astronomy subjects, all written in a style that you can understand. (If you're really knowledgeable about astronomy, there's an easy link to Imagine the Universe, a Web site intended mainly for people ages 14 and up.)

Check out the many activities, too. Watch a movie about the solar system, calculate your height and age for other planets, find addresses for astronauts, and match star charts to the myths of various cultures. Once you become an expert on things astronomical, you'll be ready to play games such as Planet Tac Toe and Pair Me Up, Scottie!

Eat Your Veggies
http://www.broccoli.com

Broccoli will become your favorite vegetable after you visit Mom's Kitchen in Broccoli Town and learn how to whip up a tuna salad wrap, some spicy buffalo potato skins, or a tasty Asian stir-fry.

Did you know that broccoli has been on the dinner menu for at least 2,000 years? And that one-third pound of broccoli stalks contains more vitamin C than 204 apples? These are among the trivia and facts you can learn at this site. And if you have a question about broccoli, there's a handy Post Office where you can send an e-mail. In the Kids Club there are games to play, a coloring book to print out, and space to write a letter to the Broccoli Bunch.

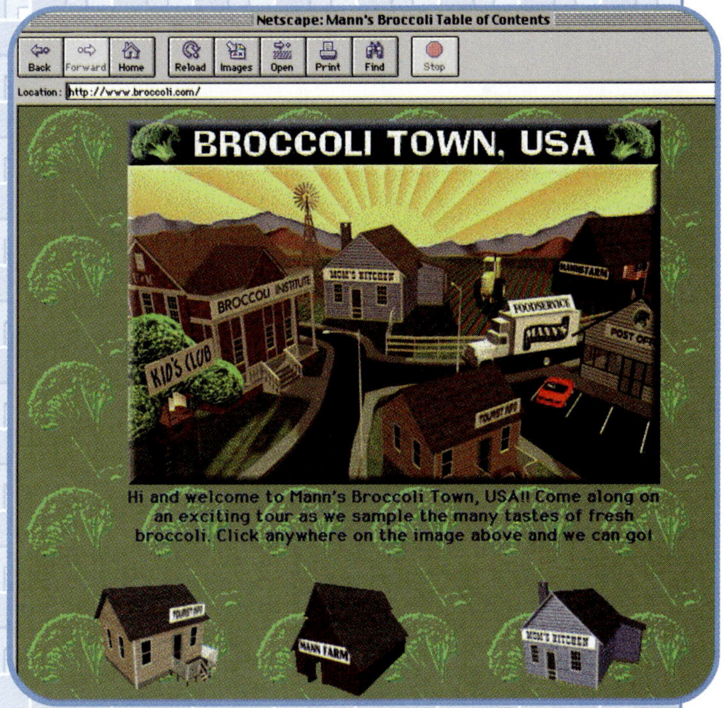

A career in writing can be a rewarding yet often demanding profession. Writers, like well-known author David Halberstam (*above*), can spend years gathering research materials before writing a book.

CAREERS IN WRITING

People often think of writing as a romantic, glamorous profession. The writer sits at a computer, turning out page after page of elegant prose. Then the work is published, and the author gains fame and fortune.

In fact, few writers fit this picture—and even fewer gain fame and fortune. But writing can be a fascinating career, with a wide range of options. People who have a way with words are in demand in publishing and politics, teaching and television, and many other areas. They may hold salaried positions, or they may work freelance (independently) for different clients. Writers come in contact with many people and ideas. And they have the satisfaction of producing work they can be proud of, whether it's a novel or a piece of advertising copy.

Here's a sampling of careers in writing. Each has its own rewards and requirements.

JOURNALISM

Journalism has been called the front line of history—**journalists** get information about current events and report that information to the public, and thus they are the first to record history. Because new events occur every day, a journalist's work is always exciting.

When people think of journalism, they think first of newspapers. On daily and weekly papers, **reporters** gather the news and write the stories that keep people informed. Often a reporter covers a "beat"—a geographic or subject area—and must keep abreast of events in that area. But some are general assignment reporters, assigned to cover different kinds of stories every day. Reporters must deal with tight deadlines. If a fire breaks out downtown at 3 P.M., the reporter assigned to cover it may have to gather the facts and write the story by 6 P.M., so the paper can be printed and distributed to its readers on time.

Most newspapers require reporters to have a four-year college degree. Many schools offer both undergraduate and advanced degrees in journalism, but a degree in liberal arts or in a specialty such as economics can also be useful. Reporters also need an avid curiosity and a willingness to work odd hours—news events don't all occur between 9 A.M. and 5 P.M.

The reporter's work is directed by **editors.** The **editor-in-chief** has the final say about what events are covered and how they will appear in the paper. On large papers, the editor-in-chief is assisted by a **managing editor,** who handles much of the day-to-day operation of the newspaper, and a staff of other editors who are in charge of certain kinds of news (such as local or international) or certain sections of the paper. There are also **copy editors,** who polish the language of the stories, check facts, write headlines, and often design the newspaper's pages. Editors usually begin as reporters and gain experience before moving into their jobs.

Newspapers also employ writers in other roles—as **editorial writers** (who give the newspaper's opinions on current events); **critics** (who review books, movies, art shows, and similar events); and **columnists** (who write their personal views of specific subjects).

But not all journalists work for newspapers. Some work for wire services, which distribute news stories to newspapers. Others work for magazines. Many magazines have full staffs of writers and editors, similar to newspaper staffs. But others are staffed mainly by editors and obtain articles from freelance writers, who may do work for many different magazines. Magazine articles tend to be longer and more thorough than newspaper stories, and the writer has more time to prepare them. The requirements for jobs on magazines are similar to those for jobs on newspapers.

Today, many journalists choose careers in television and radio, in the exciting field of broadcast news. **Broadcast news writers** work behind the scenes, gathering and writing the news stories that will be sent over the air. In television, the news writer's words must match the graphics and videotapes that viewers see on their screens. Broadcast writing must be clear, easy to read, and tight—the script for a news story may have to fit a time slot of a minute or less. But many TV news writers also work on documentaries and other long pieces.

Broadcast reporters, like news writers, gather and write about the news. But they also

The newsroom of a major newspaper is a busy place. Newspaper employees include reporters, editors, and specialty journalists such as editorial writers, critics, and columnists.

Reporters gather the news and write the stories that keep people informed. Most reporters cover events on the scene.

appear on screen and read their stories over the air. The most glamorous job in television journalism is that of the **news anchor,** who presents the major stories and links together the stories of other reporters. Many anchors write some of their own copy, particularly the lead story of the newscast. Often, however, they read material written by news writers.

News directors and **assistant news directors** coordinate the entire newscast and supervise the work of broadcast reporters and news writers. Like newspaper editors, they usually begin as reporters and move up as they gain experience. A four-year college degree in liberal arts or communications provides a good background for any of these jobs, but news directors also need managerial skills and some knowledge of the technical aspects of broadcasting.

BOOK PUBLISHING

The authors of books—whether their works are fiction or nonfiction—generally work independently. They gather the material they need and put it in the form they think is best. A book may take weeks, months, or years to write. There are no educational requirements for this work, beyond knowledge of the subjects you write about—you simply must have a talent for writing. But most book authors find that being well-read and having experi-

Television news anchors—such as CNN's Kathleen Kennedy and Leon Harris—often read material written by news writers. Broadcast writing must be clear and concise, in order to fit into tight time slots.

Stephen King—the Sultan of Spook

Stephen King is America's top author of horror fiction, and possibly the richest writer ever. His books have sold well over 100 million copies worldwide, and many have been turned into hit movies. They have made him a millionaire many times over. What's the reason for King's success? He scares people out of their skins—and they love it.

King, who turned 51 in 1998, has been at his craft for many years. He began reading horror fiction—and writing stories—as a boy in rural Maine. Before he graduated from college in 1970, he had sold two of his stories to a magazine. He kept writing, supporting himself by working as a janitor and an English teacher, among other jobs. He collected more rejection slips than checks for his work. He grew so discouraged that he tossed the unfinished manuscript for a novel into the trash. But his wife, Tabitha, saved the pages and encouraged him to complete it.

That book, published in 1974, was *Carrie,* about a rejected high-school girl who takes ghastly revenge on her town. It was a huge hit and later became a movie. King followed with *Salem's Lot,* about vampires in a small town; *The Shining,* a terrifying tale of a haunted hotel; and a string of other scary novels and short-story collections. *The Dead Zone, Firestarter, Christine,* and *Misery* are just a few of the King books that have hit the best-seller lists and been made into movies.

King's output is amazing. He writes about two books a year, under his own name and a pen name, Richard Bachman. He's also written screenplays for films and television miniseries. Critics have panned his works for being too gory. But even his critics agree that he's a genius at scaring people.

ence in writing shorter pieces is helpful in tackling a project as large as a book. Because they work independently, book authors must also be highly motivated.

The dream of every book author is to produce a best-seller, but few writers achieve this dream. In fact, far from becoming famous, some authors don't even see their names on their books. These are **ghostwriters,** who write such works as the "autobiographies" of celebrities. But like other book authors, ghostwriters are paid for their work, usually with a percentage of the proceeds from the book's sales.

When an author develops a manuscript or an idea for a book, he or she submits it to a **publisher,** who decides whether or not to produce the book. (Many authors work with **literary agents,** who help sell their works to publishers.) Publishers employ editors in a range of jobs to carry through the process of acquiring manuscripts and producing books, and writing skills are an important part of these jobs.

A **book editor** helps decide which manuscripts should be published, negotiates contracts with authors, works with designers and illustrators, oversees revisions in the manuscript, and follows the book through all the stages of production. Often the details of this work are carried out by **assistant editors, production editors,** and people in similar positions. A **copy editor** gives the language a final polish and sees that the manuscript is ready to go to the printer. In some types of publishing, such as reference book and textbook publishing, editors may be called on to do some of the actual writing.

Many editors have four-year college degrees in English or in another area of liberal arts. Most begin in low-level publishing positions, such as editorial assistant, and gradually work their way up. On the top rung are senior editors, who handle the most important books, and the publishers themselves. A publisher must have the ability to recognize good writing, but true writing skills are less important than managerial ability and good business sense.

Advertising copywriters create the slogans that make products sell. A highly successful campaign for milk uses the catchy phrases: "Got milk?" and "Where's your mustache?"

ADVERTISING

Today millions of products and services compete in the marketplace for the consumer's attention. The producers of these products and services rely on advertising to reach potential customers. If you're inventive and can turn a catchy phrase, you might consider a career in this field.

Advertising copywriters write the words that make products stand out, whether the ads appear in print or on radio and television. Their ads must be clever, informative, and persuasive—the consumer who sees or hears an ad for soap should remember the brand and want to buy it. But not all advertising is commercial. Besides everyday products and services, copywriters may prepare ads for political campaigns or nonprofit organizations. Some copywriters specialize in certain kinds of products or in certain media, such as billboards or television.

Direct mail advertising is a field that has grown in recent years. Instead of short, punchy ads for print or broadcast, the **direct mail specialist** prepares longer sales letters, brochures, flyers, inserts, and similar pieces that are mailed to potential customers. With more and more of this type of mail being sent out, the direct mail specialist must be especially creative to come up with novel approaches that will catch people's attention.

Many copywriters work freelance or for large advertising agencies, where they are part of an advertising team. The team, which includes marketing experts as well as the creative staff, develops an overall advertising campaign for each client. An **account executive** heads the team and is responsible for dealing directly with the client. This job requires the ability to come up with creative ideas, judge good advertising copy, and present proposals to clients.

A college degree in advertising, journalism, or liberal arts is recommended for most copywriting jobs. For account executives, college and graduate school degrees in business or economics can be helpful.

PUBLIC RELATIONS

In many ways, public relations is like advertising—it seeks to create a good image for the client. But public relations specialists take many different avenues to reach this goal. A number of corporations and agencies have their own public relations staffs, but there are also public relations agencies that service many clients. Public relations is a big field, and clients may range from adoption agencies to zoos.

Many **public relations writers** specialize in external publications—that is, they prepare news releases, articles, and press kits giving information about their clients. These are sent to trade journals and the news media, in the hope that they will form the basis for stories that appear in the press. Writers may also prepare brochures giving information about the company or client, and they may write speeches or scripts for slide presentations that others will deliver to the public. They may help prepare a company's annual report or letters to its stockholders.

Some public relations writers specialize in internal publications—they put out employee newsletters and magazines. This work is similar to work in journalism, but the goal is to promote good morale within the company as well as to keep employees informed. Such newsletters and magazines, called "in-house" publications, often feature profiles of employees and departments, news of promotions and hirings, and messages from executives.

Because much of public relations work is similar to journalism, the educational requirements are roughly the same. Experience in journalism is often a help in public relations. In fact, many journalists change careers and go into public relations, often because salaries tend to be higher.

SCRIPTWRITING

If you want to see your words come to life, consider a career as a **scriptwriter.** You could be a **playwright,** a **screenwriter for films,** or a **writer of television or video scripts.** Most scriptwriters specialize in one of these areas. In addition to being able to write, they must have some technical knowledge about production—at least what's possible and what isn't. There's also a small demand for writers of radio scripts.

The most glamorous forms of scriptwriting—for Broadway plays, major Hollywood

Write Now!

You don't have to wait to begin a writing career. There are plenty of opportunities for young people to develop writing skills and publish their work. Writing for school publications is a great way to start. In addition, many local newspapers devote a page to work by children. Community groups often sponsor writing contests for young people. And some children's magazines

print material by young writers. *Stone Soup,* for example, is written and illustrated by kids 8 to 13 years old. Check your school or local library for this and other magazines.

Want to compare notes with other kids who write? Find out if there's a writing club at your school. If not, perhaps you can start one. Your teachers may be able to guide you to programs and conferences for young writers, too. For example, high-school students in New England can apply to attend the yearly New England Young Writers' Conference at Middlebury College's Bread Loaf Mountain Campus in Vermont. They share manuscripts, attend readings by authors, and polish their skills.

A writer of video scripts must have technical knowledge of videotape editing and production.

films, and network television—are extremely competitive. Most scriptwriters work freelance. Producers may commission writers to prepare a script, or the writer may approach the producer with an idea. In films and television, several writers may work on a script until the final version is complete. A beginner who wants to break into this field usually has to prepare one or more complete scripts and then call on producer after producer, hoping that one will buy a script. Established writers often hire agents to help them find work. It helps to live in one of the major cities where the theater, film, and television industries are concentrated, such as New York and Los Angeles.

But there are many other outlets for script writers. Local theaters and cable television stations often produce works by writers who are just getting started. Scripts are needed for educational films and for instructional home videos. Corporations and public relations firms also employ scriptwriters. There are even video press releases, which are sent to television news departments.

At all levels, a scriptwriter must be able to visualize the way his or her material will be presented, whether it's on stage or screen. Narration and dialogue must be written to sound smooth and natural. A college degree in liberal arts provides a good basis for this career, but experience or study in theater, film, or video production also helps.

THE ELECTRONIC AUTHOR

Computers are the newest communications tool, and that means new opportunities for writers. The most exciting areas are compact discs (CDs) and the Internet, especially the part of the international computer network known as the World Wide Web. Many reference and educational books are now being published in CD versions. On the Internet, businesses are setting up Web sites to advertise their products and services. The Internet also has e-zines (electronic magazines), newsletters on just about any topic you can think of, and electronic versions of print newspapers and magazines.

Writers for electronic media must be creative and have computer know-how. Most CD's and many on-line publications combine text with graphics, animation, and sound. Writing material for them is a bit like scriptwriting. CD's and Web sites also use an interactive approach, with menus and links that allow readers to decide where they would like to go next. The writing itself

Producing E-zines (electronic magazines) on the Internet is an exciting new field for writers. The writing must be brief and effective to grab the attention of Web surfers.

must be concise and effective, to get the reader's attention.

Major publishers and other large businesses sometimes employ writers and editors who specialize in electronic media. However, many of the writers who create material for CD's and the Internet are freelance or work for small specialty firms.

OTHER WRITING CAREERS

Many other careers in writing are possible too. If music appeals to you, you might become a **lyricist** or a **jingle writer.** These are the people who write the words to songs and advertising jingles. Like many other writers, they often work freelance for a number of different clients.

Technical writers have been in great demand in recent years. They write instruction manuals, maintenance guides, and specifications for complicated pieces of equipment and devices such as computers. The job usually requires training in a specific technical field as well as writing ability.

Teaching is another avenue for someone who likes to write. Writing is an important part of the curriculum in elementary and middle schools. All colleges have English programs that involve writing, and many have journalism programs. A teaching certificate and, often, a graduate degree are required for most of these jobs. As you can see, writing offers tremendous variety when it comes to choosing a career. And if you have a way with words, that talent will serve you well in just about whatever field you choose.

Getting Started in Writing

Many successful writers offer this advice to young people who want to enter the field: Read as much as you can, and get as much writing experience as possible. For more information on writing careers, contact the following organizations:

Association of American Publishers—71 5th Avenue, New York, NY 10003

Society of Professional Journalists—16 S. Jackson Street, Greencastle, IN 46135

Freelance Editors Association of Canada—35 Spadina Road, Toronto, Ontario M5R 2S9

American Advertising Federation—1101 Vermont Avenue, N.W., Washington, DC 20005

Public Relations Society of America—33 Irving Place, New York, NY 10003

Society for Technical Communication—901 N. Stuart Street, Arlington, VA 22203

Canadian Authors Association—27 Doxsee Avenue North, Cambellford, Ontario KOL 1L0

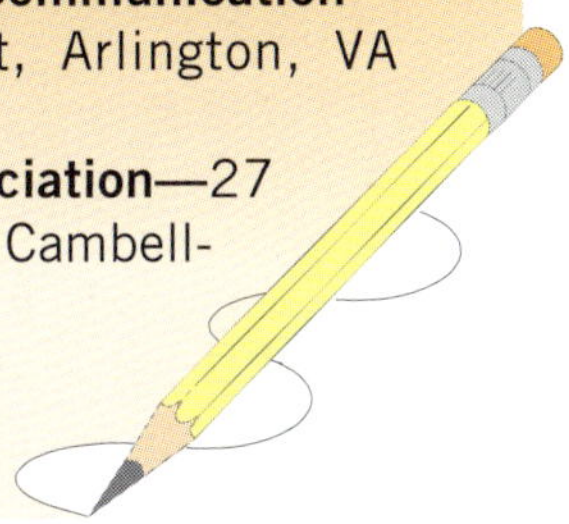

They admire their parents and worry about drugs. They work part-time, have their own television sets, and listen to alternative and rap music. They're **typical American teens,** according to a telephone poll conducted in April 1998. Among the findings were these:

- Today's teens get along with their parents. In the survey, 97 percent said they get along "very well" or "fairly well" with their parents. Many rank their parents as the people they most admired.
- Sixty-five percent of teenagers have their own television sets. On a typical weekday, today's teens spend an average of 3.9 hours watching television. Fox is the most popular network among teens.
- Teens with home computers spend an average of 2.5 hours a day at their machines. Those with Internet access spend almost 2 hours on line.
- Almost 50 percent of teens have part-time jobs.
- Eighteen percent carry beepers, and 14 percent have their own cars.
- Drugs and violence top the list of problems that worry teenagers.
- Alternative and rap tied as the teens' favorite music, followed by rhythm and blues and rock. Country ranked a distant fifth.
- Sixty-five percent of teens like tattoos—but only 5 percent have one.

What do you do with the little hangers that come on socks? Throw them out? Not **Kathleen McGowan** of Farmington Hills, Michigan. Kathleen, 24, has dozens of uses for them—hair curlers, jewelry, plant markers, and more. She won the $3,000 first prize in the 1998 National Plastic Reuse It Contest, sponsored by the American Plastics Council. What ideas can *you* come up with?

Hikaru Nakamura (right), 10, became the youngest chess master in the history of the game in February 1998. Chess players attain the master ranking by winning points in tournaments. Hikaru, who lives in White Plains, New York, started playing chess at age 7. He racked up 2,200 points by defeating players far more experienced than he is. Hikaru's brother, Asuka, 12 (left), is also a top player.

Asthma made **Franco Ripple**'s early years miserable. But in 1998, the Fort Lauderdale, Florida, teen was winning recognition for research into the cause of his misery—dust mites. These microscopic mites live in carpets and other places where dust collects. Millions of people, like Franco, are allergic to them. Franco, who has his allergies under control, has won awards for his studies of the mites, and for his use of photography and electron microscopy in his research. A top science student, 15-year-old Franco also draws and acts in community theater.

When **Christopher Haas** of Wildomar, California, noticed classmates having trouble with basic basketball skills, he figured out a way to help them. He dipped his hands in poster paint and put hand prints on the ball, to show how it should be held. The idea impressed his parents and teachers, who helped him develop it. The result: the Hands-on Basketball, a hot product that earned 13-year-old Chris $50,000 in 1998. The junior-sized ball has two sets of prints—for righties and lefties. A hands-on football and more products are in the works.

Jody-Anne Maxwell, 12, spelled "chiaroscurist" (an artist who emphasizes light and shade) to win the Scripps Howard National Spelling Bee, held in Washington, D.C., in May 1998. The National Spelling Bee is open to all kids who speak English, are 15 or under, and haven't entered ninth grade. Jody-Anne was the first winner from outside the United States and its territories in the contest's 71-year history. She's from Kingston, Jamaica, where she is an A student, and she hopes to be a lawyer one day. She beat 248 other finalists, all winners in local and regional spelling bees. Her victory brought her $10,000 and other prizes.

On safari in Africa? No—this is the Safari Ride at **Disney's Animal Kingdom,** which opened in 1998. The park is the latest addition to Disney World in Orlando, Florida. It covers 500 acres (202 hectares) and cost $800 million to build. And unlike other Disney parks, it features live animals—more than 1,000 of them. The 20-minute Safari Ride is a top attraction. It takes visitors by open truck through a section of the park that's been designed to look like the African plains. They can see white rhinos, giraffes, lions, and many other animals. Feeding stations bring the animals close to the truck route—ravines and boulders keep them away from the trucks!

Other areas in Animal Kingdom mix wildlife with the kinds of rides and shows that are a hallmark of Disney parks. At Dinoland USA, the animals aren't real and visitors can take a spine-tingling thrill ride called Countdown to Extinction. Shows featuring characters from Disney films such as *The Lion King* and *Pocahantas* are staged at Camp Minnie-Mickey. Asia, still under construction in 1998, will have a whitewater thrill ride through a rain forest. And Safari Village contains the park's centerpiece—the Tree of Life, a 14-story tower made to look like a giant tree, with a 3-D theater inside.

Amber Coffman of Glen Burnie, Maryland, is a typical teen in many ways. She goes to high school and has a busy social life. She even won a beauty pageant—she was Miss Maryland Teen in 1998. But her weekends are a little out of the ordinary. Every weekend she makes hundreds of sandwiches and delivers them to the homeless and hungry in Glen Burnie and nearby Baltimore. Amber got the idea for her food program when she was in fifth grade and worked on a report about Mother Teresa, the Roman Catholic nun who helped the poor in India. With her mother's help, she founded a nonprofit organization called Happy Helpers for the Homeless. In 1998 the organization was five years old, and Amber, 16, was still dedicated to it. Local businesses donate food, and her mother and friends help her distribute it. Her volunteer work has brought her much recognition over the years. She has received awards worth thousands of dollars. In 1997 Crayola named her the Ultimate True Blue Hero, the top honor in its community-service award program. As part of the honor, the company produced a new crayon bearing her name.

Nine-year-old **Hatty Jones** of London, England, won hearts in *Madeline,* the 1998 film based on the classic children's book. Hatty's only previous acting experience was in school plays. But the filmmakers knew that, with her red hair and impish smile, she would be a natural in the title role. The movie, about a little French schoolgirl whose adventurous spirit leads to all sorts of adventures, was shot in Paris over a twelve-week period. Hatty's parents were with her most of the time, and a tutor was on hand so she could keep up with school.

Twelve-year-old **Lindsay Lohan** also starred in her first film in 1998. In fact, she had two roles—as identical twins separated by their parents' divorce in *The Parent Trap*. Lindsay, from Cold Spring Harbor, New York, had made more than 60 TV commercials. She also had a role in a TV soap opera. The filmmakers chose her from about 4,000 girls who hoped to get the part. In the film, she played both twins—proper Annie James, raised in England, and hip Hallie Parker, from California.

Christopher Colin Mihelich of Carmel, Indiana, won first place in the 1998 Westinghouse Science Talent Search, America's most prestigious science contest. Chris studied mathematical expressions called polynomials for his project. He showed his math talent at an early age—he began taking college-level math courses in eighth grade. He got the news of the award, which includes a $40,000 scholarship, on his 17th birthday.

Brandon Keefe of Agoura Hills, California, has always loved to read. So no one was surprised when, in 1993, he decided to collect books for neglected kids as a third-grade project. But the drive turned out to be more successful than anyone expected. And in 1998, Brandon, now 13, was still at it. Twice a year, he sends out flyers and collects thousands of books, which are distributed to needy kids.

In March 1998, a controversial paper appeared in the *Journal of the American Medical Association*—one of the most important scientific journals in the United States. It suggested that a widely used healing technique called therapeutic touch (TT) didn't work. And what really set scientists buzzing was the fact that the paper's author was an 11-year-old, **Emily Rosa** of Loveland, Colorado.

Emily's paper was based on research she did for a science project in fourth grade, when she was 9. She had heard about TT from her mother, a nurse. TT is based on the idea that the body produces an energy field. TT practitioners say they can feel and manipulate the energy field by holding their hands several inches from the body, and that this promotes healing.

Emily put the claims to the test with 21 TT healers. Each healer sat behind a solid screen and put his or her hands, palm up, through holes in the screen. Emily held her hand several inches over the healer's right or left hand. The healer was asked to tell where Emily's hand was by feeling her energy field. In 280 tries, the healers did no better than they would have done by guessing randomly. Based on those results, Emily concluded that there was no scientific basis for TT. Her neat research project made her the youngest person to have a paper published in a major scientific journal.

Thanks to **Hunter Scott** of Cantonment, Florida (right), history books may carry a new account of one of World War II's most notorious disasters—the sinking of the USS *Indianapolis.* Struck by Japanese torpedoes, the *Indianapolis* went down in the Pacific Ocean on July 30, 1945. Hundreds of men bobbed in the ocean for four days, try-

ing to survive cold, thirst, and shark attacks. In all, 880 died. The Navy blamed the ship's captain, Charles Butler McVay. Survivors said the Navy was wrong, but McVay was relieved of his command. Years later, haunted by the incident, he took his own life.

Hunter first heard the story while watching the movie *Jaws*. A character in the film hates sharks because he was on the *Indianapolis* and saw sharks kill his shipmates. Hunter asked his father if the story was true, and his father said, "Look it up at the library." Hunter did more than that. Over two years, he interviewed 80 survivors and collected stacks of evidence, including documents that the Navy had kept secret for years. The evidence showed that actions the Navy failed to take might have saved the ship, or at least hundreds of lives. Partly as a result of 12-year-old Hunter's work, a bill to clear McVay's name was introduced in Congress in April 1998.

CREATIVITY

Made of exquisite silks and ivories and richly decorated with paintings, spangles, feathers, and pearls, fans have long been admired for their beauty. Today many are considered works of art and are prized by collectors. This delicate, hand-painted ivory fan was made for a fashionable French woman in the 1800s.

Ophelia (1852), by John Everett Millais, displays many features associated with the Pre-Raphaelite movement. Its tragic subject is taken from William Shakespeare's play _Hamlet._ It's filled with precise detail. And it was painted from life—using a model who floated in a bath.

THE PRE-RAPHAELITE MOVEMENT

In 1848, three young British artists started a revolution. Dante Gabriel Rossetti, 20, John Everett Millais, 19, and William Holman Hunt, 21, were fed up with the conventional art of their time, which was produced according to rigid formulas. They joined forces and set out to break those formulas, to create art that was inspiring and true to nature.

The result was the Pre-Raphaelite movement, a fascinating chapter in the story of art. The works of Pre-Raphaelite artists were extraordinary—scenes of medieval tales, Bible stories, myths, and similar subjects, in a style that was realistic and magical at the same time. The Pre-Raphaelites became some of the best-known artists of the Victorian era. And 150 years later, their paintings still cast a spell.

BREAKING THE RULES

Rossetti, Millais, and Holman Hunt met as students at a school run by the Royal Academy, the guiding force in the British art world. They were an unlikely trio. Millais, who came from a well-to-do family, was a child prodigy. He entered the Royal Academy school at age 11, and by the time he was 17 his works were hanging in prestigious academy shows. Holman Hunt was 17 when he entered the school, but he had to struggle to get in. His working class family opposed his art studies, and the school rejected him twice before finally accepting him.

Millais and Holman Hunt were already friends when they met Rossetti. The son of a poet and professor of Italian, Rossetti was sensitive and unconventional. He studied at the Royal Academy school only a short time. But he was the one who provided the spark for the movement.

Two things drew the three together—a passion for art, and a dissatisfaction with standard ideas about what art should be. Royal Academy students learned to paint according to a set of rules. Human figures, the rules said, were to be grouped in certain ways and drawn with ideal proportions. Strong light should come from one side, matched by softer light on the opposite side. Shadows should be deep, and objects in the foreground and background should be less detailed than the central subject. These rules were supposedly based on the works of the Italian Renaissance painter Raphael, which were considered ideal.

Rossetti, Millais, and Holman Hunt thought the rules produced paintings that were stilted and artificial. They also felt that the subjects considered appropriate for paintings—still lifes, landscapes, seascapes, family scenes, farm scenes—were boring and unworthy of art.

A SECRET SOCIETY

The three young artists recruited a few others to their cause and formed a secret society. They named it the Pre-Raphaelite Brotherhood—a reference to art before the time of Raphael—and worked the initials "PRB." into their paintings. Those paintings caused a stir when they were first exhibited, in 1849. The colors were bright, almost harsh. The pictures were filled with detail—everything from the patterns of fabrics to litter on the ground was rendered precisely. Settings were based on real landscapes and interiors. Figures were based on real models, not ideal proportions, and stood or sat as they might in real life. And the subjects—drawn from poetry and religion—were very different from the usual still lifes and landscapes.

At first, the Pre-Raphaelites weren't successful with their paintings. One critic scoffed at "that strange disorder of the mind or the eyes, which continues to rage with unabated absurdity among a class of juvenile artists who style themselves PRB." Others, including the novelist Charles Dickens, denounced the works as eccentric and even revolting. Then, in 1851, the Pre-Raphaelites attracted the attention of John Ruskin, one of the most respected art critics of the time. Rather than condemning the artists, Ruskin supported them. Even if their work was flawed, he said, it showed talent—and they deserved respect. Over the following years, Ruskin continued to defend the Pre-Raphaelites, and their work began to gain acceptance. A growing

Our English Coasts ("Strayed Sheep") **was painted by William Holman Hunt in 1852. Of all the Pre-Raphaelite painters, Hunt was the one most drawn to the English countryside. The strong light, bright colors, and realistic details of this scene are typical of his work. Hunt continued to paint in this style throughout his career.**

Saint George and the Dragon (1868) was painted by Edward Coley Burne-Jones. A "second-generation" Pre-Raphaelite painter, Burne-Jones was fascinated by medieval legends.

number of artists adopted aspects of the Pre-Raphaelite style.

The Pre-Raphaelite Brotherhood was short-lived, however. By 1855, the three founders were heading in different directions. Millais was accepted as an associate of the Royal Academy and began to paint in a more popular style. He chose more popular subjects, too, producing numerous paintings of adorable little girls. Hugely successful, he eventually became president of the Academy. Holman Hunt kept to the Pre-Raphaelite style, especially its vivid colors and natural settings. But his paintings preached the moral values of the Victorian era. Eventually, he argued with Rossetti, and their friendship ended.

THE SECOND GENERATION

Rossetti, meanwhile, became the center of a growing artistic circle. Sensitive to criticism, he rarely exhibited his work. But he developed an excellent reputation and many private patrons. He had a lifelong fascination with the works of the Italian Renaissance poet Dante, and he often painted scenes from the poet's work.

By the 1880s, the Pre-Raphaelite style had won an important place in British art. *The Lady of Shalott,* painted in 1888 by John William Waterhouse, shows its continuing influence. Subjects taken from the legends of King Arthur, like this one, were favorites with the Pre-Raphaelites.

Among those who gathered around Rossetti to talk of art and poetry were two young artists, Edward Coley Burne-Jones and William Morris, who helped take the Pre-Raphaelite movement to its next stage. Burne-Jones was so taken with Rossetti's works that he left school, where he was studying for a career in the church, to paint. Morris, an architect, also switched careers after meeting Rossetti. Like the other Pre-Raphaelites, Burne-Jones and Morris were in love with the past and fascinated by romantic poetry, tales of chivalry, and ancient myths. Tales of King Arthur were favorite subjects for their works.

The paintings of this new generation of Pre-Raphaelite artists had an air of romance and mystery. They were also more decorative, emphasizing patterns and composition. In fact, several of the artists branched out into decorative arts. In 1861, Morris founded a company to create interiors that reflected the Pre-Raphaelite style. The company designed rooms and produced furniture, tapestries, wallpaper, and stained glass. Rossetti and other artists contributed many of the designs. Today, Morris is best remembered as a designer and craftsman and the founder of the Arts and Crafts movement.

Dante Gabriel Rossetti painted *The Day Dream* in 1880, two years before his death. Sad, beautiful maidens like this one were among Rossetti's favorite subjects.

A LASTING LEGACY

In 1860, Rossetti married Elizabeth Siddal, the model for many of his pictures. Tragically, she died within two years of an overdose of laudanum, a pain-killing drug. Rossetti buried her with a sheaf of his poems and moved to a new house on Cheyne Walk in London. He continued to paint, and in 1870 he published his poems—after retrieving the manuscripts from his wife's grave. When they met with harsh criticism, he was crushed. He became more and more reclusive, spending his days at home with an assortment of strange pets—armadillos, hedgehogs, lizards, peacocks, wombats.

Rossetti died in 1882, Millais in 1896, and Holman Hunt in 1910. By that time, the Pre-Raphaelites were no longer revolutionary. Impressionism and other movements had taken painting in new directions. But Pre-Raphaelite influence was still strong, especially in illustration and decorative arts. The decorative style known as art nouveau, with swirling lines and natural forms, grew out of the Pre-Raphaelite style.

In their day, the Pre-Raphaelites brought new life to art. Today their paintings seem melodramatic, but people still appreciate the strange beauty of these works. Their appeal may have been summed up best by Burne-Jones, whose paintings were showcased in an exhibit at the Metropolitan Museum of Art in New York City during 1998.

"I mean by a picture," Burne-Jones wrote, "a beautiful romantic dream of something that never was, never will be—in a better light than any light that ever shone—in a land that no-one can define or remember, only desire—and the forms divinely beautiful."

Helen Hunt (best actress) and Jack Nicholson (best actor) in *As Good as It Gets*.

ACADEMY Awards 1998

CATEGORY	WINNER
Motion Picture	*Titanic*
Actor	Jack Nicholson (*As Good as It Gets*)
Actress	Helen Hunt (*As Good as It Gets*)
Supporting Actor	Robin Williams (*Good Will Hunting*)
Supporting Actress	Kim Basinger (*L.A. Confidential*)
Director	James Cameron (*Titanic*)
Cinematography	*Titanic*
Visual Effects	*Titanic*
Song	"My Heart Will Go On" (*Titanic*)
Foreign–language Film	*Character* (The Netherlands)
Documentary Feature	*The Long Way Home*
Documentary Short	*A Story of Healing*

Left: Matt Damon and Robin Williams (best supporting actor) in *Good Will Hunting*. Above: Leonardo DiCaprio and Kate Winslet in *Titanic* (best motion picture). Below: Kim Basinger (best supporting actress) in *L.A. Confidential.*

This peacock-feather fan from China was made in the 1900s. Today, beautiful fans like this one are reminders of the elegance of the past and are valued as works of art.

FAN-FARE

Hand-held fans have a practical purpose: On a hot day, they create a cooling breeze. But throughout their long history, fans have been far more than useful objects.

Delicate and richly decorated, these accessories have been symbols of rank and aristocracy and "musts" for fashionable women. Special fans have been created to commemorate important events and even to advertise products. And today, when air conditioning has replaced the fan as the most common cooling device, beautiful fans are valued as works of art.

FAN HISTORY

People may have used fans before the dawn of history—the first ones were probably large leaves or palm fronds. They were followed by fans made of ostrich plumes and other feathers. Such fans were used in ceremonies and by royalty in many ancient civilizations. But the Chinese may have been the first to have fans for ordinary use, perhaps as early as 2000 B.C. These fans were carried by both men and women.

Early Chinese fans were handscreens—flat, rigid boards—made of wood, woven rushes, and paper or embroidered fabrics stretched over wooden frames. Handles were formed of ivory, jade, gold, silver, lacquered wood, and other materials. These fans came in many shapes, including heart-shaped, moon-shaped, and pear-shaped. The Chinese are also thought to have been the first to paint designs on fans.

In the 600s A.D., the Japanese invented the folding fan, which was formed of flat sticks riveted together at one end. Folding fans were far less bulky than handscreens, and their popularity quickly spread. Again, all sorts of materials were used. There were even iron-ribbed fans that warriors could carry into battle. This wasn't as silly as it sounds—not only did these battle fans make good weapons, the Japanese commanders also used them to send signals to their troops.

Ivory and silk cockade fan, United States, mid-1800s

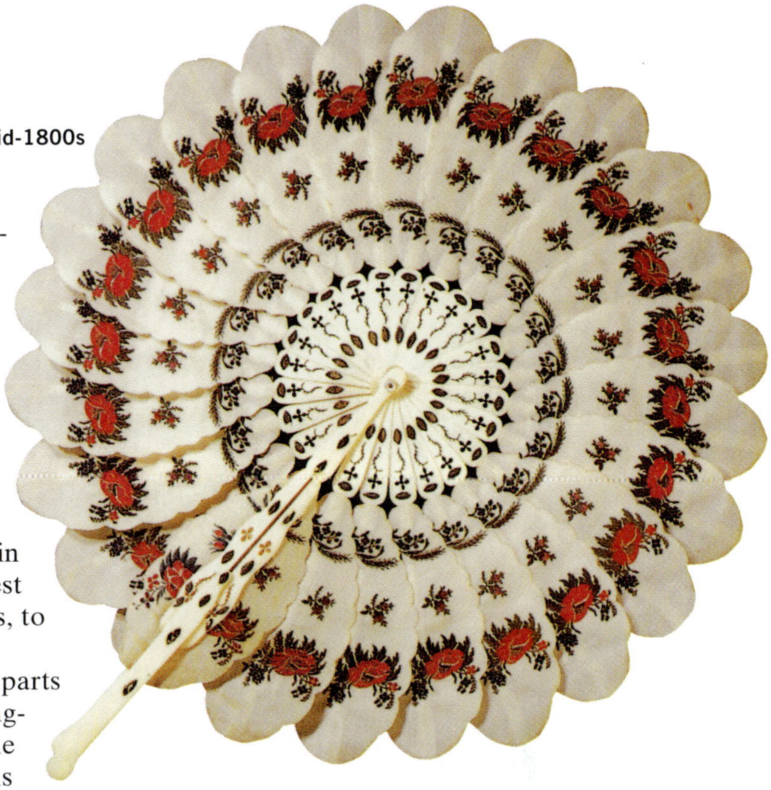

Off the battlefield, Chinese and Japanese court etiquette dictated how fans should be held and used. For example, high-ranking Chinese officials who passed each other on the street were allowed to cover their faces with their fans. That way, they wouldn't have to acknowledge each other and go through elaborate rituals of greeting. Etiquette also decreed that fans should be used only in warm weather, and certain types of fans were reserved for the hottest days. Fans were often presented as gifts, to show esteem and goodwill.

Fans have an ancient history in other parts of the world, too. Bearers carrying long-handled ostrich-plume fans attended the rulers of ancient Egypt. Feather fans were also used in ancient Greece and Rome, and women of that time often carried handscreens. Our word "fan" comes from the Latin word *vannus,* the name of a flat, fan-like tool used in winnowing grain.

Fans were an important part of Greek and Roman religious rituals, and the early Christian church used them in its ceremonies. In Medieval Europe, court ladies (and sometimes men) carried flag-shaped leather handscreens or cockades—fans that opened to a full circle, with end sticks that formed a long handle. Fans made from peacock, ostrich, and parakeet feathers, with jewel-studded handles of ivory and silver, were popular in the 1400s and 1500s.

As European explorers began to roam the world's oceans at about this time, they

Ivory and parchment pleated fan, France, mid-1700s

brought back many strange items. Among them were folding fans from China and Japan. Europeans were quick to adopt this new fashion, first in Italy and then in France and other countries. Although handscreens and cockades remained in use, folding fans soon became the most popular type.

Royalty and the nobility were the primary users of fans at this time. Queen Elizabeth I of England was said to have been especially fond of them. From the early 1600s on, however, the fan more and more became an accessory that no well-dressed, sophisticated woman could do without. European craftsmen turned out thousands of fans each year, and thousands more were imported from China.

Ivory and silk pleated fan, China, mid-1800s

By the end of the 1700s, men had stopped carrying fans. But women used fans to shield their faces from the heat of open fireplaces in winter. In summer, fluttering fans cooled them and shooed away insects and unpleasant odors. A fashionable woman needed several fans—everyday fans, fancy-dress fans, fans to go with different outfits. And special fans were made for special occasions. Bridal fans—made of ivory, satin, and lace and carrying pictures of Cupid, hearts, and other symbols of love—were given by grooms to their brides. A woman who was in mourning might carry a black or gray fan, with discreet decorations.

A fan was more than a useful accessory—it was a mark of grace and style. Etiquette manuals gave instructions on proper fan use. The way a woman held and used her fan even became a method of communication. It was said that in the language of fans, different motions had meanings. When a woman held her open fan by her left ear, for example, she was saying, "Do not betray our secret." A half-open fan pressed to the lips meant, "You may kiss me." Historians doubt that such set meanings were ever really used. But there is no question that a woman could communicate many things by the way she snapped, fluttered, and carried her fan.

Ivory and silk pleated fan, Western Europe, mid-1800s

FABULOUS FOLDING FANS

There are two basic types of folding fans, the brisé fan and the pleated fan. *Brisé* is the French word for "broken" or "collapsible." This type of fan is formed of wide, flat sticks that fold up between decorative end pieces (called guards). A rivet fastens them together at the base of the fan. At the top, a ribbon links them so that they overlap slightly when the fan is open. In a pleated fan, the upper

Tortoise shell, silk, and ostrich-feather pleated fan, United States, 1920s

parts of the flat sticks support a semicircular band of paper or other flexible material. This band, called the leaf, is pleated so that it will fold up neatly between the guards when the fan is closed.

Both methods of construction are clever. But the materials and decoration that have been used are what make folding fans truly delightful. Sticks and guards have been made of ivory, bone, mother-of-pearl, horn, tortoiseshell, metal, and wood, including bamboo and fragrant sandalwood. They have been carved, painted, gilded, lacquered, pierced to look like lace, and studded with metal pins, spangles, and gems.

The leaves of pleated fans have been made of parchment, lace, silk, linen, and other fine fabrics, as well as of paper. Like the sticks, the leaves have been pierced, painted with all kinds of scenes and designs, and decorated with spangles, feathers, tiny pearls, and pieces of ivory and mica. Modern fans are often made of plastics and other synthetics that mimic these finer materials.

Like other articles of fashion, fans have been subject to fads and whims in East and West alike. The pictures and designs painted on them generally reflected the styles of art popular at the time they were made. Chinese and Japanese fans, for example, were made in many different styles and often carried short messages or poems in delicate calligraphy. The paintings were considered works of art, and the artists signed them. Sometimes the leaves of pleated fans would be removed from their guards and collected in albums.

Like other Chinese and Japanese paintings, these fan paintings often showed birds, flowers, and scenes from nature, delicately rendered in simple brushstrokes. Silk and paper with a gold or silver sheen were popular background materials. Bright red paper with gold designs was used in fans created for special

Painted cardboard handscreen, France, late 1800s

occasions like birthdays and New Year celebrations. In China, black was a color once reserved for the lower classes, but in the late 1800s black fans with gold and silver decorations became popular even with the aristocracy.

During their heyday in the West, fans likewise had many styles of decoration. Chinese designs were always popular because they suited the folding fan's origin in Asia. Sometimes the sticks and guards of a pleated fan would have a Chinese look, while the leaf bore a Western design. The reason was that, especially in the 1700s, sticks and guards were often imported from China and fitted with leaves when they arrived. Scenes from classical, Biblical, and mythological tales were also very popular in the 1700s, and fans of this time often carried miniature copies of famous paintings.

In the mid-1800s, the Victorians turned from painted scenes to elaborately carved and decorated sticks, painted designs, and exotic materials such as satin, lace, sequins, and feathers. But after new trade links were opened between Japan and the West in the 1860s, Japanese designs enjoyed a wave of popularity. And around the turn of the century, fans reflected the art nouveau style with swirling, free designs based on peacocks, flowers, and other natural forms.

While most fans were designed to look elegant and made use of rich materials, some were designed to deliver a message. For example, after the French Revolution, the French currency collapsed, and people began to carry fans papered with worthless bank notes and IOU's. And from the late 1700s on, printed fans were very popular.

Some printed fans were aids to memory—they carried rules for card games, dance steps, the words and music of songs, historical infor-

Ivory brisé fan, China, mid-1800s

mation, and maps. Church and chapel fans had prayers and psalms. Children's fans—smaller than adults' fans—carried the alphabet.

Other special fans were made to commemorate important events, such as the first balloon flight, in 1783. Travelers brought back souvenir fans that showed scenes of the places they visited. And as time went on, advertisers got into the act. Fans carried messages that plugged everything from hotels to cologne. Because these fans were designed to be given away, they were often cheaply made, with plain wooden (or, later, celluloid) sticks and thin paper leaves. But many had lovely designs.

Some fans were conversation pieces, with riddles or cartoons that poked fun at the society or the politics of the times. Another type of fan that was sure to spark comment was the autograph fan—a plain white fan that could be "decorated" with the signatures of friends and famous people. Telescope fans became popular in the 1800s. These fans had telescoping sticks that could be shortened, so that the folded fan could be tucked in a handbag.

Trick and puzzle fans were two special types of brisé fans. A trick fan looked like any other brisé fan—as long as it was opened from left to right. If your friend tried to open it from right to left, it would appear to fall apart, as though the ribbon holding the tops of the sticks had broken. Puzzle fans showed four different pictures: one on each side when opened from right to left, and two more when opened from left to right.

Mask fans had eyeholes, so that the bearer could hide her face and peer out. Lorgnette fans featured a small magnifying glass, usually set in one of the guards. The French queen Marie Antoinette, who was nearsighted, had one of these fans. And in the late 1800s, all kinds of odd fans were invented—pistol fans, parasol fans, fans made of rubber.

By World War I, however, fans were falling out of fashion in Western countries. Women were becoming more emancipated and didn't need to hide behind their fans. Clothing was more comfortable, and houses could be cooled with electrical fans.

Flashy ostrich-plume fans made a brief comeback in the 1930s, as accessories for evening gowns. But by this time, fans no longer served a useful purpose, and they were gradually set aside. Today the delicate and lovely fans of the past can be seen in museums and private collections, where they stand as reminders of the elegance of the past.

There was no question about it—**Leonardo DiCaprio** was the big new film star of 1998. DiCaprio played the young hero in the box-office blockbuster *Titanic,* and his starring role made him famous. Legions of Leo fans flocked to theaters when his next film—*The Man in the Iron Mask,* a swashbuckling adventure tale—came out in March 1998. Girls raved about his good looks. And everyone agreed that DiCaprio, 23, had plenty of talent. He also had solid acting credentials. He had appeared in a television series, *Growing Pains.* At age 19, he had been nominated for an Academy Award for *What's Eating Gilbert Grape,* in which he played a mentally impaired teen. Two other films—*This Boy's Life* and *William Shakespeare's Romeo and Juliet*—had brought praise. After *Titanic,* DiCaprio was said to be uncomfortable with his image as a romantic idol. In October 1998, he appeared in a different sort of role—as a spoiled movie star in the film *Celebrity.*

Before she landed the title role in the TV series *Ally McBeal,* actress **Calista Flockhart** had no plans to work in television. Her career was taking off on Broadway and in the movies. But then she read a script for the series, about a young female lawyer juggling her career and personal life. Its mix of comedy, drama, and fantasy captivated her. The series captivated viewers, too. It become a hit of the 1997–98 season—and made Flockhart a star.

The Lion King ruled Broadway in 1998, winning the Tony Award as best musical. The show was based on Walt Disney's animated film of the same name. It told the story of Simba, a young lion who comes of age on the African plains. In this version, directed by Julie Taymor, actors wore giant masks and moved puppets to suggest animal characters. Even the African savanna came to life, portrayed by dancers. Composers Elton John and Tim Rice wrote three new songs for the show.

Actress **Ming-Na Wen** starred in a major film in 1998—without appearing on screen! Wen "voiced" Mulan in the animated Disney feature of that name. Many of Mulan's mannerisms were also hers. She was videotaped as she read her lines, and the animators watched the tapes. Wen, 30, was born in Macao, on the China coast, but grew up in Pennsylvania. She appeared in the 1993 film *The Joy Luck Club* and other movies.

No, it isn't a tattoo. It's **mehndi**—an ancient art that was a hot fashion in Western countries in 1998. In mehndi, intricate designs are painted on the skin using a paste made from henna, a plant. When the wet henna paste is applied, it's dark in color. When it dries it's brushed off, and red-brown designs remain. But unlike tattoos, mehndi designs aren't permanent—in a few weeks, they fade away. Mehndi is a traditional art in India, the Mideast, and North Africa.

These glittering gems are diamonds—the world's most coveted jewels. In 1998 they were featured in an exhibit, ***The Nature of Diamonds,*** at the American Museum of Natural History in New York City. The exhibit explored every facet of the diamond—its origins, its hardness, its uses, its beauty. Among the surprises: Diamonds come in almost every color of the rainbow.

When ***Dawson's Creek*** aired in February 1998, the series brought a group of fresh faces to television. From left are Joshua Jackson, Katy Holmes, James Van Der Beek, and Michelle Williams, the show's young stars. Van Der Beek, 20, took a leave from college to play Dawson Leery, a film-crazy teenager from a small town. The others, all aged 17 to 20, play his pals. The show earned high ratings with teenage viewers in its first season.

On May 14, 1998, the popular television series ***Seinfeld*** went off the air after nine years. Billed as "a show about nothing," *Seinfeld* was created by comedian Jerry Seinfeld (far right). On it, he played a stand-up comedian, joined by friends Kramer (left; Michael Richards), George (Jason Alexander), and Elaine (Julia Louis-Dreyfus). *Seinfeld* followed the lives of the four friends, all single New Yorkers, finding humor in everything from riding the subway to ordering takeout food. It won top ratings and numerous awards. In the show's last season, its stars were among the highest paid actors on television. About 108 million fans tuned in the last episode. In it, the four were arrested on charges of criminal indifference, for failing to help the victim of a carjacking. Characters from past episodes reappeared at their trial to denounce them for selfish things they'd done in the past. The "New York Four" were sent to jail for "selfishness, self-absorption, and greed"—exactly the qualities that made them so funny. Fans were sorry to see the show go, but they could look forward to years of reruns.

Look closely at the picture of the flamingo at right. It's made up of hundreds of tiny photographs, each carefully chosen and placed to form the larger image. **Photomosaics** like this, created by Robert Silvers, were a hot design trend in 1998. Several major magazines used the designs on their covers, and Silvers's work was featured on posters and in a book. The technique is simpler than it seems—because it's done with the help of a computer program that Silvers wrote. First, the main image is scanned into the computer. Then the computer searches among thousands of photos to find the perfect match for each section. Finally it arranges the photos to produce the photomosaic. Each photo must have the right colors and textures for its part of the image, and sometimes it must relate to the subject, too. Silvers used photos of money, for example, to make a portrait of Bill Gates, the world's richest man. He created a portrait of Abraham Lincoln from old Civil War photographs.

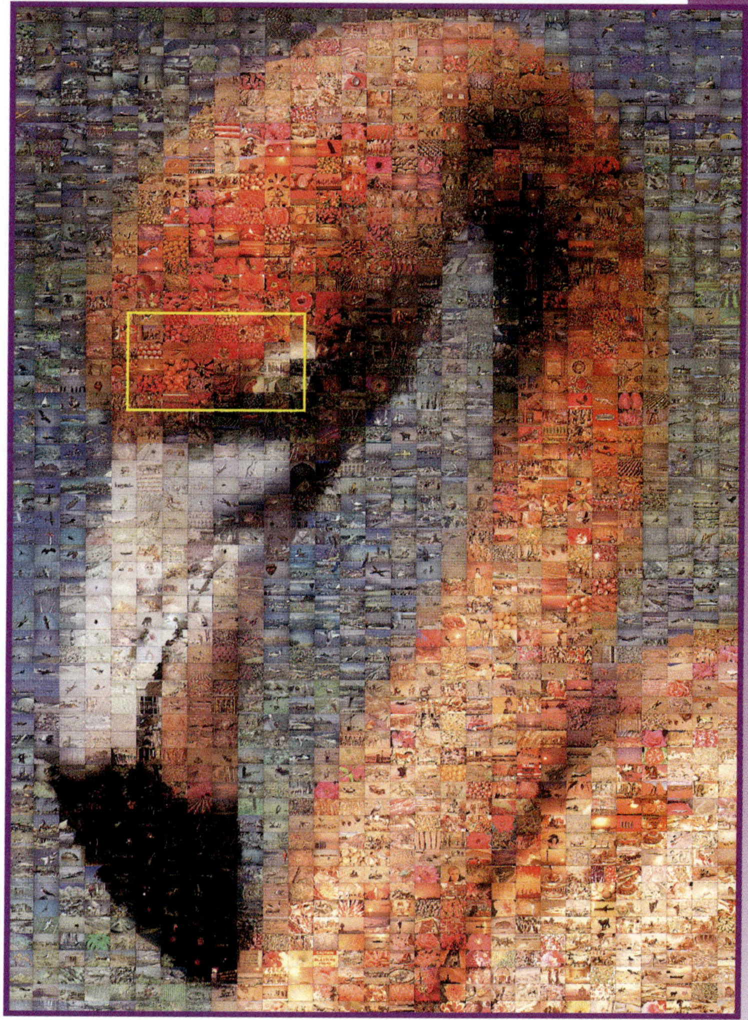

Saving Private Ryan, with Tom Hanks and Matt Damon, won high praise for its realistic battle scenes.

MOVIE TIME!

At the movies, 1998 was a *Titanic* year. The film about the sinking of the famous ocean liner broke box-office records and was the year's most talked-about movie. But other films brought plenty of excitement to the big screen. Comets, meteors, and a giant reptile threatened Earth. Swashbuckling heroes crossed swords with villains, and soldiers battled in World War II. There were plenty of warm-hearted tales, too, with films of children's classics, a famous Chinese legend, and remakes of several classic films.

LIGHTS, CAMERA...ACTION!

Director Steven Spielberg brought a classic wartime action movie to the screen with *Saving Private Ryan*. The plot of this film centers on a group of soldiers, led by Captain John Miller (Tom Hanks), who are sent behind enemy lines in Europe during World War II. Their mission: Find and rescue Pri-

Antonio Banderas starred as the masked avenger Zorro in the swashbuckling adventure film, *The Mask of Zorro.*

vate Ryan (Matt Damon), a paratrooper whose three brothers have all been killed in the war. The movie raised important questions about the nature of war and heroism. It won high praise for its realistic presentation of battle, especially for a 24-minute segment showing the D-Day landing in brutal detail.

A more dashing and romantic adventure story was *The Man in the Iron Mask,* based on the classic novel by Alexandre Dumas. Leonardo DiCaprio starred in a dual role: As the young King Louis XIV of France, he was a spoiled royal brat; and as the king's identical brother, Philippe, he was as noble as the king was shallow. At the start of the film, Philippe has been imprisoned by the king and forced to wear an iron mask to keep his identity secret. He is freed by none other than the Three Musketeers—Athos (John Malkovich), Porthos (Gérard Depardieu), and Aramis (Jeremy Irons)—heroes of other Dumas novels. Gorgeous costumes and restored castles were used to create the 17th-century setting.

Masked heroes starred in another costume adventure film, *The Mask of Zorro.* Set in Mexico during Spanish colonial days, this film brought back a character that first appeared in a 1919 novel and has been featured in numerous earlier films. Zorro is Don Diego de la Vega, a nobleman who puts on a mask to battle Spanish injustice. When this masked avenger strikes, he leaves a telltale mark—a "Z" carved with his sword. In the 1998 film, Don Diego (Anthony Hopkins) escapes after 20 years of unjust impris-

The Unsinkable *Titanic*

"WE HAVE STRUCK AN ICEBERG." This was the message received from the oceanliner *Titanic* on April 14, 1912. In less than three hours, this "unsinkable" ship was at the bottom of the Atlantic Ocean. More than 1,500 of its 2,200 passengers died. People called it "the most terrible shipwreck in history."

"WE HAVE STRUCK GOLD." This was the message from the people who made the movie *Titanic,* which opened in theaters at Christmastime 1997. Some had predicted that the film, like the ship, would be a disaster. But at the box office, *Titanic* quickly surpassed *Star Wars* as the top-grossing film of all time.

Why was *Titanic* so popular? Because the movie seemed to have something for everyone. The story is a vivid and sweeping portrayal of a true historical event. It has acts of heroism—men sacrificing their lives by choosing to go down with the ship. The special effects are eye-popping, and the suspense is heartstopping. Perhaps most of all, the movie has a tender love story, in which Jack (Leonardo DiCaprio) dies so that Rose (Kate Winslet) can live.

Few films have touched audiences in so personal a way. Fans were seeing it three, four, and even ten times. Audiences not only in the United States but also in Denmark, Mexico, China, and Slovenia loved it. Nine books about *Titanic* and its male star, Leonardo DiCaprio, appeared on the best-seller lists. And the soundtrack, which includes Celine Dion's haunting hit "My Heart Will Go On," sold like hotcakes.

Titanic also did fantastically well at the Academy Awards. It won a record-tying 11 Oscars—including best picture, best director, best visual effects, and best song. It's no wonder that *Titanic* became the first film ever to gross $1 billion worldwide!

In *Armageddon*, astronauts (led by Bruce Willis) set out to save the world from a deadly asteroid.

onment. He teams up with a young apprentice (Antonio Banderas) and teaches him how to play the Zorro role. Together, the two Zorros defeat the evil Spanish governor who sent Don Diego to jail and kidnapped his infant daughter years before. There's plenty of swashbuckling swordplay and daredevil horseback riding, as well as romance.

Not all of the year's films were so packed with action. *The Horse Whisperer* was the story of a girl and her horse, both injured in a terrible accident, who heal and regain confidence with the help of a Montana horse trainer. Robert Redford directed the film and played the trainer. Scarlett Johansson played the injured girl, who is left partly crippled and emotionally withdrawn by her accident. Kristen Scott Thomas played her mother, a brisk and determined magazine editor. One of the film's biggest stars was its beautiful Montana setting.

Another thoughtful film was *Good Will Hunting*, about a young math genius who prefers manual labor and obscurity to academic stardom. Will Hunting (Matt Damon) works as a janitor at the Massachusetts Institute of Technology, where he could easily be a top student. Will he stay in that life or realize his intellectual potential? The film's plot revolves around that question. Robin Williams plays a therapist who works with Will, and Ben Affleck plays Will's best friend. Affleck and Damon, both in their 20's, also wrote the script.

SCIENCE-FICTION THRILLS

High-tech special effects have brought science-fiction films to new levels. So it's not surprising that one of 1998's popular offerings featured a high-tech version of an old sci-fi favorite: *Godzilla*. Godzilla is a mutant reptile, grown unbelievably large due to nuclear radiation. In movies of the 1950s, the monster was played by an actor in a rubber suit. In the 1998 film, Godzilla was created through computer graphics and robotics—and this Godzilla is much bigger, and much scarier, than the old one. The beast emerges from the ocean at New York City and stomps through Manhattan, trashing most of the city's landmarks. Matthew Broderick stars as a scientist racing to stop the creature.

Earth was threatened by huge objects from deep space not once but twice in 1998—but both threats were pure science fiction. In *Deep Impact,* a comet nearly as big as Manhattan zooms toward Earth. Will the impact snuff out life, the way an earlier impact is thought to have killed off the dinosaurs? Astronauts (led by Robert Duvall) rocket into space in a last-ditch effort to divert the comet before it strikes. In *Armageddon,* an asteroid the size of Texas hurtles toward Earth. Destruction seems certain. But astronauts (led by Bruce Willis) set out to blow up the deadly asteroid with a nuclear blast.

The popular science-fiction television show *The X-Files* made the jump to the big screen in 1998, as FBI agents Fox Mulder (David Duchovny) and Dana Scully (Gillian Anderson) continued their pursuit of mysterious aliens from outer space in a feature film. The film's plot hinges on a vast government conspiracy to conceal the presence of aliens who are determined to rule Earth. The action sweeps from Texas to Antarctica, with plenty of the weird goings-on that fans of the television show have come to love.

COMEDY

One of the year's most original films was *The Truman Show.* Jim Carrey starred as Truman Burbank, a man whose entire life, from birth to age 30, has been broadcast live on television—without his being aware of it. The Florida island where he lives is nothing more than a giant set for the show. All his friends, even his mother and his wife, are actually just actors. And everything he says and does is captured by hidden cameras. Gradually, Truman begins to realize that everything in his perfect world isn't what it seems. Will he be able to escape the show, and what sort of life will he find outside it? Carrey, best known for slapstick comedy roles, won praise for his work in this funny but thought-provoking film.

Spice World, a film that was strictly for laughs, featured the singing group Spice Girls. Members of the group played themselves in this fictionalized behind-the-scenes look at their lives as pop stars. The movie was peppered with plenty of Spice Girl hits, and lots of other stars showed up in cameo roles.

What if you suddenly came face-to-face with your identical twin—a twin you never knew existed? That's what starts the action in *The Parent Trap.* This 1998 film was a remake

Going Buggy for *Antz*

It had comedy, romance, action, and suspense. It had a cast of billions. And the stars all had six legs. The animated feature film *Antz* was an instant hit—it went straight to the top of the box-office list and audiences went buggy!

Antz was the first animated film by the movie studio DreamWorks, and the filmmakers had a lot of fun with the project. They gave their insect characters human ideas and emotions. And they imagined what the world might look like from an ant's point of view. All the animation was created by computers, which allowed the animators to include lots of detail and give the insect characters a three-dimensional look. But actors, who provided the voices of the characters, gave them personality.

The movie's hero is Z-4195 ("voiced" by Woody Allen), a lowly worker ant who's unhappy with his lot. He complains about being the middle child in a family of five million. But when he meets the beautiful Princess Bala (Sharon Stone) it's love at first sight. Z trades places with a soldier ant (Sylvester Stallone) in a scheme to bring him closer to the princess. But he's soon up to his antennae in trouble.

Insects, even cartoon insects, may seem to be unlikely subjects for a feature film. But *Antz* wasn't the only 1998 film with six-legged heroes and heroines. Another "buggy" animated feature—Walt Disney's *A Bug's Life*—opened in November. It, too, featured an ant hero who defends his colony, this time from a swarm of grasshoppers.

of a movie that was a hit in 1961. Back then, Hayley Mills starred. This time Lindsay Lohan played a double role as twin girls, Hallie and Annie, who are separated at birth by their parents' divorce and meet at summer camp eleven years later. When the girls figure out the situation, they decide to switch places. And before long they are plotting to reunite their parents.

CLASSICS AND MORE

The classic fairy tale *Cinderella* came to the screen with a comic 1990s twist in *Ever After.* In this film, set in 16th-century France, the orphaned Cinderella (named Danielle, and played by Drew Barrymore) has plenty of spunk. She's forced to work as a servant by her mean stepmother (Anjelica Huston), but she wins her prince (Dougray Scott) without the help of magic. In the process, she remakes him, by raising his awareness of human rights and other issues.

Films of several famous children's books also appeared in theaters during the year. *Madeline* followed the adventures of a mischievous French schoolgirl, the heroine of six picture books by Ludwig Bemelmans. The movie, which drew on stories in several of the books, starred 9-year-old Hatty Jones as Madeline and Frances McDormand as Miss Clavel, the principal of her school.

The Borrowers explains why little household objects go missing—they've been taken by the Borrowers, tiny people who live under floorboards and in other hidden places in people's houses. Adapted from children's novels written by Mary Norton in the 1950s, this film used 1990s special-effects techniques to make the fantasy seem real. In this version, the Clock family (the Borrowers) is threatened when a lawyer schemes to buy and demolish

Mulan: A Chinese Legend

A famous Chinese legend inspired Walt Disney's *Mulan,* one of 1998's most exciting animated films. The movie was praised for its creative animation and for its depiction of the title character—a young woman as brave as she is beautiful.

The tale takes place more than 1,500 years ago, in the days of the emperors. China is being invaded by the Huns, and the emperor has ordered every household to send a man to fight in the army. The only man in Mulan's household is her father, and she knows that going to war will mean death for him because he is old and unwell.

Mulan has already disappointed her father by failing to capture a husband—she's a bit of a tomboy. But now she sees a way to help her family and her country. She cuts her hair, takes her father's armor, and rides off to serve in his place, disguised as a man. Before long she teams up with a pint-sized (and very hip) dragon named Mushu, who rides on her shoulder and offers advice.

Mulan gets through her army training without revealing her secret and goes to war. And in battle, she becomes a hero, proving that brains are just as important as strength when it comes to winning. When the Huns charge her battalion in the snowy mountains, she fires a cannon at a mountain slope. The shot sets off an avalanche that stops the Huns cold.

Audiences loved the film, which took five years to make. Ming-Na Wen provided the voice of Mulan, and Eddie Murphy was Mushu. *Mulan* was especially popular with girls, who liked its underlying message that women are as good as men. The movie was even given credit for a new wave of interest in martial arts among girls.

the house where they live. But they team up with the Lenders—the big people who own the house—to defeat the plan.

Classic children's books by Hugh Lofting were the inspiration for *Dr. Dolittle,* a film about a doctor who suddenly discovers, to his shock, that he can understand and talk with animals. The movie version updated the story and moved the setting from Britain to America, and it added a twist by featuring the sharp-tongued comedian Eddie Murphy in the title role. For the scenes in which he talked with animals, Murphy had to deliver most of his lines to stand-in objects like tennis balls. The animals, filmed separately, were animated by computer so that they seemed to speak. Then the two sets of images were blended seamlessly for the finished film.

Similar techniques were used to make several other movies that featured animal stars. In *Paulie,* the star was a parrot—a green-and-blue conure, to be exact. Unlike most parrots, which simply repeat words they're taught without understanding the meaning, this bird actually carries on conversations. In fact, he can't keep his mouth—that is, beak—shut, and his amazing ability gets him in hot water again and again. In the course of the movie, he's pawned, birdnapped, and imprisoned by an animal researcher. He also stars in a song-and-dance act at a burrito stand. Filmmakers used fourteen different conures and one animatronic figure (for dangerous or difficult scenes) to make Paulie come to life. Actor Jay Mohr provided the bird's voice and also played the birdnapper.

It's a good thing that real mice aren't as smart as the movie mouse in *Mouse Hunt.* In this film, two brothers (played by Nathan Lane and Lee Evans) inherit a run-down old house with architectural value. They decide to fix it up and auction it off to the highest bidder. They hope to make millions. But there's just one problem—the house's tenant is determined to stop them. That tenant is a mouse, and a lot of comic madness unfolds. The mouse sets booby traps for the brothers. The brothers try all sorts of schemes to eliminate the mouse, all without success. It took sixty trained mice, plus computer animation and animatronic figures, to bring this clever rodent to the screen.

Ever After,* with Drew Barrymore and Dougray Scott, put a comic 1990s twist on the classic fairy tale *Cinderella.

David Hyde Pierce (best supporting actor, comedy series) and Kelsey Grammer (best actor, comedy series) in *Frasier* (best comedy series).

EMMY

CATEGORY	WINNER
Comedy Series	*Frasier*
Actor—comedy series	Kelsey Grammer (*Frasier*)
Actress—comedy series	Helen Hunt (*Mad About You*)
Supporting actor—comedy series	David Hyde Pierce (*Frasier*)
Supporting actress—comedy series	Lisa Kudrow (*Friends*)
Drama Series	*The Practice*
Actor—drama series	Andre Braugher (*Homicide: Life on the Streets*)
Actress—drama series	Christine Lahti (*Chicago Hope*)
Supporting actor—drama series	Gordon Clapp (*NYPD Blue*)
Supporting actress—drama series	Camryn Manheim (*The Practice*)
Miniseries	*From the Earth to the Moon*
Variety, Music, or Comedy Series	*Late Show with David Letterman*

Top left: Andre Braugher (best actor, drama series) in *Homicide: Life on the Streets.* Above: Christine Lahti (best actress, drama series) in *Chicago Hope.* Left: Camryn Manheim (best supporting actress, drama series) in *The Practice* (best drama series).

The Backstreet Boys were one of the major hitmakers of 1998. The popular quintet won an MTV Video Music Award for best group video for their single "Everybody (Backstreet's Back)."

THE MUSIC SCENE

Music fans continued to prefer new bands in 1998, and many performers saw their debut albums hit number one on the charts. Listeners' willingness to give new acts a chance led to a variety of groups with fresh new sounds getting lots of exposure. And fans were trying out a wide range of music too, from rap to rock to swing to African pop.

WHAT'S NEW?

The Backstreet Boys were one of the year's major hitmakers. Their U.S. debut album, *Backstreet Boys*, had sold 6 million copies by the fall of 1998 and produced four hit singles. The five band members, all in their 20's, were especially popular among preteen and young teenage girls, who mobbed their concerts during the group's 42-

Madonna's new album *Ray of Light* was highly praised. She also won six MTV Video Music Awards.

city tour. The Boys also won the MTV Video Music Award for best group video, for their song "Everybody (Backstreet's Back)." Another new "boy group," 'N Sync, hit it big with their self-titled debut album.

Several new albums by female stars who hadn't been heard from in a while received positive reviews. Among these were Liz Phair's *Whitechocolatespaceegg*; Alanis Morissette's *Supposed Former Infatuation Junkie; Celebrity Skin,* from Courtney Love's band, Hole; and Madonna's *Ray of Light,* which was highly praised. Madonna won six MTV Video Music Awards for the videos of the singles "Ray of Light" and "Frozen." Stevie Nicks, from the 1970s supergroup Fleetwood Mac, released a boxed set, *Enchanted.* Jewel came out with her second album, *Spirit.* Sheryl Crow released *The Globe Sessions.* And Gloria Estefan received positive press for her dance-oriented *Gloria!*

Pearl Jam's new album, *Yield,* was lighter in tone than most of the band's previous music, but didn't sell particularly well. However, the longtime (17 years) band Sonic Youth's new *A Thousand Leaves* was popular. Several other bands released follow-up albums with varying degrees of success, among them Garbage (*Version 2.0*), Smashing Pumpkins (*Adore*), and Hootie and the Blowfish (*Musical Chairs*).

Several veteran rock performers released new albums in 1998. Former Beatle Ringo Starr came out with *Vertical Man,* his first release in six years. Most listeners agreed that Eric Clapton's latest, *Pilgrim,* wasn't up to his usual standards. On the other hand, Rod Stewart's *When We Were the New Boys* was well-received for its mix of traditional rock and gentle love ballads.

SPOTLIGHT ON...
Brandy and Monica

Once there were two teenaged pop stars. Each was beautiful and talented, with a string of hit songs to her credit. Brandy, 19, wore braids and had an air of youthful innocence. Monica, though two years younger, had a husky, soulful voice that gave her songs a more worldly quality. The two girls arrived on the music scene at about the same time. But Brandy, who also stars in the popular TV comedy *Moesha*, got most of the attention at first. Rumors circulated that the singers were rivals.

"That really bothered both of us," says Monica about the gossip. So Brandy decided to invite Monica to sing a duet with her on her new album, *Never Say Never.* The song, "The Boy Is Mine," also became the title song on Monica's new album. The duet did more than simply stop the rumors of a rivalry. It skyrocketed to the top of the Billboard charts, and its video was nominated for two MTV Video Music awards. The song's success promised to push sales of each of the girls' albums into the millions.

With the misunderstandings cleared up once and for all, what was next for the two ambitious young performers? Brandy spent the summer shooting her first feature film. And Monica, who graduated from high school with a perfect 4.0 average, was thinking about attending college—after her upcoming world tour.

Among the year's hit singles were Semisonic's "Closing Time"; Celine Dion's "My Heart Will Go On," featured on the *Titanic* soundtrack as well as on her new album, *Let's Talk About Love*; several songs by Brandy and by Monica, along with their duet, "The Boy Is Mine"; Savage Garden's "Truly Madly Deeply"; and Shania Twain's "You're Still the One." Natalie Imbruglia's "Torn," from her debut album *Left of the Middle,* won her an MTV Video Music Award for best new artist in a video.

Rhythm-and-blues star Usher hit it big with his second album, *My Way,* which produced two hit singles.

WOMEN ARE STRONG

Two British all-girl groups, Cleopatra and All Saints, hit it big in 1998, drawing comparisons to 1997's hottest act, the Spice Girls. Cleopatra had a hit with their first, R&B-tinged album, *Comin' Atcha.* The group's three sisters—Zainam, 17; Cleopatra, 16; and Yonah, 14—had real musical talent, as well as enthusiasm and confidence to spare. Cleopatra was also compared to Hanson, because of their soaring vocal harmonies and catchy hooks, as well as their lively, teen-friendly personalities.

All Saints featured a stronger hip-hop sound, and—with their fashion-conscious clothes and spicier lyrics—appealed to a slightly older audience. Their first album, *All Saints,* was released in November 1997 in Britain; by the time it was released early in 1998 in the United States, it had reached quadruple-platinum status abroad. The group's catchy single "I Know Where It's At" became an international hit.

The Spice Girls themselves, meanwhile, had an eventful year. Their film *Spice World* came out early in 1998 and was moderately popular among young fans if not with critics. By year's end, however, Ginger Spice (Geri Halliwell) had left the group, and the Girls' musical future was in doubt.

Women soloists also made musical news in 1998. Paula Cole's second album, *This Fire,* made her a star and garnered her a Grammy for best new artist. And one of the year's most-discussed musicians was Lilith Fair organizer Sarah McLachlan. Several of her songs, including "Adia" and "Sweet Surrender," appeared on the charts, and she was awarded two Grammys—one for best female pop instrumental album and one for best female pop vocal.

HIP-HOP, SOUL, R&B, BLUES

The year's biggest hip-hop star was Fugees member Lauryn Hill; her solo debut album, *The Miseducation of Lauryn Hill,* revealed intelligent, thoughtful lyrics backed by strong and exhilarating rhythms. Other Fugees members also released some popular work: Wyclef Jean, featuring the Refugee Allstars, won an MTV Video Music award for best R&B video for "Gone 'Til November"; and Pras Michel had a major hit with "Ghetto Supastar (That's What You Are)."

Usher was one of the year's hottest R&B names. The 19-year-old hit it big with his second album, *My Way,* which produced the hits "You Make Me Wanna" and "Nice and Slow." Other hot singles included "All My Life" from K-CI & JoJo and "Been Around the World" by Puff Daddy and the Family, featuring the Notorious B.I.G. and Mase.

Several familiar rap acts released successful new albums. Snoop Doggy Dogg's *Da*

Game Is to Be Sold, Not to Be Told hit number one, and the Beastie Boys came roaring back to the top five with *Hello Nasty.* Master P had a number-one hit with *MP Da Last Don.*

Next's debut effort, *Rated Next,* yielded the hits "Butta Love," "Too Close," and "I Still Love You." Gang Starr's first release in four years, *Moment of Truth,* was welcomed by fans and gained the group new attention.

Will Smith had two hits in 1998, and won MTV Video Music Awards for both of them. The catchy "Gettin' Jiggy Wit It" won an award for best rap video, while "Just the Two of Us," Smith's ode to fatherhood, won best male video. The father of two brought his 5-year-old son onstage with him to accept the award.

Among R&B-oriented acts, Janet Jackson's 1997 album, *The Velvet Rope,* remained on the charts in 1998 with the top single "Together Again." Aretha Franklin released a new album, *A Rose Is Still a Rose,* whose title track was produced and written by Lauryn Hill. Hill also had a hand in CeCe Winans' 1998 release, *Everlasting Love*—she penned one of its songs.

ON THE ROAD

One of the summer's hottest tours was the Dave Matthews Band's 23-city jaunt. After unseating the *Titanic* soundtrack from the number-one chart spot with their new album, *Before These Crowded Streets,* the band headed out on the road, playing to sold-out crowds nationwide.

One of the more unusual road shows of 1998 was Africa Fête, which featured African musicians relatively unknown to American audiences. These included Somalia native Maryam Mursal, Malian star Salif Keita, Papa Wembo from the Democratic Republic of the Congo, and Senegal's Cheikh Lô. The festival of music and culture traveled to 20 North American cities, exposing audiences to the innovative, fresh sounds of African pop.

The all-female Lilith Fair tour was a hit again in the summer of 1998. The Fair again

WHAT IS. . .Swing?

Step into the most popular dance club in town. The room is packed with couples jumpin' and jivin' to the music of a jazz band. Men in wide-shouldered suits and women in swirling skirts clasp hands, turn, twirl, and kick with perfect timing. As a trumpet wails, a man grasps his partner around the waist and swings her through a turn, lifting her right off the floor.

An old movie about the 1940s? Nope. It's 1998—and swing is the thing! Your grandparents, and maybe your great-grandparents, danced to swing music more than 50 years ago. Now swing dancing is back!

Swing started in the 1930s, when great jazz musicians such as "Duke" Ellington and Benny Goodman toured the country with their bands. The traditional "swinging" jazz played by these bands was made for dancing. By the 1940s swing was king! On weekend nights, couples flocked to ballrooms to hear their favorite bands and dance the night away.

Swing went out of style after rock music came on the scene in the 1950s. Young people turned to new dances—the Twist, the Frug, the Mashed Potato. But now young people are rediscovering the great jazz music of the 1940s. They're listening to new swing bands that play in the old style—Big Bad Voodoo Daddy, Cherry Poppin' Daddies, the Brian Setzer Orchestra, Royal Crown Revue. And they're finding out how much fun it is to dance to that music.

The Dave Matthews Band had one of the summer's hottest tours, playing to sold-out audiences nationwide.

featured headliner Sarah McLachlan, as well as a roster of more than 50 performers, including Joan Osborne, Paula Cole, Bonnie Raitt, Sheryl Crow, the Indigo Girls, Sinead O'Connor, Erykah Badu, Liz Phair, and other top names.

In contrast to the second-year success of Lilith Fair, another blockbuster summer tour, Lollapalooza, was canceled in 1998. Once one of the summer's most-hyped musical happenings, Lollapalooza faded because of lack of interest among top alternative bands.

Among other summer tours were the George Strait Country Festival; the Furthur Festival, featuring former Grateful Dead members; the metal tour OZZfest; Smoking Grooves, a hip-hop tour; and the blues and roots-rock H.O.R.D.E. Festival. The Family Values Tour, featuring hip-hop and metal acts, continued well into the fall; an October stop was to be taped for release as an MTV special, home video, and live album.

MUSIC NOTES

The album from the 1998 blockbuster film *Titanic* was the undisputed champion of the year in the soundtrack category. It became the first soundtrack since 1982's *Chariots of Fire* to reach number one on the Billboard pop chart. It also won Oscars and Golden Globe Awards for best original dramatic score and best original song (Celine Dion's "My Heart Will Go On"). It remained in the number-one spot for sixteen weeks.

Other soundtrack albums reaching hit status in 1998 included David Arnold's *Godzilla* (featuring the Wallflowers, Puff Daddy with Jimmy Page—the hit "Come With Me"—and others); *Armageddon* (with four tracks by Aerosmith, including "I Don't Want to Miss a Thing"); and *City of Angels* (which spotlighted Alanis Morissette, who had a hit with "Uninvited," as well as the Goo Goo Dolls, Peter Gabriel, U2, Paula Cole, Sarah McLachlan, and Eric Clapton). The album from *Hope Floats* featured a romantic collection of tunes overseen by Don Was. Meanwhile, David Was—Don's former partner in the group Was (Not Was)—headed the production of the eccentric *X-Files* soundtrack, which included songs by Noel Gallagher of Oasis, Ween, and Sting, among other modern rockers.

The trend of popular musicians performing theme songs for TV series continued, and on the hit series *Ally McBeal,* it grew into something more. Vonda Shepard, who wrote the show's theme, became a featured performer on the series as well, playing a singer at a club frequented by Ally and her friends.

A CD entitled *Songs from "Ally McBeal," Featuring Vonda Shepard* headed up the charts and turned gold during 1998.

The Rock and Roll Hall of Fame welcomed a cross-section of new members in January at its 13th annual induction ceremony. The Eagles and Fleetwood Mac, two of the most popular and influential groups of the 1970s, were inducted, along with 1960s folk musicians the Mamas and the Papas; R&B pioneer Lloyd Price; late rockabilly musician Gene Vincent, who headed the Bluecaps; and Santana, who became the first Latino group to be welcomed to the Hall of Fame. Other inductees included songwriter and producer Allen Toussaint and the late jazz composer Jelly Roll Morton.

Singer Sarah McLachlan won a Grammy as best female pop vocalist for her song "Building a Mystery."

1998 Grammy Awards

Record of the Year	"Sunny Came Home"	Shawn Colvin, artist
Album of the Year	*Time Out of Mind*	Bob Dylan, artist
Song of the Year	"Sunny Came Home"	Shawn Colvin, John Leventhal songwriters
New Artist of the Year		Paula Cole
Pop Vocal Performance—female	"Building a Mystery"	Sarah McLachlan, artist
Pop Vocal Performance—male	"Candle in the Wind 1997"	Elton John, artist
Pop Vocal Performance—group	"Virtual Insanity"	Jamiroquai, artists
Rock Vocal Performance—female	"Criminal"	Fiona Apple, artist
Rock Vocal Performance—male	"Cold Irons Bound"	Bob Dylan, artist
Rock Vocal Performance—group	"One Headlight"	Wallflowers, artists
Rhythm and Blues Vocal Performance—female	"On & On"	Erykah Badu, artist
Rhythm and Blues Vocal Performance—male	"I Believe I Can Fly"	R. Kelly, artist
Rhythm and Blues Vocal Performance—group	"No Diggity"	Blackstreet, artists
Country Vocal Performance—female	"How Do I Live"	Trisha Yearwood, artist
Country Vocal Performance—male	"Pretty Little Adriana"	Vince Gill, artist
Country Vocal Performance—group	"Looking In the Eyes of Love"	Alison Krauss and Union Station, artists
Music Video Performance	"Got 'Till It's Gone"	Janet Jackson, artist
Alternative Music Performance	*OK Computer*	Radiohead, artists
Score for a Motion Picture	The *English Patient*	Gabriel Yared, composer
Musical Show Album	*Chicago: The Musical*	Jay David Saks, producer
Classical Album	*Premieres: Cello Concertos (Works of Danielpour, Kirchner, Rouse)*	David Zinman conducting the Philadelphia Orchestra

A red pepper makes a perfect hummingbird. The pepper's own stem is the hummingbird's long beak. Celery leaves, tucked into slits in the top of the pepper, are the wings.

This wide-eyed yellow octopus started out as a plain banana. The peel is split into eight segments for the legs. Black-eyed peas make the eyes. What do you do with the rest of the banana? Eat it, of course!

PLAY WITH YOUR FOOD!

"Don't play with your food!" Have your parents ever told you that? It's bad manners to fiddle with your food at the dinner table, of course. But check out the pictures on these pages. You'll see that some creative play in the kitchen can be lots of fun.

These creations are animals—but they've all been made out of vegetables! They and many others like them are featured in a book, *Play With Your Food,* by Joost Elffers, a graphic designer. Elffers was struck by the way certain oddly shaped fruits and vegetables seemed to resemble birds, fish, and other animals. With a

A Brussels sprout goldfish looks ready to swim away. Leaves are folded out to make the fins, and an extra leaf is added for the tail.

The outside of a pineapple looks just like the plates of a turtle's shell. A few pineapple leaves make four legs and a set of snapping jaws.

little carving and some extra leaves and other additions, he helped the resemblances along. The result was a vegetable zoo.

You can make your own vegetable zoo with animal creations that *you* dream up. Take a look around your kitchen. Is there a potato that kind of looks like a pot-bellied pig, or a turnip that could turn into a turtle? Here are some tips: The stems of fruits and vegetables often make natural "noses." Dried peas, raisins, beans, and cloves are perfect for eyes. Thin stems, like cherry stems, can become insect legs and antennae. Leaves will make great tails and wings.

Look at fruits and vegetables from all different angles to see what their shapes suggest. Who knows what animals you'll find hiding in your vegetable bin!

An artichoke makes a fluffy coat, and a mushroom cap becomes a high-fashion hat. Beads and red beet juice make the face on the stem.

FUN TO READ

The hero of Ruth Brown's picture book Toad *probably isn't the sort of animal you'd like to cuddle up with. He's a "muddy toad, a mucky toad, a clammy, sticky, gooey toad," covered with warts, bumps, and stains. He plops through the mud, slurping up worms and insects, leaving a slimy trail as he goes—until he stumbles right into the mouth of a monstrous lizard! But the toad has a secret that keeps him from becoming the lizard's dinner and leaves a smile on his toady lips.*

Princess Rosette

Once upon a time there lived a King and Queen who had two handsome sons and a little daughter who was so pretty that everyone who saw her couldn't help loving her. When it was time for the Princess to be christened, the Queen sent for all the fairies to be present at the ceremony.

When it was over and the fairies were preparing to leave, the Queen said to them: "Do not forget your usual good custom. Tell me what is going to happen to Rosette."

For that was the name of the beautiful Princess.

But the fairies said they had left their book of magic at home, and they would come another day and tell her.

"Ah!" said the Queen. "I know very well what that means—you have nothing good to say; but at least I beg that you will not hide anything from me."

So, after a great deal of persuasion, they said: "Madam, we fear that Rosette may be the cause of great misfortunes to her brothers. They may even meet with their death through her. And that is all we have been able to foresee about your dear little daughter. We are very sorry to have nothing better to tell you."

Then they went away, leaving the Queen very sad, so sad that the King noticed it and asked her what was the matter. So she told him all that the fairies had predicted about Rosette, and begged him to think how the misfortunes might be prevented.

Then it was the King's turn to look sad, and at last he said: "I see no way of saving our sons except by having Rosette's head cut off while she is still little."

But the Queen cried that she would far rather have her own head cut off and that he had better think of something else, for she would never consent to such a thing. So they thought and thought, but they could not decide what to do. At last the Queen heard that in a great forest near the castle there was an old hermit who lived in a hollow tree, and that people came from far and near to consult him. So she said: "I had better go and ask his advice. Perhaps he will know what to do to prevent the misfortunes that the fairies foretold."

She set out very early the next morning, mounted upon a little white mule that was shod with solid gold, and two of her ladies rode behind her on beautiful horses. When they reached the forest they dismounted, for the trees grew so thickly that the horses could not pass, and they made their way on foot to the hollow tree where the hermit lived. When the hermit first saw them coming he was vexed, for he was not fond of ladies. But when he recognized the Queen, he said: "You are welcome, Queen. What do you come to ask of me?"

The Queen told him all the fairies had foreseen for Rosette and asked what to do. The hermit answered that she must shut the Princess up in a tower and never let her come out of it again. The Queen thanked and rewarded him, and hastened back to the castle to tell the King.

When he heard the news, he had a great tower built as quickly as possible. And there the Princess was shut up, and the King and Queen and her two brothers went to see her every day so that she might not be bored, for they all loved her very much.

When Rosette was fifteen years old, the older Prince went to the King and asked if it would not soon be time for her to be married, and the younger Prince put the same question to the Queen. Their majesties were amused at them for thinking of it but did not make any reply.

Then a terrible illness struck the kingdom, and both the King and Queen died on the same day. Everyone was very sad, especially Rosette and her two brothers. The older brother was crowned the new King, and he vowed to rule as justly as his father had done.

Soon after, the new King and his brother said to one another: "Now that we are the rulers, let us take our sister out of that terrible tower." (For the King and Queen had never told their sons or Rosette what the fairies had foretold.)

The two brothers walked across the garden to the tower, and there they found Rosette busy at her embroidery. But when she saw them she jumped to her feet, and taking the King's hand cried: "Good morning, dear brother. Now that you are King, please take me out of this dull tower, for I am so tired of it."

Then she began to cry. The King kissed her and told her to dry her tears, as that was just what they had come to do.

"Make haste," said the King, "and let us get away from this ugly tower, and very soon I will arrange a grand marriage for you."

When Rosette saw the beautiful garden, full of fruit and flowers and green grass and sparkling fountains, she was so astonished that she could not say a word, for she had never in her life seen anything like it before. She looked about her and ran hither and thither gathering fruit and flowers, while her little dog Frisk, who was bright green all over and had but one ear, danced before her, crying "Bow-wow-wow," and turning head over heels in the most enchanting way.

Everybody was amused at Frisk's antics, but all of a sudden he ran away into a little wood. The Princess was trying to follow him when, to her great delight, she saw a peacock spreading his magnificent tail in the sunshine. Rosette thought she had never seen anything so pretty. She could not take her eyes off him, and there she stood entranced until the King and the Prince came up and asked what was amusing her so much. She showed them the peacock and asked what it was, and they answered that it was a bird that people sometimes ate.

"What!" said the Princess, "do they dare to kill that beautiful creature and eat it? I declare that I will never marry anyone but the King of the Peacocks, and when I am Queen I will take very good care that nobody eats any of my subjects."

At this the King was very much astonished.

"But, dear little sister," said he, "where shall we find the King of the Peacocks?"

"Oh! wherever you like, sire," she answered, "but I will never marry anyone else."

After this they took Rosette to the beautiful castle. The peacock was brought with her, too, and was told to walk about on the terrace outside her windows so that she might always see it. Then the ladies of the court came to see the Princess, and they brought her beautiful presents—dresses and ribbons and sweetmeats, diamonds and pearls and dolls and embroidered slippers. And she was so well brought up, and said "Thank you!" so prettily, that everyone went away delighted with her.

Meanwhile, the King and Prince were considering how they should find the King of the Peacocks, if there even was such a person. First of all they had a portrait made of the Princess, which was so like her that you really would not have been surprised if it had spoken to you. Then they said to her: "Since you will not marry anyone but the King of the Peacocks, we are going to search the world for him. If we find him for you we shall be very glad. In the meantime, mind you take good care of our kingdom."

Rosette thanked them for all the trouble they were taking on her account and promised to take great care of the kingdom, and to amuse herself only by looking at the peacock and making Frisk dance while they were away.

So they set out and asked everyone they met—

"Do you know the King of the Peacocks?"

But the answer was always, "No, no."

They went on and on, so far that no one had ever been farther, and at last they came to the Kingdom of the Beetles.

They had never before seen such a very large number of beetles, and their buzzing was so loud that the King was afraid he would become deafened by it. He asked the most distinguished-looking beetle if he knew where they could find the King of the Peacocks.

"Sire," replied the beetle, "his kingdom is thirty thousand leagues from here; you have come the longest way."

"And how do you know that?" asked the King.

"Oh," said the beetle, "we all know you very well, since we spend two or three months in your garden every year."

Thereupon the King and Prince made great friends with him, and they all walked arm-in-arm and dined together. Then they set out again to finish their journey, and this time, as they knew the way, they were not long upon the road. It was easy to guess that they had come to the right place for they saw peacocks in every tree, and their cries could be heard a long way off.

When they reached the kingdom, they found it full of men and women who were dressed entirely in peacock feathers, which were evidently valued more highly than anything else.

They soon met the King of the Peacocks, who was driving about in a golden carriage that glittered with diamonds and was drawn by twelve peacocks. He was very handsome, and on his curly golden hair rested a crown of peacock feathers.

When he saw Rosette's brothers he knew at once that they were strangers, and he stopped his carriage to greet them and ask why they were visiting.

"Sire," they said, "we have come from very far away to show you a beautiful portrait."

So saying, they drew from their traveling bag the picture of Rosette.

The King looked at it in silence a long time, and at last he said: "I could not have believed that there was such a beautiful Princess in the world!"

"Sire," said the Prince, "my brother is a King, like yourself. He is called the King, I am called the Prince, and that is the portrait of our sister, the Princess Rosette. We have come to ask if you would like to marry her. She is as good as she is beautiful, and we will give her a bushel of gold pieces for her dowry."

"Oh! with all my heart," replied the King, "and I will make her very happy. She shall have whatever she likes and I shall love her dearly. Only I warn you that if she is not as wonderful as you have told me, I will have your heads cut off."

"Certainly, we quite agree to that," said the brothers.

"Very well. Off with you into prison, and you will stay there until the Princess arrives," said the King of the Peacocks.

The Princes were so sure that Rosette was far lovelier than her portrait that they went without a murmur. They were very kindly treated, and the King came often to see them.

The King and Prince sent a letter to the Princess telling her to pack up all her treasures as quickly as possible and come to them, as the King of the Peacocks was waiting to marry her. But they did not say that they were in prison for fear of making her uneasy.

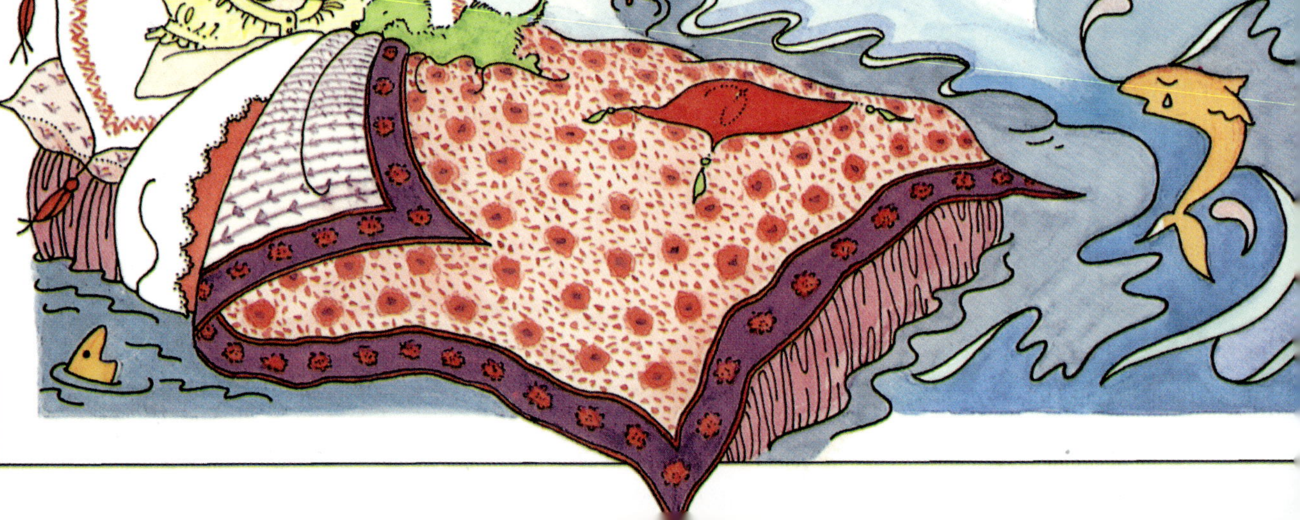

When Rosette received her brothers' letter she was so delighted that she ran about telling everyone that the King of the Peacocks had been found, and that she was going to marry him.

She entrusted her brother's kingdom to the care of the wisest men, telling them to take charge of everything and, above all, not to forget to feed her peacock. Then she set out, only taking with her her nurse, the nurse's daughter, and her little green dog Frisk.

They took a boat and put out to sea, carrying with them the bushel of gold pieces and enough dresses to last the Princess ten years, and they did nothing but laugh and sing.

They had been traveling across the sunlit sea for two days when the nurse quietly took the boatman aside and whispered: "Do you want to make your fortune?"

And he said: "Certainly I do."

"I can tell you how to get a bag of gold," said she.

"I ask nothing better," said the boatman.

"Well," said the nurse, "tonight, when the Princess is asleep, you must help me throw her into the sea. And when she is drowned I will put her beautiful clothes upon my daughter and we will take her to the King of the Peacocks, who will be only too glad to marry her. And as your reward, you shall have your boat filled with gold."

The boatman was very much surprised at this proposal and said: "But what a pity to drown such a lovely Princess!"

However, at last the nurse persuaded him to help her, and when night came and the Princess was fast asleep, with Frisk curled up on his own cushion at the foot of her bed, the wicked nurse fetched the boatman and her daughter. They picked up the Princess, feather bed, mattress, pillows, blankets, and all, and threw her into the sea, without even waking her.

Now luckily, the Princess's bed was entirely stuffed with phoenix feathers, which are very rare and have the property of always floating upon water, so Rosette and Frisk went on swimming about as if they had been in a boat. After a little while the Princess began to feel cold, and she murmured in her sleep, "How our boat does rock upon the water! I am really glad that I am not often as uncomfortable as I have been tonight."

In the meantime, the wicked nurse, her daughter, and the boatman were now quite a long way off, approaching the kingdom of the King of the Peacocks.

The King had sent a hundred carriages to meet them, drawn by every kind of strange animal. There were lions, bears, wolves, stags, horses, buffaloes, eagles, and peacocks. The carriage intended for Princess Rosette had six blue monkeys in red jackets, which could turn somersaults and dance on a tightrope and do many other charming tricks.

The nurse had taken great care to deck out her daughter. She dressed her in Rosette's prettiest frock and covered her with diamonds from head to foot. But she was so ugly that nothing could make her look nice, and what was worse, she was sulky and ill-tempered and did nothing but grumble all the time.

When she stepped from the boat and the guards sent by the King of the Peacocks caught sight of her, they were so surprised that they could not say a single word.

"Now then, look alive," cried the false Princess. "If you don't bring me something to eat I will have all your heads cut off!"

Then the guards whispered to one another: "Here's a pretty state of things! She is as wicked as she is ugly. What a bride for our poor King! She certainly was not worth bringing from the other end of the world!"

As the procession was so long, it advanced very slowly. The nurse's daughter sat up in her carriage trying to look like a Queen. But the peacocks, who were sitting upon every tree waiting to salute her, could not help crying instead: "Oh! How ugly she is!"

This offended the false Princess so much that she said to the guards: "Make haste and kill all these insolent peacocks who dared to insult me."

But the peacocks only flew away, laughing at her. And they told the King that the Princess was approaching.

"Well," said he, "did her brothers tell me truly? Is she prettier than her portrait?"

"Sire," they answered, "if she were as pretty that would do very well."

"That's true," said the King. "I for one shall be quite satisfied if she is. Let us go and meet her." For he knew by the uproar that she had arrived, but he could not tell what all the shouting was about. He thought he could hear the words: "How ugly she is! How ugly she is!" and he fancied they must refer to some dwarf the Princess was bringing with her. It never occurred to him that such words could apply to the bride herself.

The King was now all impatience to see the lovely Princess, but when he caught sight of the nurse's daughter he was furiously angry and would not advance another step. For she was really ugly enough to have frightened anybody.

"What!" he cried. "Have the two rascals who are my prisoners dared to play such a trick as this? Do they propose that I shall marry this hideous creature? Let her be shut up in my great tower, with her nurse and those who brought her here. And as for her brothers, I will have their heads cut off."

Meanwhile the King and the Prince, who knew that their sister must have arrived, were expecting to be summoned to greet her. So when the jailer came with the soldiers and carried them down into a black dungeon that swarmed with toads and bats, nobody could have been more surprised and dismayed than they were.

"This is a dismal kind of wedding," they said. "What can have happened that we should be treated like this?"

Three days passed before they heard any news, and then the King of the Peacocks came and berated them through a hole in the wall.

"You have called yourselves King and Prince," he cried, "to try to make me marry your sister, but you are nothing but beggars. I mean to make short work with you, and the sword is being sharpened that will cut off your heads!"

"King of the Peacocks," answered the King angrily, "you had better take care what you are about. I am as good a King as yourself, and have a splendid kingdom and robes and crowns and plenty of gold. You are pleased to jest about having our heads cut off; perhaps you think we have stolen something from you?"

The King of the Peacocks was taken aback by this bold speech. But he read the accusation to the prisoners—that they were imposters, and that they had promised the King a beautiful Princess in marriage who, when she arrived, proved to be an ugly peasant girl.

The brothers cried out that they had spoken the truth, that their sister was indeed a Princess more beautiful than the day, and that there was some mystery about all this that they could not fathom. Therefore they demanded seven days in which to prove their innocence. Although the King of the Peacocks was very angry, he granted them this favor.

While all this was going on at court, let us see what had been happening to the real Princess. When morning came, she and Frisk were equally astonished at finding themselves alone at sea, with no boat and no one to help them. "Alas!" she said, "the King of the Peacocks must have ordered me to be thrown into the sea because he had changed his mind and did not want to marry me. But how strange of him, when I should have loved him so much and we should have been so very happy together!"

And then she cried harder than ever. So for two days they floated in the sea, wet and shivering with cold and very hungry.

Now it happened that they floated close in to the shore, where a poor old man lived all alone in a little cottage. He heard Frisk barking and thought to himself: "There must have been a shipwreck!" (for no dogs ever passed that way by chance), and he went out to see if he could be of any use. He soon saw the Princess and Frisk floating up and down, and Rosette, stretching out her hands to him, cried: "Oh! Good old man, do save me or I shall die of cold and hunger!"

When he heard her cry out so piteously he was very sorry for her, and ran back into his house to fetch a long boat-hook. He waded into the water to his chin, and after being nearly drowned once or twice he at last succeeded in getting hold of the Princess's bed and dragging it to shore. He then brought the shivering pair into his warm cottage.

Rosette and Frisk were joyful to find themselves once more on dry land, and the Princess thanked the old man heartily. The old man realized that Rosette must be some great lady, for her bed coverings were all of satin and gold. He begged that she tell him her story. The Princess told him everything, weeping bitterly again at the thought that it was by the King's orders that she had been thrown overboard.

"And now, my dear, what is to be done?" said the old man. "You are a great Princess, and I have nothing to offer you but black bread and radishes, which will not suit you at all. Shall I go and tell the King of the Peacocks that you are here? If he sees you he will certainly wish to marry you."

"Oh, no!" cried Rosette. "He must be wicked, since he tried to drown me. Don't let us tell him, but if you have a little basket give it to me."

The old man gave her a basket, and tying it around Frisk's neck she said to him: "Go and find the best cooking pot in the kingdom and bring the contents to me."

Away went Frisk, and as there was no better lunch cooking in all the kingdom than the King's, he took the cover off the pot and brought all it contained to the Princess, who said: "Now go back to the pantry and bring the best of everything you find there."

So Frisk went back and filled his basket with white bread and every kind of sweetmeat, until it was almost too heavy for him to carry.

When the King of the Peacocks wanted his lunch there was nothing in the pot and nothing in the pantry. All the courtiers looked at one another in dismay, and the King was terribly cross.

"Oh well," he said, "if there is no lunch I cannot dine, but take care that plenty of things are roasted for supper."

When evening came the Princess said to Frisk: "Go into the kingdom and find the best kitchen, and bring me all the nicest morsels that are being roasted upon the spit."

Frisk did as he was told, and as he knew of no better kitchen than the King's, he went in softly, and when the cook's back was turned took everything that was upon the spit. He carried his basket to the Princess, who at once sent him back to the pantry to bring all the tarts and sweetmeats and sugarplums. Frisk emptied the pantry, leaving the cupboards bare.

The King, since he had had no lunch, was very hungry and wanted his supper early. But when he asked for it, lo and behold it was all gone, and he had to go to bed half-starved and in a terrible temper. The next day the same thing happened, and the next, so that for three days the King had nothing at all to eat. At last, one of the King's guards resolved to hide himself in some dark corner of the kitchen and never take his eyes off the cooking pot. His surprise was great when he saw a little green dog with one ear slip softly into the kitchen, uncover the pot, transfer all its contents into his basket, and run off. The guard followed hastily and tracked him all through the kingdom to the good old man's cottage. Then he ran back to the King and told him that he had found out where all his lunches and suppers had gone. The King, who was very much astonished, said he should like to go see for himself. So he set out and arrived just in time to find the old man and the Princess finishing his dinner.

The King ordered that they should be seized and bound with ropes, and Frisk also.

When they were brought back to the palace the King said: "Today is the last day granted to those deceiving brothers. They shall have their heads cut off at the same time as these stealers of my dinner."

Then the old man went down on his knees before the King and begged for time to tell him everything. While he spoke, the King for the first time looked attentively at the Princess. He thought she was the most beautiful maiden that he had ever seen. And when he heard the old man saying that her name was Rosette, and that she had been treacherously thrown into the sea, he ran to embrace her, declaring that he loved her with all his heart.

Messengers were sent to bring the King and Prince out of prison, and they came very sadly, believing that they were to be executed at once. The nurse and her daughter and the boatman were brought also. As soon as they came in, Rosette ran to embrace her brothers, while the traitors threw themselves down before her and begged for mercy. The King and the Princess were so happy that they forgave them, and as for the good old man he was splendidly rewarded and spent the rest of his days in the palace. The King of the Peacocks made ample amends to the King and Prince for the way in which they had been treated, and he did everything in his power to show how sorry he was.

The wedding was held at once amid great rejoicing, and the feasting and merrymaking lasted for three days. The King of the Peacocks and Rosette lived happily ever after. And Frisk, who enjoyed the greatest luxury, never had anything worse than the wing of a partridge for dinner all the rest of his life.

POETRY

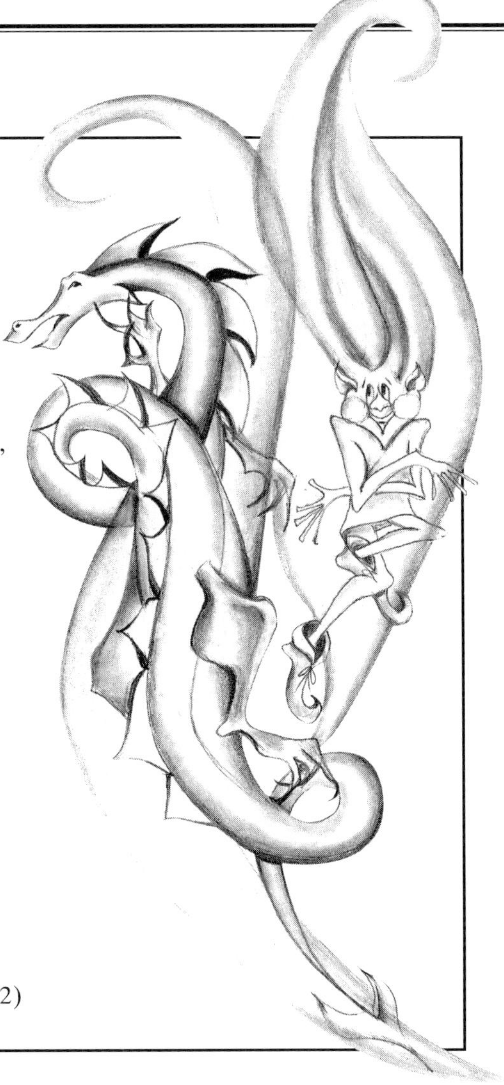

FLAME FAIRIES

Knights on golden prancing steeds,
  Elves and goblins leaping higher,
I can see the finest things
  In the dancing fire!

Sometimes dragons twist and curl
  Tails of red and purple light,
Sometimes giants, sometimes gnomes,
  Meet in fearsome fight!

Banners stream above the wood,
  Gaily-painted ships sail past
With a green or yellow flag
  Flying from the mast.

Then they change from this to that,
  Steeds to castles, ships to kings,
And a dragon vanishes
  Into golden rings.

Flames are fairies prisoned fast,
  Long within the logs they lie;
Once they're free they gaily leap
  Upward to the sky!

RUPERT SARGENT HOLLAND (1878–1952)

THINKING OF EAST MOUNTAIN

It's been so long since I headed for East Mountain—
how many times have the roses bloomed?
White clouds have scattered themselves away—
and this bright moon—whose house is it setting on?

LI PO (8TH CENTURY)

THE CAT

Within that porch, across the way,
  I see two naked eyes this night;
Two eyes that neither shut nor blink,
  Searching my face with a green light.

But cats to me are strange, so strange—
  I cannot sleep if one is near;
And though I'm sure I see those eyes
  I'm not so sure a body's there.

WILLIAM HENRY DAVIES (1871–1940)

THE STARGAZER

A stargazer out late at night,
With eyes and thoughts turned both upright,
Tumbled by chance into a well
(A dismal story this to tell);
He roared and sobbed, and roared again,
And cursed the "Bear" and "Charles's Wain."

His woeful cries a neighbour brought,
Less learned, but wiser far in thought;
"My friend," quoth he, "you're much misled,
With stars to trouble thus your head;
Since you with these misfortunes meet,
For want of looking to your feet."

UNKNOWN

AS THE WORLD TURNS

I'm up and down and round about,
Yet all the world can't find me out,
Though hundreds have employed their leisure,
They never yet could take my measure,
I'm found in almost every garden,
Nay, in the compass of a farthing;
There's not a chariot, coach, nor mill,
Can move an inch except I will.
(A circle)

JONATHAN SWIFT (1667–1745)

THE DAISY'S SONG

The sun, with his great eye,
Sees not so much as I;
And the moon, all silver-proud
Might as well be in a cloud.

And O the spring—the spring!
I lead the life of a king!
Couch'd in the teeming grass,
I spy each pretty lass.

I look where no one dares,
And I stare where no one stares,
And when the night is nigh
Lambs beat my lullaby.

JOHN KEATS (1795–1821)

Shakespeare's plays have been translated into dozens of languages. They have been performed more often than those of any other playwright. And today, the plays remain as appealing as ever. What accounts for the four centuries of popularity that these works have enjoyed?

Partly, it's the author's use of language. Famous lines and beautiful passages from his plays and poetry are still widely quoted. Shakespeare also coined many expressions that are now in common use—"in one fell swoop," "a foregone conclusion," and others. More than language however, Shakespeare's insight into human nature has kept his works alive. Even today, people find meaning in the vivid characters he created.

William Shakespeare was born in Stratford-upon-Avon, England, in April 1564. Although there are gaps in the record of his life, it is known that he married and had three children before he began his career in the theater. By 1592, he was appearing as an actor in London and had begun to write plays. And by the end of the 1500s, he was an important figure in the English theater and had also established a reputation as a poet.

In Shakespeare's day, the theater was somewhat disreputable. Actors generally formed groups and obtained the patronage of a noble, so that they wouldn't be arrested as vagabonds. Shakespeare's group, the Lord Chamberlain's Men (later the King's Men), gave many performances for royalty. But most of their plays were designed to appeal to wide audiences. Beginning in 1599, they presented outdoor performances to audiences of up to 3,000 people at the Globe Theater in London. These productions were quite different from modern ones. The stage projected into the theater, so that the audience watched from three sides. Commoners stood in the "pit," at ground level, while middle- and upper-class theatergoers sat in galleries above. There was no scenery, but costumes, props, and sound-effects were used. And no women appeared on stage—female parts were played by boys.

While Shakespeare's plays were among the most popular of his day, they weren't honored and studied then as they are now. Thus they weren't collected (and many weren't even published) until after his death in 1616. This led to some disagreement about how many plays he actually wrote. Some scholars have even contended that the plays were written by other authors who had more education than he did. But today it's generally thought that Shakespeare wrote at least 36 plays, along with parts of others, two long narrative poems, and a number of sonnets and other short verses.

The plays are usually divided into three groups: tragedies such as Hamlet and Macbeth; history plays such as Richard II that tell the story of the English monarchy; and comedies. A scene from one of the comedies, A Midsummer Night's Dream, follows. As you read it, you may find unfamiliar words and phrases—the English language has changed a great deal in 400 years. If you come across terms that you don't know, check the glossary at the end of the scene.

A Midsummer Night's Dream

This play is one of Shakespeare's lightest plays, a mixture of fantasy, comedy, and romance. It's set in Athens, where the duke is preparing to wed; and in a nearby forest—a forest filled with fairies. The main plot is a romantic tangle involving four young Athenians. And woven into this story are several subplots.

One subplot concerns a group of simple tradesmen who decide to present a play in honor of the duke's wedding. The tradesmen—Bottom, Flute, Quince, Snout, Snug, and Starveling—go to the forest to rehearse the play, which is their foolish version of the Greek tale of Pyramus and Thisbe. Another subplot involves the fairies. Oberon, king of the fairies, argues with Titania, the fairy queen, and decides to play a trick on her. He sends his jester, Puck, for a potion that will make Titania fall in love with the first living thing she sees on waking. Oberon waits until she falls asleep and then sprinkles the juice on her eyelids.

In the scene that follows, the two subplots come together. The tradesmen begin to rehearse near the spot where Titania is sleeping. (Quince is the play's director, Bottom plays Pyramus, and Flute plays Thisbe, or "Thisby.") Puck comes upon them and, as a prank, casts a spell that gives Bottom the head of a donkey. Then Titania wakes up, sees the donkey-headed Bottom, and falls wildly in love with him.

ACT THREE

Scene One: *A Wood. Titania lying asleep.*

Enter the tradesmen

BOTTOM. Are we all met?

QUINCE. Pat, pat; and here's a marvellous convenient place for our rehearsal. This green plot shall be our stage, this hawthorn-brake our tiring-house; and we will do it in action as we will do it before the duke.

BOTTOM. Peter Quince—

QUINCE. What sayest thou, bully Bottom?

BOTTOM. There are things in this comedy of Pyramus and Thisby that will never please. First, Pyramus must draw a sword to kill himself, which the ladies cannot abide. How answer you that?

SNOUT. By'r lakin, a parlous fear.

STARVELING. I believe we must leave the killing out, when all is done.

BOTTOM. Not a whit: I have a device to make all well. Write me a prologue; and let the prologue seem to say, we will do no harm with our swords, and that Pyramus is not killed indeed; and, for the more better assurance, tell them that I, Pyramus, am not Pyramus, but Bottom the weaver: this will put them out of fear.

QUINCE. Well, we will have such a prologue, and it shall be written in eight and six.

BOTTOM. No, make it two more; let it be written in eight and eight.

SNOUT. Will not the ladies be afeared of the lion?

STARVELING. I fear it, I promise you.

BOTTOM. Masters, you ought to consider with yourselves: to bring in—God shield us!—a lion among ladies, is a most dreadful thing; for there is not a more fearful wildfowl than your lion living, and we ought to look to it.

SNOUT. Therefore, another prologue must tell he is not a lion.

BOTTOM. Nay, you must name his name, and half his face must be seen through the lion's neck; and he himself must speak through, saying thus, or to the same defect, "Ladies," or "Fair Ladies," "I would wish you," or, "I would request you," or, "I would entreat you, not to fear, not to tremble: my life for yours. If you think I come hither as a lion, it were pity of my life: no, I am no such thing: I am a man as other men are." And there indeed let him name his name, and tell them plainly he is Snug the joiner.

QUINCE. Well, it shall be so. But there is two hard things, that is to bring the moonlight into a chamber; for, you know, Pyramus and Thisby meet by moonlight.

SNOUT. Doth the moon shine that night we play our play?

BOTTOM. A calendar, a calendar! look in the almanack; find out moonshine, find out moonshine.

QUINCE. Yes, it doth shine that night.

BOTTOM. Why, then may you leave a casement of the great chamber-window, where we play, open; and the moon may shine in at the casement.

QUINCE. Ay; or else one must come in with a bush of thorns and a lanthorn, and say he comes to disfigure, or to present, the person of Moonshine. Then there is another thing: we must have a wall in the great chamber; for Pyramus and Thisby, says the story, did talk through the chink of a wall.

SNOUT. You can never bring in a wall. What say you, Bottom?

BOTTOM. Some man or other must present Wall; and let him have some plaster or some loam, or some rough-cast about him, to signify wall; and let him hold his fingers thus, and through that cranny shall Pyramus and Thisby whisper.

QUINCE. If that may be, then all is well. Come, sit down, every mother's son, and rehearse your parts. Pyramus, you begin: when you have spoken your speech, enter into that brake; and so every one according to his cue.

Enter Puck behind

PUCK. What hempen homespuns have we swaggering here,
So near the cradle of the fairy queen?
What! a play toward! I'll be an auditor;
An actor too perhaps, if I see cause.

QUINCE. Speak, Pyramus. Thisby, stand forth.

BOTTOM. "Thisby, the flowers have odious savours sweet"—

QUINCE. Odours, odours.

BOTTOM. —"odours savours sweet:
So hath thy breath, my Thisby dear.
But hark, a voice! stay thou but here awhile,
And by and by I will to thee appear." *Exit*

PUCK. A stranger Pyramus than e'er played here! *Exit*

FLUTE. Must I speak now?

QUINCE. Ay, marry, must you; for you must understand, he goes but to see a noise that he heard, and is to come again.

FLUTE. "Most radiant Pyramus, most lily-white of hue,
Of colour like the red rose on triumphant brier,
Most briskly juvenal, and eke most lovely Jew,
As true as truest horse that yet would never tire,
I'll meet thee, Pyramus, at Ninny's tomb."

QUINCE. Ninus' tomb, man. Why, you must not speak that yet; that you answer to Pyramus; you speak all your part at once, cues and all. Pyramus enter: your cue is past; it is "never tire."

FLUTE. O!—"As true as truest horse, that yet would never tire."

Re-enter Puck , and Bottom with an ass's head

BOTTOM. "If I were fair, Thisby, I were only thine."

QUINCE. O monstrous! O strange! We are haunted. Pray, masters! Fly, masters! Help! *Exeunt five tradesmen*

PUCK. I'll follow you. I'll lead you about a round,
Through bog, through bush, through brake, through brier:
Sometimes a horse I'll be, sometime a hound,
A hog, a headless bear, sometime a fire;
And neigh, and bark, and grunt, and roar, and burn,
Like horse, hound, hog, bear, fire, at every turn. *Exit*

BOTTOM. Why do they run away? this is a knavery of them to make me afeard.

Rapunzel

retelling of *Rapunzel,* an old and much loved fairy tale. The best-known version of this story was set down by the brothers Wilhelm and Jacob Grimm in the 1800s, but there are older French and Italian versions as well. Zelinsky drew on all these sources to create his book. The illustrations bring to mind the art of the Italian Renaissance in both their style and their details. The flowing clothing worn by Rapunzel and the other characters, the bell tower in which she is imprisoned, and the lush gardens, red-roofed buildings, and rolling hills in the background all recall Italy of the 1500s. The book won the 1998 Caldecott Medal, which is awarded each year to the best American picture book for children.

The setting for Karen Hesse's novel *Out of the Dust* could hardly be further from the colorful fantasy world of *Rapunzel*—in time, place, or feeling. A story about a 14-year-old girl named Billie Jo, the novel is set in the heart of the Dust Bowl—Oklahoma—

LOOKING AT BOOKS

Young readers had a wealth of choices at libraries and bookstores in 1998. Outstanding recent books for children ranged from a moving novel set in rural America during the Great Depression of the 1930s, to a beautifully illustrated retelling of a classic fairy tale, to a lighthearted story about three chickens.

AWARD-WINNING BOOKS

Richly detailed oil paintings illustrate Paul O. Zelinsky's

The Etcher's Studio

The woman had an odd look about her as she strolled past a group of Confederate soldiers lounging in front of the red brick warehouse that now served as a prison for captured Union officers. She walked with a nervous gait, her head bobbing back and forth like that of a person who's a little crazy. And she seemed to be mumbling, the sound of her words carried away by the sharp wind that blew in from the James River.

The soldiers eyed her suspiciously. Her clothes were those of a woman born to wealth, although the brocaded silk dress was frayed and worn, and the expensive-looking velvet coat was spattered with mud. Her dark blond ringlets dangled from under a battered bonnet that matched her coat. And her sharp blue eyes, though lively, seemed to dart about aimlessly. She carried a large basket filled with food, clothing, and books.

A strange sight indeed, the soldiers thought as the short, slender woman ambled by them. They watched as she approached the main entrance to the warehouse. Over the large door a faded sign announced "William Libby & Son, Ship's Chandlers"—although the Libby family no longer did business there. Now the four-story building was known as Libby Prison.

The woman turned sharply as if intending to enter the building. One of the soldiers brought his long-barreled Enfield rifle to port arms and moved quickly to block her way.

"Just a minute, Miss," the soldier said curtly. "Don't you know this is a military prison? You can't enter without a pass."

The woman drew back momentarily, then thrust her head forward and replied in a loud voice, "I know full well what this horrid place is used for. I have permission to enter as I please. You must be new here or you would know that."

She drew a rumpled paper and dangled it before the face of the startled soldier, close enough so that he could read the handwriting. "The bearer of this pass, Miss Elizabeth Van Lew, is hereby authorized to freely enter all Confederate military prisons in Richmond for the purpose of caring for captured Federal soldiers." It was signed "Brigadier General John Winder, Provost Marshall."

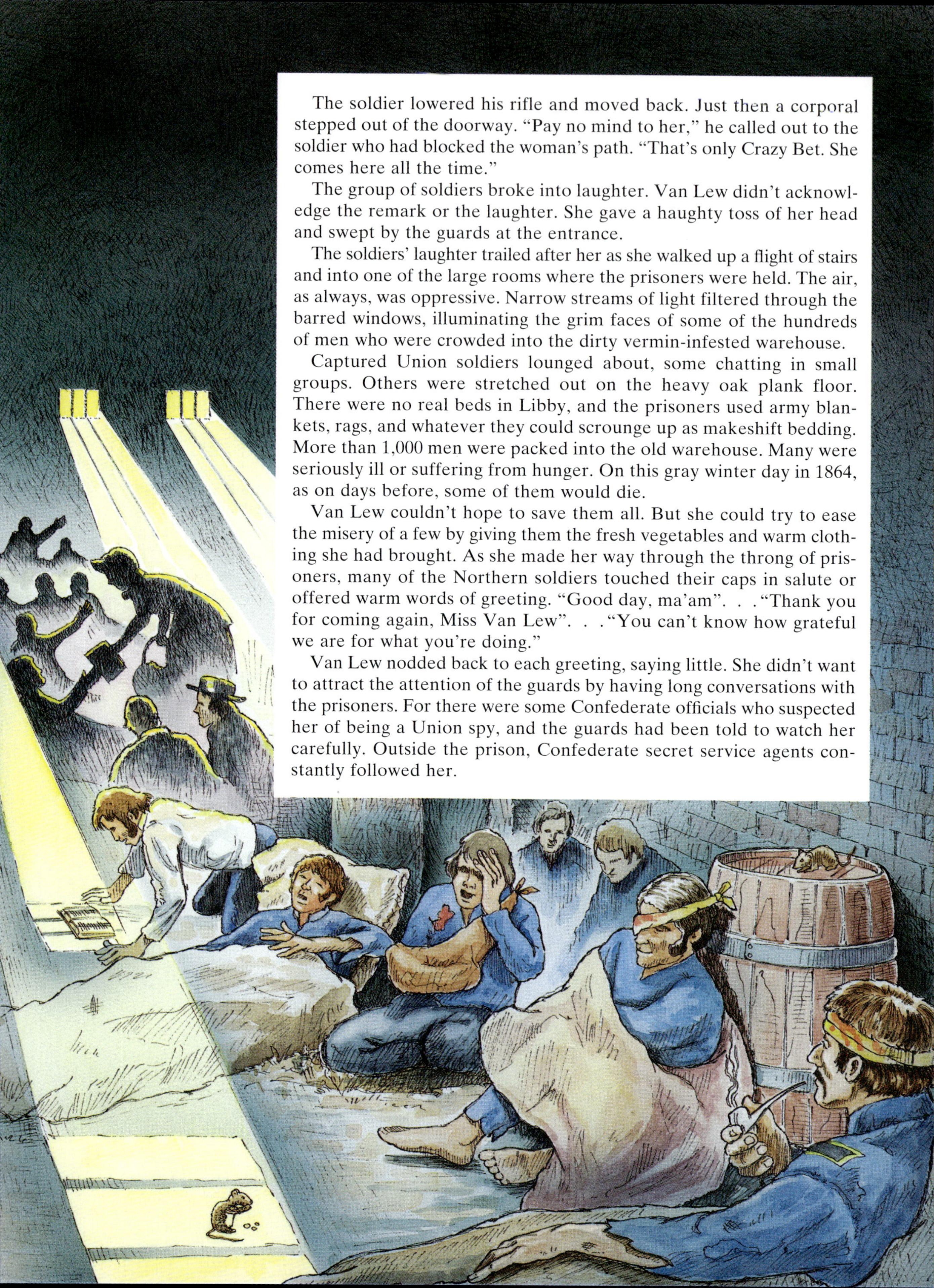

The soldier lowered his rifle and moved back. Just then a corporal stepped out of the doorway. "Pay no mind to her," he called out to the soldier who had blocked the woman's path. "That's only Crazy Bet. She comes here all the time."

The group of soldiers broke into laughter. Van Lew didn't acknowledge the remark or the laughter. She gave a haughty toss of her head and swept by the guards at the entrance.

The soldiers' laughter trailed after her as she walked up a flight of stairs and into one of the large rooms where the prisoners were held. The air, as always, was oppressive. Narrow streams of light filtered through the barred windows, illuminating the grim faces of some of the hundreds of men who were crowded into the dirty vermin-infested warehouse.

Captured Union soldiers lounged about, some chatting in small groups. Others were stretched out on the heavy oak plank floor. There were no real beds in Libby, and the prisoners used army blankets, rags, and whatever they could scrounge up as makeshift bedding. More than 1,000 men were packed into the old warehouse. Many were seriously ill or suffering from hunger. On this gray winter day in 1864, as on days before, some of them would die.

Van Lew couldn't hope to save them all. But she could try to ease the misery of a few by giving them the fresh vegetables and warm clothing she had brought. As she made her way through the throng of prisoners, many of the Northern soldiers touched their caps in salute or offered warm words of greeting. "Good day, ma'am". . . "Thank you for coming again, Miss Van Lew". . . "You can't know how grateful we are for what you're doing."

Van Lew nodded back to each greeting, saying little. She didn't want to attract the attention of the guards by having long conversations with the prisoners. For there were some Confederate officials who suspected her of being a Union spy, and the guards had been told to watch her carefully. Outside the prison, Confederate secret service agents constantly followed her.

That was why she had started wearing shabby clothes and acting a bit strange. The "Crazy Bet" routine was a clever act to throw the hounds off the scent. Now, as she paused to hand a warm shirt, a bit of food, or a book to a prisoner, she looked for some quiet signal indicating that the prisoner had some information to pass on to her.

As Van Lew passed one bearded man, who wore the yellow shoulder straps of a cavalry officer, she caught such a sign.

"Good afternoon, Captain Sloan. How are you feeling today?" she asked the officer.

"A bit better, ma'am, thank you. The doctor gave me something for the dysentery and it seems to be helping. Perhaps you have a good book to help me pass the hours."

She handed the Union officer a volume of short stories by Washington Irving. "I hope this may provide you with a few pleasant hours," Van Lew said, then hurried on.

Continuing her rounds, she spotted another prisoner coughing and moaning while several of his friends tried to comfort him. When she asked what was wrong with the ailing man, one of the officers replied: "We think he's got pneumonia, ma'am. Been coughing this way for nigh on a week."

Van Lew bristled. "Why, that's outrageous! This poor man must be taken to a hospital."

She waved at one of the guards and beckoned him over. "I insist that you remove this man to a military hospital at once."

The guard turned sullen. "Now listen, you crazy old maid," the rebel soldier snarled. "You may have permission to come into this prison, but you ain't got no right giving any orders. I don't see why you're so concerned about these Yankees anyway. Why, if you were a decent Southern woman, you'd be doing things to comfort our own brave lads. There's barely enough food and medicine for our soldiers who are suffering in the trenches as bad as these darn Yankees."

Van Lew fixed her eyes coldly on the guard. "If I report your insolent manner to General Winder, perhaps he will transfer you to General Lee's army so you can see for yourself just how our 'brave lads' are suffering."

Faced with this threat, the guard backed down. Everyone in Libby knew that old General Winder, who was both Provost Marshall and Inspector General of the Military Prison, was an old friend of the Van Lews. And they also knew how Elizabeth Van Lew had won favor with the vain general by making flattering comments about his good looks. An attractive woman in her forties, Van Lew knew, like all Southern belles of her day, how to charm a man.

There was a hasty conference among the guards. A Confederate doctor was summoned, and after examining the sick Union officer the doctor ordered him transferred to a military hospital.

Having won her victory, Van Lew finished distributing food and clothes and started to leave the warehouse. On her way out, she passed Captain Sloan again. He motioned her to stop and handed back the book she had given him.

"Beg pardon, Miss Van Lew, but I recollect now that I have read this book," he said.

Van Lew took the book and smiled knowingly at the captain. "I shall bring you another one tomorrow," she said, then walked out the door.

Once outside the prison, she hurried to where she had left her buggy in the care of one of her black servants. As the black man helped her mount the wagon, he whispered, "Best be careful, Miss Elizabeth, there's a man been watching you since we came here." The servant nodded in the direction of a group of army tents in front of the prison.

Van Lew pretended to adjust her dress, turning slightly so she could catch a glimpse of the spy. She spotted a man in a bowler hat and dark suit. He had heavy side-whiskers and harsh features. She recognized him at once as one of the Confederate detectives who had been trailing her for weeks.

"Thank you, James," she said to the servant. "Now let's go home."

The buggy made its way through the streets of Richmond to the large mansion on Church Hill where the Van Lew family had lived for nearly half a century. The house, with its magnificent columns and portico, was located just opposite the old church in which Patrick Henry had made his immortal cry, "Give me liberty, or give me death!"

While James took the horse and buggy around to the stable, Van Lew went quickly inside the house. She passed through the spacious parlor, with its large crystal chandeliers, and into the library. For a brief moment she recalled more pleasant days before the war when the Van Lews had entertained many prominent people. Jenny Lind, the great singer, had visited them, and one night Edgar Allan Poe had recited some of his poems in this very room.

Her mother was waiting for her in the library. "Mr. Haley has been in touch again," she said quietly. "He will be expecting you tonight at the usual place. Oh yes, and the seamstress is here as you requested."

"Good. I will see her shortly. And I shall not disappoint Mr. Haley."

Mrs. Van Lew, a small, quiet woman, looked concerned. "Frankly, Elizabeth, I think you are taking too many risks. The rebels have spies everywhere."

Elizabeth gently placed her hand on her mother's shoulder. "We must be willing to take risks, Mother, if we are ever to bring this awful war to an end. Come now, let's see what information our friend Captain Sloan has passed on to us."

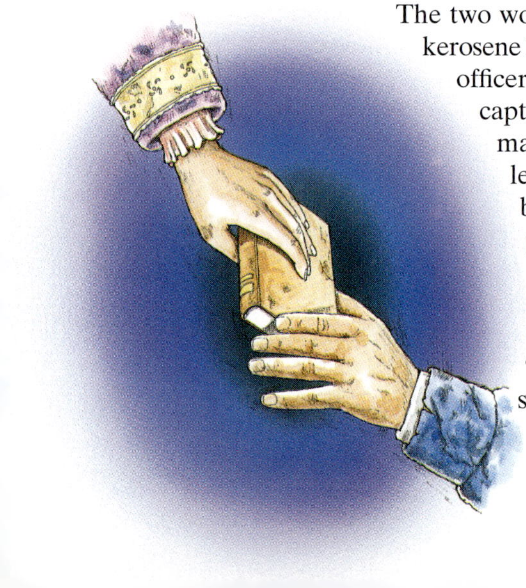

The two women sat down at a small table. Van Lew turned up a kerosene lamp and took out the volume of short stories the Union officer had returned to her. Months earlier, Van Lew and the captain had worked out a code system for getting out information. The captain would make tiny pinpricks over the letters of different words in a chapter of a book she brought him. He would tear a tiny corner from the first page of the chapter to indicate which it was.

By using a magnifying glass to spot the tiny pin marks, Van Lew and her mother pieced together letters to form words, and words to form sentences: "Rumor that Federal prisoners in Richmond to be sent to Georgia. . .New forts being built on Danville

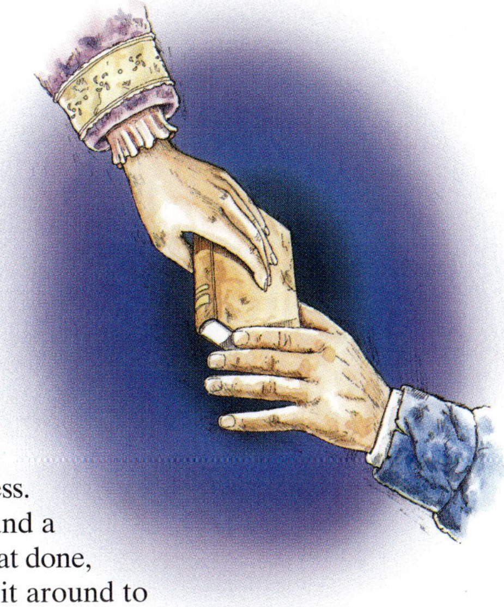

Road. . .Pickett's division now in Petersburg. . .Three regiments of rebel cavalry disbanded by Lee for want of horses."

When they were finished, Van Lew announced, "This is important information. I must get it to Mr. Haley."

Van Lew carefully printed the information on small slips of paper. Then she called in the seamstress and had her sew the slips of paper inside the folds of the dress she was planning to wear for her nighttime excursion.

When all was in readiness, Van Lew slipped into the dress. Then she put on leather leggings, a belted canvas coat, and a large bonnet so that she would look like a farm woman. That done, she ordered the stable boy to hitch the buggy and bring it around to a side entrance.

Shortly before ten o'clock, Van Lew drove off in the direction of the family summer house and farm, just south of the city. The night sky was overcast, with only an occasional glimmer of a faint star and a sliver of hazy moon. By the time Van Lew had passed through the outskirts of the city, a soft rain had begun to fall.

Van Lew preferred to travel alone on these nighttime excursions. But tonight she had an eerie feeling that she wasn't completely alone. Some sense told her that unfriendly eyes were watching her, that she was being followed. Now and then she would glance nervously over her shoulder. She could see no one.

About two miles outside the city, Van Lew spotted a small campfire. She could see the shadowy forms of men huddled around the fire as she drew closer. A Confederate patrol, she thought to herself. There was no going around them, so she rode boldly forward.

A sentry stepped forward to challenge her. "Halt and identify yourself," the soldier ordered.

"I am Elizabeth Van Lew from Richmond," she replied. "I have a pass signed by General Winder permitting me to travel in and out of the city."

Some of the other soldiers now gathered around the wagon. They were a mixture of young boys and older men, for the Confederacy was now using whatever manpower was left. Their gray and butternut uniforms were badly worn and patched. A few wore captured Union army coats and trousers and several had no shoes. Although she opposed the Southern cause, Van Lew couldn't help feeling pity for these men who continued to fight on despite great odds.

The sentry finished inspecting the pass. He was about to wave her on when the sound of a horse coming up the road distracted him. Van Lew looked over her shoulder and saw a man with side-whiskers and a bowler hat dismount and hurry forward. It was the same man who had been spying on her that afternoon.

"Hold that woman. Don't let her go through," the man shouted.

The sentry protested, "But she has a pass signed by General Winder."

The newcomer's lips curled in a sneer. "Never mind her damn pass. I am H. L. Rusk of the Secret Service, and I, too, have a paper. Mine is signed by James Seddon, Secretary of War, and it gives me the right to arrest spies."

Rusk pointed a finger menacingly at Van Lew. "This woman is a Union spy." Then he reached up, grabbed her arm roughly, and forced her to dismount.

Van Lew wrenched her arm free, her face flushing in anger. "How dare you put your hands on me," she cried. "I demand that you let me go."

The Confederate agent didn't budge. "Don't put on uppity airs with me, Miss Van Lew. I know you are carrying dispatches for your Yankee friends and I aim to prove it."

Rusk pushed her against the wagon. There was a cruel look in his eyes. Van Lew tried to squirm loose, but the man was too strong for her.

A few of the soldiers protested his handling of the woman, but Rusk waved them off. Suddenly, a voice of authority sounded from across the road. "Take your hands off that woman, sir."

Van Lew looked to her right and saw a Confederate officer approaching them. He was a tall man, with a neatly trimmed beard and the bars of a captain on the collar of his uniform.

"A gentleman doesn't treat a woman in such a manner," the captain declared. Then, turning to Van Lew, he bowed and said. "My apologies, ma'am, for this man's rude behavior."

The Confederate agent was livid. "Dammit, Captain, this woman is a spy and she carries secret messages under her clothes. I'm certain of it." The Confederate officer looked over at Van Lew. He asked her to identify herself and to tell him why she was out so late at night. For the next few minutes, Van Lew calmly explained that it was her custom to go to her family's summer house and farm at night to bring back vegetables.

"Fresh vegetables are hard to come by in Richmond, as you probably know, Captain," she concluded.

The Confederate officer nodded his understanding. "Then I have but one other question for you, madam," he said. "Are you carrying any secret papers under your—if you'll pardon my bluntness—your dress?"

Van Lew looked the captain straight in the eye. "I give you my word, sir, that I carry no messages under my clothes. Of course, if you insist, I will remove my dress. . ."

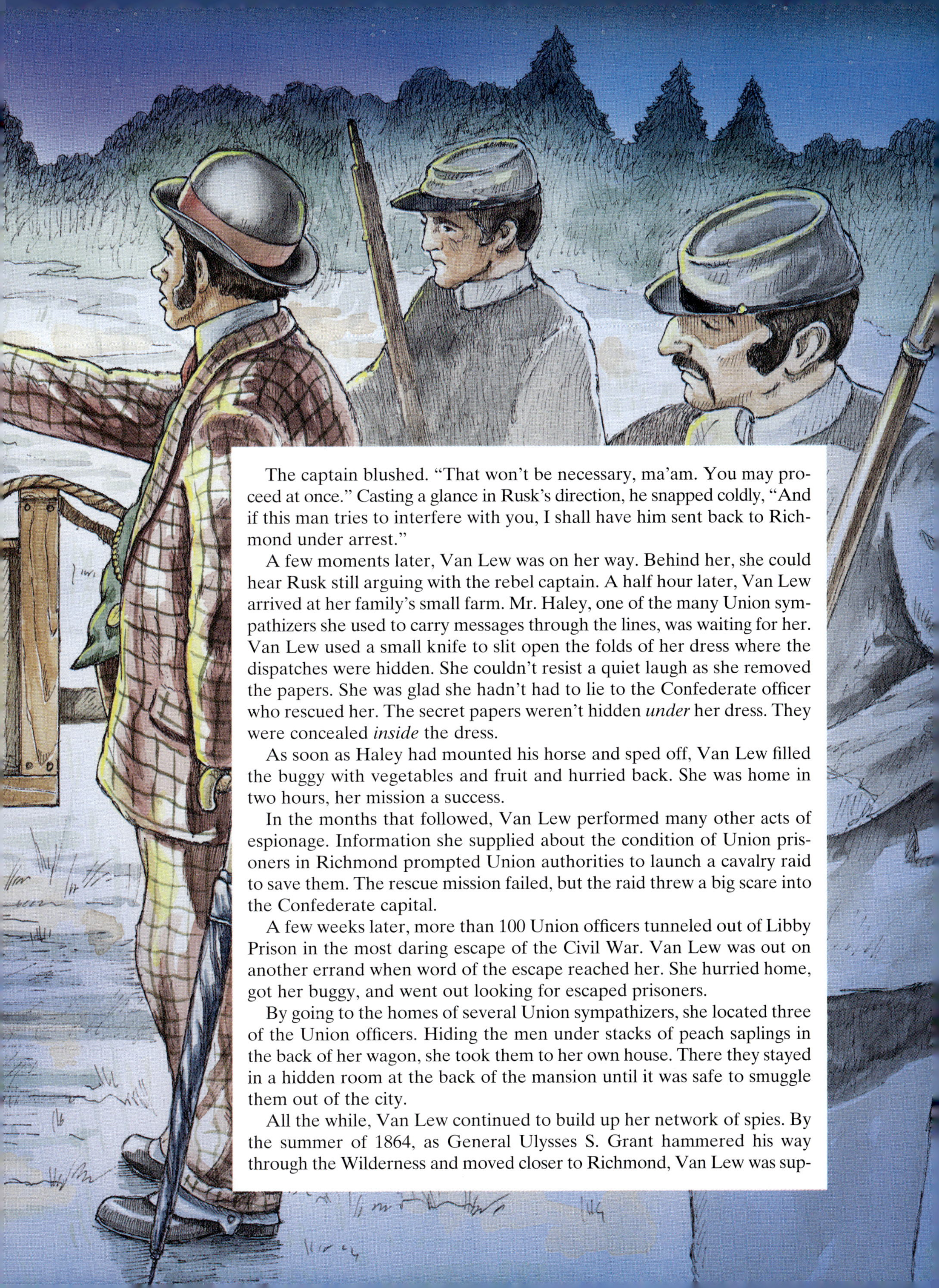

The captain blushed. "That won't be necessary, ma'am. You may proceed at once." Casting a glance in Rusk's direction, he snapped coldly, "And if this man tries to interfere with you, I shall have him sent back to Richmond under arrest."

A few moments later, Van Lew was on her way. Behind her, she could hear Rusk still arguing with the rebel captain. A half hour later, Van Lew arrived at her family's small farm. Mr. Haley, one of the many Union sympathizers she used to carry messages through the lines, was waiting for her. Van Lew used a small knife to slit open the folds of her dress where the dispatches were hidden. She couldn't resist a quiet laugh as she removed the papers. She was glad she hadn't had to lie to the Confederate officer who rescued her. The secret papers weren't hidden *under* her dress. They were concealed *inside* the dress.

As soon as Haley had mounted his horse and sped off, Van Lew filled the buggy with vegetables and fruit and hurried back. She was home in two hours, her mission a success.

In the months that followed, Van Lew performed many other acts of espionage. Information she supplied about the condition of Union prisoners in Richmond prompted Union authorities to launch a cavalry raid to save them. The rescue mission failed, but the raid threw a big scare into the Confederate capital.

A few weeks later, more than 100 Union officers tunneled out of Libby Prison in the most daring escape of the Civil War. Van Lew was out on another errand when word of the escape reached her. She hurried home, got her buggy, and went out looking for escaped prisoners.

By going to the homes of several Union sympathizers, she located three of the Union officers. Hiding the men under stacks of peach saplings in the back of her wagon, she took them to her own house. There they stayed in a hidden room at the back of the mansion until it was safe to smuggle them out of the city.

All the while, Van Lew continued to build up her network of spies. By the summer of 1864, as General Ulysses S. Grant hammered his way through the Wilderness and moved closer to Richmond, Van Lew was supplying the Union commander with daily reports about Confederate troop movements. Learning that Confederate President Jefferson Davis needed another house servant, Van Lew planted one of her own former slaves in the Confederate White House. Twice each week, the young black woman and Van Lew met after dark to exchange information.

Confederate spies, including the dogged Rusk, continued to follow her. But she was always too clever for them and eluded their traps. Van Lew also continued to make visits to Libby Prison. In addition to the pinpricks-in-the-book trick, she also used a large serving dish with a double bottom to carry messages. Once a suspicious guard demanded that she hand over the dish. But Van Lew had been warned that the guard was on to her. She had filled the dish, which she held cradled in her shawl, with boiling hot water. When the guard took the dish from her, it scalded his hands and he dropped it with a howl.

Summer gave way to autumn, and the Confederacy continued to lose ground. General William Sherman captured Atlanta and set out on his "March to the Sea." Phil Sheridan swept Confederate forces out of the Shenandoah Valley, and Admiral David Farragut took the city of Mobile, Alabama. Meanwhile, Grant's army had laid siege to Petersburg, just twenty miles from Richmond. It was only a matter of time before the Confederacy collapsed.

But Elizabeth Van Lew still went on with her work as a spy. One evening, she sent her servant James out with an important message hidden in the sole of one of his brogans. James had hardly been gone half an hour when he came dashing back with troubling news. Confederate troops were seizing all remaining horses in the area for use by the army.

"They'll get Alexander for sure," James said, referring to the family's remaining horse.

"No, they won't!" Van Lew said firmly. "Come on, James, we'll find a nice safe hiding place for him."

By the time the Confederate soldiers arrived at the Van Lew mansion, Alexander was nowhere to be seen. The Southern troops searched the stable and the smokehouse in back of the house, but they could find no trace of the animal.

One of the soldiers demanded to know where the horse was hidden. "We know that you have a horse, Miss Van Lew," the soldier said. "You might as well tell us where he's been put."

Van Lew shrugged. "Why, if you mean our old carriage horse Alexander, he's been dead for over a month."

The soldiers prowled about the grounds for more than an hour. But they couldn't find the animal. Finally, they gave up and left. After the troops had trotted off, Elizabeth's mother asked her daughter, "Whatever did you do with Alexander?"

"Come, Mother, I'll show you."

The two women walked up the stairs to the library. With a flourish, Elizabeth threw open the door. There, standing quietly amid some straw that James had put down, was the big stallion.

"He's such a good horse, not even a whinny," Elizabeth said proudly.

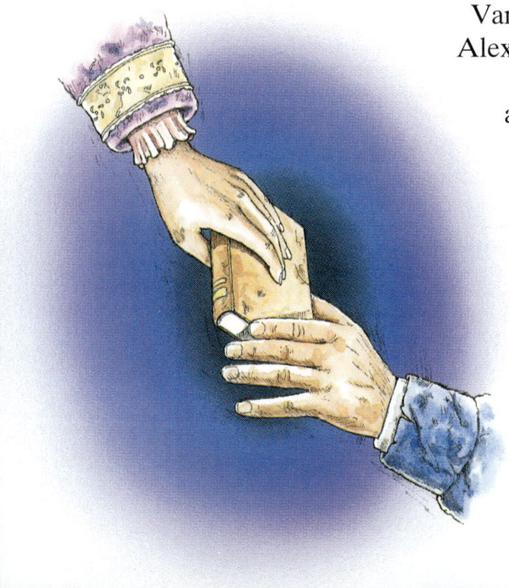

"Yes, but look, he's chewed up some of our books," her mother noted.

Elizabeth walked over to where the remains of one leather-bound volume were strewn about. "Our Alexander is a horse with good taste, Mother," she said with a laugh. "He has devoured an entire volume of plays by Mr. Shakespeare."

The final months of the war passed without much excitement for the Van Lews. Gradually, Lee's lines at Petersburg buckled. Finally, on April 2, 1865, word was flashed that Lee's army had been forced out of Petersburg. Confederate authorities had ordered Richmond evacuated. The following day, the last Confederate troops marched out of the Confederate capital. As they left, they set fire to some of the public buildings so that Confederate records wouldn't fall into Union hands. Looters set fire to other buildings, and soon much of the city was blazing.

Amid the confusion, Van Lew set herself one last task. She walked to the Capitol building to look amid the rubble for any unburned secret papers that she could turn over to the Union Army.

As she rummaged through the smoldering ruins, she was startled by the familiar figure of a man in a bowler hat. His clothes were disheveled and his face was drawn. But there was no mistaking the cruel features. It was Confederate Detective H. L. Rusk.

Van Lew recoiled as she saw him approaching. She felt a sudden chill of fear.

"I thought I might find you here, Miss Van Lew," Rusk sneered. "I've caught you red-handed, you Yankee spy! Well, you won't escape this time."

He moved closer, drawing a Colt revolver from his belt. "I'd like to see you hang like a spy should. But we've no time for that. A bullet will have to do."

Rusk cocked the pistol and raised it, his lips spread in a vicious grin. Although she was trembling with fright, Van Lew managed to blurt out, "You're a fool. Union troops will be here soon and when they find out what you've done, you'll be the one who is hanged."

Rusk paid no attention to her words. He continued to come toward her. Suddenly, Van Lew heard the clatter of horses' hooves and the jangle of sabers. Rusk heard it, too, and whirled in time to see a detail of Union cavalry galloping toward them. The rebel agent dropped his pistol and raced off. But not fast enough. Union troopers ran him down and brusquely dragged him back.

A Union officer dismounted and rushed over to Van Lew. "Are you all right, Miss?" he asked.

Van Lew's heart was pounding furiously, but she nodded.

"Would you be Elizabeth Van Lew?" asked the Union officer.

She was barely able to say "Yes."

"Well then, I'm certainly glad we found you," the officer said, smiling broadly. "General Grant sent us to offer you and your family protection. When we went to your house, your mother told us you had come here. I'm glad we arrived in time."

He pointed at Rusk. "Who is this man?"

"A rebel detective," Van Lew told him. "He has been hounding me for months."

The Union officer put a comforting hand on her shoulder. "You need not fear this man," he told her. "The Union Army now occupies Richmond, and you and your family will be well guarded."

Elizabeth Van Lew slept soundly that night, no longer troubled by thoughts of war or fears of rebel agents. In the morning, when she went to the window, she could see the Stars and Stripes fluttering from the partly burned Capitol.

Later that day, as Van Lew and her mother were having tea, they heard the tramp of marching troops and a bugle sounding flourishes. Rushing to the front door, they saw Union troops cheering and tossing their hats in the air as a group of mounted officers approached the house.

Near the entrance to the mansion, the party halted and several officers dismounted. One of them was a short man, with a thick beard and the stub of a cigar in his mouth. He carried no sword and wore a plain uniform jacket with only the three stars of a lieutenant general on his shoulder straps to mark his rank.

Van Lew knew immediately who he was. As the general came up the steps, she stepped forward and greeted him. "General Grant, I am delighted to meet you. I am Elizabeth Van Lew."

The Union commander removed his hat, clasped her hand warmly, and replied, "Miss Van Lew, I am truly honored to have this opportunity to thank you for what you have done for our cause. The United States government owes you a great debt."

Van Lew smiled. "My mother and I would be truly pleased if you would join us for tea."

"With pleasure, Miss Van Lew," said the general.

Van Lew took General Grant's arm and escorted him into the house. Outside, a fife and drum corps struck up "John Brown's Body."

Henry I. Kurtz
Author, *John and Sebastian Cabot*

THE NEW BOOK OF KNOWLEDGE
1999

The following articles are from the 1999 edition of *The New Book of Knowledge*. They are included here to help you keep your encyclopedia up to date.

Desktop computers put information at the fingertips of many people, such as these students in a geography class.

COMPUTERS

Computers help society function in many vital ways, often without our being aware of them. Computers control traffic lights and factory operations. They scan bar codes at checkout counters and track store inventories. They monitor banking, credit card, and cash machine transactions. Computer chips in our cars, home appliances, radios, televisions, and stereos help us use these and many other products every day. And computers link schools, governments, businesses, and people throughout the world.

Every time you call a friend on the telephone, you are probably using several computers. The telephone itself may have a tiny computer chip that remembers names and numbers. A computer at your local telephone company may automatically connect the call. If you are phoning long-distance, a computer on an orbiting satellite may relay your call to another part of the world. Even the operator may be a computer that answers with a human voice and recognizes your spoken commands.

TYPES OF COMPUTERS

Computers are classified by how fast they compute and how much information they can store. **Supercomputers**—the most powerful computers available—perform complex tasks and handle massive amounts of information. They are used mainly by scientists and engineers for such jobs as predicting the weather or designing automobiles.

More widely used computers today include servers, workstations, desktops, laptops, and palmtops. (Older terms such as "mainframe" and "minicomputer" are rarely used anymore.) **Servers** are usually more powerful computers that perform jobs, such as storing information or connecting to a network, for groups of people using less powerful computers. **Workstations** often sit on desks, but are more powerful than average home or business computers and are used for science, engineering, or computer graphics.

Desktops, or personal computers, usually sit on a desk and are used by one person in a home, school, or business. **Laptops** usually weigh less than 10 pounds (4.5 kilograms) and fit in a briefcase. Because of their size, laptops usually cost more than desktops for the same computing power. **Palmtops**, as their name says, fit in the palm of your hand. Many palmtops have very small screens and no keyboard. You use a special pen to write directly on the screen.

COMMON FEATURES OF COMPUTERS

Every computer is a system—a group of electronic components that work together to store, retrieve, and process data. The components that sit on your desk or that you hold in your hand are known as **hardware**. A computer also needs instructions that tell the hardware what to do. These instructions are called **software**. Computers can be programmed to perform different jobs, and this makes them different from simple calculators. Computers come in many shapes and sizes, and they serve many purposes.

Hardware

A computer's hardware has three types of components: processing units, input and output devices, and memory and storage.

Processing Units. The **central processing unit**, or **CPU**, carries out the instructions from the software by controlling millions of tiny electronic pulses every second.

The CPU is plugged into the **motherboard**, which holds other electronics needed to run the CPU. Support processors on the motherboard help the CPU manage all the parts. The motherboard also has slots that allow other boards called daughtercards to be attached. Daughtercards can also contain support processors for such jobs as controlling the disk drives or connecting the computer to the network.

Input and Output Devices. The processing units must be given information to process—the **input**. The results of the processing are called **output**. Output can be displayed on the screen of a monitor (similar to a television), printed on paper, saved on a disk, or sent to another computer over a network. Many devices, often called **peripherals**, are used to input and output information. A single computer system may have several input and output devices. Input devices usually include a keyboard for typing text and a mouse for controlling a pointer on a computer monitor. Input devices may also include a joystick for playing games, a scanner for inputting images, and a graphics tablet for drawing pictures. Output devices usually include a monitor and a printer. Some devices are used for both input and output, including communication devices called modems and storage devices called disk drives.

Memory and Storage. The CPU performs its calculations using **digital** data, which is information in the form of 1's and 0's. During calculations, the CPU must both save some data for later and find and use previously saved data. For storing and finding data, a computer has memory and disks. Memory is fast, usually temporary, and inside the computer on small electronic components called chips, which are plugged into the motherboard. Disks are slower but can hold much more information for a much longer time.

The smallest unit of memory is the **bit**, which is short for *b*inary dig*it*. A bit can be 0 or 1. As a rule, 8 bits make a **byte**. One **kilobyte** is 1,024 bytes. A computer's internal memory is usually measured in **megabytes**, each of which is 1,024 kilobytes or about 1 million bytes. A computer's hard disk space is often measured in **gigabytes**. A gigabyte is about 1 billion bytes—enough to store the full text of 30 complete sets of *The New Book of Knowledge* encyclopedia. Large computer facilities often have disks or tapes for storing **terabytes** (1 trillion bytes) and are even planning to store a **petabyte**—1 quadrillion bytes.

These girls are using laptop computers, which can be easily carried from place to place and operate on battery power.

Computers have two types of memory on chips. **Random-access memory (RAM)** holds temporary data. It is called random-access because the CPU uses it to store and retrieve data quickly. Since the late 1990's, personal computers have had at least 32 megabytes of RAM. The other type of memory is **read-only memory (ROM)**. ROM holds small amounts of data permanently, including the instructions needed to start, or boot, the computer.

Computers often need to store larger amounts of data and store it for a longer time. Computer disks are devices to hold data, and **disk drives** let the computer read data from and write data to disks. Most disks are covered with a magnetic coating, and bits are stored by arranging the microscopic magnetic particles in the coating. **Hard disks**, which are housed in devices called hard drives, stay inside the computer or in separate boxes

Palmtop computers feature touch-sensitive screens that allow a user to write on them using special pens.

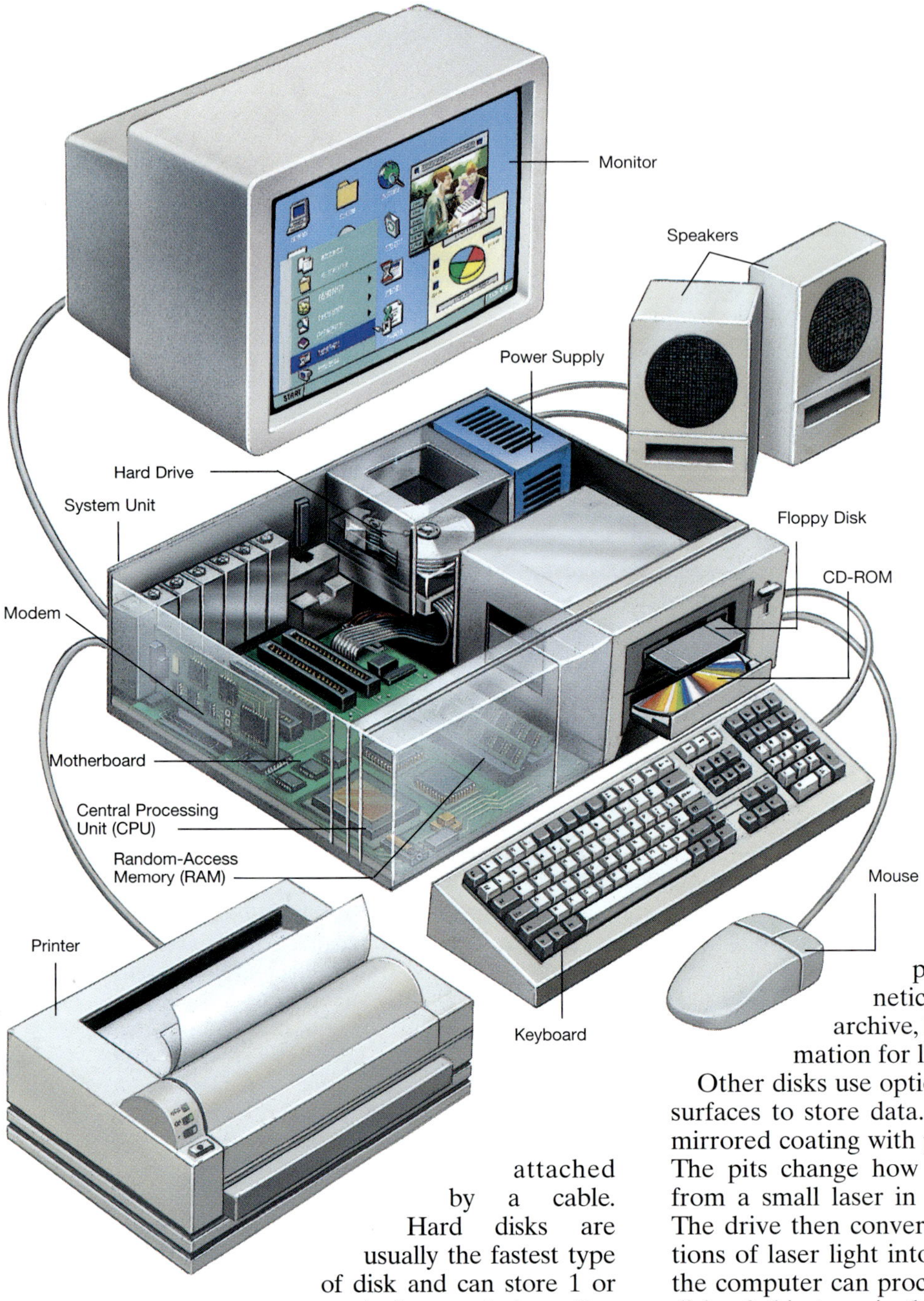

INSIDE A PERSONAL COMPUTER

A typical personal computer includes a system unit, which houses the central processing unit, hard drive, and other important components. Commands and data are entered using input devices, such as the keyboard and mouse. Information in the form of text and graphics is displayed on output devices, such as the monitor and printer. Sound from CD-ROM's and other sources can be heard over the speakers.

attached by a cable. Hard disks are usually the fastest type of disk and can store 1 or more gigabytes of data. Removable disks can be put into a disk drive and removed when they are filled or not needed. **Floppy disks** are 3½-inch (8.9-centimeter) removable disks, protected in hard plastic cases, and can hold about 1 or 2 megabytes of data. (They are called "floppy" because the disks used to come in soft, flexible cases.) Newer removable disks can hold hundreds of megabytes or even gigabytes of data.

Many large computer systems use magnetic tape to store, or archive, huge amounts of information for long periods of time.

Other disks use optical instead of magnetic surfaces to store data. An optical disk has a mirrored coating with pits that represent bits. The pits change how the disk reflects light from a small laser in the optical disk drive. The drive then converts the flickering reflections of laser light into electronic pulses that the computer can process. The most common disk of this type is the **CD-ROM** (compact disc read-only memory). CD-ROM's are thin disks about 4¾ inches (12 centimeters) in diameter. A single disk holds about half a gigabyte of information—the same as several shelves of books. Newer optical disks, called **digital video discs** or **digital versatile discs (DVD's)**, can store even larger amounts of data, including entire movies, on disks that are the same size as CD-ROM's.

A floppy disk (*left*) can store 1 to 2 megabytes of data; a newer removable disk (*center*) can store 100 megabytes or more; a CD-ROM (*right*) can store about half a gigabyte.

Software

For the computer hardware to do useful work, it needs software—instructions that tell the computer what to do and how to do it. A single set of instructions is called a **program**. One program, the **operating system**, has instructions for running all of the hardware components and for managing the actions of other programs. The operating system directs data and instructions to and from the hardware components.

Algorithms. A clearly specified set of simple steps for solving a problem is called an **algorithm**. Each step in an algorithm might become many detailed instructions for the computer. A single program may use many algorithms to do its job. For example, a program might have algorithms for sorting a list of numbers or for checking the spelling of all the words in a document. The flowchart at the bottom of this page shows one way to describe an algorithm for outputting a message to wish someone a happy birthday. The rectangles represent instructions, and the diamond represents a decision. Each of these symbols represents a step that can be written in any programming language.

Programming Languages. The language of computers is **machine language**—a series of 1's and 0's that are converted into "on" and "off" electrical pulses. The electrical pulses tell the computer what to do. Machine language is easy for the computer to understand, but it is difficult for programmers to read and write. **Assembly language** includes labels and other text in a program, and each instruction in an assembly-language program translates to a single machine-language instruction. Machine language and assembly language are called low-level languages because programmers must include every detail of what the computer must do.

Most programs are written in special languages called high-level programming languages, which use words and symbols that look more like English and make it unnecessary for the programmer to be aware of every tiny detail of instruction. Most high-level languages use special programs called **compilers** that translate an entire program into the computer's machine language. Some high-level languages use programs called **interpreters** that translate one instruction at a time into machine language and run it before translating the next instruction.

Higher-level languages, called authoring languages, make it even easier to write common programming tasks. For example, a pull-down menu—a list that appears on the screen to give users a choice of many options—can be created with a simple command, while the programming to do this requires several pages of machine-language code.

COMPUTER APPLICATIONS

A computer application can be either a job accomplished with the help of a computer or the software written for that job. Computers can accomplish many different tasks because many applications have been written for each purpose.

Managing Information

Businesses rely on computers to handle important data, including employee records, payrolls, inventories, customer records, invoices, and receipts. Most of this work is done by programs that manage large collections of information called **databases**. Libraries use databases to catalog, manage, and share their

Computer programs are based on algorithms, with steps that can be represented as symbols. This algorithm tells a computer when to wish you a happy birthday.

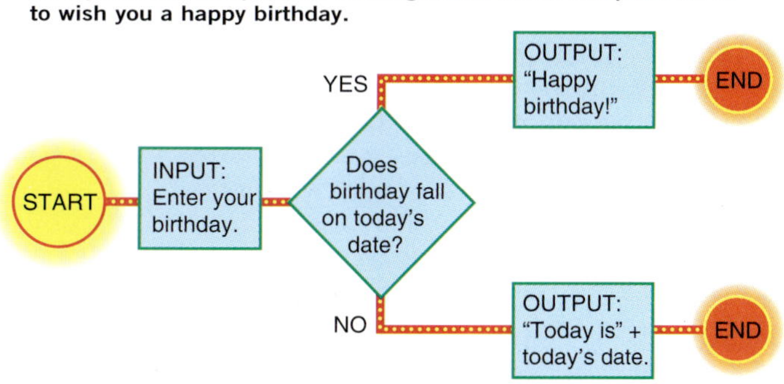

books and reference materials. Teachers and schools use databases to keep track of student grades. Government agencies, such as the Internal Revenue Service and the Social Security Administration, use huge databases to keep track of information about millions of individuals. Databases are used by just about every type of organization.

Writing and Creative Applications

One of the most common computer applications is word processing. Many kinds of programs process text, from simple children's programs to complex desktop-publishing programs. Many of these programs combine text processing with the ability to include designs and illustrations. Some programs can convert speech into text and even translate text into different languages.

Computers also have many applications in art and music. Some programs enable artists to create their own drawings or to duplicate certain styles of painting. Others imitate or alter the sounds of musical instruments and human voices, producing entirely new sounds.

Computer Graphics

Computers are also used to create graphics, or images, that can illustrate information in books, newspapers, magazines, and television. Computer graphics can become animated characters and special effects on television, in movies, and in video games. Computer graphics also have many scientific, industrial, and educational uses.

Business Uses. Many businesses hire graphic artists who use computers to create charts, graphs, maps, and illustrations for public relations, sales, marketing, and training presentations. These graphics are used in printed materials, on slides and overhead transparencies, and even in videos to present information in a pleasing and easy-to-read format.

Science and Industry. In universities and research centers, scientists use computer graphics to make complex information—such as the movement of air in a hurricane—easier to visualize and understand. In government and industry, scientists and engineers use computer graphics to design many products, from spacecraft and submarines to everyday products. Computer graphics are also used in interpreting satellite photographs of Earth and in guiding fighter jets and missiles.

Entertainment. Computer graphics have become a basic tool in creating animation as well as two- and three-dimensional visual effects in television shows, films, and video games. While many special effects now done with computers could be done in the past using traditional methods, some have been possible only through computer technology. One example of this is called **morphing**—from the word "metamorphosis," which means a change in form. In morphing, the size, shape, and characteristics of an object change until it resembles something else. A picture of a car, for example, can be morphed into a picture of a tiger.

These frames from a television ad show how computer graphics technology can be used to make a car "morph," or change its form, until it resembles a tiger.

Education. Computer graphics are now being widely used in textbooks and on instructional CD-ROM's, videodiscs, and other computer technologies. In addition, many interactive and multimedia instructional programs in schools rely heavily on graphics that designers and artists create on computers.

Robotics and Mechanical Control

Often computers are used to control complex mechanical devices. For example, computer-controlled robots perform tedious or dangerous jobs in industry and science. Robots move

CD-ROM's can combine text, images, sound, and animation, as shown in this screen view of the *Grolier Multimedia Encyclopedia*.

large automobile parts on assembly lines and put some of the pieces together. Some police departments use robots to remove suspected bombs from buildings. Robots are also used in space exploration. In 1997, the *Mars Pathfinder* probe landed on Mars. Scientists on Earth used computers to control the probe's robotic vehicle *Sojourner* as it moved from rock to rock and performed its scientific studies.

Helping People with Disabilities

Computers can also provide assistance to people with disabilities. TDD (telecommunications device for the deaf) phones let hearing-impaired people use the telephone by typing on a keyboard and reading messages on a screen. Visually impaired people use computers with software that magnifies screen text or reads text aloud. People who have difficulty speaking or moving may also use computers. Physicist Stephen Hawking, paralyzed from amyotrophic lateral sclerosis (ALS, or Lou Gehrig's disease), has delivered many lectures using a computer to speak for him.

Research and Simulation

Scientists and engineers use computers to conduct experiments that are easier, less expensive, and safer than real-world experiments. Such an experiment starts with a model of something in the real world—for example, a molecule, a car, or a galaxy. The model is built from mathematical equations, which are programmed in a computer to create a simulation of the real thing. Researchers experiment with the model to see how changing the model affects the outcome of a simulation. This tells the researcher how similar changes would affect the real-world object. Using computer models, government planners study traffic flow, economic development, and population growth; engineers test designs for buildings, bridges, and cars; astronomers study planets, stars, and galaxies.

Medical Uses. Computers help scientists design new drugs, scan patients' bodies for signs of disease, study how the brain works, and practice complicated operations. To design new drugs, for example, researchers view molecules as computer graphics. Then they can see how to build drugs that prevent harmful molecules from interfering with helpful ones. In the operating room, robotic arms handle surgical tools in some delicate operations. Computers helped American neurosurgeon Benjamin Carson rehearse the complicated surgery to separate conjoined (Siamese) twins before performing the operation in 1997. More commonly, doctors use computer-controlled devices ranging from

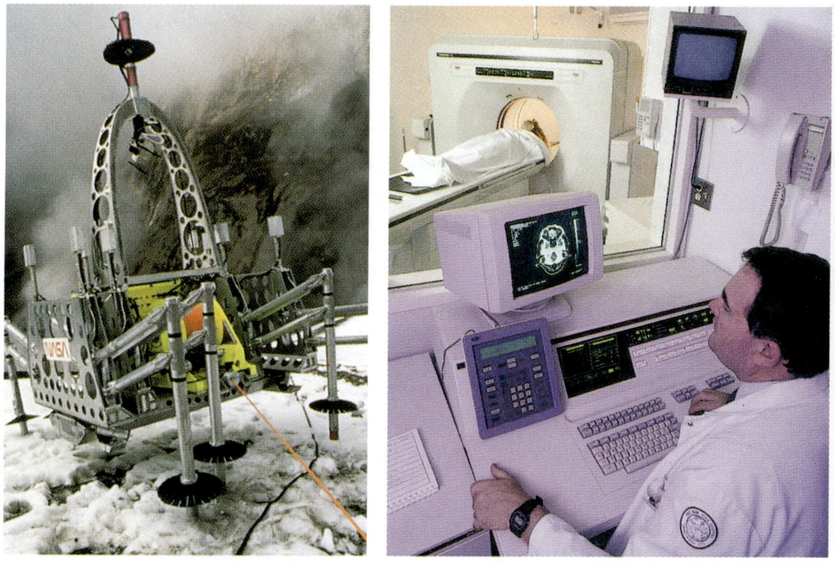

Left: **A robot named Dante 2 explores Alaska's Mount Spurr, an active volcano.** ***Right:*** **Computerized axial tomography, or CAT, scanning lets doctors see inside the body.**

digital thermometers and blood pressure monitors to CAT (computerized axial tomography) and MRI (magnetic resonance imaging) scanners. These devices help doctors better diagnose illnesses.

Weather Prediction. Television news programs use computers to display weather patterns around the world. Those predictions come from supercomputers that run daily weather simulations to forecast weather a few days into the future. More complex simulations try to predict the weather much further into the future. In 1997, scientists used supercomputers to predict the arrival of El Niño, a warming of water in the Pacific Ocean that changes weather around the world. This successful prediction allowed countries and cities to better prepare for heavy rains and flooding.

Flight Simulation. Computers help train pilots and astronauts without leaving the ground. In a flight simulator, a pilot sits inside a copy of an airplane's cockpit. Computers control how the plane moves and what the pilot sees on a large video screen during a simulated flight. Airline pilots can learn how to handle emergencies before they happen in the air. Astronauts can practice complicated missions, such as docking a space shuttle with a space station or releasing a satellite. The military can test fighter pilots' performances without going into battle.

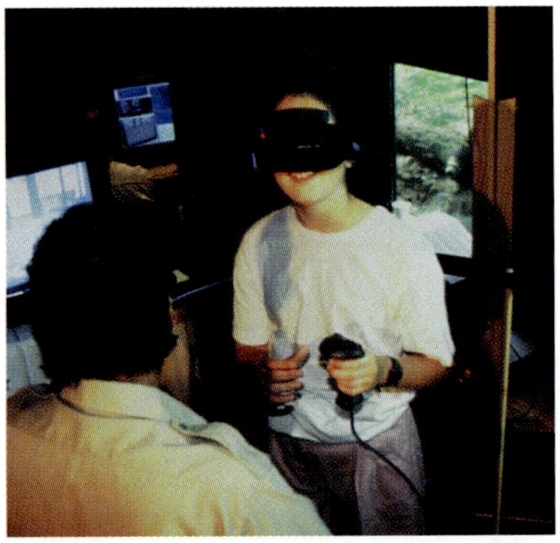

A young woman (*right*) wears special goggles with video screens that give her the impression of being inside an imaginary three-dimensional zoo, inhabited by computer-generated gorillas (*below*). Using a handheld device, she can control her views and perceived movements inside the virtual-reality zoo.

Virtual Reality. Computers can also create virtual reality—three-dimensional (3-D) models of real or imaginary worlds that you can explore with the help of special equipment. Goggles, fitted with a small video screen for each eye, let you view lifelike scenes in 3-D. Other devices, such as position sensors mounted in a headset, change your viewing angle as you move your head and body. The equipment gives you the impression of being "inside" a computer-generated, or virtual, world. Virtual worlds can be entire cities in which a psychiatrist "walks" with a person who is afraid of open spaces or heights. Biologists can create a world from the structure of a molecule and then explore this microscopic world up close. Imaginary worlds can be created for use in games. In some virtual worlds, many people can meet together even though they might be far away from each other in the real world.

COMPUTERS AND THE INTERNET

For much of their history, computers have operated as independent machines. Each computer did its work alone. Starting in the 1960's, computers separated by many miles could be connected to networks and work together. Today, millions of computers are connected to one another in a worldwide network called the Internet. Education, business, entertainment, and

BOOLEAN LOGIC

The CPU and other chips are the most vital components of a computer. These chips are made up mostly of transistors called **logic gates** that enable them to carry out the instructions of a program. The logic used by the chips is the same sort of logic that World Wide Web search engines use to find information.

Chips and search engines both use what is called Boolean logic. Boolean logic is a type of math that calculates the answers to true-or-false questions. Instead of numbers, Boolean logic uses the values "true" and "false," which equal 1 and 0 for a computer. Instead of addition, subtraction, and other math operations, Boolean logic uses three basic logical operations—AND, OR, and NOT. Each transistor in an integrated circuit is a logic gate that performs one of these operations.

You can think of the logical operations as very specific ways to combine true-or-false questions. The AND, OR, and NOT operations work very much like the words *and*, *or*, and *not* in spoken English.

The AND operation takes two inputs and produces one output. The output is true (or 1) only if the first input is true and the second input is true. If either or both of the inputs are false (or 0), then the answer is false. If you are using a search engine, searching for "computer" AND "virtual reality" will return only pages that have both terms in them.

The OR operation also takes two inputs and produces one output. The output is true if either one of the inputs is true. With an OR operation, the search engine will return any page that has either one of the search terms. Many search engines rank the matching pages. Pages that match the first search term AND the second search term rank higher than pages that match only the first term OR the second term.

The NOT operation takes only one input and returns one output, the opposite of the input. If the input is true, the output is false. If the input is false, the output is true.

For example, say you wanted to use a search engine to find weather-related Web sites about thunder or lightning, but not sites about the Tampa Bay Lightning hockey team. You could use the following Boolean phrase: weather AND (thunder OR lightning) NOT hockey.

government are changing as the Internet connects more and more people to one another and to more information.

Networks

A network is a group of computers connected by cables, optical fibers, or telephone lines so that the computers can share information. A network often has one or more servers that hold shared data and programs. A local-area network (LAN) connects computers located near one another, in the same room or building, for example. A wide-area network (WAN) connects computers that are farther apart.

The Internet

The Internet is the worldwide network of networks. Small local-area networks are connected to other local-area networks, and these groups of networks are then connected to other, larger networks. Every computer connected to the Internet, the largest network, is called a **host**. Host computers communicate with one another by sharing a common **networking protocol**, or methodical way of exchanging information.

Internet Technology. All computers on the Internet speak the same networking protocol, called **TCP/IP** (transmission control protocol/Internet protocol), which makes sure that information sent by one host arrives at the proper destination. Every computer on the Internet has a unique Internet protocol, or IP, address—the computer version of a post office box and zip code. Because IP addresses are numbers, people usually prefer to give computers names, which are easier to remember. Some computers on the Internet called domain name servers have the job of matching computer names to IP addresses that computers understand.

When a computer sends data to another computer, special software breaks up the data and bundles it into a sequence of **packets**—envelopes stuffed with data and labeled with the receiver's and sender's addresses. A packet may make many "hops" from computer to computer to get from sender to receiver, and each packet can take a different route. The receiving computer collects the packets and reassembles the message.

Internet Services. The Internet allows many forms of communication between computer users. The oldest, and still very popular, method is electronic mail, or **e-mail**. E-mail lets people send messages back and forth, just as the postal service delivers letters. E-mail led to the creation of **newsgroups**, which let many people with similar interests take part in discussions.

People can also use the Internet to "chat," or exchange messages during live sessions. Internet chats are unlike e-mail or discussion groups, where the messages are saved and may be read later. In chats, what you type appears immediately on the screens of the other participants. Groups of people can meet in chat "rooms"—screens of messages devoted to particular topics of discussion.

The **World Wide Web** is another popular way of sharing information on the Internet. The Web provides information in a standardized way that can be understood by almost any computer, as long as that computer has a Web **browser**. A Web browser is a program that can understand documents containing instructions written in **hypertext markup language (HTML)**. Web documents can include hypertext links, also called hyperlinks or links, to other documents on the same computer or to documents on another computer on the Internet. The Web lets people share many types of information—text, images, sound, animations, programs, and databases.

Each of the millions of documents on the Web has a unique address, called a **uniform resource locator (URL)**. The most common URL format looks like this:

http://www.example.edu/file.html

A browser is a computer program that lets users see documents with text, photos, sounds, and other elements on Web sites, such as *The New Book of Knowledge Online*.

The "http://" indicates that the request uses the hypertext transfer protocol, the network language of the World Wide Web. The "www.example.edu" is the name of the computer where the information can be found. And "/file.html" points to a specific file on that computer.

Internet Uses. The Internet and the World Wide Web are playing important roles in many aspects of daily life. Business, shopping, news media, education, and science are all taking advantage of these new communication technologies.

Businesses provide their customers and investors with the latest information about new products, financial successes, and company changes. Companies that have traditionally sold products through retail stores or through mail order are letting customers buy products on the Web. Hyperlinks can connect advertisements directly to an advertiser's Web site. Software companies let customers download some programs directly from Web sites to their own computers.

The news media use the Web to bring breaking news stories to a worldwide audience. The Web allows news organizations to provide up-to-date stories, photographs, and video around the clock. The Web also lets the audience view many past stories.

Schools and universities use the Web to distribute class notes and submit homework assignments. The Internet also has made what is known as distance learning much more common. Students far away from one another can listen to and see class lectures broadcast on the Internet and can communicate with teachers and other students by e-mail and chat sessions.

Scientists use the Internet to run simulations on distant computers, share information with their colleagues and their students, and meet with other scientists using e-mail and discussion groups. The Internet is even making it possible to operate complex scientific instruments, including electron microscopes and telescopes, by remote control.

A computer artist at Industrial Light and Magic works on the animation of *Tyrannosaurus rex*, one of the special effects for the movie *Jurassic Park*.

Searching for Information

The Internet and the Web have put a world of information at everyone's fingertips, and more information is becoming available every day. But information on the Web can only help solve a problem if the person with the problem can find it. Finding information on the Internet would be nearly impossible without **search engines** and other services that let users find what they want to know. These search engines often use programs called **spiders** to visit as many Web sites as possible and compile an index of them. Most Web browsers include a search button that will help start a search.

Internet users need to pay careful attention to the sources of information. There is so much information that even the largest search engines may have visited only one-third of all Web sites. The Web has made it easy for just about anyone to post information on the Internet. Depending on the source, information might be very accurate or it might be completely wrong. News from an established media source on the Web is probably more accurate than the news provided by an unhappy customer or someone promoting a hoax. Businesses or activist organizations may offer biased points of view. The Internet is a community of institutions and individuals—some may be fair and honest, others might be holding a grudge, and others might not know what they are talking about.

COMPUTER CAREERS

About half the jobs in the United States today involve processing data—gathering, analyzing, and storing information. It is not surprising, then, that working with computers is an important part of many careers, including some you might not think would be related to computers.

Computer programmers design software for homes, schools, and businesses. Programmers also "debug," or fix, faulty programs and create new ones tailored to a company's needs. There are exciting possibilities for creating programs that recognize handwriting and human speech and that sense nearby objects. Programming computers that are built into electronic devices such as telephones, televisions, and appliances provide still other challenges.

Graphic artists design magazines, Web sites, newsletters, product packaging, and advertising. Artists and animators also create computer games and multimedia software, television animations, and special effects in films.

Nearly every company, school, and organization that uses computers relies on **technicians** and **system administrators** to fix hardware and software problems.

As the Web becomes more important, many organizations are hiring employees to maintain their Web sites. **Webmasters** operate many types of software, write programs, and experiment with new technologies.

Many non-computer jobs require employees to use a computer to get their work done. Secretaries, journalists, nurses, telemarketers, air traffic controllers, assembly line workers, travel agents, real estate brokers, mechanics, bank tellers, and stock brokers—to name just a few—all use computers in more and more parts of their jobs.

HISTORY OF COMPUTERS

For thousands of years, people have needed to count and calculate. In ancient

ENIAC, the first high-speed electronic computer, could not store its own programs. Instead, it had to be rewired for each new set of calculations.

times, the Egyptians, Greeks, and Chinese began using the **abacus**, a calculating device with rows of beads on wires. The first true calculating machine, an adding machine, was built in 1642 by the French mathematician Blaise Pascal. It consisted of interlocking gears and wheels mounted on axles, and it added numbers that were dialed on its wheels. In the late 1600's, the German philosopher and mathematician Gottfried Wilhelm von Leibniz devised a system of gears that could multiply as well as add.

The First Computers

The next major advance occurred in the early 1800's, when the English mathematician Charles Babbage built what many people consider to be the first true computer. Babbage created a model of what he called an **analytical engine**, a device that could perform any set of instructions fed to it by cards with holes punched in them. Ada Byron, Countess of Lovelace, wrote instructions for Babbage's machine, which probably makes her the first computer programmer. But Babbage never produced a working machine. (In 1991, the National Museum of Science and Technology in London built a working analytical engine using Babbage's plans. Weighing hundreds of pounds and operated with a hand crank, it has never calculated a wrong answer.)

Punched cards, like those used by Babbage, turned out to be important to the development of computers. The first computer that used punched cards was created to win a contest. Because it took years to tabulate the results of the 1880 census by hand, the U.S. government sponsored a competition to devise a faster method for the 1890 census. The contest was won by Herman Hollerith, a statistician. Hollerith built a mechanical coding and decoding process based on the positions of holes punched in cards. A hole in a certain place on a card represented a piece of information, such as a person's age or occupation. Hollerith also developed machines that could "read" this data by sensing the positions of holes electrically. By the end of the 1800's, people were collecting so much information that computing machinery became a necessity.

Electricity was the next key development in computing. For forty years after the 1890 census, computers used slow mechanical parts that often broke down. During the 1900's, electrical components increased the power and efficiency of computers while reducing their size.

In the 1930's, Howard Aiken and others developed a way to use vacuum tubes instead of mechanical parts to perform many computer functions. Then, during World War II (1939–45), fast computers were needed to control sophisticated weapons systems and calculate, for example, the flight paths of missiles. John Eckert and John Mauchly built ENIAC, short for Enhanced Numerical Integrator and Calculator, to calculate these missile flight paths. ENIAC needed 18,000 vacuum tubes, 1,800 square feet (167 square meters) of floor space, and 180,000 watts of electrical power. (Today, ENIAC's functions can be performed much faster using a programmable pocket calculator.)

ENIAC and other early computers were wired for specific tasks, and to reprogram the computer, engineers had to change the wiring. According to computer lore, an insect once blocked an electrical connection in a computer's wiring, causing the computer to malfunction. That is why we call an error in a program a "bug." In the mid-1940's, mathematician John von Neumann came up with

GLOSSARY OF COMPUTER TERMS

ANALOG DEVICE: A mechanism that represents data in the form of continuous physical quantities, such as the hands on a clock.

ARTIFICIAL INTELLIGENCE: Software that can simulate certain aspects of human intelligence.

BIT: From *b*inary dig*it*; the smallest unit of memory in a computer, represented by a 0 or a 1.

BYTE: A basic unit of computer memory, usually 8 bits.

CD-ROM: Compact disc read-only memory; a storage medium consisting of a small disk that can contain half a gigabyte or more of information.

CPU: Central processing unit; the part of a computer that carries out a program's instructions.

DATABASE: A collection of information in a form computers can use.

DIGITAL DEVICE: A mechanism, such as a computer, that uses 1's and 0's to represent information.

DISK DRIVE: The hardware that places information on or retrieves information from computer disks.

E-MAIL: Electronic mail, a way of sending messages on the Internet.

GIGABYTE: An amount of memory storage equal to 1,024 megabytes; abbreviated GB.

HACKER: A person who uses a computer to break the law—for example, by gaining unauthorized access to another computer.

HARD DISK: A magnetic disk, housed in a device called a hard drive, usually inside the computer or in an external box connected by a cable.

HARDWARE: The electrical and mechanical parts of a computer system, such as the CPU, disk drives, keyboard, and printer.

HTML: Hypertext markup language; the instructions that tell a Web browser how to display information.

INPUT DEVICE: Any hardware, such as a mouse or keyboard, used to enter information into a computer.

INTEGRATED CIRCUIT: A set of interconnected logic gates and other electronic circuits on a single semiconductor chip.

IP ADDRESS: The address of a computer on the Internet.

KEYBOARD: An input device consisting of rows of keys representing numbers, letters, symbols, and functions.

KILOBYTE: An amount of memory storage equal to 1,024 bytes; abbreviated as KB.

MEGABYTE: An amount of memory storage equal to 1,024 kilobytes; abbreviated as MB.

MODEM: Short for *mo*dulator-*dem*odulator. A device that converts digital computer signals to analog telephone signals, and vice versa.

MOUSE: An input device consisting of a palm-sized box with buttons. Moving the mouse across a surface controls a cursor, or movable pointer, on a computer screen.

NETWORK: A group of computers connected by cables, optical fibers, or telephone lines that can share information and programs.

OUTPUT DEVICE: Any hardware, such as a printer or video screen, used by a computer to give out information.

PERIPHERALS: Hardware devices that are controlled by the CPU, such as printers, modems, and disk drives.

PROGRAM: A list of instructions, written in a programming language, to be followed by a computer.

RAM: Random-access memory; a temporary type of memory in which data can be added or removed in random order.

REMOVABLE DISK: A disk, such as a floppy disk, that can be taken out of its disk drive and stored separately.

ROM: Read-only memory; a permanent type of memory containing unchanging data or instructions.

SERVER: A computer for storing data or programs that are shared by other computers on a network.

SIMULATION: A type of program that represents some event, object, or process and allows the user to experiment with aspects of it.

SOFTWARE: Instructions or programs that describe tasks to be carried out by a computer.

SUPERCOMPUTER: The fastest, most powerful type of computer.

TCP/IP: Transmission control protocol/Internet protocol; a methodical way in which computers on the Internet exchange data.

TRANSISTOR: A small electronic switch.

URL: Uniform resource locator; the address of a file on the World Wide Web.

VIRUS: A small program that can attach itself to files and destroy data or damage a computer's operating system.

WEB BROWSER: A program that lets you view HTML documents and other information on the World Wide Web.

WORD PROCESSOR: A program designed for writing and editing text.

WORKSTATION: A powerful desktop computer, usually used for science, engineering, or computer graphics.

WORLD WIDE WEB: A way to share text, images, and other information on the Internet using documents connected to other documents by HTML, or hypertext, links.

WONDER QUESTION

Will computers ever outsmart humans?

Chess champion Garry Kasparov contemplates a move against IBM's Deep Blue. The computer's moves were shown on a monitor and carried out by a human assistant.

In 1997, the world's best chess player, Garry Kasparov, lost a six-game match, winning only two games against his opponent. The loss made headlines because his opponent was a computer, IBM's Deep Blue. This was the first time that a computer had defeated the world champion chess player.

However, this does not mean that computers are now smarter than humans—just faster. Kasparov examines and evaluates up to three chess positions per second. Deep Blue has 32 CPU's and examines up to 200 million chess positions per second.

The truly amazing "computer" is the human brain that can analyze a handful of moves per second and still win two games against Deep Blue. What the brain lacks in raw computing speed, it makes up for in its superior ability to think and create. Consider that Kasparov has written three books, speaks several languages, and gives talks at conferences. Deep Blue only plays chess.

Artificial intelligence (AI) researchers try to make computers think like humans, which has turned out to be very difficult. Some computer programs, called **neural networks**, are built from simple computing units connected to one other, like neurons in the brain. But like Deep Blue, a neural network is good at only one task, usually some type of pattern matching. Neural networks "learn" from examples to recognize handwriting, forecast demands for airline flights, and test tires, computer chips, and other products.

On the surface, some computers may seem smarter than humans. Computers can recognize voices and translate from one language to another. But in fact, computers must work very hard to perform tasks that are simple for humans. Other human abilities, such as consciousness and intuition, are beyond the power of computers, no matter how fast they compute.

the idea of storing programs inside computers and avoiding the need to rewire them for every new task. The first programs were written in low-level machine language or assembly language.

The Information Age

The 1950's witnessed the beginning of what is called the Information Age with the arrival of several advances in hardware and software. **Transistors**, small electronic switches, were developed that were much smaller and cheaper than vacuum tubes. Transistors also lasted longer, worked faster, and used less power, and they soon replaced vacuum tubes in computers. What had once taken up an entire room could now fit into a box the size of a small refrigerator. Programmers developed

Tiny computer chips with millions of transistors are made on wafers of silicon, which must be handled in dust-free conditions inside a manufacturing plant.

high-level languages, such as Fortran, to make programming easier. Fortran was created for scientific calculations. Stacks of punched cards were still used to load a program into a computer's memory.

Integrated Circuits

The next major advance occurred in the late 1960's with the development of **integrated circuits**, also known as IC's or chips. The first IC's contained only a few transistors. IC's made computers much cheaper, smaller, and faster. Faster computers allowed scientists and engineers to present more complex information with clear and precise computer graphics. At about the same time, computer graphics were being used to design and manufacture many everyday products. Smaller and cheaper computers meant that there were many more computers in more places. In 1969, the Advanced Research Projects Agency (ARPA) of the U.S. Department of Defense connected two universities in an experimental network called ARPANET, the forerunner to the Internet.

Computer chips continued to become smaller and more powerful. Before IC's were invented, most early computers were room-sized devices operated by special technicians and shared by many people. By the late 1970's, computer hardware was small enough for building personal computers.

Personal Computers

By the 1980's, tiny chips containing hundreds of thousands of transistors were being produced, resulting in even more powerful, faster, and smaller computers. In 1981, the International Business Machines Corporation (IBM) introduced its own personal computer, which it dubbed the PC. In 1984, the Apple Computer Corporation unveiled its revolutionary Macintosh computer. The Macintosh showed that computers had advanced far enough to use graphics to control their operations. Instead of listing computer files in lines of text on a screen, for example, the Macintosh represented files as small images, called icons, that could be moved on a screen by a person using a mouse. Later, PC's also adopted graphical operating systems, such as Windows. As personal computers became cheaper and easier to use, people began using them more in homes and schools.

The Internet remained limited mainly to universities and large computer-related businesses throughout the 1980's. In the late 1980's, many personal computer owners got their first taste of networking by using modems to dial in to on-line services such as CompuServe or by dialing in to home-grown bulletin-board systems (BBS's).

Recent Developments

By 1990, the Internet had 600,000 computers connected to 5,000 smaller networks. In 1991, researchers at CERN, a physics laboratory in Switzerland, created what became the World Wide Web. In 1992, the Web browser Mosaic, which led to Netscape Navigator, was developed at the University of Illinois.

Computer chips containing tens of millions of transistors made inexpensive computers even more powerful. The Web led to an explosion of Internet usage by small businesses, schools, and home users. By 1998, there were nearly 30 million computers connected to the Internet and more than 2.2 million Web hosts in nearly 200 countries around the world.

Every year, computer components become smaller, memory capacity becomes larger, and computer speed

E-mail

Trash

Word processing

Icons represent computer files and programs, which can be accessed by using a mouse. These icons stand for e-mail, trash (for deleting files), and word processing.

becomes faster. This trend will no doubt result in even more dramatic changes in the near future. Computers today generally use one CPU, so only one operation can proceed at a time. The latest supercomputers, however, can run many programs at once by using multiple CPU's. This will allow computers to perform incredibly complicated tasks, such as simulating the birth of the universe.

COMPUTERS AND SOCIETY

Computers have changed society in many ways. Vast amounts of information are available to anyone who has a computer and a modem. New tasks can be accomplished, and people can communicate in ways never thought possible. Along with the benefits, however, come some new problems. Understanding computers helps us prepare for changes that will influence our lives.

Problems

While the vast amounts of information in computer databases can be beneficial, such databases could also be used to abuse people's rights and privacy. For example, many databases contain private information about individuals, such as health, employment, or financial records. Because computers are connected to networks, unauthorized access to such information is possible.

Hackers use computers for activities that are generally considered illegal. One such activity is the creation of **viruses**—programs that can destroy data or damage operating systems. Another activity involves breaking into computer systems over a network and then possibly stealing or destroying data.

Another problem, illegal copying of copyrighted software, deprives software producers of income. Computers can also be used to deceive by manipulating pictures, voices, and animations in ways that change their original content or intent. Another significant problem is the loss of jobs through computerization. Since the 1980's, many jobs have been assigned to computers and robots.

Trends

Media. Televisions, stereos, and video cameras are now routinely connected to one another, as are computers and telephone lines. Cable modems provide Internet connections across the same wires through which cable television signals are sent. Computers and the Internet are also bringing print and broadcast media closer together. Newspapers are publishing Web sites that include video and sound, and television networks have Web sites with text-based stories. Radio stations are broadcasting to listeners across the Web.

Distributed Computing. Computers connected by networks can perform computations that previously only supercomputers had been able to perform. In a distributed computing project, one central computer manages a large problem by assigning small parts of it to thousands of computers. In one such effort, a 19-year-old college student's computer discovered the largest known prime number, a number that is evenly divisible only by itself and 1. The new prime number was 909,526 digits long. Distributed computing takes advantage of the time when the computer is not being used by its owner.

Artificial Intelligence (AI). Since computers were first built, people have wondered whether computers could "think" the way people do. This has turned out to be much more difficult than expected, but computer programs are getting better at imitating some aspects of human intelligence. (For more information on AI, see the Wonder Question in this article.)

Home Environments. Computers may change how you interact with your home. The home may soon have a central computer that controls electronic appliances throughout the house. Voice commands, even over the telephone, could turn appliances on or off. More people will also work from home, telecommuting to their office across the Internet.

Future Computers. Today's computer chips use electronic circuits to perform their computations. In the future, computers may not use electricity at all. Optical computers store data and perform computations with light. Biological computers use molecules such as DNA, the same molecule that encodes the genes of living things. Quantum computers use individual atoms and the laws of physics to perform calculations.

DAVID L. HART
Senior Technical Editor
San Diego Supercomputer Center

RAIN FORESTS

Rain forests are lush with plants and filled with the sounds of insects, birds, and chattering animals. They are called rain forests because they receive more than 2½ inches (60 millimeters) of rain per month, making the air inside the forests very humid. Tall trees form covers of vegetation that capture water from the air. A person living in the forest might see bats, monkeys, and birds such as toucans, hornbills, and parrots. A person might also see flying squirrels flattening their bodies and gliding through the air or snakes slithering on the ground.

Tropical rain forests are found close to the equator from the Brazilian Amazon and Central America to Southeast Asia, Northeast Australia, and Equatorial Africa. In tropical rain forests, the average annual temperature is 77°F (25°C). Rain forests farther away from the equator are called temperate rain forests because they are cooler and experience less rainfall than tropical forests. Temperate rain forests can be found in the Pacific Northwest of the United States, Southeast Australia, New Zealand, and Chile.

Life in the Rain Forests

Different layers of trees and plants grow in rain forests. The tallest trees are called **emergents** because they emerge above the rest of the forest. These emergents form a thick layer of leaves called a **canopy**, which allows little light to reach the forest floor. Plants growing beneath the emergents have large leaves to capture flecks of light passing through the canopy.

A shallow dig into a tropical rain forest floor reveals bright red and yellow soils. Soils with these colors are high in clay and low in vital nutrients. To survive in such conditions, some plants depend on cooperative relationships with fungi, which attach to plant roots. These fungi-plant associations help plants acquire nutrients from the soil. Other plants have roots that crawl out of the ground, capturing nutrients being washed down tree trunks during rains. Plants can also form deep carpets of roots on top of the soil to catch nutrients before they go into the ground.

It can be difficult to walk through rain forests because of the abundant plant growth. In the tropics, machetes are useful for cutting through thick vines hanging down from the canopy or plants creeping up tree trunks.

Tall trees emerge from a rain forest in Costa Rica (*above*). A researcher studies the forest canopy from a gondola hanging from a giant crane (*right*).

However, if a visitor were to see the rain forest only from the ground, he or she would miss a sense of the distinct living community in the forest canopy. Some animals and plants live their whole lives in the canopy, never touching the ground. Other canopy-dwellers, such as sloths, crawl down tree trunks only occasionally. Some plants, such as the strangling fig, begin their life in the canopy by growing on the branches of other trees. The strangling fig's thick roots eventually wind around its host tree and kill it.

Rain forest plants have developed many sophisticated methods to keep animals from eating their leaves, stems, or bark. The animals are often hindered by toxic compounds,

A worker in Paraguay burns part of a forest to clear land for farming. Such burning threatens many rain forests worldwide.

called alkaloids, that can either inhibit digestion or kill the animals. Some plants have developed other defenses, such as spines, to discourage vines and other climbing plants from crawling up their trunks.

The Importance of Rain Forests

Rain forests are important because they contain the highest diversity of plant, animal, and insect species in the world.

Rain forests are also important because they affect Earth's climate. Rain forests stabilize the climate by keeping temperatures from rising. The forest plants do this by absorbing carbon dioxide, a gas in the atmosphere that traps the sun's heat and warms the world. Rain forests also stabilize the climate by controlling rainfall patterns. Because rain forests capture water from the atmosphere, the loss of these forests in some areas has turned them into grasslands or deserts.

Loss of rain forests affects people all over the world in many ways. For example, the cutting down of rain forests can trigger the growth of insect populations, such as mosquitoes, which can carry malaria and other diseases deadly to humans. Habitat loss can also force diseased animals to move closer to human communities. Monkeys carrying the fatal Ebola virus are a danger to people living in some African rain forest areas.

Uses of Rain Forests. Native people living in rain forests have traditionally depended on forest resources for all aspects of life, ranging from food and shelter to medicine. Many of these resources are also harvested and used in products exported to countries around the world.

Rain forests are a source of many agricultural crops and houseplants. The cacao plant is used to make chocolate, and the chiclet plant is used in chewing gum. Other rain forest crops include coffee plants, rubber plants, and cinnamon. Rain forests also provide many medicines. Chemicals that plants produce to protect themselves have been extracted and used as treatments for disease. Extracts from one rain forest plant, the cinchona, have been used for hundreds of years to treat malaria.

Deadly fluids from some animals, such as frogs, have been used by native people on arrow tips for hunting. Cassava, a starchy root, has been a major agricultural crop. It can be dangerous if not prepared properly, since the roots have high concentrations of cyanide.

Threats to Rain Forests

Today, native people's lives are changing rapidly, and traditional knowledge of how to live in rain forests is being lost. However, the threat to rain forests does not stem simply from a change in the native people's lives. Increasing demands are being made on rain forest resources from people all over the world. Rain forests are being cleared to mine minerals and metals, ranchers are converting forests to grasslands for grazing cattle, and timber companies are harvesting valuable tree species. Even tourists can pose a threat to tropical rain forests. Visitors often pay to stay in huts with thatched roofs, resulting in the overharvesting of the palms used for thatch. Plants sold as medicines or spices are also being overharvested, and animals are being killed for their skins or sold as exotic pets.

Many attempts are now being made to protect rain forests. Some rain forest products carry a "green" label showing that they were produced using methods that sustain rather than destroy the forests. Other attempts include restoring degraded forests so that they can return to their original condition.

KRISTIINA VOGT
Professor of Ecosystem Ecology
B. BROOKE A. PARRY
Research Assistant, School of Forestry and Environmental Studies, Yale University

HAWKS

A red-tailed Krider's hawk (*left*) is a buteo, or soaring hawk. A Cooper's hawk (*above*) is an accipiter, or woodland hawk. It has just caught a bobwhite quail.

High on a tree, a red-tailed hawk closely watches the field below. The bird waits quietly for hours, until its sharp eyes spot a squirrel scurrying through the grass. With a quick beat of its wings, the hawk takes flight and swoops down to make the kill. Clutching its prey with sharp talons, the hawk returns to its perch to devour its meal.

Hawks are birds of prey, also called **raptors**. Like their relatives, eagles and falcons, hawks have curved talons that grasp and crush prey, and a hooked beak for tearing flesh. They have keen vision—eight times as sharp as a human's—and are excellent judges of distance. Hawks are found throughout the world in all kinds of habitats: forest, prairie, tundra, and desert.

TYPES OF HAWKS

The two main kinds of hawks are woodland hawks, called **accipiters**, and soaring hawks, called **buteos**. Accipiters include three North American species—the northern goshawk, Cooper's hawk, and sharp-shinned hawk. These forest birds dart through the trees, hunting birds and small mammals. With their short, rounded wings and long tail, they can easily make sharp turns and overtake prey with a quick burst of speed.

Buteos soar over fields and canyons. North American species include the red-tailed hawk, the most common species in the United States, and the ferruginous hawk, the largest North American hawk, with a wingspan of 53 inches (135 centimeters). Compared with accipiters, buteos are larger, with broad, rounded wings and a wide tail.

Did you know that...

hawks can fly hundreds of miles without getting tired? Instead of flapping their wings constantly, migrating hawks often glide on rising columns of warm air called **thermals**. This way hawks can travel long distances without using a lot of energy.

LIFE OF THE HAWKS

In general, the larger the hawk, the longer it lives. While accipiters live for only about three years, red-tailed hawks and other buteos may live ten years or more.

Red-tails court and mate in early spring, and mated pairs usually stay together for life. Working together, a male and female build a large stick nest in the fork of a tall tree. Their favorite nesting places are at forest edges, close to open areas where they can easily find prey.

The female lays two or three eggs and incubates them. After about thirty days the chicks hatch, covered with white down. Newborns need plenty of food, and both parents keep busy feeding and caring for the growing chicks. After four or five weeks, the young hawks begin to fly. In another few weeks, they are fully grown and can leave the nest.

Red-tailed hawks eat mainly small mammals such as mice, ground squirrels, and rabbits, but they will also eat birds, snakes, and lizards. Some farmers view red-tails as enemies, because young hawks will occasionally kill chickens. But overall, red-tails and other hawks benefit the environment by helping keep rodent populations under control.

Centuries ago, many people trained hawks and falcons to hunt, a sport called **falconry**. Today in the United States, falconry is strictly controlled but remains a popular activity for people who are dedicated to these majestic birds of prey.

CARRIE DIERKS
Science Writer

PIONEER LIFE

Pioneer life has a special meaning in America. In less than 300 years, civilization spread across a vast continental wilderness. From the first landings in Virginia and Massachusetts in the early 1600s, American settlers kept pushing westward behind an ever moving frontier. Into wild country went hunters, trappers, fur traders, miners, frontier soldiers, surveyors, and pioneer farmers. The farmers tamed the land and made it productive. Every part of America had its pioneers.

A pioneer family in the mid-1800s posed in front of the covered wagon that had brought them to Johnson County, Kansas.

KINDS OF PIONEERS

The pioneers were as varied as human nature. Some were adventurous and independent. Some were irresponsible and lazy, like the Indiana squatter who moved eight times without ever clearing timber or fencing a field. "To move," he said, "all I have to do is put out the fire and call the dog." But most of the pioneers were determined and industrious people. Silas Garber, for example, settled in a sod-roofed dugout on a prairie creek bank in 1871. Four years later he had succeeded in becoming the governor of Nebraska.

Most pioneers were willing to face toil and hardship for the sake of opportunity. They meant to carve homes out of the wilderness. Yankee farmers went west from the stony fields of New England, and Southern families went west from the crowded lands of Virginia and the Carolinas. Still other pioneers were immigrants newly arrived from Europe. English, Scotch, Welsh, and German pioneers went into the Ohio Valley. Scandinavian colonists settled mainly in the upper Mississippi Valley and on the Great Plains beyond the Missouri River.

REASONS FOR THE WESTWARD MOVEMENT

All the pioneers hoped to find something better over the western horizon. New England families, tired of farming rocky valleys, were attracted to broad and fertile lands beyond the Appalachian Mountains. Southern farmers, suffering from bad luck or bad management, sought a new life in the West. To European immigrants the American frontier offered political freedom and economic opportunity. In the West, you could own your own land and work for your own future. For many people the West meant new opportunities.

In the Great Migration, which began after the War of 1812, multitudes of people went to the American interior. The population was growing in the eastern states. Families were large, and only one child could inherit the family home. The rest went to the growing cities or to the frontier. During hard seasons,

when crops failed or when farm prices fell, many headed for a new beginning in the West.

Many went almost empty handed to the frontier. They traveled light and arrived with only an ax and a rifle. Others carried heirlooms and farming tools. Some took seed corn and orchard shoots, cattle, hogs, and poultry. But how does one prepare for sickness and danger, for accident and misfortune? Some settlers failed and returned to the East. Those who stayed and survived turned a wilderness into a civilization.

BUILDING A CABIN IN THE CLEARING

On every new frontier the pioneers made homes for themselves, using what the wild land provided. In the great forests of the Ohio and Mississippi valleys the land provided timber. Here the pioneers' essential tool was the ax. The ax would clear the forest for the plow. But its first task was to shape a pioneer shelter.

When a family of settlers arrived at the spot where they planned to make their home, they began chopping saplings and trimming poles to build a lean-to. Between two forked trees they laid a crosspole. With the help of oxen or horses they rolled up a log, which was banked with dirt to form a low back wall. Then they laid poles, slanted upward, from the back log to the crosspole. The sloping roof was covered with bark and branches. The ends of the lean-to were walled with shorter poles and pickets. This was the pioneers' "half-faced camp." It always faced south, away from wind and rain. In front of the open side they dug a fire pit. Logs smoldered there day and night, giving warmth and protection.

This served as a temporary home while the pioneer family prepared ground for their first crop. A real clearing took months of work, but a "deadening" could be done quickly. A few ax cuts were made in the tree trunks so that sap could not flow up to the branches. Soon the leaves withered, allowing sunlight to reach the damp soil. Seed corn was dropped into ax cuts in the ground. The crop from that crude planting provided food for the first winter.

Before winter came, the pioneer family hoped to have a small clearing and a snug

After finding a location for a homestead, the pioneers' first task was to clear a field for a vegetable garden. They used the felled trees to build a temporary shelter.

cabin. The forest was the settlers' enemy—it had to be destroyed to create their fields. At the same time, it was their friend—it gave them logs for their cabin, fuel for their fire, rails for their fences, wheels for their wagon, and a frame for their plow.

Notched logs formed the cabin walls. A ridgepole at the peak supported lighter roof poles, and a bark thatching made the roof complete. Logs, split into flat-faced planks called puncheons, were used to make the cabin floor. Two openings, a window and a door, were sawed out with patient labor. Typically the first doorway covering was an old quilt weighted with a log; later a board door would be hung on leather hinges. The first window covering was greased paper, which turned away wind and water and admitted a dim light. Pioneers used any paper they had. One settler greased his wedding certificate with bear fat and put it in his window frame.

Opposite the cabin doorway was the yawning chimney mouth. Clay from the creek bank, mixed with dried grass, was formed into clumsy bricks, which hardened in the sun. Laid against the cabin wall, the bricks formed a "cat and clay" chimney with a broad opening. The fire that smoldered there gave heat for cooking, light, and warmth. Outside, the ax thudded and the smoke of brushfires hazed the air. Slowly the field was widened; a few new acres were cultivated every year. The cabin in the clearing was the pioneer homestead. When it gave way to a frame house, with a traveled road going past, the pioneer life had ended.

TRAVELING ON THE OVERLAND TRAILS

In the 1840s and 1850s hundreds of thousands of pioneers made the long trek west to new frontiers in Oregon and California. For months they lived in covered wagons. These adventurers traveled in caravans, with 30 or more wagons rocking westward on the overland trails. On fine days a wagon train could cover 20 miles (32 kilometers); when the rains brought mud, they would be satisfied to cover half that distance.

When a caravan was large, it was divided into two groups. Behind the line of wagons came the "cow column"—milk cows and spare oxen driven by men and boys on horseback. At night the wagons drew into a circle and the oxen were turned loose to graze. Men took turns at guard duty under the western stars.

Attractive advertisements showing beautiful land and happy settlers encouraged hundreds of thousands of people to move west.

OREGON FEVER

Based on the enthusiastic reports of people who had been (or perhaps claimed to have been) to Oregon, thousands of men uprooted their families and made the overland journey across the continent. This excerpt from a young pioneer's diary describes the kinds of exaggerated stories that were told to entice people to go west.

> One Saturday morning father said that he was going . . . to hear Mr. Burnett talk about Oregon . . . . Mr. Burnett hauled a box out on to the sidewalk, took his stand upon it, and began to tell us about the land flowing with milk and honey on the shores of the Pacific . . . . He told of the great crops of wheat which it was possible to raise in Oregon, and pictured in glowing terms the richness of the soil and the attractions of the climate, and then with a little twinkle in his eye he said "and they do say, gentlemen, they do say, that out in Oregon the pigs are running about under the great acorn trees, round and fat, and already cooked, with knives and forks sticking in them so that you can cut off a slice whenever you are hungry." . . . Father was so moved by what he heard . . . that he decided to join the company that was going west to Oregon . . . . Father . . . was the first to sign his name . . . .

On Sundays, unless a wagon train was behind schedule, the pioneers would stop to rest, play, and catch up on necessary chores.

At first daylight the guards went around the circle shouting "Arise! Arise!" Cows were milked while breakfast sizzled on the fire. The oxen were yoked and the wagons pulled into line. As the long bullwhips cracked, another day's travel began.

At noon the captain called a halt on a prairie ridge or beside a creek bank. While lunch was laid out, children ran over the prairie, gathering buffalo "chips" for the evening fire. (Buffalo dung was the travelers' main source of fuel.) After an hour's rest the march started again. The sun beat down, and heat waves shimmered on the horizon. When the shadows lengthened behind them, the captain began looking for a camping place. Supper was a restful meal. Children ran from one campfire to another. Men talked about the next day's travel, and women talked about the homes they would have at the end of the journey. After a fiddler played a few tunes, the people went to bed, some in the wagons, others on the ground. When the fires died down, the night wind brought the haunting call of coyotes.

Sunday was commonly a day of rest. However, even on Sundays the women washed clothes and baked bread, and the men repaired harnesses and greased the wagon wheels. While dinner was cooking, the whole company gathered in the shade of the circled wagons as the captain read a chapter from the Bible. Most often they turned to the Book of Exodus, which told of people wandering in the wilderness, seeking a promised land.

On the plains, where fuel was scarce, pioneers collected buffalo "chips" (dung) to feed the evening fires.

▸SETTLING ON THE GREAT PLAINS

On the Great Plains, which were settled soon after the Civil War (1861–65), the pioneers built their first dwellings with the deeply rooted grass. Here farmers plowed up building material

Most pioneer homes on the plains were crude shelters made from whatever materials were available. A family in Oklahoma used sod, cloth, and bits of wood to build their dwelling (*left*). A family in Kansas dug their shelter straight into a hillside (*below*).

while breaking their first fields. With a spade they cut the furrows into 3-foot (1-meter) lengths. These they piled up like bricks, leaving openings for a door and window. Roof poles came from willow thickets along the infrequent prairie creeks. When a layer of sod covered the crisscrossed poles, the house was completed. It was cool in summer, warm in winter, windproof, and fireproof. But it did not keep out water. Spring rains seeped through the sod roof long after the sky had cleared. Sometimes a pioneer would have to hold an umbrella over the fire to cook a meal.

Outside the sod shanty a settler chopped into the broken ground and dropped seed corn into each cut. A year of wind and weather would soften the field for cultivation. But the first crop was sod corn, growing in the matted grass roots. On the prairie lay buffalo bones left by hide hunters. Pioneer settlers hauled wagon loads of bones to the nearest railroad town, trading them for a wooden door, a glass-paned window, or some joints of stovepipe. The bones were ground up for fertilizer.

Near the first sod hut other pioneers marked their claims with a "straddlebug"—three boards nailed in a flimsy pyramid. New "soddies" appeared on the prairie, with new breakings beside them. These small fields, almost lost in the blowing grasslands, were the beginning of a changed country. In a few

Sturdy cooking pots and ladles were staples of the pioneer kitchen, along with herbs prized for their medicinal value. Essential tools included (*opposite page, from left to right*): a carpenter's adze, a boring auger, a striking maul, a hitting beetle, a barking spud, a scythe, and various axes.

years roads were graded along the section lines, settlements sprang up at the township corners, and wheat and corn grew where the buffalo grass had been.

WAY OF LIFE

Whatever their surroundings, the pioneers had to depend on themselves and on the land. Self-reliance was a frontier requirement. Game provided food and leather clothing. New settlers gathered wild fruits, nuts, and berries. For salt they boiled the water of saline springs. Maple sugar was made by tapping maple trees in early spring and boiling the sap until it thickened into a tasty sweetening. Substitutes for tea and coffee were provided by boiling sassafras root and brewing parched corn and barley. With an ax and adze for cutting tools, the pioneers made beds, tables, benches, and stools. They split logs into rails to make the zigzag fence that enclosed their clearings.

On wash day, women would gather outdoors to do their weekly laundry.

Pioneer women learned to supply their own household goods. Gourds served as pails and dippers. Wood ash was sifted to make soap. Tallow (sheep and cattle fat) was molded into candles. Every cabin had two spinning wheels—a big wheel for wool and a smaller wheel for flax. With their own homewoven "linsey-woolsey," a coarse cloth of mixed linen and wool, pioneer women made their family's clothing. Clothes were also made from animal skins, which the pioneers tanned into leather.

Winter was a hard season on the frontier. In bitter weather the family huddled around the fire. When there was no leather, some people went barefoot and suffered frostbite. Food was scanty and monotonous. For months there were no fresh fruits or vegetables. In early spring, women looked eagerly for the first wild mustard and dandelion plants, which they could boil into a dish of "greens."

As long as they had their health and strength, people could stand hardship. But every family had frequent bouts of illness. The most common frontier ailment was chills and fever. Young and old suffered from "the shakes," shuddering with cold and then breaking into a drenching sweat. This disease came at the end of summer and lasted until frost. Since it was most common in marshy districts, the settlers thought it came from breathing damp air. Actually it was malaria, carried by mosquitoes. When swamps were drained, there were fewer mosquitoes and the number of malaria cases declined.

For medicines the pioneers had to provide for themselves. Women soon learned the use of herbs for healing. They used boneset for fever, pennyroyal to purify the blood, horehound for coughs, and ginseng for tonic. Syrups and salves were made from cherry root, horseradish, and witch hazel. Wild mustard, poplar root, and red sumac root went into teas, poultices, and powders. The standard cure for a chest cold was to rub the chest with goose grease and apply a mustard plaster.

Some frontier remedies were based more on superstition than science. Among these were potions of walnut bark "peeled upward," boiled nettles, and "nanny tea," made from sheep dung.

Pioneer families tended to be large. Most cabins had a cradle, hollowed from a poplar or cottonwood log, and the cradle was rarely empty. Children were helpful in new lands. Girls soon learned important household tasks—gardening, cooking, spinning, weaving, mending, sewing, making soap and candles. Boys worked in the woods and fields with their fathers. They learned to fell timber, to clear out brush, to split rails and build fences. A rail fence would keep hogs and sheep out of the corn, but deer could leap that barrier. It was the children's job to chase deer out of the fields and to keep squirrels from devouring the growing crop. Children pounded dried corn to make cornmeal. When gristmills came into the neighborhood, it was typically a boy's chore to ride to the millstream with

Pioneer children had many responsibilities on the frontier. Chores included (*clockwise from above*) mending clothes, chopping wood for fires, baking bread, hoeing fields, and fetching water.

a bag of grain behind his saddle and return with a dusty bag of meal.

Although pioneer families were extremely resourceful and nearly self-sufficient, neighbors were highly valued on the frontier. When fires went out, one could borrow a pan of glowing coals from the nearest cabin. Neighbors from miles around helped newcomers with logrolling, house-raising, and barn-raising. Entire communities joined in hunts for wolves, foxes, squirrels, and rabbits.

These common tasks, shared by pioneer neighbors, also provided amusement on the frontier. A house-raising was also a picnic, with women spreading a dinner on the grass while children swung from grapevines and the men laid up the roof poles on a new cabin. Neighbors gathered for "husking bees," competing to see who was the fastest at stripping the husks from ears of corn. The cornstalks were kept for fodder, while the husked corn was stored in a crib. Pioneer women held "quilting bees," exchanging family news while they sewed patchwork together. One amusement that did not involve household tasks was the barn dance. With a local fiddler playing such tunes as "Skip-to-my-Lou" and "Way Down in the Pawpaw Patch," men, women, and children joined in square and circle dances by lantern light on a rough barn floor.

Schools and Churches

To pioneer people, "book l'arnin'" was less important than learning to use an ax and a plow, a loom and a spinning wheel. But as settlements grew, parents wanted their children to know the three R's—reading, 'riting, and 'rithmetic. In crude log schoolhouses, shelves fastened to the wall served for desks and the students sat on three-legged stools. They used charcoal to write on hand-smoothed writing boards. Later came slates and slate pencils. A slate, wiped clean after each lesson, could be used for years.

A teacher (known as a schoolmaster or schoolmistress) sat in the front of the schoolroom at a rough plank table. In the corner the teacher kept a bundle of hickory switches to whip unruly boys. Teachers "boarded round," a week at a time, in the homes of pioneer families. Often they slept in cabin lofts. They were paid according to the number of children they taught. All grades sat in the same room. About twenty students made a typical school, and a teacher's common salary was between $1 and $2 a term for each student. In wooded regions children walked as far as 5 miles (8 kilometers) on forest trails to the schoolhouse. On the prairie frontier they often went to school on horseback. They ate their lunch in the schoolyard in good weather and around the stove on winter days.

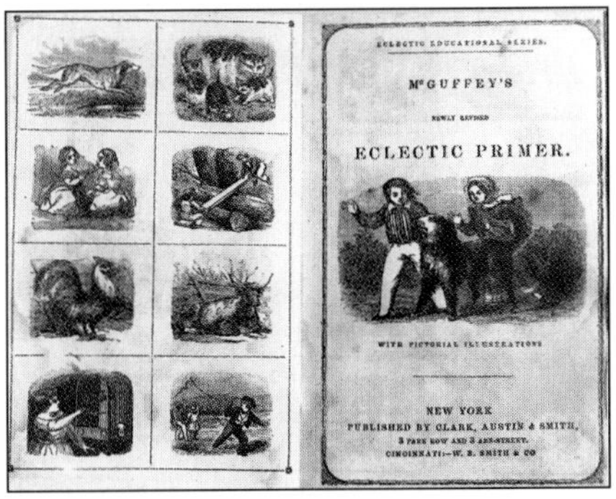

Frontier schools were usually small. Children of all ages shared a classroom and a teacher (*above*). Most students in the 1800s learned from the McGuffey Readers (*left*). In addition to reading, writing, and arithmetic, these early textbooks stressed religious faith, thrift, courage, and obedience.

In frontier schools all over America, the most common textbooks were the McGuffey Readers. Their pages were full of references to rural and pioneer America. In McGuffey's primer the first lesson was "A is for ax." After *ax* came *box, cat, dog*—all familiar things. The

Preachers on horseback came to newly settled communities to deliver sermons and perform religious rites and ceremonies.

readings described children at work and play in barnyards, fields, and forests. These schoolbooks brought learning close to pioneer life.

Before the first churches were built, religion was carried to the frontier by the circuit rider, a preacher on horseback. The circuit rider visited pioneer families in their own cabins. He carried a Bible and a hymnbook in his saddlebag. He preached at crossroad settlements, standing on a stump or a wagon bed. He read from the Bible, prayed, and "lined out" hymns, reading one line at a time, which the people sang after him. In remote cabins he performed baptisms and marriages. He prayed over the graves of the dead.

As settlements grew, communities organized congregations and built churches at the crossroads. The church became a social as well as a religious center. It was a place of community socials and suppers, of Christmas entertainments, of Sunday school parties and neighborhood gatherings. The frontier church provided the first strong social bond in new communities.

Government and Law

The first political organization on the frontier was the territorial government, with officials appointed by the president of the United States. Statehood could be sought when a region had a large enough population; 60,000 was the original requirement. With statehood the pioneers elected their own legislators and sent representatives to the U.S. Congress.

But pioneers went into new lands ahead of the law. Therefore, in its first years every frontier had its own unwritten laws, which were enforced by common consent. Some of the unwritten rules were remembered from older regions. Others evolved on the frontier to meet frontier needs. It was generally agreed that a stray horse became the property of the first man who could catch it. Horse thieves, the worst of criminals, deserved to die. Anyone involved in a quarrel had a right to defend himself. Killing another man in self-defense was not regarded as a crime. However, it was considered criminal to shoot an unarmed man or to strike anyone in the back.

In western communities bands of self-appointed vigilantes enforced their own ideas of justice. At its worst this action became mob violence. At its best it was a temporary assertion of community judgment. Though it was a necessity on the frontier, this lawless judg-

With new towns springing up overnight, lawyers, land agents, and other businessmen set up temporary shop outdoors.

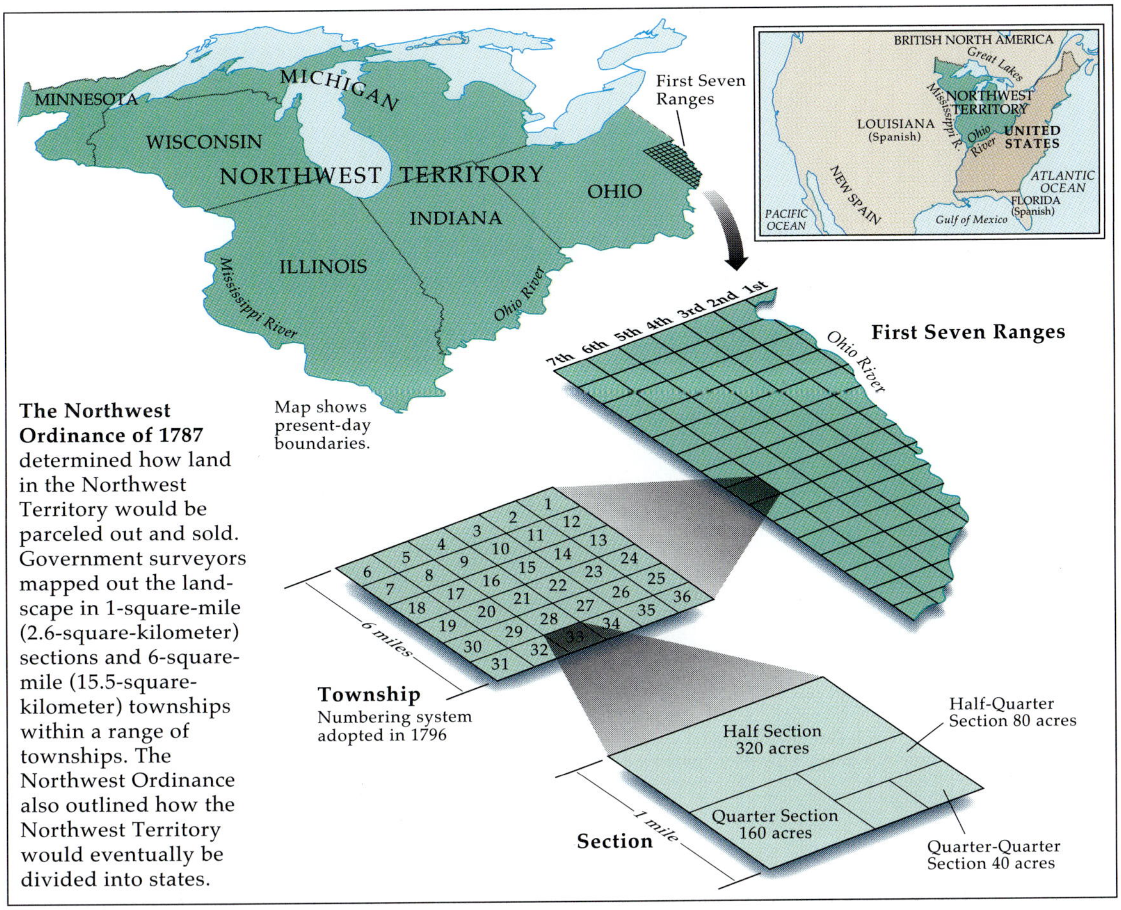

The Northwest Ordinance of 1787 determined how land in the Northwest Territory would be parceled out and sold. Government surveyors mapped out the landscape in 1-square-mile (2.6-square-kilometer) sections and 6-square-mile (15.5-square-kilometer) townships within a range of townships. The Northwest Ordinance also outlined how the Northwest Territory would eventually be divided into states.

After the Civil War, railroad companies distributed thousands of posters encouraging easterners to take the train and move west. *Left:* The Hannibal and St. Joseph Railroad advertised land available in Missouri. *Below right:* The Chicago, Milwaukee, & St. Paul Railway hoped to bring farmers to Three Forks Country, Montana.

ment had to give way to a legal system. In the process some vigilantes became officers of the law. Still, the pioneer districts had no trained officials. In west Texas, one weathered justice of the peace was called Old Necessity because he knew no law. On his bench he kept a mail-order catalog, which he always consulted before making a judgment. Once, considering a man charged with a misdemeanor, he put on his spectacles, flipped open the catalog, looked at it a moment, and announced, "I fine you $4.88." When the man jumped up to protest, a friend yanked him back. "Sit down," he said. "You're lucky he opened it at 'pants' instead of at 'pianos.'"

Roads

In the interior of America, the first roads were rivers. The great rivers, notably the Ohio and the Mississippi, became frontier highways, carrying the population and the produce of the new West. The tributary streams were only slightly less important. Settlers paddled and poled up the side rivers, finding their way into a trackless land. On flatboats they took corn, wheat, pork, lard, and apples to market. Settlers and town builders alike chose sites on running waterways.

In a land run in 1893, homesteaders eager to enter a newly opened section of Oklahoma Territory gathered on Kansas's southern border and awaited the government's permission to cross over.

Through the forest the pioneers cut primitive roads called traces. Boone's Trace was a pioneer path in Kentucky. The historic Natchez Trace led north from Natchez, Mississippi, to Nashville, Tennessee. Zane's Trace ran through the Ohio woods; it began and ended at landings on the Ohio River.

The first improved highway—straight, wide, and smooth—was the National Road, begun at Cumberland, Maryland, in 1815. It eventually ran through the frontier capitals of Columbus (Ohio), Indianapolis (Indiana), and Vandalia (Illinois). Multitudes of pioneer settlers traveled the National Road, as later emigrants to the far West traveled the overland trails to Oregon and California. Canals between the Great Lakes and the Ohio and Mississippi rivers hastened the settlement of the Midwest.

▶ LAND LAWS

After the Revolutionary War (1775–83), the United States acquired a spacious domain extending beyond the original 13 colonies to the Mississippi River. The Louisiana Purchase in 1803 extended it farther, to the Rocky Mountains. And the annexation of Oregon and California carried it to the Pacific Coast by 1850. The western regions were sparsely occupied by Indians. A piece at a time, by treaty and purchase, the tribes ceded vast lands to the United States. So the public domain was offered to settlers, at first by purchase and finally as free homesteads.

Before land could be sold and legally settled, it had to be surveyed. Government surveyors mapped it into 1-square-mile (2.6-square-kilometer) sections and 6-square-mile (15.5-square-kilometer) townships. By this system any tract of land could be precisely located and its boundaries determined. With chain and compass the surveyors went into wild country. They left a numbered post at each mile and a marked cone of dirt at the township corners.

After it was surveyed, the land was open to sale and settlement. The first federal land law offered a minimum tract of 640 acres (256 hectares) at $2 an acre, half the price to be paid to the government within 30 days and the remainder within a year. Many settlers did not have that much money. They became known as squatters—people who lived on the public land without legal ownership.

In a series of reforms the land laws were made more democratic. The Harrison Land Act of 1800 allowed sales of 320 acres (128 hectares) at $2 an acre and allowed four years to pay. In 1820 the revised law offered 80-acre (32-hectare) tracts at $1.25 an acre. This enabled a pioneer with $100 to buy a small farm. At last, in 1862, President Abraham Lincoln signed the Homestead Act, which offered land free to any adult who would live on it and improve it. People then sang a popular song: "Uncle Sam is rich enough to give us all a farm." The Homestead Act helped to fill up the Great Plains frontier.

On a stump-studded street in a raw new town stood the government land office, with survey maps on the wall and a big open ledger on a table. Steubenville, Marietta, Chillicothe, and Cincinnati had the first land offices in the Northwest Territory. As new districts were surveyed, land offices were opened at Zanesville, Vincennes, Shawneetown, and Kaskaskia. By 1820 they were extended to Detroit and St. Louis. In all these places a familiar scene was repeated. While a woman and her children waited outside in a wagon, a pioneer settler studied the survey maps in the land office. At last he counted out his advance payment and signed his name or made his mark in the ledger. He got a certificate that he could exchange for a deed of ownership when payment was completed. Then the wagon creaked on to the township and section numbered on his claim. So another pioneer family found their land.

▶ THE CLOSING OF THE FRONTIER

In 1889 central Oklahoma was opened to homesteaders. Thousands of people, on horseback, in wagons, and on foot, raced into the area to mark out homesteads. In this dramatic land rush, settlement came to the last large tract of public domain. In 1890 the U.S. Census Director declared, "There can hardly be said to be a frontier line." After more than 200 years the moving frontier had come to an end. Vast stretches of wilderness remained in the western mountains and deserts. Much of it would become national forestland. But an era of American history had closed, an era shaped by the hope, the hardship, and the toil and accomplishment of pioneer people.

Today the United States still has some remote and primitive areas, where resourceful, self-reliant people can go beyond the reach of civilization. Alaska is sometimes called the Last Frontier. With large areas of uninhabited land it attracts pioneer people as the American interior did in the 1800s.

▶ PIONEERING AND THE AMERICAN CHARACTER

From Virginia to Alaska, life on the frontier produced many common traits in pioneers. Among them were independence, resourcefulness, individualism, and belief in the future. Men especially were free and equal on the frontier, and democracy was strengthened by the pioneer experience. New lands stimulated initiative, energy, and determination.

In 1895, a group of Dutch emigrants posed in front of a picture of the ship that would bring them all to America. By the late 1800s, most of America's new pioneers were emigrants from European countries.

But today, with no land left to discover and little left to explore, modern pioneers must look to other frontiers to break new ground. They must look to the oceans or the solar system—or even to the realms of social justice, education, public health and medicine, religion, or the arts. From finding water on the moon to discovering cures for cancer, the opportunities for the modern pioneer are endless.

WALTER HAVIGHURST
Author, *First Book of Pioneers*

OVERLAND TRAILS

"Old America seems to be breaking up and moving westward," a British traveler wrote in the early 1800s. Thousands of Americans would have agreed with him. To many farmers of that time, the grass always seemed greener just over a western hill.

The mass migration into the West that began late in the 1700s, after the Revolutionary War, was greater than any previous movement like it in history. When the migration started, the American colonies were all on the eastern coast of North America. When it ended, less than 100 years later, pioneers had settled across the continent, a distance of nearly 3,000 miles (4,800 kilometers) from east to west.

The charters of seven of the American colonies granted territories from sea to sea. But in the 1600s and 1700s, when these charters were drawn up, no one knew how far it was to the western sea (Pacific Ocean) or how much of the land was free for the colonies to claim. Native American Indians roamed the Far West, and parts of it were explored and claimed by France and Spain. Early in the 1700s, France held the region from the Appalachian Mountains to the Mississippi River. England won this section after the French and Indian War (1754–63), and after the Revolutionary War (1775–83) it became part of the United States. However, even before the region belonged to the United States, Americans were settling into it.

THE FIRST TRAILS

The westward movement followed a pattern. Pioneers hungry for land and freedom pushed toward the wilderness, but barriers such as mountains stood in the way. Advance scouts found trails through the mountains. More and more settlers followed the trails until the land was filled. Then scouts found paths past the next barrier, which might be another mountain range or a vast forest or desert. Since migration was often blocked by the Indians who held the land, moving into the West meant fighting as well as trail blazing. But one by one the barriers came down.

The trails were as simple as nature would allow. The first trailbreakers were buffalo, deer, and antelope. Their trails led to low divides and shallow fords across rivers. The Indians followed these animal trails, beating them down and widening them. Later scouts—mostly hunters, trappers, and traders—followed the Indian trails.

Most animal and Indian trails were short, but trappers linked them together into routes leading from one part of the country to another. Where possible, the routes followed rivers, since river travel was easier than overland travel, especially where rivers cut through the mountain ranges.

In the 1700s, scouts from the backwoods of the eastern colonies roamed into Kentucky or Tennessee in pursuit of deer and other

In his painting ***Traders Descending the Missouri*** **(1845), American frontier artist George Caleb Bingham captured the serenity of a time when rivers were common routes of transportation.**

Cattle trails in the Old West led through wide open rangelands to railroad towns, where the animals were shipped east to market.

animals whose hides they could sell. They found that a man could live on the land with only his ax and his gun. Some hunters built lonely huts far beyond the edge of the settled colonies. There were also fur trappers who sought beaver pelts, which were much in demand. When they had trapped most of the beaver in the Appalachian hunting grounds, they moved farther west. Early in the 1800s, beaver trappers went up the Missouri River and into the Rocky Mountains. In their search for beaver they eventually explored much of the North American continent. They found the mountain passes and marked the paths that wagon trains would follow later.

Traders followed the trails the trappers had blazed and traded with the Indians for furs. Traders brought back news of beautiful lands and new trails. Government explorers also went into the wilderness. Unlike the trappers, these men published reports about their discoveries and made maps of the wilderness. Speculators saw a chance to buy land cheaply from the government and make a fortune selling it to settlers hungry for farmland. They promoted the land and nurtured among easterners a growing enthusiasm to go west along the trails that trappers, traders, and explorers were opening.

While hunting for furs, mountain men explored the western wilderness and found the best routes across the mountains.

THE APPALACHIAN WALL

By 1740 the eastern coast of North America from Maine to Georgia held a rapidly growing population. Plantations in Virginia spread into the hills and stopped before the barrier of the Blue Ridge Mountains, a chief range of the southern Appalachian Mountains. In the middle colonies German and Scotch-Irish newcomers pushed south along the Shenandoah Valley and northwest up the Susquehanna River. They settled the valleys between the Appalachian ridges. They, too, faced a mighty Appalachian barrier—the Great Allegheny Front, rising 1,000 feet (300 meters) or more above the valley. Pioneers had come up against a stone wall.

Beyond the mountains, according to traders, lay a vast saucer-shaped lowland. They knew that it stretched at least as far as the Mississippi River, but no one knew how much farther it might reach. The land was level and fertile. Through this fertile land ran a mighty network of rivers—the Mississippi and its tributaries—providing a water highway from the Appalachians to the Gulf of Mexico. Dreamers hoped that there were rivers that ran all the way to the western sea.

Two natural routes led past the mountain walls to this rich land. There was a northern route, through the Mohawk Valley, and also a southern route, around the mountains. However, the Mohawk Valley was inhabited by unfriendly Iroquois Indians, and the southern route was blocked by Cherokee Indians. Beyond the mountains lay fortified

French trading posts. In the mid-1700s, the Appalachian Mountains, the French, and the Indians all stood like a dam, holding back the flood of Americans eager to reach the new lands.

Gist's Trace

Between 1740 and 1750 brisk trading went on between the British and the Shawnee and Delaware tribes near present-day Pittsburgh, Pennsylvania. However, the trails blazed by traders were not wide enough or smooth enough for wagons. Christopher Gist (1706?–59) blazed the first wagon road in 1753. The road started in Maryland, near Fort Cumberland on the Potomac River, and followed Indian trails to the Monongahela River, which joins the Ohio River. Gist's Trace, as the road was called, was too rough to accommodate the migration of large numbers of people, but it was the first wagon road to connect the East with the Mississippi waterways.

The Cumberland (National) Road

The French and Indians resisted the invasion of traders from British colonies, and these conflicts led to the outbreak of the French and Indian War in 1754. However, in order to move their troops and supplies, armies needed roads. The British general Edward Braddock cut a road that ran near Gist's Trace, from Fort Cumberland to Fort Duquesne (now Pittsburgh) at the fork of the Ohio River. In the early 1800s, this road was extended to Vandalia, Illinois, and became known as the Cumberland, or National, Road. In 1758, General John Forbes, a British officer who captured Fort Duquesne from the French and renamed it Fort Pitt, carved another road—Forbes Road—through the Pennsylvania Alleghenies, from Fort Loudon to Fort Pitt. These early roads soon became the first of many heavily used overland trails.

After the war the French were gone, and the Treaty of Fort Stanwix (1768) opened the country south and east of the Ohio River for settlement. Pittsburgh, at the western end of the military roads, was the jumping-off place for settlers bound for Ohio. The town was filled with excitement every spring. Families poured in along the trails—about 50,000 settlers by 1774. Covered wagons and flatboats crowded the banks of the Monongahela River, waiting for the spring thaw to break the ice on the Ohio River. Then there was high water and clear sailing to Kentucky and new farm homes along the rich river valleys.

The Cumberland Road was the first national highway. Begun in Cumberland, Maryland, in 1811, it eventually led to Vandalia, an early capital of Illinois.

Boone's Wilderness Road and the Cumberland Gap

From his home in North Carolina, Daniel Boone went hunting far into the Blue Ridge Mountains. Like other frontiersmen, he knew the hunters' tales of a paradise west of the Shenandoah Valley, a place where deer crowded the grasslands and turkeys got so fat they broke the branches of trees when they perched on them. But the forbidding Allegheny wall blocked the way. People said there was a break in the wall, but no one knew where it was.

In 1769, Boone entertained a peddler, John Finley. As a captive of the Indians, Finley had seen the bluegrass meadows alive with game. He had heard that this land lay near the rumored mountain pass, and he thought he could find it. He offered to guide Boone. The men set out, and in time they came to a giant V in the ridge, beneath a 1,500-foot (457-meter) cliff. This was what they had sought—the Cumberland Gap, gateway to Kentucky.

Turning north, Finley and Boone followed the Warriors' Path (an Indian path) and hunters' trails. After many adventures, Boone came out of the mountains and looked for the first time upon the fabled bluegrass land. In 1775, with 30 men, he cut a wagon road along this route they called the Wilderness Road. At its western end, near the Kentucky River, the men built a frontier stockade and named it Boonesborough. The Wilderness Road, the most difficult trail through the mountains, never became an improved highway. But it was an important migration route during the Revolutionary War period. Between 1775 and 1790, about 70,000 people traveled the route to settle in Kentucky. They paid a high price, however, as many lost their lives to Indian attacks. With good reason this country became known as the Dark and Bloody Ground.

FROM THE APPALACHIAN MOUNTAINS TO THE MISSISSIPPI RIVER

Between 1790 and 1840, settlers filled the plains between the Appalachians and the Mississippi River. During the War of 1812 almost the last of the hostile Indian tribes was defeated. The Mississippi basin set up no barriers. Its river system provided a highway along which settlers could float their families and household goods on flatboats. Towns sprang up rapidly along the riverbanks. By 1825 the frontier had reached St. Louis.

The land of the Mississippi basin seemed to be the heaven that the pioneers had been trying for so long to find. Its soil was rich and black, and its rivers gave farmers a way to market their goods downstream as far as New Orleans. Traders often returned on horseback, following the road called the Natchez Trace from Natchez, Mississippi, to Nashville, Tennessee.

From 1804 to 1806, Lewis and Clark headed an expedition to find an overland route to the Pacific Ocean. They were guided on their journey by Sacagawea, a Shoshoni Indian woman.

Until about 1840 the Middle West supplied enough land for pioneers. Therefore the settlers' frontier paused along the Mississippi and the Missouri rivers. Beyond the rivers, a sea of grass stretched as far west as the eye could see. Farmers assumed that because there were no trees the soil must be poor. Stephen Long, a government explorer, had visited the Southwest in 1820 and called the Great Plains the "Great American Desert." Few pioneers wanted to venture beyond the rivers. But the advance scouts went on, finding new paths and trails that would carry the next wave of wagons west when the time came.

SCOUTING THE FAR WEST

Meriwether Lewis and William Clark led the most famous exploring party of pioneer days, the Lewis and Clark expedition (1804–06). They struggled through the northern Rockies, where only Indians had gone before, and reached the Pacific Ocean. Returning from Oregon, they tested new routes. They brought back the first accurate information about the Far West. The news that Rocky Mountain streams teemed with beaver aroused great excitement in the East.

Fur traders hurried in the wake of Lewis and Clark. In 1811 and 1812, traders sent west by John Jacob Astor (1763–1848) crossed the continent to Oregon and returned east. Coming back, they traced part of the route that became the Oregon Trail. They crossed the Rockies at South Pass, the main gateway through the mountains. The pass was forgotten but was rediscovered twelve years later by a great American explorer, a trapper named Jedediah Smith (1799–1831). Then, in 1826, Smith led the first explorers to reach California overland from the United States.

By the 1820s traders and trappers were already exploring the Rockies. And the earliest of the Far Western overland wagon trails was open—the road to Santa Fe.

THE SANTA FE TRAIL

The Santa Fe Trail was a traders' path. Never an actual road, it was a broad route following rivers and wagon ruts, passing known landmarks. It led from the Missouri River to Santa Fe, New Mexico.

For some time American traders had been eyeing the riches of Santa Fe. The people of that lonely Mexican mission town wanted to trade with Americans, for Missouri was nearer than Mexico City. But Mexico's Spanish rulers forbade trade and jailed American traders. When Mexico rebelled against Spain in 1820, however, Santa Fe was opened wide to the expanding American trade.

Traders Blaze the Trail

The first man to reach Santa Fe after trade opened was William Becknell (1790?–1832), who is called the Father of the Santa Fe Trail. He was on a western trading trip in 1821 when he heard that Mexico had declared its independence from Spain. He immediately turned his caravan to Santa Fe, where he traded his goods for Mexican dollars, then worth five times what the goods had cost. On the return trip, winter snow clogged the northern trail through the Raton Pass, pioneered by explorer Zebulon Pike (1779–1813). Becknell took a shortcut across the Cimarron Desert. This Cimarron Cutoff became part of the Santa Fe Trail. When Becknell returned to his home in Franklin, Missouri, in January 1822, he poured out his silver dollars onto the sidewalks, to the amazement of his neighbors. A new era had begun. By May, Becknell had organized a trading party. They planned to take wagons where wagons had never gone before.

Becknell and his 21 men had three heavily laden Conestoga wagons, each carrying more than 2 tons of goods. They crossed the Missouri, struck out across the Great Plains to the Arkansas River, and followed its course. Often they had to float or drag wagons across the river, to avoid steep cliffs.

At Cimarron, west of Dodge City, they turned south across the parched plains. Wagons could never travel the steep Raton Pass, so they would have to journey through the Cimarron Cutoff. That meant crossing 50 miles (80 kilometers) of dry, hot wasteland without a landmark to help them find their way or a sign of life. They struggled on, bitter dust stinging their throats and blinding them. At times they feared they would die of thirst.

Finally they reached the Cimarron River and crossed it. They were safely past the desert. But another 300 miles (480 kilometers) of rough travel through foothills lay ahead before they would reach Santa Fe. Nevertheless, they had proved men could

American traders celebrated their arrival in Santa Fe, New Mexico, after an arduous 780-mile (1,260-kilometer) journey from Independence, Missouri.

OVERLAND TRAILS
Bozeman Trail
California Trail
Chisholm Trail
Cimarron Cutoff
Cumberland (National) Road
First California Trail
Forbes Road
Gila Trail
Gist's Trace
Hastings Cutoff
Mohawk Trail
Mormon Trail
Natchez Trace
Old Spanish Trail
Oregon Trail
Santa Fe Trail
Sublette's Cutoff
Western Road
Western Trail
Wilderness Road
PACIFIC OCEAN
ATLANTIC OCEAN
Gulf of Mexico
ROCKY MOUNTAINS
GREAT PLAINS
APPALACHIAN MOUNTAINS
CASCADE MOUNTAINS
GREAT BASIN
Fort Vancouver
Fort Walla Walla
Whitman Mission
Fort Boise
Fort Hall
Soda Springs
Virginia City
Fort Phil Kearny
Fort Laramie
Fort Bridger
South Pass
Independence Rock
Devil's Gate
Sacramento
Carson City
Los Angeles
San Diego
Santa Fe
Las Vegas
Dodge City
Abilene
Council Grove
Fort Kearney
Winter Quarters
St. Joseph
Independence
Franklin
Sedalia
St. Louis
Vandalia
Indianapolis
Columbus
Chicago
Detroit
Nashville
Natchez
New Orleans
Boonesborough
Pittsburgh (Fort Pitt)
Fort Cumberland
Fort Loudon
Harrisburg
Philadelphia
Washington, D.C.
New York
Boston
Schenectady
Fort Stanwix
Fort Niagara
Charleston
San Antonio
Lake Superior
Lake Michigan
Lake Huron
Lake Erie
Lake Ontario
0 150 300 mi
0 150 300 km
120°W
100°W
90°W
80°W
70°W
40°N
30°N
20°N

After Mexico gained its independence from Spain in 1821, Santa Fe became Mexico's primary center of trade with the United States.

take wagons over the trail. When they returned and showed their rich profits, others flocked to the trade. From 1822 to 1843, caravans headed west each spring over the Santa Fe Trail.

The First Wagon Trains

The wagons started from Franklin, and later from Independence, Missouri. At Council Grove, Kansas, 145 miles (230 kilometers) southwest of Independence, traders camped and waited for other wagons to arrive, so they could organize into one big wagon train.

Trail life had taught people that a lonely wagon was an easy target for Indians. They had to cooperate or die. So Santa Fe traders invented the wagon train, copied by all later pioneers. They organized the train like an army, electing a captain and his aides. The captain was trail boss, and his word was law. All wagons got in line and stayed together, usually in single file but sometimes, in dangerous country, in rows of two or four. A team of eight to twelve mules or oxen pulled each wagon. Mule skinners had to catch the mules, harness them, and crack whips and shout to drive them. Spare animals were herded along. Men rode horses beside the wagons, watching for trouble, or ranged far out as scouts and hunters.

The traders learned other lessons that saved lives during later migrations. They learned to post guards at night, each man taking his turn. They learned to form their wagons into a circle or square when they camped, to make a temporary fort with animals inside. In many ways they set the pattern for trail travel.

Every inch of the wagons was crammed with trading goods. Traders could carry little for their own use. For the first 270 miles (430 kilometers), till they passed the Great Bend of the Arkansas River, they lived on bacon, bread, and bitter coffee. Then they entered buffalo country and could shoot buffalo for fresh meat. They also tied strips of meat to ropes strung along wagons, to dry for future meals.

They passed Pawnee Rock, where they stopped to carve their names, and went on, crossing many streams that joined the Arkansas River. Some riverbanks were cliffs, where wagons had to be lowered with ropes. When they crossed the Arkansas, a half mile wide, some wagons struck boulders and turned over in midstream. Others got stuck in quicksand.

Danger was always around them. Indians attacked. Rattlesnakes hid in the bed blankets. Mules ran away and left wagons stranded. If someone got hurt or fell ill, there were no doctors. Sudden flash floods turned sandy flats into roaring torrents. Most of all, they dreaded crossing the desert, where there were no landmarks to guide them.

Once across the Cimarron Desert, they could follow the Cimarron River for 85 miles (137 kilometers). Then they had to climb 200 miles (322 kilometers) through rocky foothills to reach the village of Las Vegas, New Mexico. The trail rose steeply to the Apache Canyon. It was a perfect spot for an ambush. Thanks to watchful guards, few died on the trail at the hands of Indians. But one of the few was Jedediah Smith, who was killed in 1831.

Near Santa Fe, traders would stop to wash and put on clean shirts. Then they whooped into town, cracking their long whips. The people would swarm out, cheering. Santa Fe had a permanent population of about 3,000, but Mexicans came from all around to trade with the Americans.

The caravan's arrival was the big event of the year and called for celebration. Then trading would begin. The Americans brought tools, cutlery, materials, and dresses. The Mexicans paid in mules, furs, buffalo skins, silver, gold, and Mexican silver dollars.

Protecting the Trail

The Santa Fe trade was a great adventure and also a source of profit. During the twenty years it lasted, Americans made almost $3 million. Some traders made a 300 percent profit. But it was a rough and dangerous trip. To cut their losses in suffering and lives, traders asked the government for surveyors to mark the trail and for soldiers to act as guards. The government granted their requests, but the surveyors marked a longer road, which the traders refused to use. The traders also had bad luck with soldiers. In 1829, Captain Bennett Riley and a troop of foot soldiers guarded the wagons as far as the Mexican border (at the Cimarron Crossing) and stopped. One trader said this was like running a ferry to the middle of a river.

When Indians attacked the traders in the desert, the troops rushed to their defense and went on with them for two more days. The soldiers returned to the border and camped until the wagons came back. The Indians then attacked the soldiers. The army learned that without horses, soldiers were helpless in the West. Mounted soldiers guarded later wagon trains.

Territorial disputes with Mexico stopped the trade in 1843, and in 1846 the United States went to war against Mexico. When the war ended in 1848, Santa Fe belonged to the United States, and the Santa Fe Trail began serving California gold seekers. In the 1860s dust clouds thickened as traffic increased. But in the 1870s, increased use of the railroad lessened traffic on the Santa Fe Trail.

THE GILA TRAIL AND THE OLD SPANISH TRAIL

Some traders wanted to trade between Santa Fe and California. In 1827 James Pattie (1804–50) and his father blazed a trail from Santa Fe along the Gila River through Arizona to the Colorado River. The Gila Trail ran through southern California.

In 1829 other groups blazed the Old Spanish Trail. Men under a Mexican trader, Antonio Armijo, and trappers led by Ewing Young (?–1841) took a route that swung north to bypass the worst deserts and the Grand Canyon. The routes from Santa Fe to California saw much use in this period. Both routes served prospectors during the California gold rush.

THE GREAT MIGRATION ALONG THE OREGON TRAIL

Unlike the Santa Fe Trail, the Oregon Trail was a settlers' road. Trappers and traders blazed it, missionaries traveled it, and in the 1840s farmers poured along it by the thousands. This migration differed from any before it. Earlier pioneers had pushed perhaps 100 miles (160 kilometers) west and settled. But the pioneers of the 1840s thought the land across the Missouri was useless. So they passed by prairies, deserts, and mountains, going 2,000 miles (3,220 kilometers) to the

THE GREAT MIGRATION

The following is an estimate of the number of people who traveled through Nebraska along the Oregon Trail each year between 1841 and 1866:

1841	100
1842	200
1843	1,000
1844	2,000
1845	5,000
1846	1,000
1847	2,000
1848	4,000
1849	30,000
1850	55,000
1851	10,000
1852	50,000
1853	20,000
1854	10,000
1855	5,000
1856	5,000
1857	5,000
1858	10,000
1859	30,000
1860	15,000
1861	5,000
1862	5,000
1863	10,000
1864	20,000
1865	25,000
1866	25,000
Total	350,300

More than 150 years after the first wave of pioneers traveled west along the Oregon Trail, ruts carved by their wagon wheels can still be seen.

Fort Laramie, in Wyoming, was founded by fur traders in 1834. It later served as a supply station on the Oregon Trail.

lush meadows of Oregon. This huge cross-country drive meant traveling four to six months on the trail—and living a life few families had experienced before.

In those days, Oregon Country was a vast territory that stretched from the Rocky Mountains to the Pacific Ocean, from Alaska in the north (claimed by Russia) to California in the South (claimed by Spain and Mexico). Oregon itself was claimed by both the United States and Great Britain.

Migration was spurred by the panic of 1837, which brought hard times to midwestern farmers. Poverty made them listen to missionaries' tales of an earthly paradise in Oregon Country. The Willamette River valley had land for all and a long growing season. The Hudson's Bay Company, a British fur-trading company, dominated the region with their trading post Fort Vancouver, on the Columbia River. But enough American settlers might make it qualify to become American territory.

With more than 40 years experience as a fur trapper, trader, and guide, Jim Bridger was one of the most famous mountain men.

Establishing the Route

The Oregon Trail had already been traveled, one piece at a time, by Lewis and Clark, the fur trappers, and the fur traders. But no one had tied the pieces together into a continuous route. The eastern part of the trail was the traders' path to their meeting place in the Rockies and was well known by 1832. In that year Captain B. L. E. de Bonneville (1796–1878) took twenty wagons through South Pass and across the Green River, proving that wagons could go at least halfway to the Pacific. Without wagons, large migrations of settlers were impossible.

The next year a Boston businessman, Nathaniel Wyeth (1803–56), took a caravan the entire length of the trail. In 1834, on his second trip, Wyeth took Protestant ministers with him. Jason Lee (1803–45) and his nephew, going to Oregon to convert the Indians, spearheaded a new movement of Christian missionaries. They were guided by mountain men, who knew the wilderness trails as well as others knew the streets in their hometown.

Trading Posts

Before 1834 there were no trading posts between Missouri and the Hudson's Bay Company post at Fort Walla Walla. In 1834 three of the four Oregon Trail stations went up. Fur traders built Fort Laramie, first called Fort William, on the North Platte River. Wyeth built Fort Hall on the Snake River. British traders built Fort Boise, also on the Snake River, northwest of Fort Hall. Only one post came later—Fort Bridger, completed by the famous scout Jim Bridger (1804–81) in 1843.

Missionaries Lead the Way

The Lees settled in the Willamette Valley. In 1836 the next Protestant missionaries, Dr. Marcus Whitman and Henry Spalding, brought their wives—the first white women to cross the continent. The trappers they met on the journey liked the Whitmans. Narcissa Whitman, charming and lively, lightened the boredom of trail life. Whitman, a doctor, had won their admiration earlier, when he had successfully removed a 3-inch (8-centimeter) arrowhead from Jim Bridger's shoulder. The trappers were glad to guide his party. But they told him he could not take his wagon to Oregon. No one had ever taken wagons past Fort Hall. Whitman took the wagon on anyway, but at Fort Boise he had to leave it behind. Until then the women had sometimes rested in the wagon—a bumpy ride, for it had no springs. From then on for most of the way to Oregon, they rode on horseback, sidesaddle in their long dresses, though Mrs. Spalding was sick and Mrs. Whitman was expecting her first baby. They founded the Whitman Mission in what is now southeastern Washington State.

Marcus Whitman, one of the first pioneers to blaze the trail to Oregon, founded a mission in the Oregon Territory to convert the Indians to Christianity.

Oregon Fever

In 1839 the first farmers—13 men from Illinois, led by Thomas Farnham (1804–48)—reached Oregon with packhorses. In 1842, a minister named Elijah White led the first large group—107 pioneers—over the trail. By 1843 the "Oregon fever" had spread among farmers suffering from hard times. They formed Oregon societies to plan the trip. That spring the trickle along the trail became a flood, which came to be known as the Great Migration.

Organizing the Wagon Trains

The Oregon Trail started at Independence, Missouri. From all over the Mississippi River valley, more than 1,000 men, women, and children gathered at Elm Grove, 33 miles (53 kilometers) west of Independence. Farmers were amazed to see only two elm trees there. This was not their idea of a grove. They brought covered wagons, packed with all their worldly goods, and herded over 1,400 cattle and oxen. Though they were inexperienced, mountain men and Marcus Whitman guided them.

They began their great march on May 22, 1843. At first they took the Santa Fe Trail, but 8 miles (13 kilometers) from Elm Grove the trail forked. A sign pointing northwest said "Road to Oregon." A few miles along this fork they came to Big Springs (just east of present-day Topeka, Kansas) where they organized the wagon train. They held a meeting on the plain, voting on rules and electing Peter H. Burnett (1807–95) captain. Candidates for Burnett's aides, the Council of Ten, stood up in front of the others. Then each voter (any man over 16) fell in line behind his choice. The men with the longest "tails" of voters won.

The huge size of the party meant safety from Indians, but it made problems too. Those with no cattle could travel faster. So the pioneers split into two columns, with sixty wagons in each. The "light column," with few animals, went first. The "cow column" came slowly behind. At night the cow column caught up and camped with the rest. Jesse Applegate (1811–88), captain of the cow column, wrote a famous book about the trip.

The Difficult Journey

About 300 miles (480 kilometers) from Independence they reached the Platte River, 6 inches (15 centimeters) deep and 1 mile (1.6 kilometers) wide. Pioneers said it was "too thick to drink and too thin to plow." They followed its south bank for about 100 miles (160 kilometers). The pilot, a mountain man, ranged ahead. Wagons changed places in line, so everyone could have some relief from the choking dust. Men walked beside teams, while wives and children picked wildflowers or napped in the wagons. They made a short midday lunch stop called "nooning."

Late in the afternoon they watched for the place the pilot had marked with a big circle on the ground. Men drove their teams along the circle, making a ring of wagons. They turned the oxen free to graze and locked the wagons into a fort. Children gathered buffalo chips (dung) for fuel. When the fire was hot, the women prepared dinner—usually salted meat, bread, and coffee. After dinner people told stories and sang or the council met. Tired out, all went to bed as darkness fell, except the guards, who had to keep watch all night.

At the fork of the Platte River they crossed the South Platte and followed the northern fork toward the Rockies. At Fort Laramie they stopped to rest a few days and wash clothes. Up the North Platte they came to Independence Rock—838 miles (1,349 kilometers) from their starting point—where they carved their names. Now they could see the peaks of the Rockies. Following the Sweetwater River through a canyon (Devil's Gate), they reached South Pass. Here they crossed the backbone of the continent. Beyond this point rivers flowed west. But the "great divide" seemed very tame, as the pass was a smooth stretch 20 miles (32 kilometers) wide.

At the Green River (northern branch of the Colorado) they turned south. Earlier migrants had gone north, but the Great Migration cut a fresh path, to visit Jim Bridger's new post. Then they headed north again, joining the main trail near Soda Springs. They marveled at Steamboat Spring, which spurted hot water.

At Fort Hall they rested. They were 1,288 miles (2,074 kilometers) from Independence, over halfway to their goal, but the worst part lay ahead. Here the Oregon Trail turned into a narrow pack trail. Only once had a wagon—the one belonging to Marcus Whitman seven years earlier in 1836—gone past this point. But Whitman's light wagon had been much smaller than the bulky prairie schooners, and even that he had been forced to abandon at Fort Boise.

The pioneers had babies and household goods. They could not manage without wagons. Whitman promised to get the wagons through—against the advice of mountain men. But the wagons had to be lightened. Already the pioneers had thrown away furniture and precious belongings. Women had to give up extra clothes. At the Snake River they traded party dresses to the Indians for salmon.

Whitman's wagon led the caravan through "a wild, rocky, barren wilderness, of wrecked and ruined Nature; a vast field of volcanic desolation." The burning sun beat down on the weary travelers. On they jolted, over sharp rocks that made oxen's feet bleed, along slopes so steep that men had to hold the wagons up to keep them from turning over. They rested at Fort Boise and again in a beautiful green valley, the Grande Ronde. They followed a creek along a rocky canyon and through snowcapped mountains where wagons had never gone. At last they came to Whitman's mission near the Columbia River. Where the river foams through the Cascades, they turned wagons into boats. Boys drove the cattle over mountain trails, and families

Independence Rock, on the Sweetwater River in Wyoming, was a major landmark on the Oregon Trail. It signaled the end of the journey on the plains and the beginning of the trek over the Rocky Mountains.

floated down the Columbia to the rich meadows of the Willamette Valley. It was October. They marked off their new farms—their reward for five months on the trail.

Frontier scout Kit Carson (*left*) guided the explorer John C. Frémont (*above*) on several western expeditions. Together they opened up trails to Utah, California, and Oregon.

The 49th Parallel

Every year more settlers came. By 1846 more than 5,000 pioneers had made the journey to the Willamette Valley, making it clear to the British that Americans intended to remain in Oregon. That year Great Britain signed a treaty giving up claims to land south of the present Washington-Canada border, establishing the boundary at 49 degrees north latitude, known as the 49th parallel. Then in 1848, Oregon became a U.S. territory. It covered the present-day states of Washington, Oregon, and Idaho as well as the western portions of Montana and Wyoming.

By the end of the Civil War in 1865, more than 300,000 people had followed the Oregon Trail to settle in the Far West. Some went to California. These people left the main trail at Fort Bridger or Fort Hall and headed south. From there on they had a different trail and a different and more terrible story.

▶ THE CALIFORNIA TRAIL

The California Trail had several branches where it left the Oregon Trail, and again where it entered California. It was unusual in that the pioneers themselves blazed parts of it. Most of the pathfinding was done by mountain men and explorers, particularly John Charles Frémont, Jedediah Smith, Kit Carson, and Joseph Walker (1798–1876). The trail had to cross two forbidding barriers—the desert and the Sierra Nevada mountains. Cliffs faced the eastern side of this range, with few streams cutting through.

Two of the mountain men, Smith and Walker, were the first to challenge these barriers. Walker blazed a trail across the deserts of the Great Basin along the Humboldt River. The river provided water and a handy guide partway across the desert, until it drained into the Humboldt Sink. Though the Ute Indians, who were known to steal horses, lived nearby, this was the only route for this part of the trail.

From the Humboldt Sink the trail crossed 65 miles (105 kilometers) of desert to the mountains. There was no grass, and water holes were few and far between. The explorers found several streams leading to mountain passes. Most passes were rough, narrow, and steep. In 1841 only a few trappers knew where they were. But this was the year that the first pioneers went through unguided.

Stories of California's beauty spread, and people formed California societies, ready to make the trip. Hundreds signed up to go with John Bidwell (1819–1900), known as the Prince of California Pioneers. One group of 69 people met at Sapling Grove, Tennessee, in May 1841. They had little money and less information. Everything was new to them. About the trail, as Bidwell wrote, "We knew only that California lay to the west." Their maps showed rivers running from the Great Salt Lake to the Pacific. They had tools for building canoes to float them along these nonexistent streams. These pioneers would soon travel unaided where none but trappers had dared go before.

They had one piece of good luck. At first Thomas Fitzpatrick (1799–1854), a skilled mountain man, guided them and corrected their worst mistakes. But he was bound for Oregon. At Soda Springs the party split up. About half the party went with Fitzpatrick. Another group of 32, including one woman and her little girl, struck off for California.

Mountain men told them to head straight west for the Humboldt River. If they wandered too far south, they would die in the desert. To the north they would get lost in a wild land of canyons and cliffs.

The First Trail

It was September before they reached the Great Salt Lake. Ahead lay the desert, "glimmering with heat and salt." Wagon wheels sank into the sand. Leaving the wagons, the pioneers packed goods on the animals and floundered on. They struck the Humboldt and followed it west, as Walker had done. Then they hiked south to the Walker River.

Facing the towering cliffs, they almost gave up. It was October. They saw the high peaks hooded with snow, and they feared freezing in the mountains. But if they tried to go back, they would surely starve. So they toiled up the Walker River, along a narrow Indian trail cut in the side of the canyon. They ate some of the mules to keep from starving. At last they found the Stanislaus River, flowing west, and followed it down to the San Joaquin Valley, arriving on November 4, 1841. They were the first settlers to reach California by land.

The Main Route

Others followed. Some, guided by Walker, crossed the mountains at Walker Pass and took the Kern River trail to the valley. But this route took people miles south of the direct line.

In 1844 the Stevens-Murphy party blazed a shorter trail, north of Walker's. Going straight west from the Humboldt, they struck a mountain stream, which they named Truckee, for the Paiute Indian chief who guided them. Truckee led them up the canyon and across the mountains at what became known as Truckee Pass. They followed the American River down to the Sacramento Valley, getting wagons through for the first time. News of the route spread, and it became the main trail.

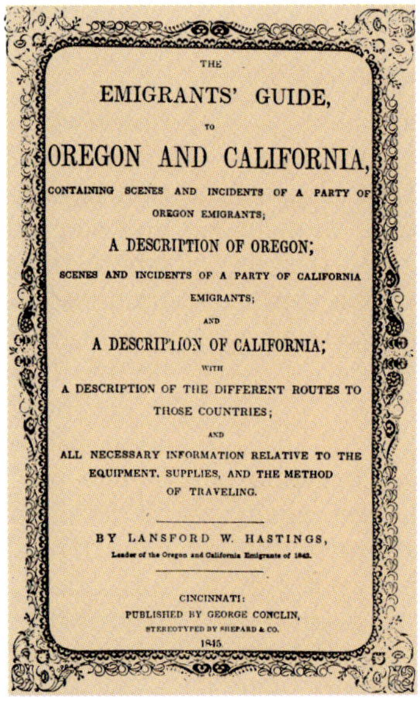
THE
EMIGRANTS' GUIDE,
TO
OREGON AND CALIFORNIA,
CONTAINING SCENES AND INCIDENTS OF A PARTY OF OREGON EMIGRANTS;
A DESCRIPTION OF OREGON;
SCENES AND INCIDENTS OF A PARTY OF CALIFORNIA EMIGRANTS;
AND
A DESCRIPTION OF CALIFORNIA;
WITH
A DESCRIPTION OF THE DIFFERENT ROUTES TO THOSE COUNTRIES;
AND
ALL NECESSARY INFORMATION RELATIVE TO THE EQUIPMENT, SUPPLIES, AND THE METHOD OF TRAVELING.

BY LANSFORD W. HASTINGS,
Leader of the Oregon and California Emigrants of 1842.

CINCINNATI:
PUBLISHED BY GEORGE CONCLIN,
STEREOTYPED BY SHEPARD & CO.
1845.

In the 1840s, numerous guidebooks were published to encourage people to go west.

Hastings Cutoff

During the 1840s, California land speculators tried to lure emigrants to California. One of them, Lansford Hastings, planned a shortcut. Instead of making the long northward loop to Fort Hall, wagons should go south to Fort Bridger and from there southwest through the Wasatch Range. They would pass the Great Salt Lake at its south end, instead of its north end as did other trails, and head west across the Great Salt Lake Desert.

This was the terrible Hastings Cutoff. It was shorter and looked fine on the map, but it crossed 80 miles (130 kilometers) of scorching desert, where nothing lived but scorpions, lizards, and snakes. There was no grass or water for oxen. A mountain man who had crossed with Hastings warned people to stay away from it. But Hastings settled down beside the trail to wait for emigrants.

The Harlan-Young party set out in 1846. Hastings guided them through the Wasatch Range to the desert and pointed out the peaks on the other side. He told them it was only 40 miles (65 kilometers), so they took hay and water for that distance. They hoped to cross in a forced march of a day and a night. But it took twice that long. Nearly fainting from heat and exhaustion, the men finally dragged themselves across. They had to leave the wagons, for the oxen had dropped in their tracks. Then they had to haul grass and water 30 miles (50 kilometers) back, to save the animals. Some say their curses against Hastings can be seen in Utah today as a blue haze over the hills. Behind them came the unluckiest pioneers of all, the Donner party. (For more information, see the feature in this article.)

The Gold Rush of 1849

After the Mexican War (1846–48), California became American territory. In 1848 gold was found on the American River. During 1849 about 80,000 gold seekers, known as

THE DONNER PARTY

Of the thousands of pioneers who experienced hardship and tragedy, the Donner party suffered perhaps the greatest misfortune.

In the spring of 1846, George and Jacob Donner led a party of 82 pioneers out of Illinois on an overland journey to California. When they reached Utah, they wasted precious days waiting for their guide, Lansford Hastings, to show them his shortcut to the California Trail. Hastings failed to appear, and the party went on without him, following an untested route through the treacherous Great Salt Lake Desert.

The Donner party reached the Sierra Nevada—the mountain range between Nevada and California—so late in the fall that early snows caught them as they tried to cross by the Truckee Pass. In mid-December, as their precious food supplies dwindled, a group of 15 set out in desperation to try to bring help from California. Only seven survived the journey.

When the rescuers returned in the spring, they found that more than two dozen men, women, and children had already died from starvation and that some of the survivors had been forced to eat the dead to keep themselves alive. Of the original 82 members of the Donner party, only 47 lived to reach California.

"forty-niners," plodded along the California Trail or the southern trails. By 1850 the California Trail was the most traveled road of all—well marked with hoofprints, wagon ruts, the bleached bones of thousands of animals, and the graves of pioneers.

▸ THE MORMON TRAIL

When the Mormons left Illinois in 1846 to seek a home in the wilderness, they traveled in stages. Advance parties moved across Iowa, stopping to build cabins and plant crops for the next group. The biggest camp, farthest west, was Winter Quarters, near today's Omaha.

On April 9, 1847, Brigham Young (1801–77) left this camp with 143 men, three women, and two children. They followed the north bank of the Platte, keeping away from other pioneers, who might be hostile to their religious beliefs. They crossed the stream near Fort Laramie, stopping to build boats for a ferry. Some waited behind to ferry the Mormon groups that were following. The band went past South Pass, turned southwest at Fort Bridger, and started along the faint track of the Hastings Cutoff. There was no trail, but scouts went ahead, finding passes and clearing a wagon path with picks and shovels.

Seeking religious freedom, Mormon leader Brigham Young led a whole community of pioneers to Utah, where they founded Salt Lake City.

On July 24 the band came through a canyon and looked upon the valley of the Great Salt Lake. They saw a curving bowl of sagebrush and cactus, rimmed with mountains. They saw nothing green. In a week came the second group, and within a month, the third. The third band, 1,500 people, saw greenery, for already grass had sprung up in the fields the first Mormons had irrigated.

The Mormon Trail, with its rest stations, was the best-managed trail of all. At the trail's end the Mormons built Salt Lake City.

▸ THE CHISHOLM TRAIL

The Chisholm Trail was the most famous of the cattle trails. Unlike other trails, cattle trails ran north and south, from southern Texas to the railroad towns in Nebraska and Kansas. Cowboys drove herds of cattle along the trails, sometimes for 1,000 miles (1,600 kilometers). This was called the Long Drive.

The Cattle Drives

During the 1860s railroads grew like vines across Kansas. If cattlemen could get their stock to a railroad station, cattle cars could take them east to market. So the idea of the Long Drive was born. The first longhorns left Texas in 1866, heading for the railroad town of Sedalia, Missouri. But the wooded hills scared range cattle, and in Missouri, farmers came out with guns to stop the cattle from trampling their fields. It was not a good trail for the drive.

The next year, an Illinois meat dealer got the Kansas Pacific Railroad to give special freight rates for cattle. He chose Abilene, Kansas, as the town where the Long Drive should end. To get there, cowboys herded stock west of the first trail—through grasslands with streams, few trees, no farms.

This route was the Chisholm Trail. It went straight north from a point near San Antonio, across Texas and the Red River, through Oklahoma, to Kansas. It crossed the Arkansas River and the old Santa Fe Trail and went north to Abilene. It proved to be a fine trail. Between 1868 and 1871, 1.5 million longhorns passed along it.

To endure the hardships of life on the cattle trails, cowboys had to be tough, spirited, and independent.

As railroads pushed west, the trail changed. Its northern end moved west to Ellsworth and to other towns on the newly built Santa Fe line. After 1876 the Western Trail led to Dodge City.

The Long Drive ended in the 1880s. Farmers were moving west, fencing in the land. Indians were charging cowboys ten cents for each head of cattle driven over their property. Kansas farmers feared the ticks carried by longhorns, which spread Texas fever. Some farmers shot cattle. In 1884 Kansas passed a law permitting the drive only in winter. The Chisholm became a ghost trail.

THE BOZEMAN TRAIL

Increasing settlement and the expanding livestock industry caused trouble between the pioneers and the Indians. The Sioux particularly resented the establishment in 1863 of the Bozeman Trail that led from Fort Laramie to the gold fields of Virginia City, Montana. The trail crossed through hunting grounds that the Sioux regarded as theirs by treaty with the United States. The establishment of Fort Phil Kearny in 1866 to protect the Bozeman Trail led to further conflict. In December of that year, Chief Red Cloud and his Sioux warriors fought U.S. troops near the fort, killing 81 soldiers as well as their commanding officer, Lieutenant Colonel William J. Fetterman. Red Cloud's victory led to a peace treaty in 1868, and the Bozeman Trail was closed.

SUMMARY

In less than 100 years the westward tide of settlers that began at the Appalachian Mountains had pushed the American frontier to the Pacific Ocean. Along the trails new cities sprang up. Trade and industry developed. A great nation began to take shape and fill the West.

Some trails faded and died. Others became arteries of commerce. Portions of most Far Western trails are now followed by highways or railroads. But overland trails are not important as ancestors of modern highways. They are important because during the century of migration, they carried a whole people west. The United States grew along its trails until it stretched "from sea to shining sea."

WILLIAM J. RAMPON
West Chester State College (Pennsylvania)

CUBAN MISSILE CRISIS

The Cuban missile crisis of October 1962 was the most dangerous episode of the Cold War, a political struggle between the world's two great superpowers, the United States and the Soviet Union. The Cold War lasted from the end of World War II until the early 1990's. No battles were actually fought. But the Cuban missile crisis for the first time raised the possibility of nuclear war between the United States and the Soviet Union.

In the spring of 1962, Soviet leader Nikita S. Khrushchev—with the permission of the Cuban leader Fidel Castro—ordered nuclear missiles to be installed on the Caribbean island of Cuba, a mere 90 miles (145 kilometers) from the United States. The military buildup took place during the summer and autumn of 1962.

The Cuban missile crisis started on October 16, 1962, when U.S. president John F. Kennedy was informed that American intelligence had detected the presence of Soviet missiles in Cuba. The crisis, which lasted 13 days, consisted of two periods.

During the first period, from October 16 to 22, President Kennedy and his advisers discussed how to react to the presence of Soviet missiles in Cuba without informing the American public or other nations of the situation. The president's advisers made a number of recommendations, including a military attack on the missile sites. But Kennedy chose instead to establish a naval blockade around Cuba in order to halt any further deliveries of Soviet missiles to the island. On October 22 in a televised speech, the president informed the American public about the missiles and his decision.

During the second phase of the crisis, from October 22 to 28, millions of people throughout the world feared that a nuclear war between the two superpowers was inescapable. On October 24 the American blockade went into effect. Soviet ships approached the line of blockade, and for a time a U.S.-Soviet clash on the seas seemed likely. Much to Kennedy's relief, however, the Soviet ships stopped before crossing the line of blockade and headed back toward the Soviet Union.

Ultimately, Kennedy and Khrushchev used diplomacy to end the crisis. Through an exchange of letters between the two men, a settlement was reached. The Soviet leader agreed to remove the nuclear weapons from Cuba, while Kennedy publicly pledged that the United States would not invade the island. Privately, Kennedy also pledged in due course to remove American missiles stationed in Turkey near the Soviet border. But this fact was not made known to the public.

Aerial photos taken over Cuba in 1962 showed evidence of Soviet missile erectors and launch stands. After the Cuban missile crisis ended, all the Soviet missile bases in Cuba were dismantled.

The Cuban missile crisis changed Soviet-American relations. Both Kennedy and Khrushchev, sobered by the events of October 1962, moved to reduce tensions between the superpowers and to minimize the possibility of another dangerous confrontation.

In the summer of 1963, Kennedy called for a more tolerant attitude toward the Soviet Union. Shortly afterward, the two countries signed the Soviet-American Test Ban Treaty, designed to limit further nuclear testing.

MARK J. WHITE
Author, *The Cuban Missile Crisis*

Hispanic Americans are united by the Spanish language, which most continue to use, and by their most common religion, Roman Catholicism. Both are legacies of Spain and its conquest of vast areas of the Americas beginning in the 1500s. However, other aspects of Hispanic American heritage spring from African and American Indian cultures. The African influence came from the importation of African slaves into the Spanish colonies.

WAY OF LIFE

The Hispanic American way of life emphasizes family values, religious and other holidays, community celebrations, and a wide range of food and ways of speaking that have come to influence all Americans.

Above left: **Early Spanish settlers in colonial America built Roman Catholic missions to serve as parish churches. Today most Hispanic Americans remain Roman Catholic.**

Left: **In many U.S. cities, Mexican Americans of all ages celebrate their ethnic heritage on *Cinco de Mayo*, or May 5th.**

HISPANIC AMERICANS

Hispanic Americans are Americans who were born in Spanish-speaking lands or whose ancestors emigrated from Spanish-speaking lands. With a population of nearly 30 million, or approximately 12 percent of the U.S. total, they are the nation's fastest-growing minority. By the year 2050, Hispanic Americans will likely number 100 million, or 25 percent of the population. Their music, food, and customs are a part of everyday life in cities such as Los Angeles, New York, Miami, Chicago, Denver, and San Antonio.

Hispanic Americans—also called Latinos—come from a variety of ethnic backgrounds. Almost two-thirds are of Mexican origin. Puerto Ricans and Cuban Americans are the next largest groups. In addition, more than 1 million Dominicans have moved to the United States since the late 1950s. More than 4 million Spanish-speaking Americans come from other countries in Central and South America. A small number trace their lineage to Spain.

Language. Many English words that Americans use today are Spanish in origin.

Weather words such as "tornado" and "El Niño" are Spanish. So is "hurricane," which is derived from a word of the Taino people, the original inhabitants of Puerto Rico. Their native language was incorporated into Spanish.

Several states and cities retain names given them by the Spanish settlers. Some of these familiar names are Florida ("floral"), Colorado ("red-colored"), San Francisco ("Saint Francis"), and Sacramento ("sacrament").

Some other words incorporated into English are "mosquito," "plaza," "patio," and "guerrilla."

Almost everything to do with cowboys is Spanish or Mexican in origin. Descendants of the early Spanish settlers taught newly arrived English-speaking settlers techniques of irrigation and mining, how to tame wild horses, and how best to raise cattle. "Stampede," "corral," "rodeo," "lasso," "bronco," "mesa," "adobe," and "canyon" are all Spanish words.

Religion. Roman Catholicism plays a major role in daily life. Some Hispanic Americans of Caribbean origin practice the *Santería* religion. *Santería* is an ancient African practice that combines Catholic religious beliefs and saints with African beliefs and deities. Evangelical and other Protestant sects have begun attracting many Hispanic American followers.

Family Life. Hispanic Americans also share a heritage emphasizing close family ties. Often several generations live under one roof. Grandparents, cousins, aunts, and uncles are all included in important family events. Traditions of hospitality and *compadrazco* (godparenting) provide a bond of unity that goes beyond the family to the community.

Holidays. Hispanics celebrate several festivals and special holidays. Religious holidays include observances such as Christmas' *El Día de Los*

Right: **A 15-year-old girl celebrates her coming of age at a special religious mass.**

Below left: **Cuban American men in Miami, Florida, play a game of dominoes. The Miami area is home to more than half of today's Cuban American community.**

Below right: **Traditional Spanish lights during Christmastime bring beauty to Santa Fe, New Mexico. The state has a large Hispanic population.**

Ethnic Origins of Hispanic Americans

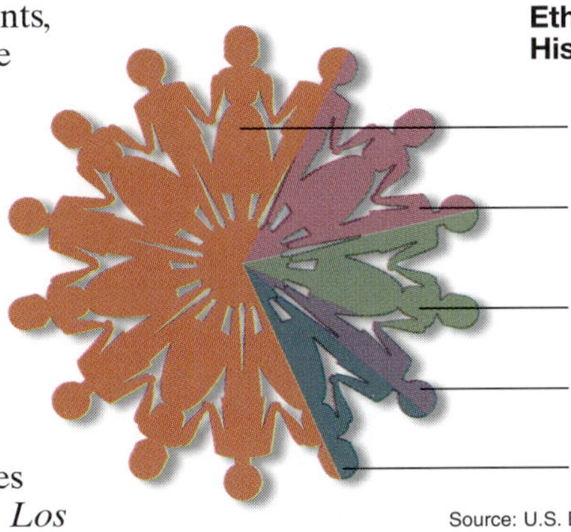

Source: U.S. Bureau of the Census (1997 estimates).

Below: Gloria Estefan, a Cuban American, is one of the world's most popular musicians. She sings in both Spanish and English. *Right:* Talented Hispanic street artists have created colorful and expressive murals on walls in many California cities.

Reyes, or Three Kings Day, on January 6. Children and adults take part in pageants that tell the story of the kings who journeyed to see the infant Jesus. Another holiday is Easter's *Semana Santa*, or Holy Week, when many pilgrimages to holy sites take place. On *El Día de los Muertos* (The Day of the Dead), celebrated in autumn, families take symbolic gifts to the cemeteries where loved ones are buried. Carnival is held at different times of the year according to local traditions.

These are all occasions for community-wide celebrations. Local saints and feast days are also recognized with pilgrimages and rituals. A girl's *quinceañera*, or 15th birthday celebration, is a special occasion marking her passage to womanhood. Holidays that have a special historical significance include *Cinco de Mayo*, or May 5th, which commemorates the defeat of the French by the Mexican Army in 1862, and January 28, the birthday of Cuban poet and patriot Jose Martí. Puerto Rican Day parades are celebrated in a number of cities. Hispanic Heritage Month, which runs from September 15 to October 15, continues to be a source of much pride for Hispanic Americans.

Food. No holiday would be complete without specially prepared tamales, paella, or decorated cookies and cakes and flan (a type of pudding). Caribbean specialties such as *sancocho*, a delicious stew, or the unique dishes of the Southwest with hot chili peppers and refried beans, have a place on the everyday table in many Hispanic homes. Some of these dishes, such as chili, tacos, fajitas, and nachos, have become as American as apple pie.

Puerto Rican actor Raul Julia appeared in many films and on television. He was also well known for his Shakespearean roles in theater.

▸ CULTURAL HERITAGE

Hispanic Americans have made important contributions to music, art, literature, theater, cinema, television, and sports.

Music. From the traditional Mexican *corridos*, or ballads, and Texan/Mexican accordion and guitar melodies, to the salsa beat of the Caribbean, Hispanic Americans have brought their story and sounds to American jazz, pop, and folklore. Salsa melodies are rooted in sacred African music. The unique musical styles of the mambo, cha-cha, and rhumba have enjoyed widespread popularity through such greats as Tito Puente, Celia Cruz, and Willie Colón. The huge followings of Cuban American singer Gloria Estefan, Mexican Americans Jon Secada and Selena Quintanilla Pérez, and Panamanian Rubén Blades reflect the importance of Hispanic Americans on the popular music scene.

In jazz, Afro-Cuban rhythms by Chick Corea, Willie Bobo, and Mongo Santamaría have inspired an entire improvisational style. The rock scene changed forever when Carlos Santana hit the charts in the late 1960s with his unique rhythms and Latino sound.

Art. Sculptors and painters, such as Luis Jiménez and Arnaldo Roche Rabell, and muralists, such as Judith Baca, Willie Herron, and Frank Romero, have transformed the art landscape with their original visions. (A mural is a wall painting.) During the 1970s and 1980s, the Chicano mural movement brought color and beauty to city walls. The hundreds of murals produced in Los Angeles made that city the undisputed mural capital of the world. The works of Puerto Rican painter Juan Sánchez, Cuban Americans Luis Cruz Azaceta and José Bedia, and Mexican American Carmen Lomas Garza are part of major museum exhibits.

Many Hispanic Americans have become professional athletes. Among them are Rafael Santana of the New York Yankees baseball team (*left*) and tennis champion Gigi Fernandez (*above*).

Literature. A number of Hispanic writers and poets have become key figures in American literature. Contemporary Mexican American writer Sandra Cisneros, Puerto Rican writer Nicholasa Mohr, and Puerto Rican poet Judith Ortiz Cofer are famous for their works focusing on their experiences as Hispanic females in a largely different culture. Chilean born Fernando Alegria devoted much of his work to exploring the Hispanic reality of the United States. Puerto Rican writer Piri Thomas is particularly noted for *Down These Mean Streets* (1967), an autobiography. Cuban American Oscar Hijuelos wrote the Pulitzer Prize-winning *The Mambo Kings Play Songs of Love* (1989).

Theater, Film, and Television. During the 1960s and 1970s, the community-based Teatro Campesino group of actors and actresses dramatized the plight of migrant farmworkers to audiences throughout a number of cities in the United States. Luis Valdez, a founder of Teatro Campesino, went on to write and produce Broadway hits and film successes such as *Zoot Suit* (1981) and *La Bamba* (1987).

The emergence of Hispanic American themes in Hollywood films marked a turning point from the days when Hispanic artists downplayed their heritage in order to succeed. Rita Hayworth and Raquel Welch, both earlier Hispanic actresses, became American cinema icons. Hispanics who have achieved lasting stardom include Dolores del Rio, Anthony Quinn, Lou Diamond Phillips, Raul Julia, Edward James Olmos, Rosie Perez, and Jimmy Smits.

Sports. A large number of Hispanics are enthusiastic about sports, and many have become professional athletes. Champion tennis players have included Pancho Gonzalez, Rosemary Casals, Gigi Fernandez, and Mary Joe Fernandez. Hall of Fame jockey Angel Cordero set a standard in horse racing that is unmatched. Golf greats Juan "Chi Chi" Rodriguez, Nancy Lopez, and Lee Trevino toured the world with their talents. In baseball, Hispanics often made up half the major leagues' All Star Game selections in the 1990s . Rafael Santana and Orlando Hernández of the New York Yankees were popular players.

HISTORY

With the founding of St. Augustine in Florida in 1565, the Spanish became the first group of Europeans to settle in what is now the United States. Spanish traders, miners, and priests settled the Southwest, often displacing Native American peoples or intermarrying with them. Centuries later, at the end of the Mexican War (1846–48), a defeated Mexico ceded to the United States a vast territory known as New Mexico. Today the area consists of Texas, California, New Mexico, and Arizona and sections of Colorado, Utah, and Nevada.

Mexican Americans. When the border between the United States and Mexico was established in 1848, small numbers of Mexicans started to come north to look for work and a better way of life. From the 1890s to 1930, one-eighth of Mexico's population entered the United States. They worked for the railroads, mines, timber industry, steel mills, automobile plants, and textile plants that made the United States an industrial giant. Many harvested and processed crops in different areas. They lived in crowded camps or trailers, and they moved on when the work was completed.

Youngsters march in New York City's annual Puerto Rican Day parade. Hispanics make up a large part of the city's population.

After years on the road, a family was often relieved to settle in a city. The Mexican American population remained concentrated in Texas, New Mexico, Arizona, and California. Los Angeles became home to more people of Mexican descent than any other place except Mexico City.

From early on, Spanish-speaking neighborhoods became known as *barrios*. There, Mexican American families lived, worked, and attended schools and churches apart from the rest of the population. Yet they were still met with prejudice and hostility. Many restaurants refused to serve them. At schools, children were often physically punished for speaking or writing Spanish. Mexican workers were also paid less than half the amounts earned by non-Hispanics. The nation's first labor unions excluded them.

One Mexican American, Lucia Eldine González, founded the Chicago Working Woman's Union to demand equal pay for equal work. Lucia González's efforts forced other unions to admit women into their ranks. Mexican Americans and other Hispanic Americans went on to help lead major strikes against big businesses that eventually won the eight-hour day and ended child labor.

Aided by prominent civil rights leaders like Guatemala-born Luisa Moreno and Mexico-born Josefina Fierro de Bright, Hispanic Americans and other minorities were able to find job opportunities in war production plants when the United States entered World War II in 1941. The status of Mexican Americans gradually began to change.

In the mid-1960s, the civil rights movement awakened the nation to many injustices. The Mexican Americans' struggle became known as the Chicano Movement. (The word "chicano" is derived from a Spanish word that had once been considered degrading.) A strike by California grape workers organized by labor union leaders Cesar Chavez and Dolores de la Huerta brought before the public the bad conditions of migrant workers of all backgrounds. It also brought the history of Mexican Americans and their hardships before the entire nation.

Puerto Ricans. Puerto Rico is a commonwealth of the United States, acquired in 1898 at the close of the Spanish-American War. Its people were declared U.S. citizens in 1917.

Since the mid-1940s , thousands of people have left Puerto Rico to try their luck in the job markets of the eastern United States. Some shuttled back and forth. Most stayed. In New York and other eastern cities, they found low-wage jobs in restaurants, hotels, factories, and hospitals.

Because they were Spanish-speaking, Puerto Ricans encountered great hostility. This was compounded by prejudice against those among them who were predominantly of African heritage. Despite everything, a growing Puerto Rican middle class has carved out a secure place for itself.

Cuban Americans, Dominican Americans, and Other Hispanic Americans. U.S. immigration requirements are sometimes lifted to allow entry of a group of people thought to be in special need of shelter in the United States. This was the case for hundreds of thousands of Cubans who fled the revolutionary regime established in Cuba in 1959 by President Fidel Castro. The Cuban exiles received government assistance in finding good homes and decent paying jobs. This was because the U.S. government opposed Cuba's communist government. Today, Florida's Miami area remains home to more than half the Cuban American community.

People from the Dominican Republic, a Caribbean island near Cuba, also entered the United States. This was especially the case after 1965, when the Dominicans were fleeing the political turbulence of their homeland. They were soon joined by thousands of immigrants from South American nations, including Ecuador, Peru, Bolivia, Argentina, Brazil, and Chile, as well as Central Americans from El Salvador, Guatemala, Nicaragua, and Honduras. Most of these people were fleeing right-wing dictatorships in their countries.

For the most part, these immigrants were not viewed as political refugees the way the Cubans had been. The U.S. government, which backed the dictatorships they were fleeing, asserted that most of them had left their homes for economic reasons rather than political ones. It therefore restricted their admission.

Modern-Day Issues. For more than a century, Hispanic Americans not only organized labor unions and strikes to improve their working conditions. They also established civil rights groups like the League of United American Citizens, the National Hispanic Leadership Conference, and the National Council of La Raza. These groups still work to achieve such goals as equal education, an end to discrimination in employment and law enforcement, and increased participation in local, state, and national elections.

As head of the United Farm Workers of America, union leader Cesar Chavez brought to the public's attention the unfair working conditions of many Mexican Americans.

By uniting not only among themselves but with African Americans, Asian Americans, and others, Hispanic Americans achieved passage of the Bilingual Education Act in 1968. This law made funds available for teaching in both English and Spanish (or another language), so that children could be taught in their native tongue while learning English. Other measures, such as expanded higher education facilities and open admissions policies, made it possible for thousands of Hispanics to attend college and graduate school.

These gains were undermined, however, by the U.S. Supreme Court's 1995 decision against earlier affirmative action laws that helped create equal opportunities for minorities. New acts of discrimination and anti-immigrant expression occurred during the 1990s . These included moves to end bilingual education and highly publicized cases of immigrants being abused. Consequently, Hispanics had to unite more than ever to create a better and just world for all Americans.

JAMES D. COCKCROFT
Author, *Latinos in the Making of the United States*

WATERGATE

The American political scandal known as Watergate resulted in the resignation, on August 9, 1974, of President Richard M. Nixon, the only president in the nation's history to resign. The scandal began to unravel on June 17, 1972, when five men were arrested for breaking into the headquarters of the Democratic National Committee, located in the Watergate apartment and office complex in Washington, D.C. It was soon discovered that one of the men was employed by the Committee to Re-elect the President (CRP or CREEP) and that the break-in had been planned by two others with close ties to the White House.

From the outset President Nixon sought to cover up any connection between the Watergate burglary and the CRP or the White House staff. But during hearings to investigate the matter, it became clear that Watergate had been only part of a wide array of questionable activities ordered by White House personnel. The hearings also revealed that since early 1971 the president had tape-recorded all his private conversations in the Oval Office.

Evidence of a cover-up, revealed by the Watergate investigation, forced President Richard Nixon to resign on August 9, 1974.

In February 1973, a U.S. Senate committee, headed by Senator Sam Ervin, Jr., of North Carolina, was formed to investigate matters relating to Watergate. A special prosecutor, Archibald Cox, was also engaged. The Senate committee and Cox soon demanded to hear the White House tapes, but Nixon refused to release them, citing executive privilege. Nixon

---

Profiles

John Wesley Dean III (1938–) served as legal counsel to President Nixon. During the Watergate scandal, Dean broke ranks with the White House. He informed the Justice Department of a cover-up and provided an incriminating picture of White House activities to the Senate investigative committee. Dean served four months in prison for his initial participation in the obstruction of justice.

John Dean

John Ehrlichman

John Ehrlichman (1925–) was President Nixon's assistant for domestic affairs. In 1971, while trying to discredit a man named Daniel Ellsberg, who had released classified defense department studies known as *The Pentagon Papers* to the *New York Times*, Ehrlichman authorized an illegal search of Ellsberg's psychiatric files. Details of the operation were revealed during the Watergate investigation. Ehrlichman served 18 months in prison for his role in the affair.

H(arry) R(obbins) "Bob" Haldeman (1926–93), President Nixon's chief of staff, conspired with Nixon and others to cover up the Watergate and the Ellsberg affairs. He served 18 months for his involvement.

E(verette) Howard Hunt (1918–), a presidential aide and former employee of the Central Intelligence Agency (CIA), planned the Watergate break-in. Hunt served 33 months in prison for burglary, obstruction of justice, and illegal wiretapping.

G(eorge) Gordon Liddy (1930–) participated in the illegal search of Daniel Ellsberg's psychiatrist's office and helped plan the Watergate break-in. Liddy refused to answer any questions and was held in contempt of court. He served four and a half years in prison.

John Newton Mitchell (1913–88) served as attorney general in Nixon's administration from 1969 to 1972, when he stepped down to become head of CRP, Nixon's re-election committee. For his role in the Watergate scandal, Mitchell served 19 months in prison for perjury and obstruction of justice.

held out until July 1974 when the Supreme Court, in *United States* v. *Richard M. Nixon*, ruled that the tapes be released. The tapes revealed that Nixon had been personally involved in a conspiracy to obstruct the Watergate investigation.

Even before this revelation, the Judiciary Committee of the U.S. House of Representatives had voted 27 to 11 to start impeachment proceedings against Nixon on the first of three eventual charges. With his political support in the Senate rapidly crumbling, Nixon resigned his office rather than face removal through the impeachment process.

Bob Woodward and Carl Bernstein, two investigative reporters for the *Washington Post* newspaper, were awarded Pulitzer Prizes for their ongoing coverage of the Watergate cover-up. Their stories often revealed new dimensions of the scandal based on information and leads provided by an individual they called Deep Throat. Speculation still continues about the identity of Deep Throat, but it remains a closely kept secret.

The effects of Watergate were far-reaching and profound. The discovery that Nixon had misused campaign funds led to the Campaign Reform Act in 1974, which limits campaign contributions and expenditures in presidential elections. In 1978, Congress also provided that the attorney general, under certain circumstances, could ask for court-appointed special prosecutors to investigate the president and other high-ranking executive officers. These special prosecutors, who can be removed by the attorney general only for supportable reasons, are virtually free of any presidential control.

Perhaps Watergate's most notable and enduring legacy has been a sense of erosion of public confidence in the institutions of government. The scandal broke toward the end of the Vietnam War era, a time when many people felt the government had misled them about the conduct and progress of the war. Watergate only served to compound a growing disillusionment with the president and members of Congress. Polls taken since the time of Watergate consistently reveal a markedly heightened public skepticism about the truthfulness and intentions of elected public officials.

GEORGE W. CAREY
Georgetown University

A CHRONOLOGY OF THE WATERGATE SCANDAL

	1972
June 17	Five individuals are arrested at Watergate complex for breaking into the headquarters of the Democratic National Committee.
September 15	White House associates are linked to the Watergate break-in.
	1973
January 8	Five defendants plead guilty to the Watergate break-in; two others are soon tried and convicted.
February 7	A Senate committee to investigate Watergate is established.
April 6	John Dean, the White House counsel, meets with Justice Department prosecutors investigating Watergate.
April 30	Attorney General Richard Kleindienst and presidential aides John Ehrlichman and H. R. Haldeman resign. President Nixon fires John Dean.
May 17	Televised coverage begins of the Senate's investigation into Watergate.
May 18	Archibald Cox is named special prosecutor for the Watergate investigation.
June 25	John Dean testifies at the Senate hearings that Nixon has participated in a Watergate cover-up.
July 16	The taping of Oval Office conversations is revealed.
July 25	President Nixon asserts executive privilege in refusing to turn over White House tapes to the Senate Watergate committee.
October 20	Nixon orders the firing of Archibald Cox as special prosecutor for seeking to obtain White House tapes. Attorney General Elliot Richardson and Deputy Attorney General William Ruckelshaus resign rather than fire Cox. Robert Bork, who became Acting Attorney General after the others' resignations, carries out Nixon's order and fires Cox. This episode becomes known as the Saturday Night Massacre.
November 1	Leon Jaworski replaces Archibald Cox as special prosecutor.
	1974
March 1	Seven White House aides are indicted for the Watergate cover-up. President Nixon is named as an unindicted co-conspirator.
May 9	The House Judiciary Committee begins impeachment hearings against Nixon.
July 24	The Supreme Court orders Nixon to surrender tapes subpoenaed by Jaworski.
July 27	The House Judiciary Committee votes 27 to 11 for an impeachment, charging Nixon with obstruction of justice.
August 5	Nixon complies with the U.S. Supreme Court order to release the tapes, which reveal his involvement in the cover-up.
August 9	Nixon resigns.
September 8	President Ford grants Nixon a full pardon for offenses he "committed" or "may have committed" in the Watergate scandal.

MAGNETS AND MAGNETISM

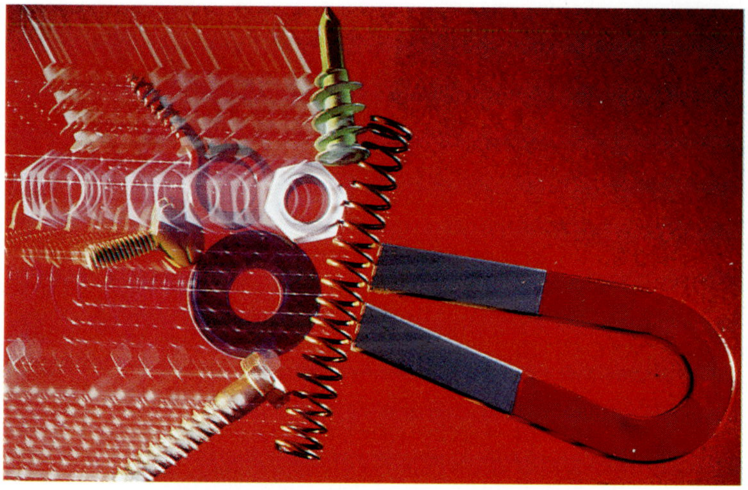

This horseshoe magnet exerts an invisible force that can attract certain metal objects containing iron, such as nuts, bolts, and springs.

If ancient sailors came back from the past, they would be surprised by modern navigational instruments such as radar scopes and satellite receivers. Inside those instruments would be things that would not surprise them: magnets.

Magnets are as important today as they were hundreds of years ago when sailors used them as compasses to guide them on their voyages. In ancient times magnets were viewed as magical, with a mysterious ability to pull certain metals or be pulled in a certain direction. Today we understand that the magic of magnets is a basic force of nature, related to electricity and light.

Even though we understand the mystery, we still marvel at what modern magnetic machines can do. Because of our knowledge of magnets, we can create images of the organs inside the body and write encyclopedias on spots no larger than pinheads.

DISCOVERING MAGNETS

Humans discovered magnets and magnetism thousands of years ago. Pieces of a certain kind of black stone exerted forces on each other and on objects made of iron. The stones became known as **magnets** and the force as **magnetism**. According to one story, those names came from a place called Magnesia in Asia Minor where magnetic rocks were first found. Another story credits the discovery of magnetism to a shepherd named Magnes, who stood on a large black rock and felt it pulling on the metal nails in his sandals.

Lines of magnetic force stretch across two opposite poles, which attract one another. Lines of force from two like poles push away, or repel, one another.

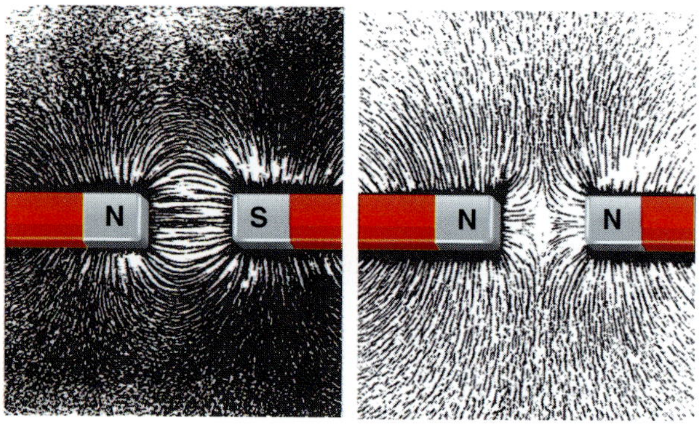

Magnetic Poles

After some time, people discovered that long, thin magnets hanging from threads would always point in a north-south direction. The same end of the magnet would always point north. The opposite end would point south. These ends became known as the **poles** of the magnet, the north pole pointing north and the south pole pointing south. Soon sailors learned to use magnets to keep track of their direction on the open sea where there were no landmarks to guide them. The black rock then became known as **lodestone**, meaning "leading stone," because it enabled sailors to find their destination. The first magnetic device that humans ever made was the sailor's compass, which used a lodestone to measure the direction in which a ship was traveling.

Magnetic Fields and Lines of Force

If you put two magnets close to each other, you can feel forces between their poles. Two north poles or two south poles push each other away (or **repel**); a north and a south pole pull toward each other (**attract**). When an object experiences a push or pull through empty space, scientists describe the effect as a **field**.

Even though a magnetic field is invisible, you can imagine it as a pattern of lines that loop from one pole of a magnet to the oppo-

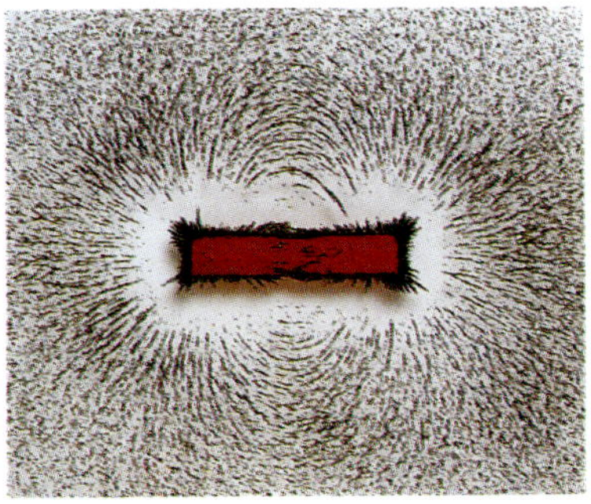

Iron filings sprinkled near a bar magnet reveal its lines of force. The area around the magnet is called a magnetic field.

site pole. You can see these lines if you put a magnet under a piece of cardboard and sprinkle iron filings on top. The filings will arrange themselves along the **lines of force**. The lines bunch together near the edges of the magnet by the poles, because that is where the field is strongest. If you put a north pole of one magnet near a south pole of another, the lines of force will connect the two poles. If two north poles or two south poles are close together, the lines follow paths that push away from one another.

Earth's Magnetic Field

A compass works because our planet has a magnetic field, with a north pole and a south pole. Earth's magnetic poles are not at exactly the same spots as the north and south geographic poles. The north magnetic pole, also known as magnetic north, is located in northern Canada. Compass needles point toward the north magnetic pole, not toward the north geographic pole, or true north. The difference between true north and magnetic north is known as the **magnetic deviation**. Knowing the deviation is important if you are using a compass to find your way in an area with few landmarks, such as a forest.

The direction of Earth's magnetic field is usually not perfectly horizontal. If you had a compass needle that could turn in any direction—north, south, east, west, up, or down—you would find that it would point generally northward but also somewhat upward or downward. The **magnetic dip** angle measures the amount that the field at a place points up or down. Together, magnetic deviation and magnetic dip describe the direction of the lines of force of Earth's magnetic field in your location.

Spectacular effects of Earth's magnetic field can be seen near the poles. Particles from the sun are drawn toward the poles and zip through the atmosphere, producing colorful **auroras** in the night sky.

The magnetized needle of a compass always points toward Earth's north magnetic pole. Hikers can use compasses to find out the direction in which they are traveling.

Earth is surrounded by a magnetic field, with poles that are different from our planet's geographic poles. That difference is called magnetic deviation.

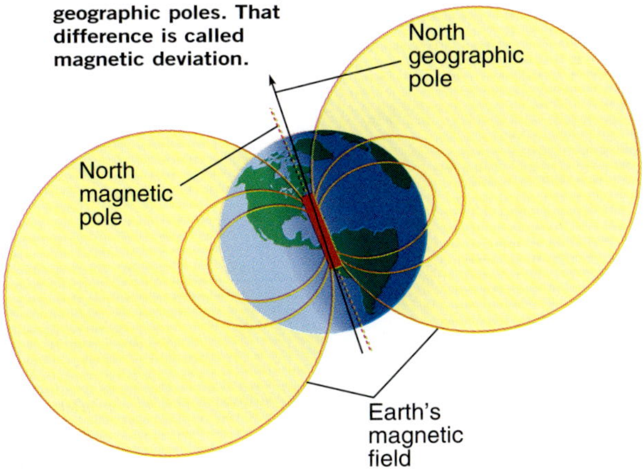

MAGNETISM AND ELECTRICITY

As scientists in the 1700's and 1800's began to study magnetism and electricity, they discovered many similarities between the two. Just as magnets have north and south poles, electricity has positive and negative charges. Just as two north or two south magnetic poles repel each other, so do two positive or two negative electric charges. And just as a north and a south magnetic pole attract each other, so do a positive and a negative electric charge.

Scientists studied the strength of those attractive or repulsive forces and learned that it depends on the distance between the charges or poles. They also learned that the strength of those forces depends on the amount of charge or the closeness of the lines of force at the poles. For both electricity and magnetism, they came up with similar mathematical formulas to describe what they observed.

They found one important difference between electricity and magnetism. Positive and negative electrical charges can exist sepa-

The northern lights, or aurora borealis, occur when particles from the sun are drawn toward Earth's north magnetic pole and zip through the atmosphere.

rately. An object or particle can have a positive or a negative charge. Magnets, however, always have both a north and south pole. If you break a magnet in the middle, you will create two magnets. The half with the original north pole now has a south pole at its end of the break. The half with the original south pole now has a north pole at its end of the break. A large magnet is made up of many small magnets with their north and south poles aligned. A magnet is sometimes called a dipole ("di" is from the Greek word for "two") because it must have two poles. Scientists continue to look for isolated north or south poles, called **magnetic monopoles** ("mono" is from the Greek word for "one"). However, no monopoles have yet been found.

Electric Motors and Generators

In the early 1800's, scientists began applying their knowledge of the relationships between electricity and magnetism to make useful devices. In 1820, Danish physicist Hans Christian Oersted discovered that an electric current passing through a wire near a compass would cause the compass needle to move. The current created a magnetic field that circled the wire. Soon after that, French scientist André Marie Ampère developed the first **electromagnet**—a magnet produced by electricity—by wrapping a current-carrying wire into a coil. In 1821, the English scientist Michael Faraday invented the electric motor. He used the magnetic

See For Yourself

How to Make an Electromagnet

You can turn an ordinary nail into an electromagnet using only an iron nail, an insulated metal wire with exposed metal ends, and a household battery, such as a 9-volt battery (a type used in some transistor radios).

Step 1: Make sure the nail is unmagnetized by bringing its head and its point close to the north pole of a compass. If both ends attract the north pole, then you know the nail is not magnetized.

Step 2: Wrap the insulated metal wire around the nail in a spiral, and connect one of its exposed metal ends to the battery's positive terminal and the other to the negative terminal for a few seconds. As long as the current is flowing in it, the wire will be an electromagnet.

Step 3: Remove the wire's ends from the battery and slide the nail out of the coil. If you were successful in magnetizing the nail, one end of it will attract the north pole of the compass, and the other end will repel it.

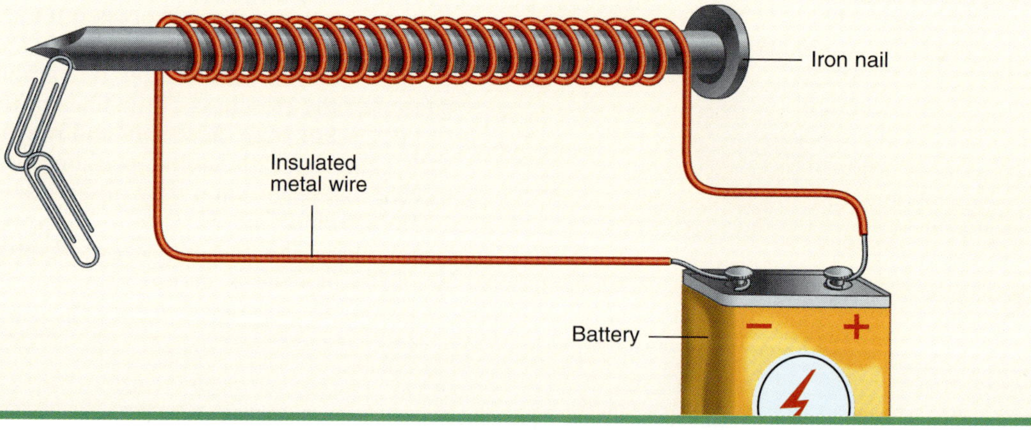

force between a wire carrying a current and a magnet to produce rotary motion. The motor turned electrical energy into mechanical energy.

In 1831, Faraday discovered a way to convert mechanical energy into electrical energy.

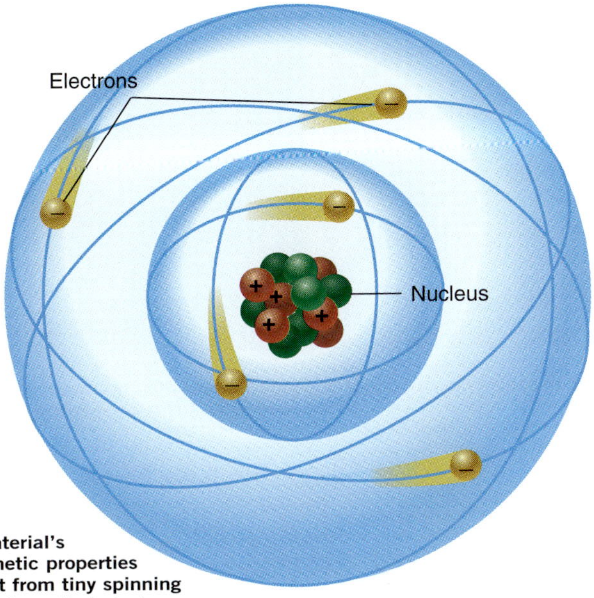

A material's magnetic properties result from tiny spinning particles called electrons, which orbit a nucleus at the center of each atom.

He showed that moving a coil of wire through a magnetic field would cause an electric current to flow through the wire. That discovery paved the way for the invention of the electric generator.

Magnetism and Light

In 1865, Scottish physicist James Clerk Maxwell made a momentous discovery about the relationship between electricity and magnetism. He produced a new set of equations describing the two forces as one force called **electromagnetism**. Maxwell's equations predicted the existence of waves of energy called **electromagnetic waves** that would travel through empty space at a particular speed. When he compared that predicted speed with the measured speed of light, they were nearly the same. Could light be an electromagnetic wave? Maxwell said yes. Furthermore, he said, many other electromagnetic waves would exist. Maxwell's prediction was correct.

MAGNETISM AND MATTER

By the end of the 1800's, scientists understood the basic relationships between electricity and magnetism, but they did not know where the forces came from. From chemistry, they knew that matter was made up of tiny particles called **atoms**. However, in the late 1800's and early 1900's, they discovered that atoms were made up of even tinier particles. Furthermore, these particles appeared to have certain magnetic and electric properties.

Magnetism of Atoms

Scientists soon discovered that the magnetism of a substance comes mainly from particles called **electrons**. Inside a substance's atoms, negatively charged electrons orbit positively charged centers called **nuclei** (singular: nucleus). Orbiting electrons produce a very weak "orbital" magnetism, just as an electrical current in a wire produces a magnetic field. Orbiting electrons also act as if they were tiny spinning balls of negative charge, creating a stronger type of magnetism called **spin**. Each orbit can be occupied by no more than two electrons, one with its spin in the same direction as the orbital magnetism and one with its spin in the opposite direction. In most atoms, electrons pair off, leaving little magnetism overall. In certain atoms, such as iron, a few orbits have only one electron. These unpaired electrons make the atoms magnetic.

The atoms of most solid materials are arranged in a repeating pattern called a crystal. Even if the atoms are magnetic, the crystal may not be. The atoms may line up so that the magnetism of one atom is opposite to its neighbor's. However, when the atoms tend to align with one another, the material is powerfully magnetic.

Magnetic Domains

A magnetic material does not always show its magnetism. Sometimes you have to study it very closely. Then you will discover it is made up of many small regions, called **domains**, where the magnetic fields of the atoms point in the same direction. However, not all

Did you know that...

some living creatures can detect and use Earth's magnetic field to survive? Some migratory birds have small magnetically sensitive structures in their heads. Scientists believe these structures help the birds find their way between their winter and summer homes. And certain bacteria produce needle-shaped crystals of **magnetite**, a magnetic form of iron oxide, within their bodies. Those crystals enable them to follow magnetic lines of force through the mud to find the nutrients they need for life. Similar, but much smaller, crystals of magnetite have been found in a meteorite that most scientists believe was once part of the planet Mars. Those crystals and other findings within the extraterrestrial rock have led some scientists to believe that bacteria once lived—and may still live—on Mars.

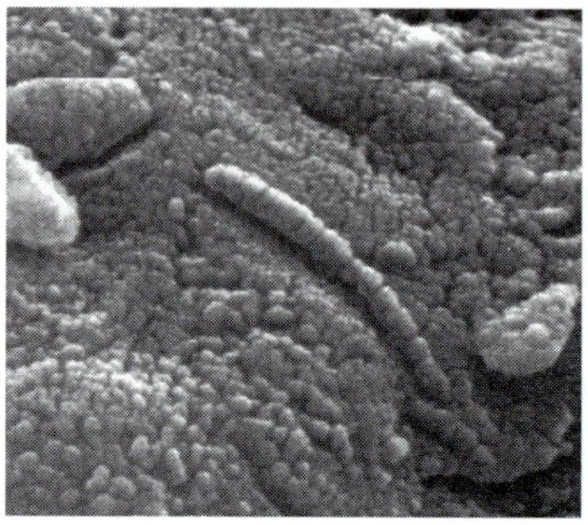

Left: **A Martian meteorite was found to contain magnetite crystals, perhaps produced by what appear to be fossilized bacteria.** ***Right:*** **Snow geese may sense Earth's magnetic field to guide them during migration.**

a material's domains have their fields pointing in the same direction. Often, the magnetism of one domain cancels out the magnetism of another, and the material is said to be unmagnetized. By putting the material in a strong external magnetic field, you can magnetize it. Magnetizing makes the different magnetisms of a material's domains line up with the external field.

Unmagnetized metals have tiny areas, called domains, whose magnetic fields point in many directions. A strong magnet magnetizes a metal by making these fields line up.

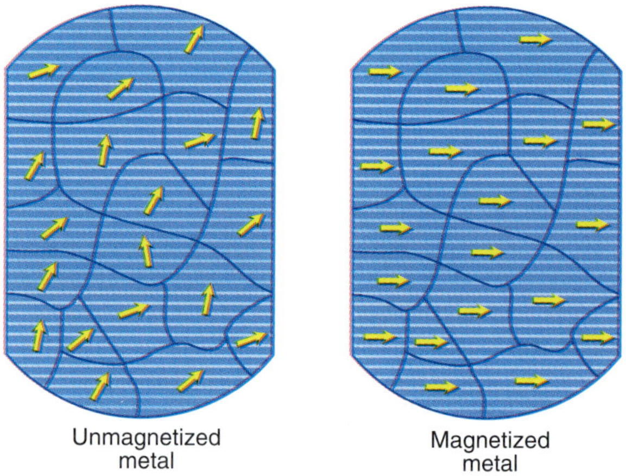

TYPES OF MAGNETS

Magnets and magnetic materials are often divided into two classes: **permanent magnets** and **electromagnets**. Permanent magnets are made from materials that remain magnetized even after they are removed from a magnetic field. Although iron is the best-known type of permanent magnet, many other substances can be magnetic. The most powerful magnetic substance known is a chemical compound combining the element neodymium with iron and the very light element boron. The compound produces a magnetic field hundreds of times stronger than a similar piece of magnetic iron.

Electromagnets are coils of wire that become magnetic when electricity passes through them. Sometimes the coils are wrapped around the easily magnetized core of a permanent magnet to increase their strength. Electromagnets are particularly useful because the shape and strength of their magnetic fields can be easily controlled.

To create a very strong field, a very large current is required. Unfortunately, in a coil of normal wire, a large current uses a great amount of energy and produces a lot of heat. To eliminate that problem, the most powerful electromagnets—and the most powerful magnets of any kind—use coils made of a **superconductor**. A superconductor is a material that carries electricity without any loss of energy. All known superconductors work only at extremely low temperatures, so superconducting coils must be kept chilled in frigid fluids such as liquid helium.

MODERN MAGNETIC DEVICES

Magnets and magnetic materials are used in many modern devices. Although high magnetic field strength can be very desirable, sometimes less strength is needed. Refrigerator magnets, which are usually made of a magnetic substance called ferrite embedded in plastic, must have a strong enough field to stick to the steel of a refrigerator door but not so strong that you cannot remove them. To store a sound or television picture, a magnetic audiotape or videotape must be made of a material that can have its magnetization changed easily by passing close to a small electromagnet, called the recording head.

One of the most important modern magnetic devices is the disk drive used to store information in a computer. The surface of the disk is coated with a special magnetic material that can have microscopic domains. The information is stored as a pattern of magnetic field directions in those domains. A nearly microscopic electromagnet is used to "write," or create, that pattern, and an even smaller magnetically sensitive device is used to "read," or detect, a pattern that was previously written. New magnetic information storage materials are constantly being developed. Some have domains so tiny that the entire set of *The New Book of Knowledge* could be stored on a spot no larger than a pinhead.

Another very important modern device is the **magnetic resonance imaging (MRI)** machine. It has improved medical care by creating detailed images of organs and structures inside the human body, especially the brain. These images would be difficult or impossible to obtain with X rays, and MRI does not damage body cells as X rays can in high doses. MRI uses the magnetic properties of the nuclei of atoms in the body.

MAGNETISM IN THE FUTURE

In some parts of the world, **magnetic levitation (maglev)** trains float above their rails, lifted by the force between electromagnets in the train and electromagnets below the tracks. Some of these trains use superconducting magnets; others use powerful normal electromagnets. These trains can travel smoothly at speeds up to 300 miles (about 480 kilometers) per hour—half the usual speed of a jet plane.

This maglev train in Sydney, Australia, uses very powerful electromagnets to levitate, or float, above its track and travel smoothly.

Maglev trains may be an important part of our transportation future. Since they can travel to the heart of a downtown area, just as regular trains do, people may find maglev travel ultimately quicker and more convenient than taking a plane.

In every other area where magnets and magnetism are important today, advances in technology will make them even more important in the future. Those ancient sailors would be astonished to see all the places magnetism will take us—and so, no doubt, will we.

ALFRED B. (FRED) BORTZ
Author, science books for children

CUBISM

Pablo Picasso's ***Woman with a Mandolin*** **(1914) has the flat shapes that are characteristic of cubism.**

Cubism is one of the most important art movements of the twentieth century. Cubist artists transformed the way typical subjects—people, places, and things—were presented in art by breaking them up into basic geometric shapes and patterns. Cubists also departed from traditional painting methods by depicting figures and objects from several different viewpoints at once. For example, a woman might be painted with three eyes in order to show her face from the front and the side at the same time. (This style of painting, in which subjects are distorted and difficult to recognize, is known as **abstract** art.)

Spanish artist Pablo Picasso and French artist Georges Braque invented many of cubism's characteristics. Between 1908 and 1914, these two artists worked closely together in France to create a new style of painting that went beyond realism. For centuries, artists had used perspective, a technique that gives a painting the appearance of depth, to render subjects as they appear in the real, three-dimensional world. Picasso and Braque, however, wanted to emphasize the flat, two-dimensional surface of the canvas. So they began dividing their subjects into flat surfaces, or planes. Their collaboration led to two phases of cubism: analytic and synthetic.

Analytic cubism began about 1910. During this phase, Picasso and Braque made paintings that were more about thought than emotion, using neutral colors such as black, brown, gray, and white rather than their usual vivid colors. They obscured their subjects in a puzzle of broken planes that seem to shift before one's eyes. In a typical analytic cubist work, such as Picasso's *Ma Jolie* (*Woman with a Zither or Guitar*, 1911–12), it is a challenge to find the subjects themselves. It takes a keen eye to piece together the musician's triangular head at the top of the painting with her bent arm strumming just a fragment of the instrument at the painting's center.

Synthetic cubism emerged in 1912. Now Picasso and Braque's subjects are easier to identify because they appear as flatter, more colorful shapes. In Picasso's *Woman with a Mandolin* (1914), which has the same subject matter as *Ma Jolie*, the woman and instrument are more visible—even though she has two overlapping faces. During this phase, Picasso and Braque also glued cloth, newspaper, and other materials directly onto their canvases. This technique became known as **collage**, derived from the French verb *coller*, "to glue."

By 1913, many cubist innovations were being tested by other artists. In Paris, French painters Fernand Léger and Robert Delaunay, Spanish-born artist Juan Gris, and Russian-born sculptor Alexander Archipenko made significant contributions to cubism. In Italy, a group of artists calling themselves futurists borrowed the shifting, broken shapes of analytic cubism to suggest the motion of machinery in their art. In Russia, an art movement led by Kazimir Malevich took cubism's abstraction of forms even further. These artists, who were known as suprematists, chose to paint only basic geometric shapes such as squares and circles.

Picasso and Braque's collaboration ended when Braque was called to fight in World War I (1914–18). But they and numerous other artists continued to devise new styles based on cubism into the second half of the 1900s. In fact, many cubist techniques are still used today, especially collage. Pasting real materials onto a canvas or paper has become a popular activity for artists of all ages.

Cheri L. Coffin
The Museum of Modern Art

CLIMATE

This Italian coastal town enjoys a mild climate because of its latitude and the effects of the nearby sea.

Climate is the overall state of weather in a region over a long period of time. The weather at a specific place may be cold and rainy on a particular day. But that place may have a warm, dry, sunny climate. This is because weather and climate are not the same. Weather comes from the temporary, often changing conditions in the atmosphere. Climate is the combination of weather conditions over a period of many years. Scientists learn about the climate of a place by studying its weather patterns and the types of plants that grow there. These scientists are called **climatologists**, and the study of climate is known as **climatology**.

Temperature and precipitation (moisture that falls to the ground, such as rain or snow) are the two most important weather conditions that describe the climate of a place. Other conditions include humidity (moisture that stays in the air), cloudiness, fog, storms, sunshine, and wind.

CAUSES OF DIFFERENT CLIMATES

What makes one place hot all year long while another place is cold, one place a desert and another place a rain forest, one place sunny and another place cloudy? The differences in climate from place to place are caused by **climatic controls**. The most important climatic control is latitude. Other major climatic controls are altitude, land and water bodies, prevailing winds, pressure centers, ocean currents, mountains, and urbanization.

Latitude

The main factor that determines the climate of any place is its distance from the equator. This distance is measured in degrees of latitude. Near the equator (0° latitude), the sun is never very far from being directly overhead at noon. Near the North Pole (90° north latitude) and the South Pole (90° south latitude), the sun is never very high in the sky. Regions close to the equator remain warm throughout the year. At higher latitudes, farther away from the equator, there are colder climates. In the middle latitudes, the sun is high in the sky in summer and low in winter. So places like Portland, Maine (about 45° north latitude), have warm summers and cold winters.

Altitude

Temperature typically decreases as altitude increases. At high altitudes the air is less dense, and it does not absorb and hold as much heat. On the average, the temperature drops about 3.5° Fahrenheit for every 1,000 feet (2° Celsius for every 300 meters). Thus snow may fall on a cold mountaintop and stay there without melting while rain falls in the warmer valley below.

Land and Water Bodies

Land warms up rapidly when the air is warm and cools off rapidly when the temperature drops. But large bodies of water change temperature more slowly. When air temperatures rise, land heats up more quickly than nearby water. Because the water is cooler, it has a cooling effect on the land. Similarly, when air temperatures fall, land cools down more quickly than nearby water. In this case, the warmer water has a warming effect on the land. As a result, seacoasts usually have milder winters and cooler summers than mid-continental places with little water.

Prevailing Winds

Winds affect climate because they carry heat and moisture. Winds that blow from the same direction most of the time are called

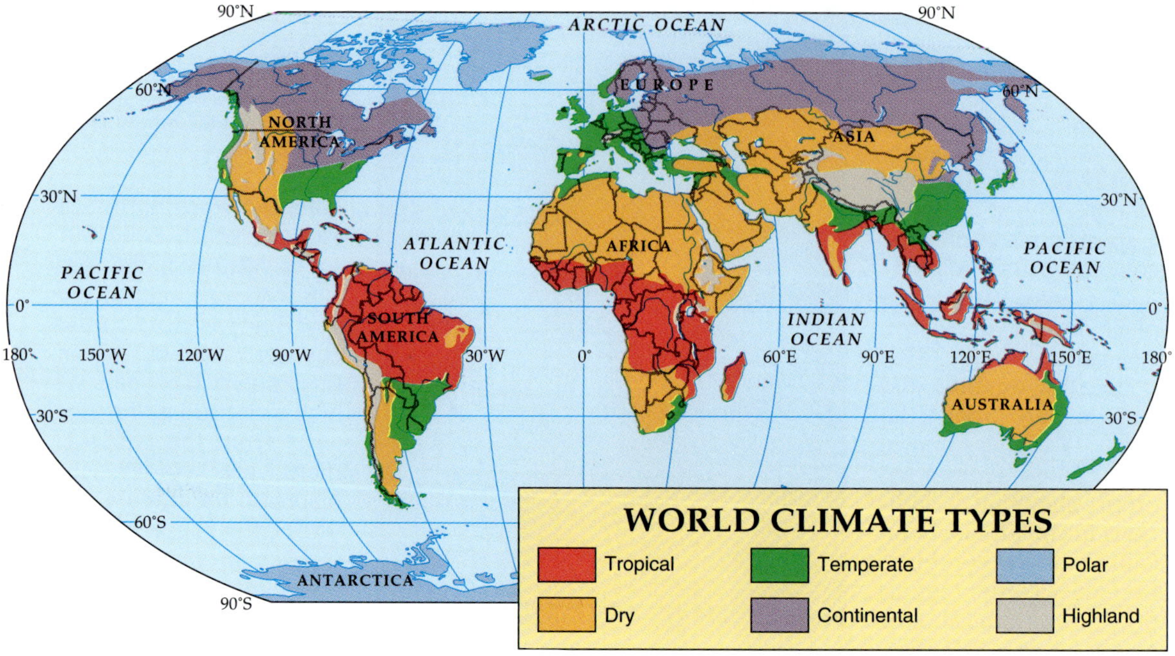

Climates of the world can be classified according to their latitudes and the plants that grow there. The descriptions of climate types below are based on a system developed in the early 1900's by Wladimir Köppen, a German climatologist and amateur botanist.

Tropical Climates

Between 20° south latitude and 20° north latitude are three types of tropical climates. A **tropical wet** climate (near the equator or on windward mountainsides) is warm and rainy all year. This gives rise to dense rain forests. Places farther from the equator have a **tropical savanna** climate. Tall grasses and scattered trees grow here because the climate is too dry for forests. A region with a **monsoon** climate has both a wet and a dry season.

Dry Climates

Between 20 and 40° latitude, in both the northern and southern hemispheres, are three types of dry climates. Toward the equator are warm **subtropical deserts** where little vegetation can grow. These can be found in Northern Africa, the Middle East, the coast of Peru, and central Australia. Farther from the equator are cooler **mid-latitude deserts**, such as the Gobi desert in Asia and the deserts of the southwestern United States. On the leeward side of mountains are **steppe** climates, where short grasses grow. Steppes are found in the high plains of the United States from Montana to Texas, as well as western Argentina and parts of central Asia and southeastern Europe.

Temperate Climates

Between 30 and 60° latitude in both hemispheres are three types of mild, or temperate, climates. These generally occur in the mid-latitudes where prevailing westerly winds blow. Rainy **marine west coast** climates can be found on the North American west coast, north of California, as well as in much of northwestern Europe. Closer to the equator lie the **Mediterranean** climates. Named for the southern European region, climates here have dry summers. Coastal California and New Zealand also have Mediterranean climates.

Continental Climates

These climates occur between 40 and 70° north latitude across vast areas of the major continents—North America, Europe, and Asia. In contrast to temperate climates, continental climates have greater extremes in temperatures, with cold winters and warm summers. Much of the northern United States eastward from the Dakotas, southern Canada, and parts of eastern Europe have **humid continental** climates. Locations farther north are colder and have less precipitation in all seasons. Even farther north lie **sub-Arctic** climates, which have generally less forest growth than more southerly climates do.

Polar Climates

These climates occur from roughly 60° north and south latitude to the poles. The **tundra**, where the climate is too cold for trees, is home to grasses, mosses, and lichens. Greenland and Antarctica have a **polar** climate, where great ice caps exist because of year-round temperatures below freezing.

Highland Climates

Unlike the other five types of climate, which are determined largely by latitude, highland climates are due to the effects of altitude. These climates are cooler than the climates of the surrounding lowlands. Highland climates are found on the highest mountains of the world, even on the equator. In the mid-latitudes and tropics, climates can vary greatly with altitude. This gives rise to different kinds of vegetation growing in zones up the slopes of mountains to the permanent snowfields.

Left: Northern Pakistan has a highland climate, with various types of vegetation at different altitudes. *Right:* Areas of Alaska have a polar climate, in which it is too cold for trees to grow.

prevailing winds. For example, the prevailing westerlies (winds that blow from the west) pick up moisture in the air over the central plains of the United States and carry that moisture in an eastward direction. This shift leads to less rainfall and short grasses in the western parts of Texas, Oklahoma, and Kansas. Rainfall is greater toward the Mississippi River, where forests and tall grasses are more common.

Pressure Centers

Pressure centers are large parts of the atmosphere where the pressure is much lower or much higher than in surrounding areas. Low-pressure centers usually cause stormy weather. High-pressure centers usually bring clear, sunny weather. If low- or high-pressure centers tend to form or move over an area at certain times of the year, this weather pattern helps determine the climate of that area. Heavy rains in warm belts of low pressure near the equator create a tropical rain forest climate. Dense tropical forests grow well in this climate. High-pressure centers are the primary cause of tropical desert climates like those of central Australia or the Sahara in northern Africa.

Ocean Currents

Ocean currents are great streams of water moving in the oceans. Some currents carry warm water to cool regions. Others carry cool water to warm regions. These currents affect climate in many parts of the world. The Gulf Stream, for example, is a warm ocean current. It carries warm water from the western tropical Atlantic toward the coasts of northwestern Europe. As a result, winters in western France are warmer than winters in the state of Maine in the United States, even though both are at about the same latitude.

Mountains

Mountains form barriers that affect the movement of prevailing winds. As winds approach mountains, air is forced to rise. The air uses energy to rise and becomes colder in the process. If the rising air contains enough water vapor, the vapor cools and condenses to form clouds and precipitation. This creates a "rain shadow" effect: More precipitation falls on the **windward** side of mountains (the

WONDER QUESTION

How can scientists tell what climates were like a long time ago?

People have been keeping accurate records of temperature and rainfall for only the past hundred years or so. To learn about ancient climates, scientists turn to nature's own weather records. For example, cross sections of tree trunks reveal alternating wide and narrow rings in the wood. These rings, which reflect the changing growing conditions from season to season, can provide clues about the temperatures of a place hundreds of years ago. Fossils of tiny organisms from lakebeds and ice from glaciers can provide clues about temperature and precipitation thousands of years ago.

Shifts in rainfall and vegetation growth can bring about changes in climate. Such changes can turn grasslands into deserts, similar to the one above.

side against which the wind blows) than on the **leeward** side (the side protected from the wind). A clear example of this effect is the two different climates on either side of the Sierra Nevada mountains in California. The windward slopes on the west side are covered with trees. The leeward slopes on the east side have scrubby vegetation.

Urbanization

Scientists have discovered that as cities and urban areas grow, local temperatures rise. This is partly caused by the greater amount of concrete and asphalt, which absorb the sun's heat. The result is the creation of "urban climates" that may be different from the surrounding climates.

CHANGES IN CLIMATE

Climates have changed throughout Earth's history. Those changes have had major impacts on nature and people as well. Large populations of people and animals have migrated to new locations because of changes in rainfall patterns and vegetation growth. This occurs especially in areas called **transition zones**, which lie between one type of climate and another. During the 1970s, drought in northern Africa caused people to flee drying areas for nearby grasslands.

There are many theories that attempt to explain climatic changes. Among the possible causes are changes in the amount of energy put out by the sun, changes in Earth's orbit, or changes in the tilt of Earth's axis. Some scientists believe that dark patches on the sun, known as **sunspots**, are responsible for certain cycles of drought.

Dust in the atmosphere can lower the amount of solar energy that reaches Earth's surface, causing temperatures to drop. Volcanic eruptions can push ash high into the atmosphere. Large clouds of dust can also be lifted into the atmosphere by meteor impacts. Ancient impacts could have caused major changes in Earth's climates, resulting in the extinction of dinosaurs and other creatures.

Climate is also influenced by the amount of certain gases in the atmosphere. The two most important gases are carbon dioxide (produced in part by volcanoes, forest fires, and other natural processes) and water vapor. Decaying organic matter produces another gas, methane. These three gases trap part of the heat generated by incoming sunlight and prevent that heat from radiating back into outer space. This is known as the **greenhouse effect** because the gases in the atmosphere act somewhat like a very large glass greenhouse. Without the greenhouse effect, Earth would be too cold to support life.

Since the early 1980s, however, scientists have gathered evidence indicating that temperatures are gradually rising around the world. Many scientists believe that this trend, known as **global warming**, may be caused by the burning of fossil fuels in homes, factories, and automobiles. These fuels (coal, oil, and gasoline) release carbon dioxide and other greenhouse gases when burned. Over the past 200 years or so, the release of these gases may have been so great that they have enhanced Earth's natural greenhouse effect.

Changes in the land and oceans are other possible causes of climatic change. Geologists have found evidence of shifts in Earth's crust. The movement of continents and the building up and wearing down of mountains would change temperature, rainfall, and wind patterns. A difference in the strength or direction of ocean currents could also be a factor in widespread changes of climate.

Several factors probably have acted together to change climates during Earth's history. Climatologists are still searching for complete answers. If they can learn more about how climates change, people may be able to plan for those changes in the future.

H. MICHAEL MOGIL
Meteorologist

SUPPLEMENT

DEATHS

Abzug, Bella. Former Democratic U.S. Representative from New York and feminist leader; died on March 31, at the age of 77. Abzug was a forceful advocate of women's rights and a strong opponent of the Vietnam War. A colorful character, she was known for her wide-brimmed hats, loud, raspy voice, and outspoken opinions. She served three terms in Congress, from 1971 to 1976.

Autry, Gene. American entertainer; died on October 2, at the age of 91. The genial Autry was the first singing movie cowboy. Beginning in the 1930s, he appeared in numerous films and later on radio and TV. Autry recorded 635 songs, including his theme song, "Back in the Saddle Again," and the popular Christmas song "Rudolph the Red-Nosed Reindeer."

Bono, Sonny. U.S. Representative from California and entertainer; died on January 5, at the age of 62. Bono achieved stardom in the 1960s as part of the husband-and-wife singing duo Sonny and Cher. Their most successful single was "I Got You Babe." *The Sonny and Cher Comedy Hour* was a popular television variety show that ran from 1971 to 1974, when Sonny and Cher divorced. Bono, a Republican, was first elected to Congress in 1994.

Bradley, Tom. Former mayor of Los Angeles, California; died on September 29, at the age of 80. Bradley, a Democrat, was the first African American to be elected mayor of Los Angeles. An immensely popular figure, Bradley served in office for 20 years from 1973 to 1993—an era in which Los Angeles experienced enormous growth and became the second largest city in the nation.

Bridges, Lloyd. American actor; died on March 10, at the age of 85. During his 57-year career, the rugged Bridges was a familiar presence in film and television. He gained the most recognition for his starring role as a former Navy frogman on the television series *Sea Hunt* (1957–61).

Caray, Harry. American baseball announcer; died on February 18, at the age of about 80. The boisterous Caray was beloved by baseball fans for his raucous play-by-play broadcasts. During his 50-year career, he announced games for the St. Louis Cardinals, the Oakland A's, the Chicago White Sox, and the Chicago Cubs.

Goldwater, Barry. Former U.S. Senator from Arizona; died on May 29, at the age of 89. Goldwater, a Republican, served in the Senate from 1953 to 1964 and 1969 to 1987. Blunt

Gene Autry

Roy Rogers (with Dale Evans)

Florence Griffith Joyner

and outspoken throughout his career, he was one of the architects of the modern conservative movement in the United States. Goldwater was defeated in a landslide by President Lyndon B. Johnson in the 1964 U.S. presidential election.

Griffith Joyner, Florence. American sprinter; died on September 21, at the age of 38. Called FloJo, Griffith Joyner was known as the fastest woman in the world. She won three gold medals and one silver at the 1988 Summer Olympics; and a silver medal at the 1984 Games. Her world records in the 100- and 200-meter dashes still stand. Griffith Joyner was admired not only for her lightning speed, but also for her beauty and humanitarian work.

Kurosawa, Akira. Japanese film director, died on September 6, at the age of 88. A master storyteller, Kurosawa was considered one of the most important and influential directors in film history. His film *Rashomon* won an Academy Award for best foreign film in 1951.

Lewis, Shari. American entertainer; died on August 2, at the age of 65. Lewis, a skilled ventriloquist and puppeteer, delighted children for four decades with her hand-puppets Lamb Chop, Hush Puppy, and Charlie Horse. During her long television career, Lewis won 12 Emmy Awards. Among her TV series were *The Shari Lewis Show* (1960–63) and *Lamb Chop's Play-Along* (1991–97).

Marshall, E. G. American actor, died on August 24, at the age of 84. A character actor who often portrayed authoritative figures, Marshall appeared in hundreds of stage, film, and television dramas. He won renown for his Emmy Award-winning role as Lawrence Preston, the crusading lawyer on the television series *The Defenders* (1961–65).

McDowall, Roddy. British-born actor; died on October 3, at the age of 70. A versatile character actor, McDowall's career spanned more than 60 years on stage, screen, and television. As a child star, he appeared in the classic films *How Green Was My Valley* (1941) and *Lassie Come Home* (1943). As an adult, his most popular role was as the chimpanzee Cornelius in the *Planet of the Apes* film series.

O'Sullivan, Maureen. Irish-born actress; died on June 23, at the age of 87. O'Sullivan was a leading actress of the 1930s and 1940s, appearing in more than 60 films. She was best remembered for playing Jane in a series of six Tarzan jungle-adventure movies between 1932 and 1942.

Shari Lewis

Sinatra, Frank. One of the world's top entertainers; died on May 14, at the age of 82. Known affectionately as "Ol' Blue Eyes," "The Voice," and "Chairman of the Board," Sinatra had millions of fans. In the 1940s, when he was a skinny young crooner from Hoboken, New Jersey, thousands of these screaming fans attended his performances. Sinatra's unique musical phrasing and clear baritone voice continued to thrill listeners for more than 50 years. Because of Sinatra's extraordinary voice, his fans believed that he was America's greatest pop singer.

Also a popular movie star, Sinatra appeared in musicals such as *On the Town* (1949) and *Guys and Dolls* (1955), and in dramas such as *The Man with the Golden Arm* (1955) and *From Here to Eternity* (1953), for which he won an Oscar for best supporting actor.

His recordings sold millions of copies. And his appearances in nightclubs and in concerts continued to attract sell-out audiences until his retirement in 1995.

Powell, Lewis F., Jr., U.S. Supreme Court justice; died on August 25, at the age of 90. Powell served on the Supreme Court from 1972 to 1987. He was widely regarded as a centrist, who served as a balance between the conservative and liberal sides of the Court. Powell often cast the deciding vote in controversial cases.

Robbins, Jerome. American choreographer and director; died on July 29, at the age of 79. Noted for his dazzling orginality, Robbins was a giant in the worlds of ballet and musical theater. Robbins choreographed many classic Broadway musicals, including *The King and I* (1951), *West Side Story* (1957), and *Fiddler on the Roof* (1964).

Rogers, Roy. American entertainer; died on July 6, at the age of 86. To his devoted fans Rogers was known as the "King of the Cowboys," a beloved hero who symbolized the American West. He appeared in movies and on television with his trusty horse Trigger and later with his wife and costar Dale Evans. His TV series, *The Roy Rogers Show* (1951–57), always ended with the signature song "Happy Trails to You."

Alan B. Shepard, Jr.

Flip Wilson

Shepard, Alan B., Jr., American astronaut; died on July 21, at the age of 74. Shepard was one of the original seven U.S. astronauts, known as the Mercury Seven. On May 5, 1961, aboard the *Freedom 7* space capsule, he became the first American launched into space. He later walked on the moon as the commander of the Apollo 14 mission in 1971.

Spock, Benjamin. American pediatrician and author; died on March 15, at the age of 94. One of the most influential childcare experts in the world, Dr. Spock took a relaxed approach toward childrearing that encouraged several generations of parents to trust their own instincts and use common sense. His book *Baby and Childcare,* first published in 1946, sold almost 50 million copies worldwide.

Wallace, George. Former governor of Alabama; died on September 13, at the age of 79. Wallace, a Democrat, was elected governor of Alabama four times—in 1962, 1970, 1974, and 1982. Early in his career, he became a national symbol of the fight to maintain racial segregation in the South. But in his later years he renounced segregation, and he won his last election as governor largely with black support. While campaigning for the presidency in 1972, Wallace was paralyzed by an assassin's bullet.

Wilson, Flip. American comedian; died on November 25, at the age of 64. The likable Wilson was the first African-American entertainer to host a successful weekly variety show on television—*The Flip Wilson Show* (1970–74). He was best known for creating outrageous characters such as the flamboyant Geraldine. Some of Wilson's trademark quips—like "the devil made me do it"—became national catchphrases.

Wynette, Tammy. American country music singer; died on April 6, at the age of 55. Known as "the first lady of country music," Wynette recorded more than 50 albums and sold more than 30 million records during her career. She was best known for her 1968 hit "Stand By Your Man."

Young, Robert. American actor; died on July 21, at the age of 91. The kindly Young was best known for portraying the patient and understanding father on the television series *Father Knows Best* (1954–60) and a compassionate doctor on *Marcus Welby, M.D.* (1969–76).

Youngman, Henny. American comedian; died on February 24, at the age of 91. Youngman entertained audiences for more than six decades with his rapid-fire delivery of one-line jokes and his horrendous violin playing.

Robert Young

INDEPENDENT NATIONS OF THE WORLD

NATION	CAPITAL	AREA (in sq mi)	POPULATION (estimate)	GOVERNMENT
Afghanistan	Kabul	250,000	24,800,000	The Taliban—Muslim fundamentalist group
Albania	Tirana	11,100	3,300,000	Rexhep Mejdani—president Pandeli Majko—premier
Algeria	Algiers	919,595	30,200,000	Liamine Zeroual—president
Andorra	Andorra la Vella	175	100,000	Marc Forne Molne—premier
Angola	Luanda	481,354	12,000,000	José Eduardo dos Santos—president
Antigua and Barbuda	St. John's	171	100,000	Lester Bird—prime minister
Argentina	Buenos Aires	1,068,297	36,100,000	Carlos Saúl Menem—president
Armenia	Yerevan	11,500	3,800,000	Robert Kocharyan—president
Australia	Canberra	2,967,895	18,700,000	John Howard—prime minister
Austria	Vienna	32,374	8,100,000	Thomas Klestil—president Viktor Klima—chancellor
Azerbaijan	Baku	33,500	7,700,000	Heydar A. Aliyev—president
Bahamas	Nassau	5,380	300,000	Hubert A. Ingraham—prime minister
Bahrain	Manama	240	600,000	Isa bin Salman al-Khalifa—head of state
Bangladesh	Dhaka	55,598	123,400,000	Shahabuddin Ahmed—president Sheik Hasina Wazed—prime minister
Barbados	Bridgetown	168	300,000	Owen Arthur—prime minister
Belarus	Minsk	80,154	10,200,000	Aleksandr Lukashenko—president
Belgium	Brussels	11,781	10,200,000	Albert II—king Jean-Luc Dehaene—premier
Belize	Belmopan	8,867	200,000	Manuel Esquivel—prime minister
Benin	Porto-Novo	43,484	6,000,000	Mathieu Kerekou—president
Bhutan	Thimbu	18,147	1,800,000	Jigme Singye Wangchuck—king
Bolivia	La Paz Sucre	424,165	8,000,000	Hugo Banzer Suarez—president
Bosnia and Herzegovina	Sarajevo	19,800	4,000,000	3-member presidency
Botswana	Gaborone	231,804	1,400,000	Festus Mogae—president
Brazil	Brasília	3,286,478	162,100,000	Fernando Henrique Cardoso—president
Brunei Darussalam	Bandar Seri Begawan	2,226	300,000	Hassanal Bolkiah—head of state
Bulgaria	Sofia	42,823	8,300,000	Petar Stoyanov—president Ivan Kostov—premier
Burkina Faso	Ouagadougou	105,869	11,300,000	Blaise Compaoré—president
Burma (Myanmar)	Rangoon	261,218	47,100,000	Than Shwe—head of government
Burundi	Bujumbura	10,747	5,500,000	Pierre Buyoya—president

NATION	CAPITAL	AREA (in sq mi)	POPULATION (estimate)	GOVERNMENT
Cambodia	Phnom Penh	69,898	10,800,000	Norodom Sihanouk—king Hun Sen—prime minister
Cameroon	Yaoundé	183,569	14,300,000	Paul Biya—president
Canada	Ottawa	3,851,809	30,300,000	Jean Chrétien—prime minister
Cape Verde	Praia	1,557	400,000	Antonio Mascarenhas Monteiro—president
Central African Republic	Bangui	240,535	3,400,000	Ange Patasse—president
Chad	N'Djamena	495,754	7,400,000	Idriss Deby—president
Chile	Santiago	292,257	14,800,000	Eduardo Frei Ruíz-Tagle—president
China	Beijing	3,705,390	1,242,500,000	Jiang Zemin—communist party secretary Zhu Rongji—premier
Colombia	Bogotá	439,736	38,600,000	Andrés Pastrana Arango—president
Comoros	Moroni	838	500,000	Tadjidine Ben Said Massonde—president
Congo (Zaire)	Kinshasa	905,565	49,000,000	Laurent Kabila—president
Congo Republic	Brazzaville	132,047	2,700,000	Denis Sassou-Nguesso—president
Costa Rica	San José	19,575	3,500,000	Miguel Angel Rodriguez—president
Croatia	Zagreb	21,829	4,200,000	Franjo Tudjman—president
Cuba	Havana	44,218	11,100,000	Fidel Castro—president
Cyprus	Nicosia	3,572	700,000	Glafcos Clerides—president
Czech Republic	Prague	30,469	10,300,000	Vaclav Havel—president Milos Zeman—premier
Denmark	Copenhagen	16,629	5,300,000	Margrethe II—queen Poul Nyrup Rasmussen—premier
Djibouti	Djibouti	8,494	700,000	Hassan Gouled Aptidon—president
Dominica	Roseau	290	100,000	Edison James—prime minister
Dominican Republic	Santo Domingo	18,816	8,300,000	Leonel Fernandez Reyna—president
Ecuador	Quito	109,483	12,200,000	Jamil Mahuad Witt—president
Egypt	Cairo	386,660	65,500,000	Mohammed Hosni Mubarak—president Kamal Ahmed al-Ganzouri—premier
El Salvador	San Salvador	8,124	5,800,000	Armando Calderón Sol—president
Equatorial Guinea	Malabo	10,831	400,000	Teodoro Obiang Nguema Mbasogo—president
Eritrea	Asmara	45,405	3,800,000	Issaias Afworki—president
Estonia	Tallinn	17,413	1,400,000	Lennart Meri—president
Ethiopia	Addis Ababa	426,372	58,400,000	Negasso Ghidada—president
Fiji	Suva	7,055	800,000	Kamisese Mara—president
Finland	Helsinki	130,120	5,200,000	Martti Ahtisaari—president Paavo Lipponen—premier
France	Paris	213,000	58,800,000	Jacques Chirac—president Lionel Jospin—premier
Gabon	Libreville	103,346	1,200,000	Omar Bongo—president
Gambia	Banjul	4,361	1,200,000	Yahya Jammeh—head of state
Georgia	Tbilisi	27,000	5,400,000	Eduard Shevardnadze—president

NATION	CAPITAL	AREA (in sq mi)	POPULATION (estimate)	GOVERNMENT
Germany	Berlin	137,744	82,300,000	Roman Herzog—president Gerhard Schröder—chancellor
Ghana	Accra	92,099	18,900,000	Jerry Rawlings—president
Greece	Athens	50,944	10,500,000	Costis Stefanopoulos—president Costas Simitis—premier
Grenada	St. George's	133	100,000	Keith Mitchell—prime minister
Guatemala	Guatemala City	42,042	11,600,000	Alvaro Arzu Irigoyen—president
Guinea	Conakry	94,926	7,500,000	Lansana Conté—president
Guinea-Bissau	Bissau	13,948	1,100,000	João Bernardo Vieira—president
Guyana	Georgetown	83,000	700,000	Janet Jagan—president
Haiti	Port-au-Prince	10,714	7,500,000	René Préval—president
Honduras	Tegucigalpa	43,277	5,900,000	Carlos Flores Facusse—president
Hungary	Budapest	35,919	10,100,000	Arpad Goncz—president Viktor Orbán—premier
Iceland	Reykjavik	39,768	300,000	Olafur Grimsson—president David Oddsson—premier
India	New Delhi	1,269,340	988,700,000	Kocheril Raman Narayanan—president Atal Bihari Vajpayee—prime minister
Indonesia	Jakarta	735,358	207,400,000	Bacharuddin Jusuf Habibie—president
Iran	Tehran	636,293	64,100,000	Ayatollah Ali Khamenei—religious leader Mohammed Khatami—president
Iraq	Baghdad	167,925	21,800,000	Saddam Hussein—president
Ireland	Dublin	27,136	3,700,000	Mary McAleese—president Bertie Ahern—prime minister
Israel	Jerusalem	8,019	6,000,000	Ezer Weizman—president Benjamin Netanyahu—prime minister
Italy	Rome	116,303	57,700,000	Oscar Luigi Scalfaro—president Massimo D'Alema—premier
Ivory Coast	Yamoussoukro	124,503	15,600,000	Henri Konan-Bédié—president
Jamaica	Kingston	4,244	2,600,000	Percival J. Patterson—prime minister
Japan	Tokyo	143,751	126,400,000	Akihito—emperor Keizo Obuchi—premier
Jordan	Amman	35,475	4,600,000	Hussein I—king Fayez al-Tarawnah—prime minister
Kazakhstan	Almaty	1,049,000	15,600,000	Nursultan A. Nazarbayev—president
Kenya	Nairobi	224,959	28,300,000	Daniel arap Moi—president
Kiribati	Tarawa	264	83,000	Teburoro Tito—president
Korea (North)	Pyongyang	46,540	22,200,000	Kim Jong Il—president Hong Song Nam—premier
Korea (South)	Seoul	38,025	46,400,000	Kim Dae Jung—president Kim Jong Pil—premier
Kuwait	Kuwait	6,880	1,900,000	Jabir al-Ahmad al-Sabah—head of state
Kyrgyzstan	Bishkek	76,641	4,700,000	Askar Akayev—president
Laos	Vientiane	91,429	5,300,000	Khamtai Siphandon—president Sisavat Keobounphan—premier
Latvia	Riga	24,600	2,400,000	Guntis Ulmanis—president

NATION	CAPITAL	AREA (in sq mi)	POPULATION (estimate)	GOVERNMENT
Lebanon	Beirut	4,015	4,100,000	Emile Lahoud—president Rafik al-Hariri—premier
Lesotho	Maseru	11,720	2,100,000	Letsie III—king Pakalitha Mosisili—premier
Liberia	Monrovia	43,000	2,800,000	Charles G. Taylor—president
Libya	Tripoli	679,362	5,700,000	Muammar el-Qaddafi—head of government
Liechtenstein	Vaduz	61	30,000	Hans Adam II—prince
Lithuania	Vilnius	25,174	3,700,000	Valdas Adamkus—president
Luxembourg	Luxembourg	998	400,000	Jean—grand duke Jean-Claude Juncker—premier
Macedonia	Skopje	9,928	2,000,000	Kiro Gligorov—president
Madagascar	Antananarivo	226,657	14,000,000	Didier Ratsiraka—president
Malawi	Lilongwe	45,747	9,800,000	Bakili Muluzi—president
Malaysia	Kuala Lumpur	127,317	22,200,000	Jaafar bin Abdul Rahman—king Mahathir bin Mohamad—prime minister
Maldives	Male	115	300,000	Maumoon Abdul Gayoom—president
Mali	Bamako	478,765	10,100,000	Alpha Oumar Konare—president
Malta	Valletta	122	400,000	Ugo Mifsud Bonnici—president Eddie Fenech Adami—prime minister
Marshall Islands	Majuro	70	100,000	Imata Kabua—president
Mauritania	Nouakchott	397,954	2,500,000	Maaouya Ould Sid Ahmed Taya—president
Mauritius	Port Louis	790	1,200,000	Cassam Uteem—president Navinchandra Ramgoolam—premier
Mexico	Mexico City	761,602	97,500,000	Ernesto Zedillo Ponce de León—president
Micronesia	Colonia	271	120,000	Jacob Nena—president
Moldova	Kishiniev	13,000	4,200,000	Petru Lucinschi—president
Monaco	Monaco-Ville	0.6	30,000	Rainier III—prince
Mongolia	Ulan Bator	604,248	2,400,000	Natsagiin Bagabandi—president
Morocco	Rabat	172,413	27,700,000	Hassan II—king Abderrahmane El Youssoufi—premier
Mozambique	Maputo	309,494	18,600,000	Joaquím A. Chissano—president
Namibia	Windhoek	318,260	1,600,000	Sam Nujoma—president
Nauru	Yaren District	8	11,000	Bernard Dowiyogo—president
Nepal	Katmandu	54,362	23,700,000	Birendra Bir Bikram Shah Deva—king Giriji Prasad Koirala—premier
Netherlands	Amsterdam	15,770	15,700,000	Beatrix—queen Willem Kok—premier
New Zealand	Wellington	103,736	3,800,000	Jenny Shipley—prime minister
Nicaragua	Managua	50,193	4,800,000	José Arnoldo Aleman—president
Niger	Niamey	489,190	10,100,000	Ibrahim Bare Mainassara—president
Nigeria	Abuja	356,667	121,800,000	Abdulsalam Abubakar—head of government
Norway	Oslo	125,056	4,400,000	Harald V—king Kjell Magne Bondevik—premier

NATION	CAPITAL	AREA (in sq mi)	POPULATION (estimate)	GOVERNMENT
Oman	Muscat	82,030	2,500,000	Qabus ibn Said—sultan
Pakistan	Islamabad	310,404	141,900,000	Mohammad Rafiq Tarar—president Nawaz Sharif—prime minister
Palau	Koror	192	20,000	Kuniwo Nakamura—president
Panama	Panama City	29,761	2,800,000	Ernesto Pérez Balladares—president
Papua New Guinea	Port Moresby	178,260	4,300,000	William Skate—prime minister
Paraguay	Asunción	157,047	5,200,000	Raúl Cubas Grau—president
Peru	Lima	496,222	26,100,000	Alberto Fujimori—president
Philippines	Manila	115,830	75,300,000	Joseph Estrada—president Gloria Macapagal-Arroyo—vice-president
Poland	Warsaw	120,725	38,700,000	Aleksander Kwasniewski—president Jerzy Buzek—premier
Portugal	Lisbon	35,553	10,000,000	Jorge Sampaio—president Antonio Guterres—premier
Qatar	Doha	4,247	500,000	Hamad bin Khalifa al-Thani—head of state
Romania	Bucharest	91,700	22,500,000	Emil Constantinescu—president Radu Vasile—premier
Russia	Moscow	6,600,000	146,900,000	Boris N. Yeltsin—president
Rwanda	Kigali	10,169	8,000,000	Pasteur Bizimungu—president
St. Kitts and Nevis	Basseterre	105	40,000	Denzil Douglas—prime minister
St. Lucia	Castries	238	100,000	Kenny Anthony—prime minister
St. Vincent and the Grenadines	Kingstown	150	100,000	James F. Mitchell—prime minister
San Marino	San Marino	24	30,000	Gabriele Gatti—head of state
São Tomé and Príncipe	São Tomé	372	200,000	Miguel Trovoada—president
Saudi Arabia	Riyadh	830,000	20,200,000	Fahd ibn Abdul-Aziz—king
Senegal	Dakar	75,750	9,000,000	Abdou Diouf—president
Seychelles	Victoria	107	100,000	France Albert René—president
Sierra Leone	Freetown	27,700	4,600,000	Ahmed Tejan Kabbah—president
Singapore	Singapore	224	3,900,000	Ong Teng Cheong—president Goh Chok Tong—prime minister
Slovak Republic	Bratislava	18,933	5,400,000	Michal Kovac—president
Slovenia	Ljubljana	7,819	2,000,000	Milan Kucan—president
Solomon Islands	Honiara	10,983	400,000	Bartholomew Ulufa'alu—prime minister
Somalia	Mogadishu	246,200	10,700,000	no functioning government
South Africa	Pretoria Cape Town Bloemfontein	471,444	38,900,000	Nelson Mandela—president
Spain	Madrid	194,896	39,400,000	Juan Carlos I—king José María Aznar—premier
Sri Lanka	Colombo	25,332	18,900,000	C. Bandaranaike Kumaratunga—president
Sudan	Khartoum	967,500	28,500,000	O. Hassan Ahmed al-Bashir—president

NATION	CAPITAL	AREA (in sq mi)	POPULATION (estimate)	GOVERNMENT
Suriname	Paramaribo	63,037	400,000	Jules Wijdenbosch—president
Swaziland	Mbabane	6,704	1,000,000	Mswati III—king
Sweden	Stockholm	173,731	8,900,000	Carl XVI Gustaf—king Goeran Persson—premier
Switzerland	Bern	15,941	7,100,000	Ruth Dreifuss—president
Syria	Damascus	71,498	15,600,000	Hafez al-Assad—president Mahmoud Zubi—premier
Taiwan	Taipei	13,885	21,700,000	Lee Teng-hui—president Vincent Siew—premier
Tajikistan	Dushanbe	55,250	6,100,000	Yakhyo Azimov—premier
Tanzania	Dar es Salaam	364,898	30,600,000	Benjamin Mkapa—president
Thailand	Bangkok	198,457	61,100,000	Bhumibol Adulyadej—king Chuan Leekpai—premier
Togo	Lomé	21,622	4,900,000	Gnassingbe Eyadema—president
Tonga	Nuku'alofa	270	108,000	Taufa'ahau Tupou IV—king Baron Vaea—premier
Trinidad & Tobago	Port of Spain	1,980	1,300,000	A.N.R. Robinson—president Basdeo Panday—prime minister
Tunisia	Tunis	63,170	9,500,000	Zine el-Abidine Ben Ali—president
Turkey	Ankara	301,381	64,800,000	Suleyman Demirel—president Mesut Yilmaz—prime minister
Turkmenistan	Ashkhabad	188,455	4,700,000	Saparmurad Niyazov—president
Tuvalu	Funafuti	10	10,000	Bikenibeu Paeniu—prime minister
Uganda	Kampala	91,134	21,000,000	Yoweri Museveni—president
Ukraine	Kiev	231,990	50,300,000	Leonid D. Kuchma—president
United Arab Emirates	Abu Dhabi	32,278	2,700,000	Zayed bin Sultan al-Nuhayyan—president
United Kingdom	London	94,226	59,100,000	Elizabeth II—queen Tony Blair—prime minister
United States	Washington, D.C.	3,618,467	270,200,000	William J. Clinton—president Albert A. Gore, Jr.—vice-president
Uruguay	Montevideo	68,037	3,200,000	Julio Sanguinetti—president
Uzbekistan	Tashkent	172,750	24,100,000	Islam A. Karimov—president
Vanuatu	Vila	5,700	200,000	Jean Marie Leye—president
Vatican City	Vatican City	0.17	1,000	John Paul II—pope
Venezuela	Caracas	352,143	23,300,000	Hugo Chávez—president-elect
Vietnam	Hanoi	128,402	78,500,000	La Kha Phieu—communist party secretary Phan Van Khai—premier
Western Samoa	Apia	1,097	200,000	Malietoa Tanumafili II—head of state
Yemen	Sana	203,849	15,800,000	Ali Abdullah Saleh—president Abd al-Karim Iryani—premier
Yugoslavia	Belgrade	39,390	10,600,000	Slobodan Milosevic—president Momir Bulatovic—premier
Zambia	Lusaka	290,585	9,500,000	Frederick Chiluba—president
Zimbabwe	Harare	150,333	11,000,000	Robert Mugabe—president

THE CONGRESS OF THE UNITED STATES

UNITED STATES SENATE

(55 Republicans, 45 Democrats)

Alabama
Richard C. Shelby (R)**
Jefferson B. Sessions (R)

Alaska
Ted Stevens (R)
Frank H. Murkowski (R)**

Arizona
John S. McCain III (R)**
John Kyl (R)

Arkansas
Tim Hutchinson (R)
Blanche L. Lincoln (D)*

California
Barbara Boxer (D)**
Dianne Feinstein (D)

Colorado
Ben Nighthorse Campbell (R)**
Wayne Allard (R)

Connecticut
Christopher J. Dodd (D)**
Joseph I. Lieberman (D)

Delaware
William V. Roth, Jr. (R)
Joseph R. Biden, Jr. (D)

Florida
Bob Graham (D)**
Connie Mack (R)

Georgia
Paul D. Coverdell (R)**
Max Cleland (D)

Hawaii
Daniel K. Inouye (D)**
Daniel K. Akaka (D)

Idaho
Larry E. Craig (R)
Mike Crapo (R)*

Illinois
Richard J. Durbin (D)
Peter Fitzgerald (R)*

Indiana
Richard G. Lugar (R)
Evan Bayh (D)*

Iowa
Charles E. Grassley (R)**
Thomas R. Harkin (D)

Kansas
Sam Brownback (R)**
Pat Roberts (R)

Kentucky
Mitch McConnell (R)
Jim Bunning (R)*

Louisiana
John B. Breaux (D)**
Mary L. Landrieu (D)

Maine
Olympia J. Snowe (R)
Susan Collins (R)

Maryland
Paul S. Sarbanes (D)
Barbara A. Mikulski (D)**

Massachusetts
Edward M. Kennedy (D)
John F. Kerry (D)

Michigan
Carl Levin (D)
Spencer Abraham (R)

Minnesota
Paul Wellstone (D)
Rod Grams (R)

Mississippi
Thad Cochran (R)
Trent Lott (R)

Missouri
Christopher S. Bond (R)**
John Ashcroft (R)

Montana
Max S. Baucus (D)
Conrad Burns (R)

Nebraska
Robert Kerrey (D)
Chuck Hagel (R)

Nevada
Harry Reid (D)**
Richard H. Bryan (D)

New Hampshire
Judd Gregg (R)**
Robert C. Smith (R)

New Jersey
Frank R. Lautenberg (D)
Robert G. Torricelli (D)

New Mexico
Pete V. Domenici (R)
Jeff Bingaman (D)

New York
Daniel P. Moynihan (D)
Charles E. Schumer (D)*

North Carolina
Jesse Helms (R)
John Edwards (D)*

North Dakota
Kent Conrad (D)
Byron L. Dorgan (D)**

Ohio
Mike DeWine (R)
George Voinovich (R)*

Oklahoma
Donald L. Nickles (R)**
James M. Inhofe (R)

Oregon
Gordon Smith (R)
Ron Wyden (D)**

Pennsylvania
Arlen Specter (R)**
Rick Santorum (R)

Rhode Island
John H. Chafee (R)
John Reed (D)

South Carolina
Strom Thurmond (R)
Ernest F. Hollings (D)**

South Dakota
Thomas A. Daschle (D)**
Tim Johnson (D)

Tennessee
Bill Frist (R)
Fred D. Thompson (R)

Texas
Phil Gramm (R)
Kay Bailey Hutchinson (R)

Utah
Orrin G. Hatch (R)
Robert F. Bennett (R)**

Vermont
Patrick J. Leahy (D)**
James M. Jeffords (R)

Virginia
John W. Warner (R)
Charles S. Robb (D)

Washington
Slade Gorton (R)
Patty Murray (D)**

West Virginia
Robert C. Byrd (D)
John D. Rockefeller IV (D)

Wisconsin
Herbert H. Kohl (D)
Russell D. Feingold (D)**

Wyoming
Craig Thomas (R)
Michael Enzi (R)

(D) Democrat
(R) Republican

* elected in 1998
** re-elected in 1998

UNITED STATES HOUSE OF REPRESENTATIVES
(222 Republicans, 211 Democrats, 1 Independent, 1 Vacancy)

Alabama
1. H. L. Callahan (R)
2. T. Everett (R)
3. B. Riley (R)
4. R. Aderholt (R)
5. B. Cramer (D)
6. S. Bachus (R)
7. E. Hilliard (D)

Alaska
D. Young (R)

Arizona
1. M. Salmon (R)
2. E. Pastor (D)
3. B. Stump (R)
4. J. Shadegg (R)
5. J. Kolbe (R)
6. J. D. Hayworth (R)

Arkansas
1. M. Berry (D)
2. V. F. Snyder (D)
3. A. Hutchinson (R)
4. J. Dickey (R)

California
1. M. Thompson (D)*
2. W. Herger (R)
3. D. Ose (R)*
4. J. T. Doolittle (R)
5. R. T. Matsui (D)
6. L. Woolsey (D)
7. G. Miller (D)
8. N. Pelosi (D)
9. B. Lee (D)
10. E. Tauscher (D)
11. R. Pombo (R)
12. T. Lantos (D)
13. F. H. Stark (D)
14. A. Eshoo (D)
15. T. Campbell (R)
16. Z. Lofgren (D)
17. S. Farr (D)
18. G. Condit (D)
19. G. Radanovich (R)
20. C. Dooley (D)
21. B. Thomas (R)
22. L. Capps (D)
23. E. Gallegly (R)
24. B. Sherman (D)
25. H. McKeon (R)
26. H. L. Berman (D)
27. J. E. Rogan (R)
28. D. Dreier (R)
29. H. A. Waxman (D)
30. X. Becerra (D)
31. M. G. Martinez (D)
32. J. C. Dixon (D)
33. L. Roybal-Allard (D)
34. G. Napolitano (D)*
35. M. Waters (D)
36. S. Kuykendall (R)*
37. J. Millender-McDonald (D)
38. S. Horn (R)
39. E. Royce (R)
40. J. Lewis (R)
41. G. Miller (R)*
42. G. E. Brown, Jr. (D)
43. K. Calvert (R)
44. M. Bono (R)
45. D. Rohrabacher (R)
46. L. Sanchez (D)
47. C. C. Cox (R)
48. R. Packard (R)
49. B. Bilbray (R)
50. B. Filner (D)
51. R. Cunningham (R)
52. D. Hunter (R)

Colorado
1. D. DeGette (D)
2. M. Udall (D)*
3. S. McInnis (R)
4. R. W. Schaffer (R)
5. J. Hefley (R)
6. T. Tancredo (R)*

Connecticut
1. J. Larson (D)*
2. S. Gejdenson (D)
3. R. DeLauro (D)
4. C. Shays (R)
5. J. H. Maloney (D)
6. N. L. Johnson (R)

Delaware
M. N. Castle (R)

Florida
1. J. Scarborough (R)
2. A. Boyd, Jr. (D)
3. C. Brown (D)
4. T. Fowler (R)
5. K. Thurman (D)
6. C. B. Stearns (R)
7. J. Mica (R)
8. B. McCollum (R)
9. M. Bilirakis (R)
10. B. Young (R)
11. J. Davis (D)
12. C. Canady (R)
13. D. Miller (R)
14. P. J. Goss (R)
15. D. Weldon (R)
16. M. Foley (R)
17. C. Meek (D)
18. I. Ros-Lehtinen (R)
19. R. Wexler (D)
20. P. Deutsch (D)
21. L. Diaz-Balart (R)
22. E. C. Shaw, Jr. (R)
23. A. L. Hastings (D)

Georgia
1. J. Kingston (R)
2. S. Bishop (D)
3. M. Collins (R)
4. C. McKinney (D)
5. J. Lewis (D)
6. vacant**
7. B. Barr (R)
8. S. Chambliss (R)
9. N. Deal (R)
10. C. Norwood (R)
11. J. Linder (R)

Hawaii
1. N. Abercrombie (D)
2. P. T. Mink (D)

Idaho
1. H. Chenoweth (R)
2. M. Simpson (R)*

Illinois
1. B. Rush (D)
2. J. Jackson, Jr. (D)
3. W. O. Lipinski (D)
4. L. V. Gutierrez (D)
5. R. R. Blagojevich (D)
6. H. J. Hyde (R)
7. D. K. Davis (D)
8. P. M. Crane (R)
9. J. Schakowsky (D)*
10. J. E. Porter (R)
11. G. Weller (R)
12. J. F. Costello (D)
13. J. Biggert (R)*
14. J. D. Hastert (R)
15. T. W. Ewing (R)
16. D. Manzullo (R)
17. L. Evans (D)
18. R. LaHood (R)
19. D. Phelps (D)*
20. J. M. Shimkus (R)

Indiana
1. P. J. Visclosky (D)
2. D. McIntosh (R)
3. T. Roemer (D)
4. M. Souder (R)
5. S. Buyer (R)
6. D. L. Burton (R)
7. E. Pease (R)
8. J. Hostettler (R)
9. B. Hill (D)*
10. J. Carson (D)

Iowa
1. J. Leach (R)
2. J. Nussle (R)
3. L. L. Boswell (D)
4. G. Ganske (R)
5. T. Latham (R)

Kansas
1. J. Moran (R)
2. J. Ryun (R)
3. D. Moore (D)*
4. T. Tiahrt (R)

Kentucky
1. E. Whitfield (R)
2. R. Lewis (R)
3. A. Northup (R)
4. K. Lucas (D)*
5. H. Rogers (R)
6. E. Fletcher (R)*

Louisiana
1. R. Livingston, Jr. (R)
2. W. J. Jefferson (D)
3. W. J. Tauzin (R)
4. J. McCrery (R)
5. J. Cooksey (R)
6. R. H. Baker (R)
7. C. John (D)

Maine
1. T. Allen (D)
2. J. Baldacci (D)

Maryland
1. W. T. Gilchrest (R)
2. R. L. Ehrlich, Jr. (R)
3. B. L. Cardin (D)
4. A. Wynn (D)
5. S. H. Hoyer (D)
6. R. Bartlett (R)
7. E. E. Cummings (D)
8. C. A. Morella (R)

Massachusetts
1. J. Olver (D)
2. R. E. Neal (D)
3. J. McGovern (D)
4. B. Frank (D)
5. M. Meehan (D)
6. J. F. Tierney (D)
7. E. J. Markey (D)
8. M. Capuano (D)*
9. J. J. Moakley (D)
10. W. D. Delahunt (D)

Michigan
1. B. Stupak (D)
2. P. Hoekstra (R)
3. V. Ehlers (R)
4. D. Camp (R)
5. J. Barcia (D)
6. F. S. Upton (R)
7. N. Smith (R)
8. D. A. Stabenow (D)
9. D. E. Kildee (D)
10. D. E. Bonior (D)
11. J. Knollenberg (R)
12. S. M. Levin (D)
13. L. Rivers (D)
14. J. Conyers, Jr. (D)
15. C. C. Kilpatrick (D)
16. J. D. Dingell, Jr. (D)

Minnesota
1. G. Gutknecht (R)
2. D. Minge (D)
3. J. Ramstad (R)
4. B. F. Vento (D)
5. M. O. Sabo (D)
6. W. Luther (D)
7. C. C. Peterson (D)
8. J. L. Oberstar (D)

Mississippi
1. R. Wicker (R)
2. B. Thompson (D)
3. C. W. Pickering, Jr. (R)
4. R. Shows (D)*
5. G. Taylor (D)

Missouri
1. W. L. Clay (D)
2. J. Talent (R)
3. R. A. Gephardt (D)
4. I. Skelton (D)
5. K. McCarthy (D)
6. P. Danner (D)
7. R. Blunt (R)
8. J. Emerson (R)
9. K. Hulshof (R)

Montana
R. Hill (R)

Nebraska
1. D. K. Bereuter (R)
2. L. Terry (R)*
3. B. Barrett (R)

Nevada
1. S. Berkley (D)*
2. J. Gibbons (R)

New Hampshire
1. J. E. Sununu (R)
2. C. Bass (R)

New Jersey
1. R. E. Andrews (D)
2. F. LoBiondo (R)
3. H. J. Saxton (R)
4. C. H. Smith (R)
5. M. Roukema (R)
6. F. Pallone, Jr. (D)
7. B. Franks (R)
8. W. J. Pascrell, Jr. (D)
9. S. R. Rothman (D)
10. D. M. Payne (D)
11. R. Frelinghuysen (R)
12. R. Holt (D)*
13. R. Menendez (D)

New Mexico
1. H. Wilson (R)
2. J. R. Skeen (R)
3. T. Udall (D)*

New York
1. M. Forbes (R)
2. R. Lazio (R)
3. P. T. King (R)
4. C. McCarthy (D)
5. G. L. Ackerman (D)
6. G. Meeks (D)
7. J. Crowley (D)*
8. J. Nadler (D)
9. A. Weiner (D)*
10. E. Towns (D)
11. M. R. Owens (D)
12. N. Velazquez (D)
13. V. J. Fossella, Jr. (R)
14. C. Maloney (D)
15. C. B. Rangel (D)
16. J. E. Serrano (D)
17. E. L. Engel (D)
18. N. M. Lowey (D)
19. S. W. Kelly (R)
20. B. A. Gilman (R)
21. M. R. McNulty (D)
22. J. Sweeney (R)*
23. S. L. Boehlert (R)
24. J. McHugh (R)
25. J. T. Walsh (R)
26. M. Hinchey (D)
27. T. Reynolds (R)*
28. L. M. Slaughter (D)
29. J. J. LaFalce (D)
30. J. Quinn (R)
31. A. Houghton, Jr. (R)

North Carolina
1. E. Clayton (D)
2. B. R. Etheridge (D)
3. W. Jones, Jr. (R)
4. D. E. Price (D)
5. R. Burr (R)
6. J. H. Coble (R)
7. M. McIntyre (D)
8. R. Hayes (R)*
9. S. Myrick (R)
10. T. C. Ballenger (R)
11. C. H. Taylor (R)
12. M. Watt (D)

North Dakota
E. Pomeroy (D)

Ohio
1. S. Chabot (R)
2. R. Portman (R)
3. T. P. Hall (D)
4. M. G. Oxley (R)
5. P. E. Gillmor (R)
6. T. Strickland (D)
7. D. L. Hobson (R)
8. J. A. Boehner (R)
9. M. Kaptur (D)
10. D. Kucinich (D)
11. S. Jones (D)*
12. J. R. Kasich (R)
13. S. Brown (D)
14. T. C. Sawyer (D)
15. D. Pryce (R)
16. R. S. Regula (R)
17. J. A. Traficant, Jr. (D)
18. B. Ney (R)
19. S. LaTourette (R)

Oklahoma
1. S. Largent (R)
2. T. Coburn (R)
3. W. Watkins (R)
4. J. C. Watts (R)
5. E. J. Istook (R)
6. F. Lucas (R)

Oregon
1. D. Wu (D)*
2. G. Walden (R)*
3. E. Blumenauer (D)
4. P. DeFazio (D)
5. D. Hooley (D)

Pennsylvania
1. R. Brady (D)
2. C. Fattah (D)
3. R. A. Borski (D)
4. R. Klink (D)
5. J. E. Peterson (R)
6. T. Holden (D)
7. W. C. Weldon (R)
8. J. Greenwood (R)
9. E. G. Shuster (R)
10. D. Sherwood (R)*
11. P. E. Kanjorski (D)
12. J. P. Murtha, Jr. (D)
13. J. Hoeffel (D)*
14. W. J. Coyne (D)
15. P. Toomey (R)*
16. J. R. Pitts (R)
17. G. W. Gekas (R)
18. M. Doyle (D)
19. W. F. Goodling (R)
20. F. Mascara (D)
21. P. English (R)

Rhode Island
1. P. Kennedy (D)
2. R. A. Weygand (D)

South Carolina
1. M. Sanford (R)
2. F. D. Spence (R)
3. L. Graham (R)
4. J. DeMint (R)*
5. J. M. Spratt, Jr. (D)
6. J. Clyburn (D)

South Dakota
J. Thune (R)

Tennessee
1. W. Jenkins (R)
2. J. J. Duncan, Jr. (R)
3. Z. Wamp (R)
4. V. Hilleary (R)
5. B. Clement (D)
6. B. J. Gordon (D)
7. E. Bryant (R)
8. J. S. Tanner (D)
9. H. E. Ford, Jr. (D)

Texas
1. M. Sandlin (D)
2. J. Turner (D)
3. S. Johnson (R)
4. R. M. Hall (D)
5. P. Sessions (R)
6. J. Barton (R)
7. W. R. Archer (R)
8. K. Brady (R)
9. N. Lampson (D)
10. L. Doggett (D)
11. C. Edwards (D)
12. K. Granger (R)
13. W. Thornberry (R)
14. R. Paul (R)
15. R. Hinojosa (D)
16. S. Reyes (D)
17. C. W. Stenholm (D)
18. S. Jackson-Lee (D)
19. L. Combest (R)
20. C. Gonzalez (D)*
21. L. S. Smith (R)
22. T. D. DeLay (R)
23. H. Bonilla (R)
24. J. M. Frost (D)
25. K. Bentsen (D)
26. D. Armey (R)
27. S. P. Ortiz (D)
28. C. Rodriguez (D)
29. G. Green (D)
30. E. B. Johnson (D)

Utah
1. J. V. Hansen (R)
2. M. Cook (R)
3. C. Cannon (R)

Vermont
B. Sanders (I)

Virginia
1. H. H. Bateman (R)
2. O. B. Pickett (D)
3. R. C. Scott (D)
4. N. Sisisky (D)
5. V. H. Goode, Jr. (D)
6. R. Goodlatte (R)
7. T. Bliley, Jr. (R)
8. J. P. Moran, Jr. (D)
9. F. C. Boucher (D)
10. F. R. Wolf (R)
11. T. Davis III (R)

Washington
1. J. Inslee (D)*
2. J. Metcalf (R)
3. B. Baird (D)*
4. D. Hastings (R)
5. G. Nethercutt (R)
6. N. D. Dicks (D)
7. J. McDermott (D)
8. J. Dunn (R)
9. A. Smith (D)

West Virginia
1. A. B. Mollohan (D)
2. R. E. Wise, Jr. (D)
3. N. J. Rahall II (D)

Wisconsin
1. P. Ryan (R)*
2. T. Baldwin (D)*
3. R. Kind (D)
4. G. D. Kleczka (D)
5. T. Barrett (D)
6. T. E. Petri (R)
7. D. R. Obey (D)
8. M. Green (R)*
9. F. J. Sensenbrenner, Jr. (R)

Wyoming
B. Cubin (R)

(D) Democrat
(R) Republican
(I) Independent

*elected in 1998
all others: re-elected in 1998
**N. Gingrich (R) resigned in 1998

UNITED STATES SUPREME COURT

Chief Justice: William H. Rehnquist (1986)
Associate Justices:
John Paul Stevens (1975)
Sandra Day O'Connor (1981)
Antonin Scalia (1986)
Anthony M. Kennedy (1988)
David H. Souter (1990)
Clarence Thomas (1991)
Ruth Bader Ginsburg (1993)
Stephen G. Breyer (1994)

UNITED STATES CABINET

Secretary of Agriculture: Daniel R. Glickman
Attorney General: Janet Reno
Secretary of Commerce: William M. Daley
Secretary of Defense: William S. Cohen
Secretary of Education: Richard W. Riley
Secretary of Energy: Bill Richardson
Secretary of Health and Human Services: Donna E. Shalala
Secretary of Housing and Urban Development: Andrew M. Cuomo
Secretary of Interior: Bruce Babbitt
Secretary of Labor: Alexis M. Herman
Secretary of State: Madeleine K. Albright
Secretary of Transportation: Rodney E. Slater
Secretary of the Treasury: Robert E. Rubin
Secretary of Veteran Affairs: Togo West

Newt Gingrich (R, Georgia), the powerful Speaker of the House, resigned in 1998 after the House suffered unexpected losses in the November elections.

STATE GOVERNORS

State	Governor	State	Governor
Alabama	Donald Siegelman (D)*	**Montana**	Marc Racicot (R)
Alaska	Tony Knowles (D)**	**Nebraska**	Mike Johanns (R)*
Arizona	Jane Dee Hull (R)**	**Nevada**	Kenny Guinn (R)*
Arkansas	Mike Huckabee (R)**	**New Hampshire**	Jeanne Shaheen (D)**
California	Gray Davis (D)*	**New Jersey**	Christine Todd Whitman (R)
Colorado	Bill Owens (R)*	**New Mexico**	Gary Johnson (R)**
Connecticut	John Rowland (R)**	**New York**	George Pataki (R)**
Delaware	Thomas R. Carper (D)	**North Carolina**	Jim B. Hunt, Jr. (D)
Florida	Jeb Bush (R)*	**North Dakota**	Edward Schafer (R)
Georgia	Roy Barnes (D)*	**Ohio**	Bob Taft (R)*
Hawaii	Ben Cayetano (D)**	**Oklahoma**	Frank Keating (R)**
Idaho	Dirk Kempthorne (R)*	**Oregon**	John Kitzhaber (D)**
Illinois	George Ryan (R)*	**Pennsylvania**	Thomas J. Ridge (R)**
Indiana	Frank L. O'Bannon (D)	**Rhode Island**	Lincoln Almond (R)**
Iowa	Tom Vilsack (D)*	**South Carolina**	Jim Hodges (D)*
Kansas	Bill Graves (R)**	**South Dakota**	William Janklow (R)**
Kentucky	Paul Patton (D)	**Tennessee**	Don Sundquist (R)**
Louisiana	Mike Foster (R)	**Texas**	George W. Bush (R)**
Maine	Angus King (I)**	**Utah**	Mike Leavitt (R)
Maryland	Parris N. Glendening (D)**	**Vermont**	Howard Dean (D)**
Massachusetts	Paul Cellucci (R)**	**Virginia**	James S. Gilmore III (R)
Michigan	John Engler (R)**	**Washington**	Gary Locke (D)
Minnesota	Jesse Ventura (RF)*	**West Virginia**	Cecil H. Underwood (R)
Mississippi	Kirk Fordice (R)	**Wisconsin**	Tommy G. Thompson (R)**
Missouri	Mel Carnahan (D)	**Wyoming**	Jim Geringer (R)**

*elected in 1998 **re-elected in 1998 (D) Democrat (R) Republican (I) Independent (RF) Reform

CANADA

Capital: Ottawa
Head of State: Queen Elizabeth II
Governor General: Romeo LeBlanc
Prime Minister: Jean Chrétien (Liberal)
Leader of the Opposition: Preston Manning (Reform Party)
Population: 30,300,400
Area: 3,851,809 sq mi (9,976,185 km^2)

PROVINCES AND TERRITORIES

Alberta
Capital: Edmonton
Lieutenant Governor: H. A. Bud Olson
Premier: Ralph Klein (Progressive Conservative)
Leader of the Opposition: Nancy MacBeth (Liberal)
Entered Confederation: Sept. 1, 1905
Population: 2,913,400
Area: 255,285 sq mi (661,188 km^2)

British Columbia
Capital: Victoria
Lieutenant Governor: Garde Gardom
Premier: Glen Clark (New Democratic Party)
Leader of the Opposition: Gordon Campbell (Liberal)
Entered Confederation: July 20, 1871
Population: 4,014,300
Area: 366,255 sq mi (948,600 km^2)

Manitoba
Capital: Winnipeg
Lieutenant Governor: Yvon Dumont
Premier: Gary Filmon (Progressive Conservative)
Leader of the Opposition: Gary Doer (New Democratic Party)
Entered Confederation: July 15, 1870
Population: 1,141,000
Area: 251,000 sq mi (650,090 km^2)

New Brunswick
Capital: Fredericton
Lieutenant Governor: Marilyn Trenholme Counsell
Premier: Camille Thériault (Liberal)
Leader of the Opposition: Bernard Lord (Progressive Conservative)
Entered Confederation: July 1, 1867
Population: 752,400
Area: 28,354 sq mi (73,436 km^2)

Newfoundland
Capital: St. John's
Lieutenant Governor: Arthur Max House
Premier: Brian Tobin (Liberal)
Leader of the Opposition: Ed Byrne (Progressive Conservative)
Entered Confederation: March 31, 1949
Population: 543,200
Area: 156,185 sq mi (404,517 km^2)

Nova Scotia
Capital: Halifax
Lieutenant Governor: J. James Kinley
Premier: Russell MacLellan (Liberal)
Leader of the Opposition: John Hamm (Progressive Conservative)
Entered Confederation: July 1, 1867
Population: 936,100
Area: 21,425 sq mi (55,491 km^2)

Ontario
Capital: Toronto
Lieutenant Governor: Hilary M. Weston
Premier: Mike Harris (Progressive Conservative)
Leader of the Opposition: Dalton McGuinty (Liberal)
Entered Confederation: July 1, 1867
Population: 11,404,800
Area: 412,582 sq mi (1,068,582 km^2)

Prince Edward Island
Capital: Charlottetown
Lieutenant Governor: Gilbert R. Clements
Premier: Patrick Binns (Progressive Conservative)
Leader of the Opposition: Keith W. Milligan (Liberal)
Entered Confederation: July 1, 1873
Population: 136,200
Area: 2,184 sq mi (5,657 km^2)

Quebec
Capital: Quebec City
Lieutenant Governor: Lise Thibault
Premier: Lucien Bouchard (Parti Québécois)
Leader of the Opposition: Jean Charest (Liberal)
Entered Confederation: July 1, 1867
Population: 7,334,100
Area: 594,860 sq mi (1,540,700 km^2)

Saskatchewan
Capital: Regina
Lieutenant Governor: John N. Wiebe
Premier: Roy Romanow (New Democratic Party)
Leader of the Opposition: Ken Krawetz (Saskatchewan Party)
Entered Confederation: Sept. 1, 1905
Population: 1,025,600
Area: 251,700 sq mi (651,900 km^2)

Yukon
Capital: Whitehorse
Premier: Piers McDonald (New Democratic Party)
Leader of the Opposition: John Ostashek (Yukon Party)
Commissioner: Judy Gingell
Organized as a Territory: June 13, 1898
Population: 31,600
Area: 186,299 sq mi (482,515 km^2)

Northwest Territories
Capital: Yellowknife
Commissioner: Helen Maksagak
Government Leader: Jim Antoine
Reconstituted as a Territory: Sept. 1, 1905
Population: 67,900
Area: 1,304,896 sq mi (3,379,684 km^2)

INDEX

A

B

C

D

E

F

G

H

I

J

K

L

M

N

O

P

Q

R

S

T

U

V

W

X-Y-Z

ILLUSTRATION CREDITS AND ACKNOWLEDGMENTS

The following list credits or acknowledges, by page, the source of illustrations and text excerpts used in this work. Illustration credits are listed illustration by illustration—left to right, top to bottom. When two or more illustrations appear on one page, their credits are separated by semicolons. When both the photographer or artist and an agency or other source are given for an illustration, they are usually separated by a slash. Excerpts from previously published works are listed by inclusive page numbers.

6 © Soprintendenza Archaelogica, Salerno/AP/Wide World Photos; Courtesy, Cooper-Hewitt Museum; Photo courtesy of The Robot Zoo/Silicon Graphics
7 © Richard Pasley/Gamma Liaison; ©Superstock, Inc.; © Agence France Presse/Corbis-Bettmann
12–13 © Brad Markel/Gamma Liaison;
16 ©Dave Chan/Ottawa Citizen/AP/Wide World Photos
17 © Paul Hanna/AP/Wide World Photos
18 ©INA, Pool/AP/Wide World Photos
19 © Fernando Llano/AP/Wide World Photos; © Carolina Jiminez /Reuters/Archive Photos
20 © Soprintendenza Archaeologica, Salerno/AP/Wide World Photos
21 © Volkswagen/AP/Wide World Photos
22 © Cynthia Johnson/Gamma Liaison
23 © Agence France Presse/Corbis-Bettmann
24 © Cesar Rangel/AP/Wide World Photos
25 © Dave Martin/AP/Wide World Photos
26 © Reuters/Corbis-Bettmann
27 © Jean-Marc Giboux/Gamma Liaison
28 © Mike Derer/AP/Wide World Photos
29 © Stephen Moitessier/AP/Wide World Photos
30 © Sayyid Azim/AP/Wide World Photos
31 © Greg Baker/AP/Wide World Photos
32 © Dave Martin/AP/Wide World Photos
33 © Gilles Bassignac/Gamma Liaison
34 © Mike Sega/Sipa Press
36 © Pornvilai Carr/AP/Wide World Photos
37 © Win McNamee/Reuters/Archive Photos
38 © Paul Hosefros/NYT Pictures
39 © Ed Bailey/AP/Wide World Photos
40 © Dirck Halstead/Gamma Liaison
41 © Khue Bui/AP/Wide World Photos; © Laurie Driver/Sygma
42 © Steve Grayson/Sipa Press
43 Kean Archives/Archive Photos; Consolidated News/Archive Photos
44 © Sayuri Inoue/Reuters/Archive Photos
45 TOLES © 1998 *The Buffalo News.* Reprinted with permission of Universal Press Syndicate. All rights reserved.
46 © Ajit Kumar/AP/Wide World Photos; © Baldev/Sygma
47 © Zahid Hussein/Reuters/Archive Photos
48 © V. Sumovsky/Sygma
49 Archive Photos
50 © Craig Strong/Gamma Liaison
51 © David Butow/Saba
52 © Gamma Liaison
53 Sygma
54 © Claude Salhani/Gamma Liaison
55 © Brad Markel/Gamma Liaison
56 © Tsafrir Abayov/Impact Visuals
57 © Paul Paith/Pacemaker Press Intl. Ltd.
58 © Yannis Behrakis/Reuters/Archive Photos
59 © Georges De Keerle/Gamma Liaison; © Demange-Vioujard/Gamma Liaison
60 © Roger Lemoyne/Gamma Liaison
61 © Brennan Linsley/AP/Wide World Photos
62 © Jim Mone/AP/Wide World Photos
63 © Andy Manis/Reuters/Archive Photos; © Andrew Medichini/AP/Wide World Photos
64 UPI/Corbis-Bettmann
65 © Ian Waldie/Reuters/Archive Photos; © Jockel Finck/AP/Wide World Photos
66–67 © Pascal Goetgheluck-Pho.n.e/AUSCAPE
68 © Ron Cohn/The Gorilla Foundation
69–70 © Michael Nichols
71 © Tim Davis/Tony Stone Images
72–75 Photos courtesy of The Robot Zoo/Silicon Graphics
76 © John Cancalosi/Peter Arnold, Inc.; © Jean-Claude Carton/Bruce Coleman Inc.
77 © Stephen Frink/Waterhouse Stock Photography; © R. Andrew Odum/Peter Arnold, Inc.
78 © Michael Dick/Animals Animals
79 ©Neal J. Menschel/*Christian Science Monitor*
80 © Michael Dick/Animals Animals
80–81 © S. Michael Bisceglie/Animals Animals
81 © Renee Lynn/Photo Researchers, Inc.
82 © Zig Lezczynski/Animals Animals
83 © Michael Habicht/Animals Animals
84 © Mary Ann Chastain/AP/Wide World Photos
85 © Greg Gibson/AP/Wide World Photos; Doug Marlette ©1997 Newsday
86 © Richard Kolar/Animals Animals; © Antje Gunnar/Bruce Coleman Inc.
87 © Tui De Roy/Bruce Coleman Inc.
88 © Frans Lanting/Photo Researchers, Inc.
89 © Phyllis Greenberg/Animals Animals
90 © Linda Haas/Courtesy, The Computer Musuem; © 1998 Nearlife, Inc./Courtesy, The Computer Museum
91 © Richard P. Smith; © Jeff Christensen/Reuters/Archive Photos
92 © Bob Cranston; © Don Ryan/AP/Wide World Photos
93 © Mike Watson/Animal Planet
94–95 © Richard Ellis/Sygma
96 © Earth Satellite Corporation/Science Photo Library/Photo Researchers, Inc.
97 © Mark Spencer/AUSCAPE; © Gregory Ochocki/Photo Researchers, Inc.
98 © Superstock, Inc.; © Jon Levy/Gamma Liaison; © Superstock, Inc.
99 Artist, Vince Caputo
100 © Nancy Simmerman/Tony Stone Images
101 © Tom Bean/DRK Photos; © Tom & Pat Leeson/Photo Researchers, Inc.
102–105 Artist, Vince Caputo
106 © Superstock, Inc.
108–113 NASA
114 © Brooks Kraft/Sygma
115 NASA/AP/Wide World Photos; NASA
117 NASA
118 © Michelle Bridwell/PhotoEdit; © Jeffrey MacMillan/*U.S. News and World Report*
119 © Spencer Grant/PhotoEdit
120 © Lawrence Migdale/PhotoEdit
121 © Rick Chard; © Michael Newman/PhotoEdit
122 Superstock, Inc.
123 © Art Stein/Photo Researchers, Inc.
124–125 © Victoria Sayer Pearson/Ventura County Star
125 © John Elk III/Bruce Coleman Inc.
126 © Patrick Robert/Sygma
127 Superstock, Inc.; © David Hundley/The Stock Market
128 © Bildarchiv Okapia/Photo Researchers, Inc.
129 © Timothy O'Keefe/Bruce Coleman Inc.
130–133 Designed and created by Jenny Tesar
138 SOLUTION: Sutter's Mill
140–141 From *Make Sculptures!* ©1991 by F&W Publications. Used by permission of North Light Books, a division of F&W Publications, Inc.
142 © Jean Paul Naci/Leo de Wys, Inc.
144 © Nina Fuller/Gamma Liaison
145 © Guilio Andreini/Gamma Liaison
146 © Mike Nelson
147 © John McCoy/Gamma Liaison; © Guilio Andreini/Gamma Liaison; © Guilio Andreini/Gamma Liaison
150–151 From *Many Friends Cooking: An International Cookbook for Boys and Girls,* by Terry Touff Cooper and Marilyn Ratner. Illustrations by Tony Chen. Reprinted by permission of Philomel Books, a division of the Putnam Publishing Group
152–155 Courtesy, *Crafts 'n Things* magazine. For more detailed information on these craft projects, write to Crafts 'n Things, 701 Lee St., Suite 1000, Des Plaines, IL 60016–4570
156–157 Courtesy, Krause Publications, Inc.
158–159 © Ray Stubblebine/Reuters/Archive Photos
160 © Agence France Presse/Corbis-Bettmann; © Al Bello/Allsport

161 © Agence France Presse/Corbis-Bettmann
162 © Allsport/IOC/NAOC
163 © Luca Bruno/AP/Wide World Photos
164 © Jamie Squire/Allsport
165 © Shaun Botteril/Allsport; © Doug Pensinger/ Allsport
168 © Jeff Vinnick/Reuters/Archive Photos
169 © Lou Requena/AP/Wide World Photos
171 © Rusty Kennedy/AP/Wide World Photos
172 © Tom Smart/Gamma Liaison
174 © David J. Phillip/AP/Wide World Photos
175 © Paul Battaglia/AP/Wide World Photos
176 © Mike Segar/Reuters/Archive Photos
177 © Jeff Christensen/Reuters/Archive Photos
178 © Jeff Christensen/Gamma Liaison
179 David E. Klutho/Sports Illustrated © Time Inc.
180 © Craig Melvin/Allsport
182 © Karin Cooper/Gamma Liaison
183 © Gary Hershorn/Reuters/Archive Photos
184 © Mike Blake/Reuters/Archive Photos
185 © Jeff Christensen/Reuters/Archive Photos
186 © Rick Bowmer/AP/Wide World Photos
187 © Luca Bruno/AP/Wide World Photos
188–189 © Chad Slattery/Tony Stone Images
190 The Granger Collection; © Stock Montage
190–191 Courtesy, The Oakland Museum of California
192 George Johnson, Collection of W. Bruce Lundberg
193 © Arnold Fisher/Science Photo Library/Photo Researchers, Inc.; © M. Claye/Jacana/Photo Researchers, Inc.
194 The Granger Collection
195 © David Young-Wolff/Photo-Edit
196 © Guy Gillette/Photo Researchers, Inc.
197 © Franke Keating/Photo Researchers, Inc.; © Jeffery Greenberg/The Picture Cube, Inc.
198 Courtesy, The Abby Aldridge Rockefeller Folk Art Center, Colonial Williamsburg; © Richard Pasley/Gamma Liaison
199 © Charles D. Winters/Photo Researchers, Inc.; © J. D. Sloan/The Picture Cube, Inc.
200–201 © Everett Collection
201 The New Haven Colony Historical Society, Bequest of George W. Crawford, 1973. Photo by William K. Sacco
202 AP/Wide World Photos
203 Blank Archives/Archive Photos
204–205 Courtesy, Six Flags/Magic Mountain
206 The Granger Collection
207 Scott Brown/Busch Gardens; © Busch Entertainment Corporation
208 © Linda Hill
209 © Chad Slattery/Tony Stone Images
210 The Granger Collection
211 Culver Pictures, Inc.
212 The Granger Collection
213 © Kunsthistorisches Museum/The Bridgeman Art Library
214 Artist, Vince Caputo
215 Art Resource
216–217 © Chuck McGowen/The News Journal/AP/ Wide World Photos
218 Courtesy, Washington State University; Courtesy Elaine Lindy
219 Courtesy, NASA; Courtesy, Mann Packing Company, Inc.
220 © Mark Lennihan/AP/Wide World Photos
221 Courtesy, Fayetteville Publishing Company
222 © J. Marshall/The Image Works; © Michael Schwartz/The Image Works
223 © Andrea Renault/Globe Photos, Inc.
224 © 1996 National Fluid Milk Processor Promotion Board/International Dairy Foods Association, Milk Industry Foundation
225 © Bob Daemmrich/The Image Workds
226 © Jon Levy/Gamma Liaison
227 © The Image Works Archives
228 © Scott J. Witte/The Picture Cube, Inc.
229 *People* Weekly © 1998 Black/Toby; © Richard Harbus/NYT Pictures
230 *People* Weekly © 1998 Jeffrey Salter; *People* Weekly © 1998 Steve Labadessa
231 © Mike Theiler/Reuters/Archive Photos
232 © Joe McNally
233 © Christopher Little/Outline
234 © Eika Aoshima/Everett Collection; *People* Weekly © 1998 Robin Bowman
235 Courtesy, Westinghouse; *People* Weekly © 1998 Steve Labadessa
236 *People* Weekly © 1998 Jeffrey Lowe
237 © Ken Ige/Star Bulletin/AP/Wide World Photos
238–239 Courtesy, Cooper-Hewitt Museum
240–241 Tate Gallery, London/Art Resource
242 *St. George and the Dragon,* 1868 (gouache) by Sir Edward Burne-Jones (1833–98) William Morris Gallery, Walthamstow, UK/Bridgeman Art Library, London/New York; Tate Gallery, London/Art Resource
243 Victoria & Albert Museum/London/Art Resource
244 © Columbia/TriStar/The Kobal Collection
245 © Everett Collection; © Everett Collection; © W.B./Monarchy/Regency Ent./Photofest
246 © Sipa Press/Art Resource
247–251 Courtesy, Cooper-Hewitt Museum
252 © Armando Gallo/Retna Ltd.
253 © John Kelly/Retna Ltd.; © Joan Marcus
254 © Barry King/Gamma Liaison; © Douglas Healey/AP/Wide World Photos
255 Erica and Harold Van Pelt/© American Museum of Natural History; © Frank Ockenfels/WB/ AP/Wide World Photos
256 © Columbia/TriStar Television Distribution/AP/ Wide World Photos
257 © Robert Silvers/Henry Holt & Co.
258 © David James/AP/DREAMWORKS/Wide World Photos; © Rico Torres/Everett Collection
259 © Merie W. Wallace/Everett Collection
260 © Frank Masi/Everett Collection
261–263 © Everett Collection
264 © Archive Photos
265 © Chris Haston/Everett Collection; © Twentieth Century Fox/Everett Collection; © Twentieth Century Fox/Everett Collection
266 © Janet Gough/Celebrity Photo; © Gilbert Flores/Celebrity Photo
267 © Kevin Winter/Celebrity Photo
268 © Craig Skinner/Celebrity Photo
269 © Jean-Marc Giboux/Gamma Liaison
270 © Patrick McMullan/Gamma Liaison
271 © Mark Lennihan/AP/Wide World Photos
272–273 From *Play With Your Food* ©1997 Joost Elffers/ Saxton Freymann/Published in the USA by Stewart, Tabori & Chang
274–275 From *Toad* by Ruth Brown. Copyright © 1997 by Ruth Brown. Used by permission Dutton Children's Books, a division of Penguin Putnam Inc.
276–285 Artist, Laine Roundy
286–287 Artist, Michele A. McLean
288 Folger Shakespeare Library
289–292 Artist, Linda Graves
294 From *Rapunzel* by Paul O. Zelinsky. Copyright © 1997 by Paul O. Zelinsky. Used by permission of Dutton Children's Books, a division of Penguin Putnam Inc.; Illustration from *The Etcher's Studio* by Arthur Geisert. Copyright © 1997 by Arthur Geisert. Reprinted by permission of Houghton Mifflin Company. All rights reserved.
295 Text and illustrations from *The Party* copyright © 1997 by Barbara Reid. Reprinted by permission of Scholastic Canada Ltd.
296 From *Nothing Ever Happens on 90th Street* by Roni Schotter, illustrated by Krysten Brooker. Illustrations copyrigth © 1997 by Kyrsten Brooker. Reprinted by permission of Orchard Books, New York; Copyright © 1997 by Sharleen Collicott. Used by permission of HarperCollins Publishers
297 Reprinted with the permission of Margaret K. McElderry Books, an imprint of Simon & Schuster Children's Publishing Division from *A Summertime Song* by Irene Haas. Copyright © 1997 by Irene Haas
298 © C. Steele-Perkins/Magnum Photos, Inc.
299 © Kennan Ward/Corbis; © Michael Nichols/ Magnum Photos, Inc.
300 © Kennan Ward/Corbis
301 © Karl Ammann/Corbis
302 The Granger Collection
303–312 Artist, Gary Torrisi
314 © Richard T. Nowitz/Corbis
315 © Porter Gifford/Gamma Liaison; Courtesy Palm Pilot III
318 Courtesy of Exxon and Pacific Data Images
319 © Remi Benali/Gamma Liaison; © Larry Mulvehill/Rainbow
320 Courtesy, Zoo Atlanta
323 © ILM-Universal. All Rights Reserved
324 Courtesy, Unisys Corporation
326 © Adam Nadel/AP/Wide World Photos
327 © Laurent Zylberman/Sygma
329 © Laguna Photo/Gamma Liaison; © Michael Melford
330 © Chris R. Sharp/DDB Stock Photo
331 © Brownie Harris/The Stock Market; © Tom Brakefield/Bruce Coleman Inc.
332 Kansas State Historical Society
334 Oregon Historical Society
335 Kansas State Historical Society
336 Western History Collections, University of Oklahoma Library; Kansas State Historical Society
337 Kansas State Historical Society
339 Kansas State Historical Society; © Culver Pictures
340 Western History Collections; University of Oklahoma Library
341 Missouri Historical Society; DeGolyer Library, Southern Methodist University
342 Archives & Manuscripts, Division of the Oklahoma Historical Society
343 Mark O. Thiessen, © National Geographic Society
344 The Metropolitan Museum of Art, Morris K. Jesup Fund, 1933

344–345 Buffalo Bill Historical Center, Cody, WY
345 © The Bettmann Archive
346 Maryland Historical Society, Baltimore, MD
347 The Granger Collection
348 The Denver Public Library, Western History Collection
350 Courtesy, Palace of Governors, Musuem of New Mexico
351 © Ron Cronin
352 The Walters Art Gallery, Baltimore, MD; The Kansas State Historical Society, Topeka, KS
353 © The Bettmann Archive
354 Denver Public Library
355 The Granger Collection; © National Portrait Gallery, Smithsonian Institution/Art Resource
356 Oregon Historical Society
357 © The Bettmann Archive; The Granger Collection
358 © Superstock, Inc.
359 © UPI/Corbis-Bettmann
360 © Michael J. Howell/Liaison International; © Sophie Dauwe/Robert Fried Photography
361 © Robert Fried; © Allan Tannenbaum/Sygma; © Buddy Mays/Travel Stock
362 © Anthony Neste/Gamma Liaison Network; © Nik Wheeler; © George Rose/Liaison
363 © UPI/Corbis-Bettmann; © Tobias Everke/Gamma Liaison
364 © Richard B. Levine
365 © Bob Fitch/Black Star
366 © UPI/Corbis-Bettmann; © Jim Wells/Archive Photos; © AP Photo
368 © Lyle Leduc/Liaison International
369 © Martyn F. Chillmaid/Science Photo Library/Photo Researchers, Inc.; © David R. Frazier/Photolibrary
370 © Kennan Ward/The Stock Market
372 NASA; © Tim Davis/Tony Stone Images
373 © Dale E. Boyer/Photo Researchers, Inc.
374 © 1998 The Museum of Modern Art
375 © Jose Fusta Raga/Leo de Wys, Inc.
377 © Jonathan Blair/Woodfin Camp; © H. Steenmans/Leo de Wys
378 © Victor Engelbert/Photo Researchers, Inc.
380 © Everett Collection
381 © Sygma; © Adam Scull/Globe Photos, Inc.
382 Captiol Records/AP/Wide World Photos; NASA/Gamma Liaison
383 UPI/Corbis-Bettmann; © Everett Collection
393 © Ron Sachs/Archive Photos